Programming with
Java

Barry Holmes

Oxford Brookes University, England

JONES AND BARTLETT PUBLISHERS

Sudbury, Massachusetts

BOSTON   TORONTO   LONDON   SINGAPORE

World Headquarters
Jones and Bartlett Publishers
40 Tall Pine Drive
Sudbury, MA 01776
978-443-5000
info@jbpub.com
www.jbpub.com

Jones and Bartlett Publishers Canada
2100 Bloor St. West
Suite 6-272
Toronto, ON M6S 5A5
CANADA

Jones and Bartlett Publishers International
Barb House, Barb Mews
London W6 7PA
UK

Disclaimer
The computer programs presented in this book have been included for their instructional value. They have been computer-tested with considerable care and are not guaranteed for any particular purpose. The author does not offer any warranties or representations, nor does he accept any liabilities with respect to the computer programs.

Trademark Acknowledgments
Java™ is a trademark of Sun Microsystems, Inc.

ISBN: 0-7637-0707-4

Cover image: © SPENCER JONES/FPG INTERNATIONAL.

Printed in the United States of America
02 01 00 99   10 9 8 7 6 5 4 3 2

Preface

Audience

I have assumed that the reader has no prior knowledge of computer programming. However, the reader is expected to be familiar with the fundamentals of operating a home-computer.

The text book **Programming with Java** is written for the ACM-recommended curriculum for CS1 in the USA and first-year college/university programming courses worldwide. The book is aimed at a broad audience of students in science, engineering and business, where a knowledge of programming is thought to be essential.

Overview

In the first five chapters of the book, much emphasis is placed upon you becoming familiar with, and using, the pre-written Java classes and methods. Once you have gained confidence in creating and manipulating objects derived from the Java Application Programming Interface (API), the remainder of the book explains how you can progress to building your own classes and apply these classes to the creation of graphical user interfaces, Web-based programming and multimedia applications.

Chapters 1 to 5 provide a gradual introduction to the fundamentals of programming, where much emphasis is placed upon good practice involving program design, testing and implementation. These chapters broadly cover primitive data types, classes and class hierarchy; program design, implementation, compilation and error correction if ..else and switch selection statements; while, do and for loop statements; and arrays.

Once you have understood the fundamentals of programming, and can use API classes competently, it is then possible to explore the object-oriented paradigm to a much greater depth. Chapters 6 to 9 cover the topics of class methods, construction of classes, instance methods, constructors, finalizers, abstract data types, object properties, inheritance, polymorphism, genericity and exception handling.

Graphical user interfaces (GUIs) are so important in the development of modern software that Chapter 10 is devoted to the production of graphical interfaces using the classes supplied by the Java language.

Chapter 11 is a complete coverage of writing and running Java Applets on the World Wide Web. This chapter is designed to introduce you to the creation of multimedia based systems.

In striking a balance between a text book that is designed to be useful for beginners and a text book that covers Java to an adequate depth and completeness, Chapter 12 includes topics on recursion, sorting, searching, linked lists, queues, and stacks.

Synopsis

Chapter 1 explores the different characteristics of data such as type, size, and format and introduces you to four data types: integer, real, character, and string. Having explored how numbers are stored in the memory of the computer, you can then look at how arithmetic is performed in Java. The chapter also introduces you to the an extension of a data type known as a class. Classes feature very prominently in the Java language, and you need to start to understand their implications at this early stage. Finally we look at the Java statements required for the input of data and the output of information.

Chapter 2 continues the theme of classes by exploring the overall format of a computer program. The first step in programming is designing and planning your programs away from the computer. This chapter focuses your attention upon a prescriptive method for program development. By the end of the chapter you will be writing simple programs consisting of a sequence of instructions.

Chapter 3 introduces the techniques of coding conditions and branching on the result of a condition to alternative statements in a program. The chapter introduces `if, if else` and `switch` statements and the `boolean` data type.

Chapter 4 introduces you to three methods for repeating statements that are based on the control structures known as `while, do while,` and `for`. The chapter also contains information on an alternative means of data input and screen output using files.

Chapter 5 introduces the array, which is the most common of the data structures. The array is available in most computer languages and uses techniques for accessing data that can lead to simple and more effective programming solutions.

Chapter 6 emphasizes the construction and use of class methods, constructors and instance methods. It introduces parameter-passing and focuses upon the building of programs from several classes.

Chapter 7 introduces the idea of encapsulation and the creation of classes that support data abstraction.

Chapter 8 extends your knowledge of object-oriented programming by showing you how one class can inherit the characteristics of another class to build a hierarchical relationship between classes.

Chapter 9 explains the features of exception handling. Exception handling helps to reduce the probability of program malfunction and contributes the design and creation of safer computerized systems.

Chapter 10 marks a departure from the traditional input of data via a keyboard and the display information in textual form on a screen. You will be introduced to many of the components found in Java that contribute the construction of a graphical user interface (GUI).

Chapter 11 introduces you to applets and multimedia, showing you how Java may be used on the World Wide Web.

Chapter 12 introduces you to a number of data structures and algorithms that you should find useful when you continue to develop programs using Java. Many of the techniques and methods discussed in this chapter are part of a computer science course. Their inclusion here is for completeness and to explain how Java supports these concepts.

Language and Computer Requirements

Studying from this book can be more effective and enjoyable if you use a computer to run the example programs, case studies and your answers to the programming problems.

All the programs written in this book have been compiled and tested using Sun Microsystems, Inc. **Java Development Kit (JDK) version 1.1** (release 1.1.5) on both a PC compatible microcomputer under Windows 95 and a Sun Workstation under Solaris.

The programs have also been compiled and tested using the **JDK beta-test version 1.2**.

The **Introduction** explains how to download the latest version of the Java Development Kit from the World Wide Web to your computer.

Pedagogical Features

Objectives

Each chapter begins with a set of learning objectives.

Case Studies

Many chapters contain fully designed case studies with comprehensive documentation, program listings and output.

Example Programs

All chapters contain example programs used to demonstrate the key features of each chapter. All computer programs are followed by a listing of the output from the program.

End of Chapter Summary

Every chapter contains a summary of its key points. This provides you with a check list of topics you should understand before you progress to the next chapter.

Review Questions

All chapters contain review questions to enable you to test and reinforcing your knowledge.

Exercises

All chapters contain pencil-and-paper exercises designed to test your understanding of aspects of the programming topics introduced in the chapter. The exercises should normally be tackled before the programming problems.

Programming Problems

All chapters contain a set of programming problems that require the use of a computer to solve. You are expected to write fully working solutions to each problem.

Icons

The chapters include icons for quick reference on:

These statements express the grammar of the language, and illustrate how language statements are constructed. The terminal symbols are shown in a `fixed width bold` font, and non-terminal symbols in an *italic typeface*.

Information the author feels should be brought to your attention.

Cautionary advice.

Directs you, part-way through a chapter, to questions you should answer to build your confidence in understanding and mastering a topic.

Supplements

Program Disk

You may download the example programs, including case study programs for every chapter in this book. The program disk is available through the Jones and Bartlett World Wide Web site on the Internet at:

`http://www.jbpub.com/disks/`

The Web site will allow for down-loading programs in either an MSDOS or UNIX format.

On-Line Instructor's Guide

A comprehensive web-based instructor's guide is available, free of charge, to adopters of *Programming with Java*. The instructor's guide is accessible via a password-protected page on the Jones and Bartlett web site. This guide contains hints and tips on teaching the material, together with all the answers to the review questions, exercises and programming problems that do not appear in Appendix A. To utilize the guide, qualified instructors should contact the Jones and Bartlett Marketing Department at 800-832-0034 or info@jbpub.com to receive a URL and password.

Acknowledgments

I would like to express my thanks to the following technical reviewers, whose comments I found to be most constructive and helpful, and have gone towards shaping this book into its present form.

Dr. Mike Fry - Lebanon Valley College
Prof. Craig Graci - SUNY Oswego State University
Prof. Dale Skrien - Colby College
Prof. Deborah Trytten - University of Oklahoma

Barry Holmes - Oxford, England - March 1998

Brief Contents

Table of Contents

Chapter 2 Program Design   49

Chapter 3 Selection   79

Chapter 4 Repetition   111

Chapter 5 Arrays   147

Programming with
Java

Introduction

Welcome to the world of Programming with Java. **Please take your time to read this introduction, since it instructs you how to access the latest version of the Java Development Kit (JDK) from Sun Microsystems, Inc.**

The JDK is free-of-charge, and subject to the licensing agreement set out by Sun Microsystems, Inc.

Sun's JDK will be used exclusively throughout this book, therefore, it is important that you get off to the right start, by using the Internet to download all the Java software and documentation that will you need to build and run Java programs on your computer.

By the end of this introduction you should have an understanding of the following topics.

- Java - a brief overview.

- Connecting to the Internet.

- Downloading Sun's JDK software.

- Java documentation.

- Examples of what Java can do.

- JDK tools.

- Compiling and running your first Java program.

- Downloading all the program examples found in this book.

- Compiling and running graphics and multimedia example programs.

What is Java?

Java is a computer language, designed and implemented by Sun Microsystems, Inc. The term Java is not an acronym, but adopted to reflect a favorite drink (coffee?) of many programmers - hence Sun's logo for Java is a cup of steaming coffee.

Java is a very young language in comparison with such languages as Pascal and C (both early 1970's). Although Java was first brought to the attention of the public in 1995, it started life back in 1990. A team at Sun, headed by James Gosling, designed a new programming language known as Oak, for the development of consumer electronics software.

In 1993 the World Wide Web appeared on the Internet. The Sun development team soon realized that the Java language would be suitable for writing programs to run on different computers connected to the Internet. This was a milestone, since Java was the first language to provide features to allow programs to be downloaded as part of a Web page, and run on a user's computer. To demonstrate this new feature, Sun developed the first Web browser to support Java applets (a Java program designed to run using a Java-enabled Web browser) and named it HotJava.

In addition to applets, the Java language can be used to develop stand-alone application programs that do not involve the use of the Web pages.

Java is an object-oriented language, unlike Pascal and C that are procedural languages. As a programmer, object-oriented programming means that you focus on building classes to represent the data in your application, rather than thinking of the solution to a problem as a set of procedures that must be followed in a set order.

The Java language is small in size and simple to learn and to use. The power of the language comes from the extensive library of utilitarian software components that a programmer may use.

You are not restricted to developing and running your programs on just one type of computer. Java programs are portable - for example, a program written and compiled for a PC may be transferred without modification to run on, say, a Sun Workstation.

Java offers improvements over other computer languages, in that it is robust, secure and may be used for networking applications.

As a young language, Java is still evolving. Although the core of the language is small, the evolution appears to be coming from the addition of more and more useful libraries to the development environment. The launch of the language in 1995 used version 1.0, followed by major additions to the libraries, and minor modification to the core language in 1997 bringing about version 1.1.

All the programs in the book have been developed using version 1.1, and despite version 1.2 becoming available in the near future this text should prove a useful source for beginners to Java programming for many years to follow.

Using the Internet

If you already have access to the Internet on your computer then please go to the section on downloading the Java Development Kit. However, if you are new to computers and would like to know how to link your computer to the World Wide Web then please read on.

There are three essential stages you need to check off before you can connect to the Web.

- Your computer must have installed a *modem* to connect it with your domestic 'phone line or mobile 'phone. If you don't have such equipment then contact your computer dealer for more information.

- You need an account with an *Internet provider*; this is an organization that your computer will dial into, and enable you to gain access to the Internet. There are many Internet providers, all competing for your custom. Many providers will allow you hours and hours of free connect time before they start billing you for their service. Many Internet providers advertise in popular computer magazines, so read around, and make your own informed choice as to which provider to sign-up with. Once you have an account you will be given a *user id* and a *password*, which must be used each time you need to gain access to Internet via the provider.

- You need an *Internet browser*. A browser is a computer program that will enable you to move around the World Wide Web looking for information. There are several popular browsers available, for example Microsoft Internet Explorer, Sun HotJava and Netscape Navigator.

To connect with the World Wide Web on the Internet, use your browser to connect with your Internet provider. You may need to type your password when prompted. Once connected with your Internet provider you then have access to all those many millions of people and companies who subscribe to the Internet World wide.

Downloading the Java Development Kit

The following illustration shows the link you need to make with Sun Microsystems, Inc to enable you to download the Java Development Kit. Once you have logged on to the Internet via your provider, input the following address to your Web browser.   `http://java.sun.com`

If your connection is successful, you will have access to Sun's Web pages for downloading the Java Development Kit. The Web page may be similar to the illustration in Figure 1.

⚠️ Sun's Web pages are regularly updated, so don't be alarmed if the pages are not exactly the same as those shown in Figures 1, 2, 3 and 4.

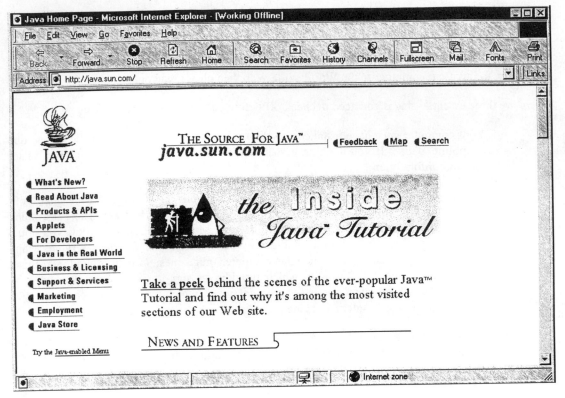

Figure 1 Access to the source for Java

Scroll down the Web page, by pressing the page down key at your keyboard, or use your mouse to pull the right-hand scroll bar down the page. Eventually you will reach the part of the page that contains a reference to Java Development Kit under the Spotlight heading on the left-hand side of the page.

Place your mouse pointer over the words Java Development Kit and press the mouse button. You will be taken to another Web page containing all the instructions to download the very latest version of the Java Development Kit.

Figure 2 illustrates part of the Web page for downloading the JDK. You are advised to follow the instructions and download:

1. The JDK Software

This contains the essential software (compiler and interpreter) for writing and running programs on your computer.

2. The JDK HTML documentation

Throughout the book you will be asked to make reference to this documentation.

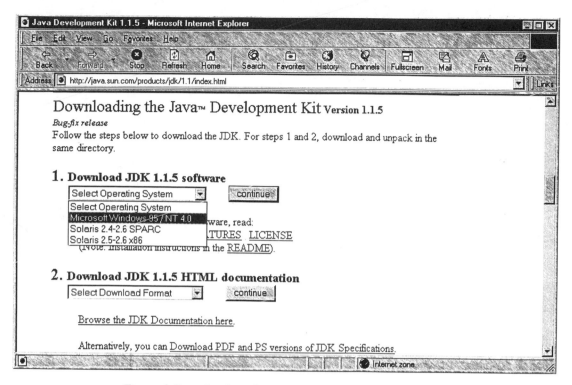

Figure 2 Downloading the JDK software and documentation

By following the instructions on the screen, the software and documentation will be downloaded to the hard drive on your computer, unless you request otherwise. The time to download the complete development kit can take anything from 15 minutes to 90 minutes, but this depends upon the speed of your connection to your provider, and the time of day you access the Internet. However, you only need to download the JDK once, and it is well worthwhile the small expense in telephone charges.

Remember by downloading your software in this manner, you can always guarantee having the very latest release of Sun's Java on your computer.

Once you have downloaded the JDK, you will need to follow the instructions for installing the JDK on your computer.

JDK Documentation

The JDK documentation is found in a subdirectory **docs** of the **jdk** directory on your computer. Upon opening docs you will see a file named **index**. By clicking on the index icon you will open the JDK documentation that is viewed using the Web browser on your computer. You do <u>not</u> need to be connected to your Internet provider in order to use your Web browser. Figure 3 illustrates a typical opening page to the documentation. You navigate through the documentation by placing your mouse pointer over the hot links (those words either underlined or appearing in a different color), and mouse-click to take you to the relevant section of the documentation. A number of hot links appear at the top of the Web page shown in Figure 3, these are:

JDK Release Notes
JDK API Documentation
JDK Guide to New Features
JDK Tool Documentation
JDK Demos
JRE Documentation
Related Documents

Be curious, explore what is contained under each heading. You may not have a clue about the technical content of the documentation at this stage, however, you will start to get a feel for how to access the documentation, and how it is organized.

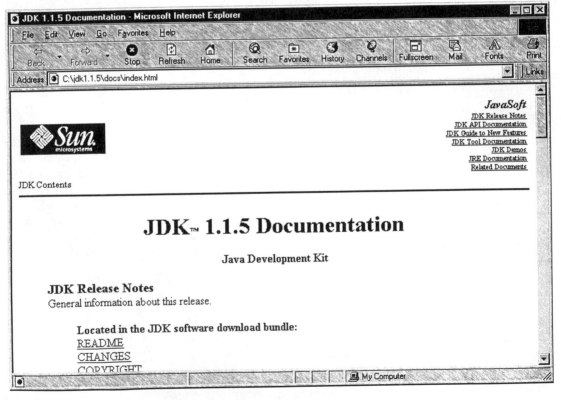

Figure 3 An opening page of the JDK documentation

Playing with Java

Rather than moving straight into the theory of the Java language, spend a little time in exploring the potential of the language. Have fun in running some of the demonstration programs that you have downloaded with the JDK. At the top of the JDK Documentation page, using your mouse pointer, click on the hot link <u>JDK Demos</u>, then click on the hot link <u>Demonstration Applets and Applications</u>. Figure 4 illustrates some of the names of the demonstration programs. Use the names as hot links to allow the computer to load and run the programs for you.

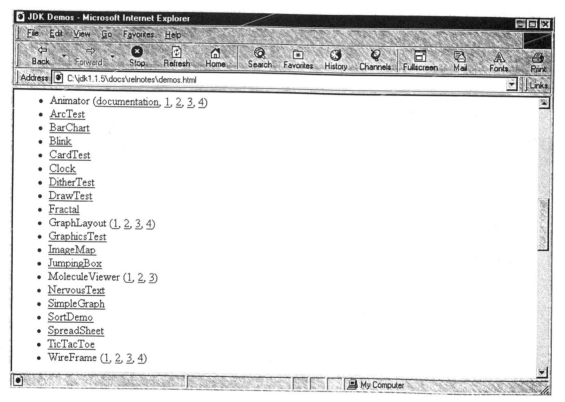

Figure 4 A selection of demonstration programs

JDK Tools

In order to build Java programs on your computer, the JDK contains a set of tools for compiling, and running your programs, plus a variety of other utilitarian features. Using your mouse pointer click on the <u>JDK Tool Documentation</u> hot link, then click on <u>Tool Docs</u> hot link for the operating system you are using. Two tools that you will use extensively throughout this book are:

javac - the **Java Language Compiler** that you use to compile programs written in the Java programming language into bytecodes;

java - the **Java Interpreter** that you use to run programs written in the Java programming language;

Take your time to browse through the JDK tool documentation using your mouse pointer to click on the hot links for each tool command. This way you will be given a full explanation of the function of each tool.

Your First Program

To get a feel for what is in store for you, why not attempt to compile and run the following program on your computer. This will also serve as a good test as to whether you have installed the JDK software correctly.

At this stage you are not expected to understand any Java statements, or the terms compilation and execution. However, through prior experience you should already be familiar with your computer environment, and how to create and edit text files and open windows.

Create a text file for the Java program illustrated in Figure 5. This involves typing the statements exactly as they are printed in Figure 5. If you are a Windows 95/NT user, then use, say Notepad, to create the file; if you are a Sun Solaris user then open a text file window to input the program.

```java
// My first program

import java.io.*;

class MyFirstProgram
{
    static BufferedReader keyboard = new
            BufferedReader(new InputStreamReader(System.in));
    static PrintWriter screen = new PrintWriter(System.out, true);

    public static void main(String[] args) throws IOException
    {
        String name;

        screen.print("Please type your name? "); screen.flush();
        name = keyboard.readLine();

        screen.print("\n\nHello " + name );
        screen.println(" - Welcome to Programming with Java\n\n");
    }
}
```

Figure 5 - Your first program

Save the program using the filename `MyFirstProgram.java`

If you are a Windows 95/NT user, open the MSDOS window. If you are a Sun Solaris user open a terminal window. In both cases change the directory to the one containing the file `MyFirstProgram.java`.

Type the following command to compile the program.

`javac MyFirstProgram.java`

There should be no errors reported. If there are errors, closely examine each line of your text file against each line in Figure 5, in an attempt to find any typographical errors. In addition you may need to refer back to the documentation for installing the JDK and check that you followed the document correctly.

In the same window you used to compile the program, type the following command to execute (run) the program.

`java MyFirstProgram`

Did your program run? If it did you should have a message displayed on your screen similar to that shown below.

```
Please type your name? Barry

Hello Barry - Welcome to Programming with Java
```

Example Programs

All the demonstration programs that are listed in this book are also available on the Jones and Bartlett Web site on the Internet. Using your browser input the following address:

`http://www.jbpub.com/disks/`

Follow the instruction for downloading all the programs on to your computer. When you have downloaded all the example programs, you may notice that the subdirectories are organized by chapter number, and the names of the programs are the same as those listed in each chapter.

As further examples of the capabilities of the Java language, you may care to examine two of these programs.

The first program, taken from chapter 10, is an example of an application. The name of the program file is: `Ex_7.java`. Compile and run the program using this filename. If all goes well, a new window should open on the screen to display a drawing package for a graphical user interface. Play with the program to get a feel for what the Java language is capable of doing.

The second program, taken from chapter 11, is an example of an *applet*. You will need a computer with a sound card and speakers to run this program correctly. The name of the program file is: `Ex_4.java`. Compile the program. Since the program is an *applet* you must run it using the command: **appletviewer Ex_4.html**. If all goes well, a new window should open on the screen, displaying a menu that allows you to select and play various prerecorded sounds.

Hopefully, playing with the demonstration programs from Sun Microsystems, Inc and those suggested from this book, has fired you with enthusiasm to write your own programs in Java!

The next step in your education is for you to understand the theory behind programming using the Java language. However, you should have already reached the first milestone down the road to Programming with Java, by installing the JDK and being able to run some of the demonstration software.

What if you cannot get the JDK to function correctly on your machine? JDK is a well proven reliable product, the chances are you have made a fundamental error in setting up your system. Either re-read the set-up documentation, or consult your teacher for further advice.

Similarly, the example programs from this book have all been thoroughly tested on both a PC using Windows 95 and on a Sun Workstation using Solaris. If you cannot get the programs to load then re-check the filenames and directory names that you are using. If the programs do not compile or run on your machine re-check your JDK settings.

Chapter 1
Data Types

This chapter is deliberately split into two halves since it covers a large amount of fundamental material. In the first half of the chapter we start our exploration of the Java language by examining data. Data types are represented by the majority of computer languages, and the use of data in programming becomes a very important aspect in your studies.

This opening chapter explores the different characteristics of data such as type and size, and introduces you to the data types for numbers, characters and strings.

We also examine how the arithmetic on numbers is performed in Java.

In the second half of the chapter you are introduced to an extension of a data type known as a class. Classes feature very prominently in the Java language, and it is necessary for you to start to understand their implications at such an early stage in the book.

Finally we look at the Java statements required for the input of data and the output of information.

By the end of the chapter you should have an understanding of the following topics.

- How to recognize data and classify it by type.

- The identification of variables and constants and their representation in a program.

- The construction of arithmetic expressions for the purpose of making calculations.

- The fundamentals of packages, classes, class hierarchy and methods.

- Input of data at a keyboard and the output of information on a screen.

1.1 Data

We are surrounded by information. Just look at the assortment of signs in Figure 1.1 we may encounter when out and about. We can classify this information into characters and numbers. From the signs you can identify single characters such as P (for Parking) T (weight limit in Tons); groups of characters such as WEAK BRIDGE, CAFÉ, breakfast, soups, etc.; and numbers such as 10 (in the 10 T weight limit for the weak bridge) or 2 (in the waiting limited to 2 hours).

Figure 1.1 An assortment of signs

Figure 1.2 illustrates more information; this time from a newspaper, and from bank and credit card statements. In the newspaper you find a listing of World share markets containing groups of characters representing a name of a company, followed by a numerical value. For example All Share +14.85, DJ Industrial -85.66 and S&P Composite -12.67 show the changes in the values of shares over a week. On both the partial listings of the bank and credit card statements a similar format exists; for example SOUTHERN ELECTRIC 23.00 and SOFTWARE WAREHOUSE 89.24 show charges for a direct debit towards the cost of electricity and the cost of a computer software package.

Data is the name given to characters and quantities operated upon by a computer. For example, in the bank and credit card statements in Figure 1.2 the names of the companies are groups of characters and the respective charges for goods or services are quantities. A computer **program** consists of a series of instructions for the computer to execute and provides a method for processing data. The data from either bank or credit card transactions can be processed by a computer into information for bank or credit card statements

From the information shown in the two figures, we can identify four data types: **integer** (a positive or negative whole number), **real** (a positive or negative number with a decimal fraction), **character** (a single character), and a **string** (a group of characters). For example, in Figure 1.1 the numbers 2 and 10 are both whole numbers and can be classified as integers. In the same figure the single characters P and T can be classified as characters, and the groups of characters WEAK BRIDGE, CAFÉ, sandwiches, and soups can be classified as strings. In Figure 1.2 the numbers -85.66, 23.00 and 89.24 are positive or negative numbers containing a decimal fraction and can be classified as reals.

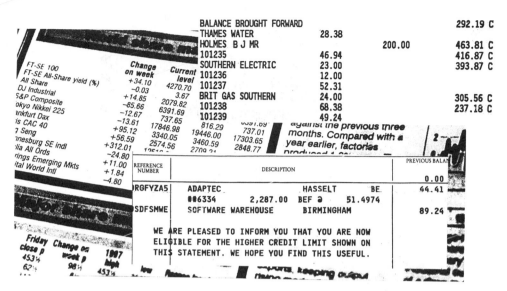

Figure 1.2 An illustration of information from a newspaper and various statements

1.2 Data Storage

Figure 1.3 illustrates a memory board from a digital computer. The term **digital** implies that all information is represented by numbers within the computer. The memory is composed from many millions of storage cells. The unique numeric address of each cell identifies the location of the cell within the memory. Figure 1.3 illustrates several separately addressed storage cells from 20000 to 20005, which contain information represented by voltage levels. The voltage levels are shown as a series of peaks and troughs, where a peak represents the binary digit 1, and a trough the binary digit 0.

A **binary digit** has one of two possible values either 0 or 1. A **binary number** is composed of a series of 0's and 1's. The figure illustrates that within memory address 20003, the voltage levels represent information having a binary number of 11010101. The number of binary digits or **bits** stored in this memory cell is 8, and is known as a **byte** sized storage capacity. Each of the memory cells in the illustration are capable of holding a byte (8 bits) of information. The memory board illustrated in Figure 1.3 has a storage capacity of 32 megabytes! A megabyte is 1,048,576 bytes (2^{20}) and not 1,000,000 as the name implies.

Despite all information being stored in the computer in a binary format, there is no equivalent representation for binary numbers in Java. A **hexadecimal** number system has 16 digits and is used in Java as a shorthand representation of binary numbers. From Figure 1.4 you will notice that the hexadecimal digits 0 to 9 are the same as those for a decimal number, however, to represent the 6 extra hexadecimal digits it is necessary to use the letters A to F which are equivalent to the decimal numbers 10 to 15.

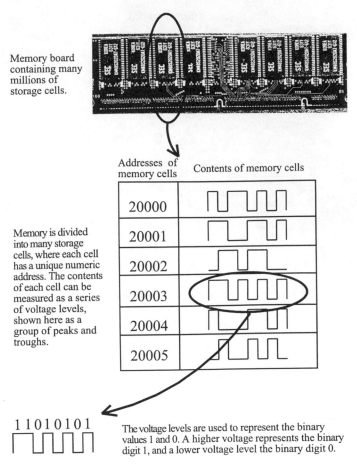

Memory board containing many millions of storage cells.

Memory is divided into many storage cells, where each cell has a unique numeric address. The contents of each cell can be measured as a series of voltage levels, shown here as a group of peaks and troughs.

Addresses of memory cells

Contents of memory cells

20000

20001

20002

20003

20004

20005

1 1 0 1 0 1 0 1

The voltage levels are used to represent the binary values 1 and 0. A higher voltage represents the binary digit 1, and a lower voltage level the binary digit 0.

Figure 1.3 Computer Memory

Figure 1.4 shows that a hexadecimal digit is a convenient representation of four bits; for example the four bits 0000 is represented as hexadecimal digit 0, the four bits 0001 is represented as hexadecimal digit 1, the four bits 0010 is represented as hexadecimal digit 2, and finally the four bits 1111 is represented as hexadecimal digit F.

A binary number can be converted to a hexadecimal number by partitioning the binary number into groups of four bits, starting at the least significant end of the number and evaluating each group as a hexadecimal digit. The binary number 11010101 shown in Figure 1.3 can be split into two groups of four bits 1101 | 0101 and converted to the hexadecimal number D5. Similarly larger binary numbers such as 0111001100011110 can be split into groups of four bits 0111 | 0011 | 0001 | 1110 and converted to the hexadecimal number 731E.

Each hexadecimal digit represents the base 16 raised to a power, with the least significant digit representing 16^0, the next most significant digit 16^1, the next most significant digit 16^2, and so on. To convert a hexadecimal number to a decimal number multiply each digit by it appropriate place weight. For example, the hexadecimal number D5 is $13 \times 16^1 + 5 \times 16^0$, which is equivalent to 213 in decimal. Note the hexadecimal digit D is evaluated to its decimal equivalent of 13 (see Figure 1.4).

Similarly, the hexadecimal number 731E is $7 \times 16^3 + 3 \times 16^2 + 1 \times 16^1 + 14 \times 16^0$, which is equivalent to 29470 in decimal. Therefore, the binary number 0111001100011110 evaluated earlier, is also equivalent to the decimal number 29470. In Java hexadecimal numbers are prefixed by 0x, for example 0x731E.

binary	decimal	hexadecimal
0000	0	0
0001	1	1
0010	2	2
0011	3	3
0100	4	4
0101	5	5
0110	6	6
0111	7	7
1000	8	8
1001	9	9
1010	10	A
1011	11	B
1100	12	C
1101	13	D
1110	14	E
1111	15	F

Figure 1.4 Representation of 0 to 15 in binary, decimal and hexadecimal

The remainder of this section explains how data of type character, integer and real are organized in the computer's memory. The explanation of the data type for a string is covered in the second half of this chapter. As a Java programmer you are not expected to remember the ranges of the numbers that are quoted; these are given to indicate to you the relative sizes of the numbers that the computer can store in memory.

Characters

In Java a character is stored in two bytes of memory using a 16 bit Unicode.

The type declaration for a character is declared in Java as `char`.

A character literal is always delimited by single quotes, for example the character literal A is written as `'A'`. The term **literal** refers to the stated value. In Java a character literal may also be expressed by its Unicode. A Unicode is prefixed by \u to distinguish it from a numeric literal. The character literal 'A' may also be written as '\u0041' (see Figure 1.5), however, this representation is not as clear as using the literal value of the character.

Unicode	Character	Unicode	Character	Unicode	Character
0020	space	0040	@	0060	`
0021	!	0041	A	0061	a
0022	"	0042	B	0062	b
0023	#	0043	C	0063	c
0024	$	0044	D	0064	d
0025	%	0045	E	0065	e
0026	&	0046	F	0066	f
0027	'	0047	G	0067	g
0028	(	0048	H	0068	h
0029	)	0049	I	0069	i
002A	*	004A	J	006A	j
002B	+	004B	K	006B	k
002C	,	004C	L	006C	l
002D	-	004D	M	006D	m
002E	.	004E	N	006E	n
002F	/	004F	O	006F	o
0030	0	0050	P	0070	p
0031	1	0051	Q	0071	q
0032	2	0052	R	0072	r
0033	3	0053	S	0073	s
0034	4	0054	T	0074	t
0035	5	0055	U	0075	u
0036	6	0056	V	0076	v
0037	7	0057	W	0077	w
0038	8	0058	X	0078	x
0039	9	0059	Y	0079	y
003A	:	005A	Z	007A	z
003B	;	005B	[	007B	{
003C	<	005C	\	007C		
003D	=	005D	]	007D	}
003E	>	005E	^	007E	~
003F	?	005F	_		

Figure 1.5 US-ASCII printable character set

> The **Unicode Worldwide Character Standard** is a character coding system designed to represent the characters of the languages of the modern world. Currently the Unicode standard contains 34,168 distinct coded characters. The characters used in the computer programs in this book are confined to those illustrated in Figure 1.5. This character set is known as the US-ASCII or Basic Latin character set. Notice that each Unicode has been defined as a four digit hexadecimal number.

Integer Numbers

An integer is stored within four bytes of computer memory. The range of integer values that can be stored in the memory is -2,147,483,648 to +2,147,483,647.

In Java the type integer is declared as `int`.

If you want to store an integer number that lies outside of the range for `int` types, then Java can also store much larger integers defined as `long`. These numbers are represented within eight bytes (64 bits) and have a range of -9,223,372,036,854,775,808 to +9,223,372,036,854,775,807.

The use of a plus sign (+) is optional for positive integer literals. All decimal integer literals must begin with a digit in the range 1 .. 9 after the sign if one is present. Integer literals must not begin with 0 (zero). A `long` integer literal, either decimal or hexadecimal, has the character `l` or `L` appended immediately after the number.

Real Numbers

A real number is stored in the computer memory in two parts, a mantissa (the fractional part) and an exponent (the power to which the base of the number must be raised in order to give the correct value of the number when multiplied by the mantissa). For example, 437.875 can be rewritten as 0.437875×10^3, where 0.437875 is the mantissa and 3 is the exponent. A four-byte representation of a real number will give a maximum value of $\pm 3.40282347 \times 10^{38}$ and the smallest value as $\pm 1.40239846 \times 10^{-45}$. The majority of decimal fractions do not convert exactly into binary fractions; therefore, the representation of a real number is not always accurate.

In Java the type real is declared as `float`.

If the float range is too restrictive for the real numbers being stored, Java can store much larger real numbers using the type `double`. The number of bytes used to store a double precision number is increased to eight. This increase in storage space will give a maximum value of $\pm 1.79769313486231570 \times 10^{+308}$ and the smallest value as $\pm 4.94065645841246544 \times 10^{-324}$.

A real literal can be written in one of two ways. For example the literal -123.456 can be written as depicted or using a scientific notation -1.23456E+2. The character E represents the base 10, so the number can be interpreted as -1.23456×10^2 which of course evaluates to -123.456 when you adjust the decimal point.

> ℹ️ All real literals in Java are stored in double-precision (double) by default. To distinguish a single precision literal, that is a real number stored as float, from its default value append the letter f or F after the number. For example, -123.456f or -1.23456E+2f. Although it is not strictly necessary a double precision real literal may have the letter d or D appended after the number.

The data types char, int, long, float and double are known as **primitive** data types.

1.3 Identifiers

Data may be thought of as occupying areas of the computer's memory in the same way as people occupy houses in a street. To distinguish different families in different houses, we could use either the surname of the family or the number of the house. To distinguish data in different areas of memory, we could give the data a name or use the numeric memory address of the first byte of where the data is stored.

In Java it is much easier to refer to data by name and let the computer do the work of finding out where in memory the data is stored. Figure 1.6 illustrates the use of names to represent data stored at memory addresses. The generic term for the name you give to a datum is an identifier. Java uses the following rules for the composition of identifiers.

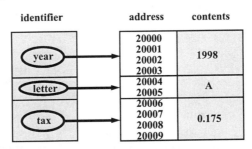

Figure 1.6 Use of identifiers to represent data

An identifier may contain combinations of the letters of the alphabet (both upper case A-Z and lower-case a-z), an underscore character _, a dollar sign $ and decimal digits 0-9. The identifier may start with any of these characters with the exception of a decimal digit. Java is a **case-sensitive** language, meaning that upper-case letters and lower-case letters of the alphabet are treated as different letters. Identifiers can normally be of any practicable length. An identifier must not be the same as those Java keywords listed in Figure 1.7. A programmer uses keywords to construct statements in a program for the computer to obey. Therefore, we will use keywords in program statements, but not as identifiers.

Those words in Figure 1.7 in a non-bold regular typeface are reserved by Java but currently unused.

abstract	default	goto	operator	synchronized
boolean	do	if	outer	this
break	double	implements	package	throw
byte	else	import	private	throws
byvalue	extends	inner	protected	transient
case	false	instanceof	public	true
cast	final	int	rest	try
catch	finally	interface	return	var
char	float	long	short	void
class	for	native	static	volatile
const	future	new	super	while
continue	generic	null	switch	

Figure 1.7 Keywords

A programmer should always compose identifiers so they convey meaning. The identifiers name, street, town, and zipcode imply the meaning of the data that they represent, unlike the non-descriptive identifiers N, S, T and Z. When an identifier is constructed from more than one word, each successive word should begin with an upper-case letter; an identifier should be easy to read, and its meaning should be clear.

Examples of legal identifiers are subTotal, salesTax, unitCost, and rateOfPay.

 Resist the temptation of beginning an identifier with an underscore _ or using a dollar $ character in your identifiers. Often such characters are used in other variables by the computer.

1.4 Variables and Constants

A Java program contains data declarations and instructions. The data declarations must appear before the instructions, since the declarations describe the type of data used by the instructions. Although a declaration may appear anywhere in a program, subject to the restrictions mentioned, you should attempt to group your declarations before the instructions that use them.

If the values of the data in the storage cells can be changed by the instructions in a computer program, the values of the data will vary, and the data identifiers are known as **variables**. The syntax for making a variable declaration follows.

syntax

Variable Declaration:

```
data-type identifier;
data-type identifier-list;
```

For example, the data declarations for the information displayed in Figure 1.2 might be:

```
float costOfElectricity;
float costOfSoftware;
float shares;
```

When variables are of the same type you may declare the type followed by a list of identifiers separated by commas, for example:

```
float costOfElectricity, costOfSoftware, shares;
```

Although Java automatically initializes all data of a primitive type at the point of declaration, such that integer types and real types are both initialized to zero and characters to the Unicode \u0000, data can be initialized at its point of declaration to other values by using the following syntax.

 Variable Initialization: *data-type identifier = literal;*

For example, from the data of Figures 1.1 and 1.2

```
char      parkingSymbol  = 'P';
int       weightLimit    = 10;
float     conversion     = 51.4974f;
```

Reminder! Notice the use of f after the value 51.4974. The f signifies that the numeric literal is stored as a single-precision value. This is an important point to remember since real numeric literals are stored in double precision by default.

Many programs have data values that remain constant during the running of the program. Examples of constants are sales tax at 5% (0.05f), mathematical PI at 3.14159, and the Earth's gravitational constant (g) at the surface 9.80665 ms^{-2}. Rather than using the literal value of a constant in an expression, it is far better to name the constant, thus giving greater clarity to the expression in which the constant is found. Using this technique a program does not become littered with numbers, whose meanings are often difficult to understand.

The syntax for a constant declaration follows.

 Constant Declaration: **final** *data-type identifier = literal;*

Such constants can be declared in Java as follows.

```
final float   SALES_TAX  = 0.05f;
final double  PI         = 3.14159;
final float   G          = 9.80665f;
```

The keyword `final` implies that the constant identifier is initialized to a value that will not change during the execution of the program. Convention dictates that constant identifiers should be coded in upper-case letters to distinguish them from variables in a program, hence the identifiers `SALES_TAX`, `PI` and `G`.

1.5 Arithmetic

Arithmetic operations are among the most fundamental instructions that can be included in a program. The following symbols are used to perform arithmetic on data stored in memory.

Unary operators

+ unary plus   **−** unary minus

Unary operators have one operand and are used to represent positive or negative numbers.

Binary multiplicative operators

* multiplication   **/** division   **%** remainder

Note - the % operator will compute the remainder after the division of two <u>integer</u> values; for example 33%16 computes remainder 1 after 33 is divided by 16; 16%33 computes remainder 16 after 16 is divided by 33 (the result of the division is 0, remainder 16).

Binary additive operators

+ addition   **−** subtraction

Both multiplicative and additive operators have two operands.

To understand arithmetic operations, it is helpful to conceptualize how a computer uses memory. In the previous section we saw how data can be referred to by name in the memory of a computer. Figure 1.8 illustrates numbers being referred to by the names `total`, `subTotal` and `tax` in three separate locations in memory before arithmetic is applied to the data.

Figure 1.8 Numbers stored by Identifier

Arithmetic may be performed on this data and the result assigned to a memory location, using the assignment operator **=** . The syntax of an assignment follows.

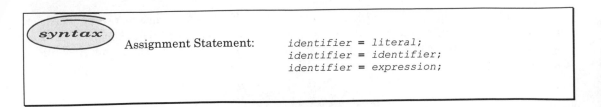

For example, the assignment statement `total=subTotal+tax` adds the contents of `subTotal` to the contents of `tax` and stores the result in `total`, destroying or overwriting the previous contents of `total`. Therefore, after the computer executes the statement `total=subTotal+tax`, the contents of `total` is changed. The result of the computation is shown in Figure 1.9.

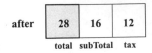

Figure 1.9 Result of the computation total = subTotal+tax

Similar before and after situations can be applied to the following computations.

```
total = score - penalty;
tax = price * taxRate;
time = distance / speed;
result = sum % divisor;
counter = counter + 1;
```

The results of the arithmetic from these statements is illustrated in Figure 1.10.

The destination of an assignment will always be on the left-hand side of an assignment - `score=9` implies that `score` is assigned the value 9. The statement `9=score` has no meaning, since 9 is not a legal identifier. However, `score=result` implies that `score` is assigned the value of `result`, whereas `result=score` implies that `result` is assigned the value of `score`.

In the last example in Figure 1.10 the expression `counter = counter + 1` may seem a little unusual, since the variable `counter` appears on both sides of the expression. The statement should be read as follows: on the right-hand side of the expression, the current value of `counter` (3) is increased by 1, giving a result of (4). This result is then assigned to the variable on the left-hand side of the expression, which also happens to be the variable `counter`. The old value of `counter` (3) is overwritten or destroyed by the new value (4). The effect of this statement has been to increase the value of the variable `counter` by 1.

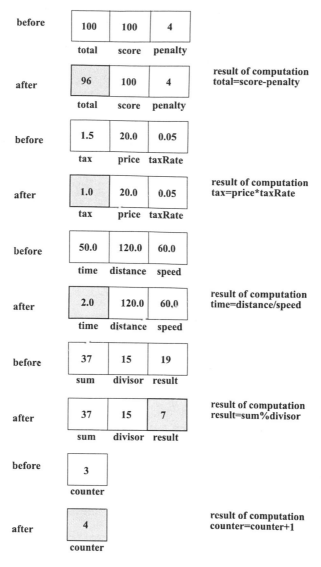

Figure 1.10 Results of various computations

The storage of integer and real numbers are organized differently, and may use different amounts of memory. For example, the internal representation of the types int and float are organized differently, and int and long as well as float and double use different amounts of memory. Therefore, when operands are of different types, one or more of the operands must be converted to a type that can safely accommodate all values before any arithmetic can be performed.

Type conversion is performed automatically when the type of the expression on the right-hand side of an assignment can be <u>safely</u> promoted to the type of the variable on the left-hand side. For example,

```
long   largeInteger;
int    smallInteger;

largeInteger = smallInteger;
```

This assignment involves `smallInteger` of type `int` being promoted to type `long` for the purpose of performing the assignment. However, the original type declaration `int` for the variable `smallInteger` does not change.

Note. The assignment `smallInteger = largeInteger;` is not allowed since the variable `largeInteger` cannot be promoted from type `long` to type `int` without possible loss of digits.

Type conversion may also be explicit through the use of a cast operation. A **cast** is an explicit conversion of a value from its current type to another type. The syntax of this operation follows:

Cast operation: `(data-type) expression;`

where data-type in parenthesis indicates the type to which the expression should be converted. For example,

```
float money;
int    looseChange;
money = (float) looseChange;
```

The cast expression `(float) looseChange`, is used to convert `looseChange` in the expression to a number of type `float`. This does not imply that `looseChange` has altered its type from `int` to `float`; only the value has been converted to type `float` for the purpose of the assignment.

Java will allow the statement `smallInteger = (int) largeInteger;` even though digits may be lost in the assignment.

1.6 Operator Precedence

If an expression was written as A+B*C-D/E, how would it be evaluated? There is a need to introduce a set of rules for the evaluation of such expressions. All operators have an associated hierarchy that determines the order of precedence for evaluating an expression. Unary operators have a higher order of precedence than multiplicative operators, and multiplicative operators have a higher order of precedence than additive operators (see Figure 1.11).

Expressions are evaluated by taking the operators with a higher priority before those of a lower priority. Generally, where operators are of the same priority, the expression is evaluated from left to right.

Expressions in parenthesis will be evaluated before non parenthesized expressions. Parenthesis, although not an operator, can be considered as having an order of precedence after unary operators.

priority level	type	operator	symbol	example
1	unary	negate	–	-A
		plus	+	+B
	cast	a data type	(type)	(float)
2	multiplicative	multiply	*	A*B
		divide	/	A/B
		remainder	%	A%B
3	additive	add	+	A+B
		subtract	–	A-B
13	assignment	equal	=	A=B

Figure 1.11 Priority levels of operators

The expression A+B*C-D/E can be evaluated by inspecting the operators and grouping operations according to the above rules. This process is illustrated in Figure 1.12; the numbers indicate the order of evaluation. The equivalent algebraic expression is given at each stage of the evaluation.

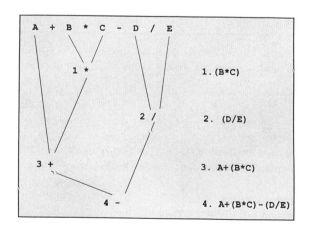

*Figure 1.12 Evaluation of A+B*C-D/E*

The expression (X*X+Y*Y)/(A+B) can be evaluated in the same way, as illustrated in Figure 1.13.

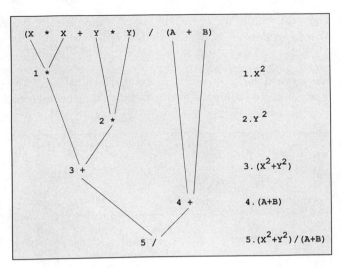

Figure 1.13 Evaluation of (X*X+Y*Y)/(A+B)

You should adopt the habit of using parenthesis in order to make the meaning of an expression as clear as possible. For example, the algebraic expression $\frac{uv}{wx}$ can be written in Java as U*V/W/X; however, (U*V)/(W*X) is clearer to understand.

Similarly, $x^2 + y^2 + \frac{4}{z^2}(x + y)$ can be written in Java as (X*X)+(Y*Y)+4*(X+Y)/(Z*Z).

With the exception of the % remainder operator, which must have integer operands, all other operators can have integer or real operands or a mixture of both types. In a division, if both the operands are integer, then the fractional remainder in the result will be truncated.

NOW DO THIS

Before continuing with this chapter you are recommended to consolidate your knowledge and turn to the following questions at the end of the chapter.

Review Questions: attempt questions 1 to 26 inclusive. The answers to these questions may be found by reading through the first part of the chapter again!

Exercises: attempt questions 41 to 51 inclusive. The answers to these questions are available in Appendix A.

1.7 Classes and Methods

Classes form the backbone of the Java language. There are numerous predefined classes for your use as a programmer. You may also invent your own classes - but more of this later in the book!

If you inspect the Java documentation you were asked to install during the Introduction, you will find listings of all the predefined classes found in the Java language.

Using your Java documentation and a Web browser follow these instructions.

Look up the JDK API Documentation (API is an acronym for Application Programming Interface); mouse-click on Java Platform Core API; you will see on the screen a list of Java API Packages. From this list mouse-click on the package `java.lang`; you will see on the screen a class index for the java.lang package. Mouse-click on **Math** and you will see on screen a full description of the Math class.

After this brief trip into the documentation did you get the feeling that the API is arranged in a hierarchical structure? Figure 1.14 attempts to capture the nature of this hierarchy.

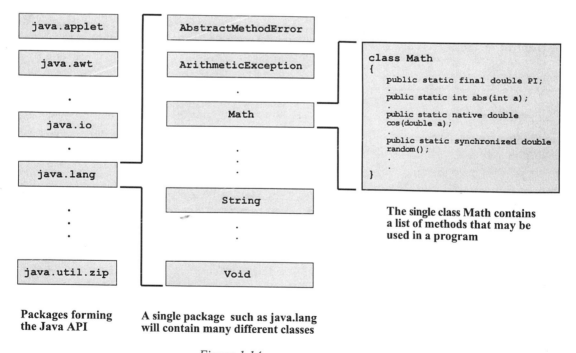

Packages forming the Java API

A single package such as java.lang will contain many different classes

Figure 1.14

The Java API is composed from many packages. At the time of writing this book there are 23 packages, however, this number is expected to increase as the Java language evolves.

A **package** is a convenient way of grouping together many different classes that have a common purpose. For example, the java.lang package contains the classes that are most central to the Java language; the java.io package contains all the classes that may be used for input and output.

A **class** may contain data, methods or a combination of both data and methods. For example, if you examine Figure 1.14 the Math class illustrates the inclusion of a constant PI, and a sample of methods abs, cos and random.

A **class method** is a group of declarations and executable program statements that perform a particular activity. A method's **signature** is the first line of a method, terminated by a semicolon. The purpose of a signature is to uniquely identify a method in terms of its return type, name and formal parameter list. The syntax of a signature is:

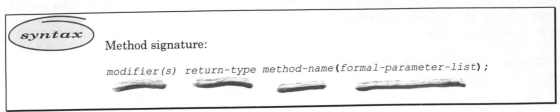

You may notice from Figure 1.14, that the documentation of a class normally contains the signatures of the methods for the class. We shall analyze the sample of signatures taken from the java.lang.Math class by parsing each of the tokens defined by the syntax.

Sample 1:   public static int abs(int a);

The keywords public and static are modifiers. The keyword **public** implies that the method may be used anywhere the class is used. The meaning of the keyword static will be explained later in the chapter. The return type is int; the method's name is abs; and the formal parameter list requires a value of type int. The function of the method is to return the absolute value of an int value.

The class method is called by using the name of the method, followed by a suitable value known as an **argument** that matches the data type of the formal parameter. Figure 1.15 illustrates the various components in a call to a class method.

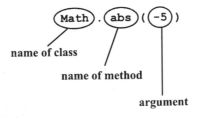

Figure 1.15 The components in a class method call

If the value of the argument is not negative, the value of the argument is returned. If the value of the argument is negative, the negation of the value of the argument is returned.

For example, if we wanted to use the abs method to return the absolute value of the integer variable value, we may write:

```
int value = -5;
int newValue;

newValue = Math.abs(value);
```

The method abs returns +5; this value is assigned to the variable newValue. It becomes clear which class has supplied the method abs since the name of the class Math is used to qualify the name of the method, hence Math.abs(value).

— requires argument double.

Sample 2:   public static native double cos(double a);

If we analyze the second signature we see that the keywords public, static and native are modifiers (don't be concerned about the keyword native); the return type is double; the name of the method is cos; and the formal parameter list requires an argument of type double. The function of the method is to return a value for the trigonometric cosine of an angle. Incidentally, the value of the argument must be measured in radians.

For example, if we wanted to find the cosine of the angle 90º (approximately 1.570795 radians); we might write the following code. You may recall that the constant PI is available in the Math package.

```
double angle = Math.PI/2.0;
double cosineOfAngle;

cosineOfAngle = Math.cos(angle);
```

The method cos returns the value of zero - the cosine of 90º.

return type.
method

Sample 3:   public static synchronized double random();

modifiers

Finally, in the third signature we see that the keywords public, static and synchronized are modifiers (don't be concerned about the keyword synchronized); the return type is double; the name of the method is random; and since the parenthesis for the formal parameter list are empty, we may deduce there is no formal parameter list. The function of the method random is to return a pseudo-random number between 0.0 and 1.0. Note - random number generators are often referred to as pseudo-random number generators because the numbers produced tend to repeat themselves after a period of time.

For example, if we wanted to generate a random number in the range 0.0 to 1.0, we might write the following code.

```
double randomNumber;

randomNumber = Math.random();
```

The variable randomNumber will be assigned any real number in the range 0.0 to 1.0.

You need to remember the following information about methods before continuing with the rest of the chapter.

- A method will allow you to perform a particular function within your program. You are advised to make full use of the predefined methods in Java rather than duplicating effort by writing your own methods.

- A method call may often require an argument. **You must ensure that the data type for the argument is the same data type as specified in the formal parameter list by the signature.**

- A method may return a value which can be assigned to a variable of the same type as the returned value, or used as an argument in a call to another method.

1.8 String Class

A string is a group of characters, that are stored as consecutive characters in the memory of a computer, with each character being represented by a 16-bit Unicode.

A string literal in Java is delimited by double quotes. For example the string literal ABC is written as "ABC", or by using the Unicodes as "\u0041\u0042\u0043".

The type declaration for a string is declared in Java as **String**.

For example, the class String will allow us to declare data of type string. If we examine a partial listing of the predefined class String then we may begin to understand the difference between a primitive type and a class.

```
public final class String extends Object
{
    // constructors
    public String();
    public String(String value) throws NullPointerException;
    .
    .

    // class methods
    public static String valueOf(char c);
    public static String valueOf(int i);
    public static String valueOf(float f);
    .
    .

    // instance methods
    public String concat(String str) throws NullPointerException;
    public int length();
    public String toUpperCase();
    .
    .
}
```

From the partial listing of the class `String`, it is evident that a class may contain up to three different types of methods.

- a constructor

- a class method

- an instance method

Constructors

You may wonder about the methods that have the same name as the class? These are special methods known as **constructors**, and their purpose is to initialize data of the type `String` to specified values. A constructor does not return a value.

How can we declare data of type string? A variable or constant of type `String` is declared by using the name of the class in the same way as you would use any of the primitive types.

A class containing a constructor and instance methods, may be thought of as a data type.

For example

```
String alphabet;
```

The declaration on its own is not much use, since the memory location `alphabet` does not refer to any data. Java recognizes this fact, and has designated the contents of this location as `null` (see Figure 1.17). We can initialize `alphabet` by using either of the constructors. This initialization is known as creating an **instance** of the class or creating an **object**.

The syntax of the instantiation of a class or the creation of an object follows.

---

syntax

Instantiation:
```
class-name object-name = new class-constructor();
class-name object-name = new class-constructor(argument-list);
```

where argument-list is one or more values used by the constructor to initialize the data of the object.

Examples of creating the object `alphabet` follow.

`String alphabet = new String();` using the first `String` constructor with no arguments.

`String alphabet = new String("abcdefghijklmnopqrstuvwxyz");` using the second `String` constructor that accepts a string as an argument.

The first statement will initialize `alphabet` to the empty string `""` and the second statement will initialize `alphabet` to the string `"abcdefghijklmnopqrstuvwxyz"`. But what is the purpose of the reserved word `new`? Let us recall for a moment how primitive data types are stored. Figure 1.16 illustrates how three primitive types `char`, `int` and `float` can be conceptually represented in the memory of the computer.

```
char letter = 'A';          [   A   ]
                              letter

int counter = 156;          [  156  ]
                             counter

float tax = 0.175;          [ 0.175 ]
                               tax
```

Figure 1.16 Primitive types stored by value

In Figure 1.16 the *values* of the identifiers `letter`, `counter` and `tax` are stored at the memory locations depicted by the names of the identifiers. Hence the primitive data is stored by **value**.

Figure 1.17 illustrates that when an identifier of the type `String` is initialized, the value of the string is not stored at the memory location depicted by the identifier, but stored in a different location pointed at or *referenced* by the identifier. The object `alphabet` is stored by **reference**.

```
String alphabet;            [  null  ]
                             alphabet
```

`String alphabet = new String("abcdefghijklmnopqrstuvwxyz");`

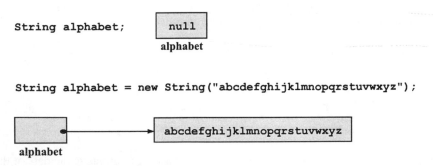

Figure 1.17 An object is stored by reference

The purpose of the reserved word `new` is to allocate a new memory storage area for holding the value of the string. Notice from Figure 1.17 that the memory location `alphabet` contains a reference to the memory area that stores the string.

> (i) Since the string data type is so commonly used, Java provides a shortcut method for initializing a string. The reserved word `new` may be omitted and an object `name` of type `String` can be declared as follows.
>
> ```
> String alphabet = "abcdefghijklmnopqrstuvwxyz";
> ```

If you wish to assign one string to another, then the assignment does not provide a copy of the value but merely a *reference* to the value. For example, Figure 1.18 illustrates that although the string `alphabet` is assigned to the string `lowerCase`, `lowerCase` is only allowed to reference the object `alphabet` and not obtain a copy of the string `"abcdefghijklmnopqrstuvwxyz"`.

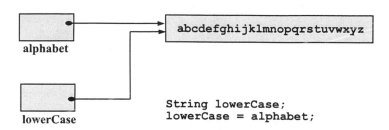

Figure 1.18 Assignment of strings

Class Methods

You have already encountered class methods in the class `java.lang.Math`. Class methods are called by stating the name of the method. The class methods defined in the class `String`, are called or invoked in the same way as for the methods in the class `java.lang.Math`. For example, if we wanted to change an integer value into a string object we might write:

```
int value = 16;
String integer = new String();

integer = String.valueOf(value);
```

At this point it is worth explaining the meaning of the keyword static. A **static** method is one that cannot be invoked by an object. A `static` method is a class method and is invoked by using the name of the method.

Instance Methods

From the partial listing of the class `String` you can see a group of methods that appear to describe the characteristics and operations you might associate with an object such as a string of characters.

For example, the identifier `length` would suggest that it returns the number of characters in a string. The identifier `concat` suggests the concatenation or appending one string after another, and the identifier `toUpperCase` suggests that the characters in the string are converted to the upper case letters if appropriate.

A class contains a group of methods that belong together in the context of the description of the class to describe the state and behavior of an object. These activities, such as `length`, `concat`, and `toUpperCase` are known as **instance methods**.

The methods defined in the class `String`, may be used to obtain information about the string. The object is allowed to invoke the appropriate instance method using the following syntax.

syntax

Invoking an instance method:

```
object.method-name();
object.method-name(argument-list);
```

For example, the statement `alphabet.length()` will return the length of the string as 26;

the statement `String alphaNumeric = alphabet.concat("0123456789")` will assign to `alphaNumeric` the new string `"abcdefghijklmnopqrstuvwxyz0123456789"`.

`String capitals = alphabet.toUpperCase()` will assign to `capitals` the new string `"ABCDEFGHIJKLMNOPQRSTUVWXYZ"`.

⚠ Once an object of a particular class has been declared, you are only allowed to perform operations upon objects of that class using the instance methods defined by the class.

1.9 Wrapper Classes

The five primitive types `char`, `int`, `long`, `float` and `double` introduced in this chapter have corresponding classes that provide some general methods that are useful when dealing with data of the specified type. These classes are known as `Character`, `Integer`, `Long`, `Float` and `Double` respectively (note that the class names begin with an upper case letter). The classes are known as **wrapper** classes since they literally wrap the primitive data type in a class. Inspect your Java documentation for a full listing of wrapper classes. A partial listing of the `Integer` class follows.

```
public final class Integer extends Number
{
    public static final int MIN_VALUE = 0x80000000;
    public static final int MAX_VALUE = 0x7fffffff;
```

```
    public Integer(int value);
    public Integer(String s) throws NumberFormatException;
    public int intValue();

}
```

From this listing you can see the class Integer contains useful maximum and minimum constants that define the size (in hexadecimal notation) of the largest negative int MIN_VALUE and the largest positive int MAX_VALUE; constructors to convert an int or a String to an Integer object; and methods to convert an Integer object to an int value. From the following declaration of a primitive type int

```
            int primitiveValue = 36;
```

an object newValue of type Integer can be created by the statements

```
            Integer newValue;
            newValue = new Integer(primitiveValue);
```

Both statements may be combined into one as

```
            Integer newValue = new Integer(primitiveValue);
```

The original integer value for primitiveValue has been wrapped in the class Integer, and an object newValue created that refers to the original value of primitiveValue. The only way of retrieving this value is by using the instance method intValue in the statement

```
            primitiveValue = newValue.intValue();
```

These facts are illustrated in Figure 1.19.

`int primitiveValue = 36;`   `Integer newValue = new Integer(primitiveValue);`

primitiveValue

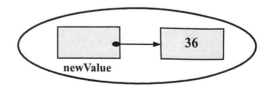

The datum 36 is now wrapped by the class Integer.

Figure 1.19 Use of the Integer wrapper class

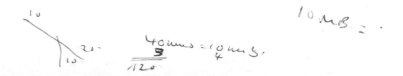

1.10 Class Hierarchy

Despite a complete chapter being devoted to class hierarchy later in the book, it is necessary to introduce the subject at a superficial level, so that you may start to understand more about predefined classes.

When you examined the partial listing for the `String` class you may have wondered about the inclusion of the keyword `extends` in the clause:

```
public final class String extends Object
```

The keyword **extends** implies that all the methods and data defined in the class `Object` are inherited by the class `String`. The class `Object` is known as a superclass of the subclass `String`. The superclass/ subclass relationship may be represented in a **hierarchy diagram** as depicted in Figure 1.20. Convention dictates that the arrow in the figure always points up the hierarchy to the superclass.

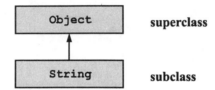

Figure 1.20 Hierarchy diagram showing superclass and subclass relationship

Figures 1.21 and 1.22 also indicate that a hierarchy of classes may contain more than just two levels as illustrated in Figure 1.20.

When one class inherits from another class anywhere in the hierarchy, an object of any subclass in the hierarchy is also a legal superclass object. From this statement two important features regarding object assignment and parameter passing follow.

- An object of a subclass may be assigned to an object of its superclass without a data type violation.

- An object of a subclass may be passed as an argument to a method that requires a parameter of its superclass type.

For example, given the following declarations:

```
Object objectDatum = new Object();
String stringDatum = new String("ABC");
```

The first bulleted point states the assignment `objectDatum = stringDatum;` is legal.

An example of the second bulleted point will be given in the next section.

1.11 Stream Classes

The term **stream** refers to any input source or output destination for data. Java provides the stream classes `BufferedReader` and `PrintWriter`, for the input and output of data respectively. The physical source and destination of the data is specified by the argument of the constructor of the appropriate class.

If we examine the class `BufferedReader`, we see that one of its constructors has the format:

```
public BufferedReader(Reader in);
```

To instantiate an object of type `BufferedReader` it is necessary to supply the constructor with a parameter of the correct type - `Reader`. If you inspect the hierarchy diagram in Figure 1.21 you will notice that the class `Reader` is a superclass to the class `InputStreamReader`. You may recall the second bulleted point will allow an object lower down a class hierarchy to be passed as an argument to a method that requires a parameter of class further up the class hierarchy. Because of this hierarchical relationship we may substitute the type `Reader` with the type `InputStreamReader`.

A constructor from the class `InputStreamReader` has the format:

```
public InputStreamReader(InputStream in);
```

We need to find a constant that represents the standard input stream. The class **java.lang.System** contains a constant **in** of type `InputStream` that represents the standard input stream and corresponds with the keyboard of a computer. Therefore, it is possible to instantiate an object of type `InputStreamReader` as follows:

```
InputStreamReader stream = new InputStreamReader(System.in);
```

The object `stream` may be used to instantiate the object `keyboard` as follows:

```
BufferedReader keyboard = new BufferReader(stream);
```

Alternatively, we can dispense with `stream` as an intermediate variable and combine the two instantiations into one as follows.

```
BufferedReader keyboard = new
BufferedReader(new InputStreamReader(System.in));
```

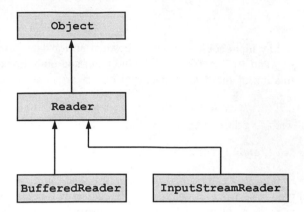

Figure 1.21 Hierarchy diagram for java.io.BufferedReader and java.io.InputStreamReader

The class `PrintWriter` is a character output stream, and its position in the class hierarchy is illustrated in Figure 1.22.

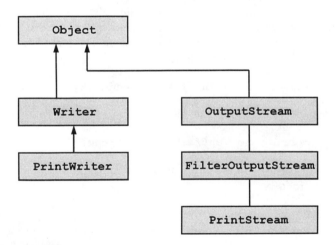

Figure 1.22 A hierarchy diagram for java.io.PrintWriter and java.io.PrintStream

A constructor for the class `PrintWriter` is:

```
public PrintWriter(OutputStream out, boolean autoFlush);
```

This constructor requires two arguments, the first argument is of type the `OutputStream` and the second argument is of the type `boolean`. If you inspect the hierarchy diagram in Figure 1.22, you will notice that a class of type `OutputStream` may be substituted for a class of type `PrintStream` (remember the second bulleted point in the previous section?). Why should we make the substitution? We need to find a constant that will represent the standard output stream. The class `java.lang.System` contains a constant **out** of type `PrintStream` that represents the standard output stream, and corresponds with the screen of a monitor.

What about the type `boolean` referred to in the second parameter of the `PrintWriter` constructor? What is it and why was it not mentioned earlier?

> ⓘ A **boolean** data type is another primitive data type. A variable of type `boolean` is permitted to have only one of two values, either **true** or **false**. The use of the `boolean` data type will be covered in detail in Chapter 3.

You are advised to set the `autoFlush` argument to `true`, otherwise, you may not get any information to appear on the screen of a monitor.

Now we have the complete picture, it is possible to instantiate an object of type `PrintWriter` as follows:

```
PrintWriter screen = new PrintWriter(System.out, true);
```

Note the dot (.) convention for showing where a class variable has originated from, hence `System.in` and `System.out`.

Figure 1.23 illustrates the concept of the object `keyboard` providing a source of input to the computer, and the object `screen` providing a destination for output from the computer.

1.12 Input and Output

This final section explains how to write Java statements to allow data to be input to the computer via a keyboard and information output from the computer and displayed on the screen of a monitor.

The class `BufferedReader` contains a method `readLine` that will allow you to input data of type `String` at the keyboard, by using `keyboard.readLine()`. You may wonder how we input data of other types such as `int` and `float`? **The answer is to input a number as a string and use the appropriate wrapper class to provide the value of the number**.

If you look back at section 1.9, you will notice that one of the constructors for the wrapper class `Integer` defines a constructor that requires a `String` type for initialization. The data we input at the keyboard is also of type `String`, therefore, this string value may be used in the constructor. For example, `new Integer(keyboard.readLine())`. In doing this we have created an object of type `Integer`.

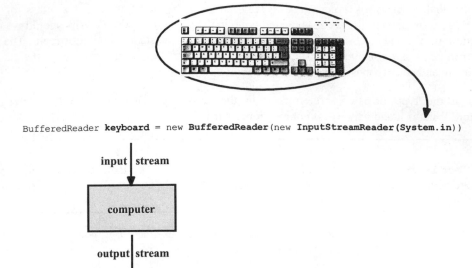

```
BufferedReader keyboard = new BufferedReader(new InputStreamReader(System.in))
```

input | stream

computer

output | stream

```
PrintWriter screen = new PrintWriter(System.out, true)
```

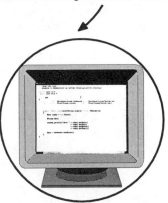

Figure 1.23 Input and output streams

To convert the string into a primitive data type `int`, simply use the wrapper class instance method `intValue()`. The whole operation can be performed using the following statements.

Firstly, declare a primitive type

```
int number;
```

then assign to the variable `number` the result of the converted string data that was input at the keyboard.

```
number = new Integer(keyboard.readLine()).intValue();
```

This technique can be applied to the data types `long`, `float` and `double` since they all have the corresponding wrapper classes and methods for conversion. For example, given the declaration of the primitive type `float realNumber;` the equivalent statement to input this number at the keyboard would be as follows.

```
realNumber = new Float(keyboard.readLine()).floatValue();
```

Unlike input, output to the screen is very straightforward. The class `PrintWriter` contains methods for displaying data as strings for all the types dealt with in this chapter. The methods from the class `PrintWriter` that will be used most often are `print`, `println` and `flush`. For example, to display text on the screen, and then move the line cursor to the next new line, can be accomplished by the statement

```
screen.println("Hello World");
```

To display a line of text and leave the cursor on the same line, can be performed using the statements

```
screen.print("Err.. what's up Doc? "); screen.flush();
```

Note - without the `flush` method the output will not be displayed on the screen until the next `println` statement is executed by the computer.

The strings that you output can have special characters embedded into them. You have already come across one such special character - the Unicode \uxxxx, where xxxx is a four digit hexadecimal number. There are other special characters, known as **escape sequences**, the most common are **\t** for a tabulation and **\n** for a new line.

If you examine the Java documentation for the class `PrintWriter`, you will notice that the methods `print` and `println` are defined for all the primitive types discussed in this chapter. The methods convert the various Java primitive types to `String` representations then output the resulting string. This not only means that either `print` or `println` can be used to display numbers but also combinations of text and numbers. For example, the following segment of Java code can be used to output text and the value of an initialized variable.

```
float grossWage = 250.00f;

screen.println("Gross weekly wage = " + grossWage);
```

Java allows a plus sign + to be used as a **string concatenation operator**. Since the Java primitive types are converted to string representations before being output, the string defined between the inverted commas `"Gross weekly wage = "` is appended with the string value of `grossWage` before the entire string is displayed on the screen.

During the course of this chapter you have been introduced to declaring variables and constants in a program; performing arithmetic on data; the input of data to a program and the output of information from a program. These are the basic ingredients that go into coding simple computer programs. In the next chapter you will be shown how to construct programs, on the basis that you have a fairly complete knowledge of the material found in this chapter.

Use the review questions and exercises to test and reinforce your knowledge before you proceed to Chapter 2.

Summary

- Data is the name given to characters and quantities operated upon by a computer.

- The integer data types are int and long; the real data types are float and double; the character data type is char. All five data types are known as primitive types in Java.

- Integers may be represented as either decimal or hexadecimal numbers.

- A boolean data type is also a primitive data type and has the values true and false.

- The data type String is a class and not a primitive data type.

- The size of data that can be stored in a computer's memory is limited by the data's type. All numerical data must be stored within pre-defined ranges.

- Data stored in the memory of a computer can be accessed through an identifier invented by the programmer and the name should be self-documenting.

- Data names must conform to the rules for identifiers.

- Numeric data that reside in memory locations can be manipulated by use of the following operators: + (addition); - (subtraction); * (multiplication); / (division); % (remainder).

- The only operator a String type may use is + for concatenation.

- With the exception of the % remainder operator, which must have integer operands, all other operators can have integer or real operands or a mixture of both.

- Arithmetic operations in Java are evaluated in order of highest to lowest operator precedence. Expressions in parenthesis have higher precedence than non parenthesized expressions. Where operators have equal precedence, the expressions are generally evaluated from left to right.

- The result of a computation is assigned to a variable using the = operator.

- When operands are of different types, one or more of the operands must be converted to the type that can safely accommodate the values before the operation can be performed. The conversion can occur in one of two ways: (1) implicitly, by which Java automatically converts the value on the right-hand side of the assignment to the type of the variable on the left-hand side, or (2) by the use of cast operation, which the programmer must write into the program code.

- Variable declaration specifies the type of data followed by the name of the data.

- Variables may be initialized at the point of declaration.

- Data values that do not change during the running of a program may be declared as constants.

- Constants must be initialized at the point of declaration.

- A package is a convenient structure for grouping together classes that represent some common purpose, such as input/ output, graphics, and so on.

- A class may contain constants, variables, constructors, class methods and instance methods.

- A class containing a constructor and instance methods may be used as a data type.

- A class method is invoked by a direct call to the method.

- An instance method is invoked by an object of the same class.

- The instance methods of a class are used to perform a variety of operations that pertain to the object.

- A variable declared as a class type does not become an object until a constructor within the class has been executed.

- Arguments in a method call must be of the same type as the parameters of the method.

- Wrapper classes are used to provide constants and general methods for the primitive data types.

- A subclass may inherit both data and methods from a superclass, in a class hierarchy.

- When one class inherits from another class anywhere in the hierarchy, an object of any subclass in the hierarchy may be treated as a superclass object.

- An object of a subclass may be assigned to an object of its superclass; and an object of a subclass may be passed as an argument to a method that requires a parameter of its superclass type.

- The assignment of one object to another of the same type does not create a copy of the object.

- A stream refers to any input source or output destination for data. Java provides stream classes for the input and output of data. `BufferedReader` and `PrintWriter` are just two of many stream classes provided by Java.

In this chapter all data input at the keyboard and displayed on a screen are treated as `String` type. Numbers input at the keyboard are converted to their correct type by the use of methods in the appropriate wrapper classes.

Review Questions

1. Describe the meaning of the data types integer, real, character and string.

2. How are the four types listed in question (1) represented as data types in Java?

3. How would you declare an integer variable that had an initial value of 67AF?

4. Distinguish between the mantissa and exponent of a real number.

5. True or false - real numbers may be described as type `float`.

6. True or false - a character is stored as an integer value.

7. True or false - an identifier may begin with an underscore.

8. What range of integers can be stored within 4 bytes?

9. What is the smallest real number that can be stored as type `float`?

10. What is a variable?

11. Is `return` a keyword?

12. What is a constant?

13. Is the declaration of a constant `final PI = 3.14159;` correct?

14. True or false - an identifier described as being constant may have its initial value changed by statements in a program.

15. True or false - 0x3GF is a legal hexadecimal literal.

16. True or false - 032767 is a legal decimal literal.

17. True or false - single precision real constants contain the letter f after the number.

18. Which operator calculates the remainder after the division of two integer numbers?

19. What is the result of the integer division 3/2?

20. If the variable counter has an initial value of 8, what is the value of counter=counter+1?

21. Describe the term operator precedence.

22. What is the result of evaluating the expression 2 * 6 + 20 / 4?

23. True or false - the multiplication operator has a higher priority than the subtraction operator.

24. What does the expression `(int)alpha` do, if `alpha` is declared as a real number?

25. What is the difference when the expressions `(float)(x/y)` and `(float)x/(float)y` are evaluated? Assume that both x and y are integers.

26. What is the Unicode for the letter H?

27. True or false - `Integer` is a primitive type.

28. True or false - an object is created by executing a class constructor.

29. True or false - a primitive data type is stored by reference.

30. True or false - a class type is stored by value.

31. True or false - assigning one string object to another string will result in a copy of the string object being made.

32. Using the wrapper class `Float` is the following statement legal?

```
Float alpha = new Float(36.89);
```

33. What is the result of the evaluation `alpha.intValue();` where `alpha` is defined in the previous question, and `intValue` is a method defined in the wrapper class `Float`?

34. What is wrong with the following declaration?

```
static BufferedReader keyboard = new BufferedReader(System.out);
```

35. If you inspect the class `PrintStream` why is it possible to use the methods `print` and `println` to output numbers of type `int`, `long`, `real` and `double`?

36. True or false - You may invoke an instance method in the same way as you call a class method.

37. How does a package differ from a class?

38. Write the signature of any `String` constructor listed in this chapter.

39. True or false - a subclass inherits from a superclass.

40. Why can an object of a subclass be assigned to an object of its superclass without a type violation?

Exercises

41. From the illustrations in Figures 1.24 and 1.25 of items found in everyday life, discuss what you consider to be data and classify the data by type as variables declared in Java.

COMMUTER RAIL FARES

Zone	One-Way	Half-Fare	Monthly Pass	Family Fare
1	2.00	1.00	64.00	8.00
2	2.25	1.10	72.00	9.00
3	2.50	1.25	82.00	10.00
4	3.00	1.50	94.00	12.00
5	3.25	1.60	104.00	13.00
6	3.50	1.75	112.00	14.00
7	3.75	1.85	120.00	15.00
8	4.00	2.00	128.00	16.00

Figure 1.24 Commuter rail fares

In Figure 1.25 the numbers refer to high and low temperatures in degrees Fahrenheit, and the abbreviations describe the following weather conditions: s - sunny, pc - partial cloud, r - rain, sh - showers and c - cloud.

World Forecasts

City	Today
Acapulco	90/79 s
Athens	79/59 pc
Bangkok	90/78 pc
Beijing	62/38 pc
Berlin	63/51 r
Bermuda	81/74 pc
Budapest	72/52 pc
Buenos Aries	83/62 pc
Cairo	89/68 pc
Dublin	53/39 c
Frankfurt	63/56 sh
Hong Kong	84/74 s

Figure 1.25 Temperatures around the world

42. Identify the illegal variable names in the following list of identifiers. Explain why you think the names are illegal.

(a) priceOfBricks   (b) net-pay   (c) x1   (d) cost of paper
(e) INTEGER   (f) ?X?Y   (g) 1856AD   (h) float

43. Describe the Java types for the following items of data:

(a) "Lexington"   (b) ';'   (c) +156   (d) +2147483648
(e) 247.9   (f) 0.732E+01f (g) 0xAB0   (h) 23.96d

44. Use Figure 1.5 to determine the Unicodes of the following characters:

(a) A   (b) M   (c) *   (d) a   (e) m   (f) 9

45. Write the following numbers using E notation for real numbers; only one nonzero digit should precede the decimal point.

(a) -874.458   (b) +0.00123456   (c) 123456789.0

46. Explain why the following numbers cannot be stored as type float within the ranges defined in this chapter.

(a) 30.16E+38   (b) -0.000456E-39

47. Write suitable type declarations for the following constants:

(a) -45678   (b) 0xFABC   (c) "The Big Apple!"   (d) '\u0041'

48. Convert the following hexadecimal numbers into decimal numbers, and convert the following binary numbers into hexadecimal numbers.

(a) 0xFF   (b) 0x1A2C   (c) 01110011   (d) 0111001100001111

49. What are the values of the following variables after the execution of the respective assignments?

(a)	B=A; C=A; D=A;	A 36	B 98	C 45	D 29

(b)	D=A+B+C+D;	A 10	B 14	C 29	D 36

(c)	A=B-2;	A 17	B 50

(d)	Y=X-Y;	X 19	Y 32

(e)	Z=X*Y;	X 18	Y 3	Z 27

(f)	B=B/A;	A 12.5	B 25.0

(g)	X=A/B;	A 16	B 3	X 25

(h)   Y=C%D;   C   D   Y
                     19   5   2

(i)   D=D+1   D
                     34

50. Write the following expressions in Java.

(a) $\dfrac{A+B}{C}$ (b) $\dfrac{W-X}{Y+Z}$ (c) $\dfrac{D-B}{2A}$ (d) $\dfrac{(A^2+B^2)}{2}$

(e) $(A-B)(C-D)$ (f) B^2-4AC (g) AX^2+BX+C

51. Rewrite the following Java expressions as algebraic expressions.

(a) X+2/Y+4   (b) A*B/(C+2)   (c) U/V*W/X   (d) B*B-4*A*C
(e) A/B+C/D+E/F

52. How would you expect the following output statements to display information?

(a) `screen.println("Hello World");`
(b) `screen.println("\tname: ");`
(c) `screen.println("\tname: " + name);`
where name is declared as `String name = "Mickey Mouse";`
(d) `screen.println("a=" + a + " b=" + b + " c=" + c);`
where a=3, b=4 and c=5.
(e) `screen.print("area covered " + area); screen.flush();`
where area = 635.8658.
(f) `screen.println("\u0041\u0042\u0043");`

53. Detect the errors in the following statements.

(a) `println("value of beta is ", beta);`
(b) `String alpha = 'X';`
(c) `int beta = new Float(keyboard.readLine()).intValue();`

54. What are the errors in the following method calls?

(a) `Math.sin(2);`   (b) `log(1.4793);`
(c) `String.valueOf("abc");`   (d) `String.toLowerCase();`

55. Draw hierarchy diagrams for the following classes.

(a) `Float`   (b) `BufferedOutputStream`

Chapter 2
Program Design

In Chapter 1 you were introduced to a considerable amount of theory to enable you to understand some of the fundamentals of the Java language and programming. The first part of Chapter 2 helps you to consolidate your new found knowledge, by explaining how to construct, compile and run simple programs.

Once you have gained a little experience of writing your own programs, it is important to stress that programming involves more than just typing statements into a computer. The first step in programming is to design and plan your programs away from the computer.

The second part of Chapter 2 focuses your attention upon a prescriptive method for program development. By the end of this chapter you should have an understanding of the following topics.

- The construction of a Java program.

- Implementing a program on a computer.

- Designing simple programs.

- Using pseudocode in the construction of an algorithm.

- Testing algorithms.

- Planning input and output.

- Coding algorithms into simple programs for the input and processing of data and the output of results.

2.1 Program Construction

A Java program is constructed from many classes. Figure 2.1 illustrates the outline of a program that has been composed from just three separate classes A, B and C. Each class may contain any combination of constants, variables, constructors, class methods and instance methods, and use data and methods from the set of Java API classes.

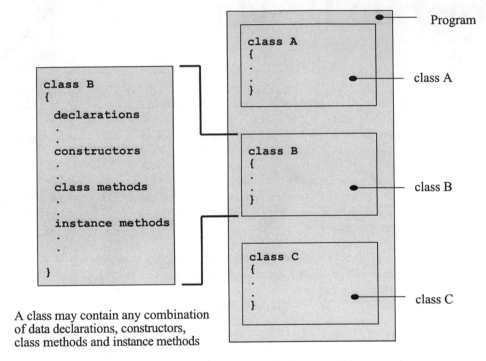

Figure 2.1 Construction of a Java program

We will begin writing programs that contain just one class and one class method. After you have gained confidence in using many of the classes from the Java API, and many of the fundamental statements of the language we will progress to constructing programs using many of our own classes.

A template for constructing a Java application program is illustrated in Figure 2.2. I say application program, because Java code can be written as either an application or an applet. However, don't concern yourself at the moment with applets, these are dealt with in detail later in the book. For the moment you need to concentrate your mind on application programming.

In the explanation that follows the key parts of the template illustrated in Figure 2.2 are used as suitable section subheadings.

heading giving details of the name and purpose of the program

import *list*

class *name*
{

    declarations of input and output streams

    main *method*
    {

        declarations of constants
        declaration of variables
        program statements

    }

}

Figure 2.2 A template for constructing a Java application program

heading giving details of the name and purpose of the program

This is simply a set of comments written on as many lines as necessary. In Java, a comment begins with a double slash **//** at the start of every line. The comments normally document the name and purpose of the program. Comments may also include the name of the author of the program and the date it was written, plus other facts that you care to document.

import list

You may recall from Chapter 1, that stream input and output required objects to be created of type `BufferedReader` and `PrintWriter`. Both of these classes are found in the `java.io` package. The **import** statement makes Java classes available to the program. You can specify each class in the import statement, for example `java.io.BufferedReader` and `java.io.PrintWriter`, but it is a lot simpler to use an asterisk as a wildcard to make all the classes of the package `java.io` available, hence the statement `java.io.*`.

A **wildcard** is a character that can represent a number of different characters. The wildcard * may represent any of the class names.

> The `java.lang` package is automatically imported, therefore, there is never any need to include it in the import list.

class name

The name of the class containing the `main` method must be the same as the name given to the program file (omitting the .java suffix). The naming of the class must follow the same rules as for the naming of any other identifier. The use of braces **{ }** indicate the beginning and ending of the class.

> ⚠️ When creating a name for a class, be careful about the rules for naming identifiers in Java and the naming of program files for the operating system being used. **The Java convention also dictates that the name of a class should always begin with an upper-case letter.**

declarations of input and output streams

You have already encountered the creation of the keyboard and screen objects in the previous chapter. Both variables `keyboard` and `screen` are initialized at their point of declaration, thus creating objects of their respective classes.

```
static BufferedReader keyboard = new
        BufferedReader(new InputStreamReader(System.in));
static PrintWriter    screen   = new PrintWriter(System.out, true);
```

main method

In the construction of a Java application program there must be one **main** method present in only one of the classes. The computer will start the execution of the program at the first statement in the `main` method, and terminate execution after the last statement. The `main` method is a class method with the following signature:

```
public static void main(String[] args);
```

The keyword **void** implies that the `main` method does not return a value. The formal parameter list will allow arguments to be passed to the `main` method at the time of giving the command to execute the program - but more of this later in the book.

Notice that the beginning and ending of the `main` method is denoted by the use of an open **{** and a closed **}** brace respectively. Notice also from the example, how the declaration of the variables is kept separate from the program statements.

2.2 Writing Simple Programs

You now have enough knowledge to be able to construct your own simple programs in Java. We will begin this exercise by looking at a program that has become the traditional opening program in many text books. I refer to the Hello World program. The function of the program is to display on the screen of the monitor the string literal `"Hello World"`. The program has been constructed using the template illustrated in Figure 2.2. Notice since there is no input via a keyboard into this program, the declaration of an input stream is not declared. Since there is no data to process, there will be no data declarations in the program.

Program Example 2.1: Hello World

```
// chap_2\Ex_1.java
// program to display a string literal on the screen

import java.io.*;

class Ex_1
{
    static PrintWriter screen = new PrintWriter(System.out,true);

    public static void main(String[] args)
    {
        screen.println("Hello World");
    }
}
```

The second program demonstrates the use of the five binary arithmetic operators +, -, *, / and % applied to the two integer constants 23 and 5. For example, 23+5, 23-5, etc. The result of each computation is displayed on the screen.

Program Example 2.2: Using Arithmetic Operators

```
// chap_2\Ex_2.java
// program to demonstrate the use of arithmetic operators on integer values

import java.io.*;

class Ex_2
{
    static PrintWriter screen = new PrintWriter(System.out, true);

    public static void main(String[] args)
    {
        // declare constants
        final int first = 23;
        final int second = 5;

        // display results of using +, -, *, / and %
        screen.println("sum        " + (first+second));
        screen.println("difference " + (first-second));
        screen.println("product    " + (first*second));
        screen.println("quotient   " + (first/second));
        screen.println("remainder  " + (first%second));
    }
}
```

Notice in this example the use of the string concatenation operator +, to combine into one string the text and the result of the computation. To avoid the ambiguity of the addition operator being mistaken for the string concatenation operator, it is necessary to enclose the computation of addition in parenthesis.

The third program calculates the circumference and area of a circle using a radius input at the keyboard. You may notice that the statement **throws IOException** has been included in the first line of the main method. If you inspect the Java documentation for the method readLine() in the class BufferedReader, you will notice that this method also throws an IOException. For the moment, simply accept that when any predefined method throws an exception, you should append a throws clause to the first line of the main method, listing the name of the exception(s). A complete chapter is devoted to exception handling later in the book.

Program Example 2.3: Calculation of the Circumference and Area of a circle

```
// chap_2\Ex_3.java
// program to calculate the circumference and
// area of a circle

import java.io.*;

class Ex_3
{
    static BufferedReader keyboard = new
            BufferedReader(new InputStreamReader(System.in));
    static PrintWriter screen = new PrintWriter(System.out, true);

    public static void main(String[] args) throws IOException
    {
        // data declarations
        float radius;
        float circumference;
        float area;

        // prompt and input radius
        screen.print("Input radius "); screen.flush();
        radius = new Float(keyboard.readLine()).floatValue();

        // calculate circumference and area
        circumference = 2.0f * (float) Math.PI * radius;
        area = (float) Math.PI * radius * radius;

        // display statistics of circle
        screen.println("Statistics of Circle\n");
        screen.println("Radius         " + radius);
        screen.println("Circumference " + circumference);
        screen.println("Area          " + area);
    }
}
```

2.3 Program Implementation

Now that you have seen how to code a program, the program must be implemented on a computer. Figure 2.3 illustrates three phases to program implementation.

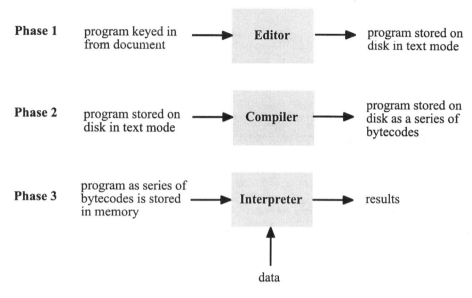

Figure 2.3 Three phases of program implementation

Phase 1 - The creation of a Java program in text mode using an editor

In order to type a Java program at the keyboard and save the program on a disk, it is necessary to run a program called an **editor**. In addition to enabling program entry, an editor allows a program to be retrieved from disk and amended as necessary. A Java program is stored in text mode so that the programmer can read the program as it was written. The Java program does not require translation to a machine recognizable form at this stage. In phase 1 the format of the program is known as **source code**. The name of the file used to store the program must be the same as the class name containing the main method, and have a .java suffix appended to it. For example the name of the file used to display the Hello World message is Ex_1.java.

Phase 2 - The translation of a program using a compiler

The computer cannot execute the Java statements as they currently appear in the program and the statements must be translated to an intermediate form for execution. The compiler is resident in the memory of the computer and uses the Java source program code as input data. The output from the compiler is the program represented by a set of Java byte codes. **Java byte codes** are a set of instructions written for a hypothetical computer, known as the **Java virtual machine**. Regardless of the computer you are using, whether it is a PC, Apple™ or Sun™ computer, the compiler will generate the same Java byte code program. For this reason programs written in Java are portable. A program written in Java to run on say a PC, that also runs without modification on a different computer, for example a Sun™, and produces exactly the same results, is said to be **portable** between the two computers.

In addition to translation, a compiler reports on any grammatical errors made by the programmer in the language statements of the program. If errors are reported it is necessary to return to phase 1, correct the errors and then recompile the program.

The command to compile a Java program using the Java Development Kit is `javac`. To compile the program listed under the heading of Program Example 2.1: Hello World, you would issue the following command in either a terminal window of a Solaris environment or an MSDOS window in Windows 95/NT environment.

```
javac Ex_1.java
```

Phase 3 - The execution of the program stored as Java byte codes

The program stored as Java byte codes is loaded into the memory of the computer, and is read and translated by an interpreter. There exists a different interpreter for different computers, for example the interpreter for a PC will be different to the interpreter for an Apple™. The interpreter reads the respective byte codes and instructs the computer to execute the meanings of the instructions.

The command to run or execute a Java program using the Java Development Kit is `java`. To execute the Hello World program you would issue the following command in the same window as you compiled the program.

```
java Ex_1
```

It is possible for a program to fail during the execution stage phase, in which case it must be stopped from any further execution. If modifications to the program are required, it is necessary to perform the amendments at phase 1, and repeat phases 2 and 3.

Inspect the JDK Tool Documentation, this provides you with a comprehensive description of using the `javac` and `java` tools.

Compile and execute the programs listed in the Program Examples 2.1, 2.2 and 2.3.

Turn to the Exercises at the end of this chapter. Write, compile and execute the programs described in questions 21 to 26 inclusive. The answers are available in Appendix A.

2.4 Software Development

The stages in the development of a software project are illustrated in Figure 2.4. Notice that although the software development cycle consists of a set of four phases, each phase is not deemed to be entirely completed before moving on to the next phase. Because the development of software evolves through the experience gained at each stage, it is possible to go back to any of the stages and modify the solution to the problem.

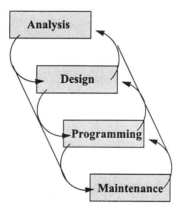

Figure 2.4 Software development life cycle

During *analysis*, the customer who commissioned the system to be built and the software developers who construct the system, meet to agree upon a description of the problem. The outcome of the analysis phase is a description of the functionality of the system, which conveys the behavior of the software system to be constructed.

In the *design* phase plans are generated for building the system. After a design is completed it is possible to look for any shortcomings in the proposed system, and iterate back to the analysis phase and, if necessary, make appropriate modifications to the requirements.

The *programming* of a software project, in the context of this book, is the area you will concentrate upon most. It is the evolutionary phase that combines coding, testing and the integration of the various software components to construct the software system.

A software system is not static. With use, and changes in requirements, the system may need to be modified to meet changing demands. The *maintenance* may take the form of simply changing and re-testing small amounts of code. Alternatively, a modification to the software system may require further analysis, design, coding and testing.

Figure 2.5 illustrates five major activities that form the *programming* part of the software development life cycle. These activities concentrate on the development of software components that have already been identified at the higher level *design* stage.

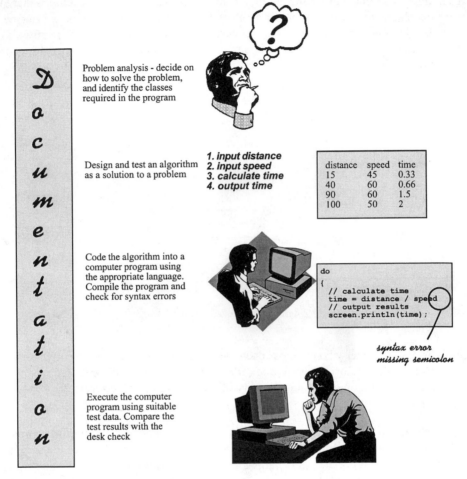

Figure 2.5 The programming phase in software development

Problem Analysis

The first activity involves studying the problem, in order to understand the nature of the problem and determine how to solve it. At this stage it is also possible to define classes and class relationships.

Designing and Testing an Algorithm

An algorithm is a solution to a problem and normally consists of a series of steps. The algorithm may be represented as a narrative of the solution written in English, and known as **pseudocode**.

Having designed a solution, the next step is to trace through the algorithm with test data to verify that the solution contains no logical errors. **Logical errors** are mistakes in the design of the program, such as a branch to a wrong statement, or the use of a wrong mathematical formula.

Coding the Algorithm

The third activity is to use a computer language to code the algorithm into a corresponding computer program. The operations defined in the pseudocode should translate directly into instructions in the computer language. After coding, the program must be compiled. During compilation, errors may be detected in the way the grammar of the computer language has been used. These errors are known as **syntax errors** and are associated with the wrong construction of computer language statements.

Testing the Code

At the stages of design and after coding the program, it is necessary to test the solution to the problem and verify that the program does indeed function correctly. Programs can be tested, either by the programmer tracing through the design and program code or by **peer-group** inspection. In the latter technique, members of the programming team review the accuracy of a design or program and determine whether it meets the original specification. Further testing, often using the same test data as the desk check, is always carried out with the program being run on the computer.

Documentation

Despite documentation being discussed as the fifth activity in programming, it is used and produced during the other four activities, and for this reason documentation can be regarded as an activity that occurs throughout the entire programming cycle.

Over a period of time a program may be changed, and indeed evolve as the computer project to which it contributes evolves. Documentation involves stating the purpose of the program, the method of solution (both pseudocode and program code), the stages of testing that it has undergone, and other necessary facts. The documentation of a program will usually conform to the in-house standards of an organization.

To conclude, programming, therefore, contains the activities of problem analysis, designing an algorithm, coding a program from the algorithm, testing the code, and documenting the program.

2.5 Program Design

Before attempting to design and code a computer program, however, we need to state a few guidelines. These guidelines will be used in the following case studies, and should help you to develop a systematic approach to problem-solving and good programming habits. The seven necessary stages for constructing a computer program are explained next.

Problem Analysis Document in English how you plan to tackle the problem from the information provided. Problem analysis should include sifting through the information and determining what classes are required; what data is to be input, how it is processed, and the information that is to be output. Also show any calculations that will be used on the data. In the case of simple problems, little analysis will be required.

At this stage you should identify the classes and methods that will be used to create the program.

Algorithm Document in English, not Java code, the sequence of operations that are necessary to solve the problem. This is in fact the algorithm or method of solving the problem, and uses pseudocode.

Data Dictionary Determine the items of data that are required. Classify this data into constants, primitive variables and objects, and specify the data type for each item. At this stage, it is possible to write declarations in Java to describe the constants, primitive variables and objects.

Desk Check Invent suitable test data such that the type and nature of the data is representative of the problem. Numerical data should be chosen for ease of calculation. Use the variables defined in the data dictionary to construct headings for the desk check table. Use the test data to trace through the algorithm line by line, obeying the instructions and modifying the values of the variables in the table as required. The desk check makes it possible to predict the results before the program is coded and run.

Screen Layout Design the final screen layout showing the screen text, specimen data and expected results.

Coding From the information documented in the algorithm, data dictionary and screen layout, code the program using the Java language. The process of compiling will not be shown in the examples in this book, although it is assumed that this stage will have been successfully completed before the program can run.

Test results When the compilation is successful, run the program using the same test data and inspect whether the results are the same as those predicted by the desk check.

The following case study illustrates the topics discussed.

Case Study: Time Taken to Fill a Swimming Pool

Problem. Write a program to input the length, width and depth of a rectangular swimming pool of uniform depth and calculate the time it takes to fill the swimming pool. Assume the rate of flow of water into the pool is 50 US gallons per minute, and a cubic foot of water has a capacity of 7.48 US gallons.

Problem Analysis. The solution involves calculating the volume of the swimming pool, and multiplying the volume by 7.48 to obtain the capacity of the pool. The time it takes to fill the pool is calculated by dividing the capacity by rate of flow.

In the implementation of this program there is only one class containing the `main` method.

Algorithm

The solution to the problem can be refined into the following four parts:

1. input the size of the pool
2. calculate the volume of the pool
3. calculate the time to fill the pool
4. output the results

Notice that each part in the first level of the solution has been given a number in the range 1 to 4. In the design it may be possible to refine each of these parts into smaller parts. For example,

1. input the size of the pool

can been refined to:

1.1 input length
1.2 input width
1.3 input depth

which in themselves have been represented as subdivisions of operation 1, hence the numbering convention 1.1, 1.2, 1.3.

2. calculate the volume of the pool

can be refined to

2.1 volume = length * width * depth

3. calculate the time to fill the pool

can be refined to

3.1 capacity = volume * capacity of 1 cu ft
3.2 time = capacity / rate of flow

4. output results

can be refined to

4.1 output volume of the pool
4.2 output the capacity of the water in gallons
4.3 output the time to fill the pool

The approach of braking a problem down into parts, and further refining each part is known as **stepwise refinement**. The expression of each statement of the algorithm in words and mathematical symbols is known as **pseudocode**. Do not make the mistake of thinking that pseudocode is just a description of the program statement in Java. Used correctly, pseudocode helps to describe the operations in the algorithm prior to these statements being coded into Java. To reinforce this point, notice that the pseudocode written in this section makes no reference to the input and output statements of Java described in section 1.12 of the previous chapter.

Data Dictionary. The constants in the problem are the rate of flow of water in the pool, and the capacity of the pool. The primitive variables are of type float and represent the length, width and depth of the pool; the volume and capacity of the pool; and the time to fill the pool.

The only two objects are the input and output streams representing the keyboard and the screen.

```
// constants
final float RATE_OF_FLOW = 50.0f;
final float CAPACITY = 7.48f;

// primitive variables
float lengthOfPool;
float widthOfPool;
float depthOfPool;
float volumeOfPool;
float capacityOfPool;
float timeToFillPool;
```

Desk Check. A desk check may be applied to the pseudocode to verify that the logic and calculations that lie behind the solution to the problem are correct. A desk check of the algorithm to calculate the time to fill a swimming pool follows. The names of items of data in the pseudocode are used as table headings in a desk check.

variable	value
lengthOfPool	50.0
widthOfPool	20.0
depthOfPool	5.0
volumeOfPool	50.0 * 20.0 * 5.0 = 5000.0
capacityOfPool	5000.0 * 7.48 = 37400.0
timeToFillPool	37400.0 / (50 * 60) = 12.46

Screen Layout

Often it is a good idea to know what your final output will look like on the screen. If you can design this information on ruled paper, showing the positions and nature of the input and output then it becomes far easier to code the input and output statements in the program. A typical screen layout for this problem might be designed as illustrated in Figure 2.6.

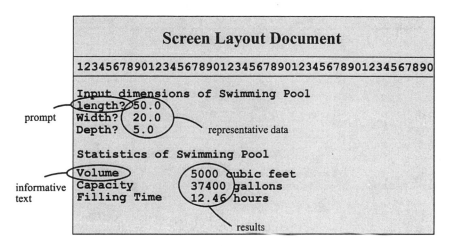

Figure 2.6 Screen layout

The screen prompts can be coded using the screen layout document to ensure that the spacing is correctly programmed. For example

```
screen.println("Input dimensions of Swimming Pool\n");
screen.print("Length? ");  screen.flush();
.
screen.print("Width?   ");  screen.flush();
.
screen.print("Depth?   ");  screen.flush();
```

Similarly, the output of the results is coded using the screen layout document.

```
screen.println("\n\nStatistics of Swimming Pool\n");
screen.println("Volume        \t" + volumeOfPool + " cubic feet");
screen.println("Capacity      \t" + capacityOfPool + " gallons");
screen.println("Filling time\t" + timeToFillPool + " hours");
```

Coding

The following program has been coded using the pseudocode, data dictionary and screen layout document.

```
// chap_2\Ex_4.java
// program to calculate the time to fill a swimming pool

import java.io.*;

class Ex_4
{
    static BufferedReader keyboard = new
    BufferedReader(new InputStreamReader(System.in));
    static PrintWriter screen      = new PrintWriter(System.out, true);
```

```
public static void main(String[] args) throws IOException
{
    // rate of water flow into pool is 50 gallons per minute
    final float RATE_OF_FLOW = 50.0f;

    // cubic foot of water has a capacity of 7.48 gallons
    final float CAPACITY = 7.48f;

    float lengthOfPool;
    float widthOfPool;
    float depthOfPool;
    float volumeOfPool;
    float capacityOfPool;
    float timeToFillPool;

    // input size of pool

    screen.println("Input dimensions of Swimming Pool\n");
    screen.print("Length? "); screen.flush();
    lengthOfPool = new Float(keyboard.readLine()).floatValue();

    screen.print("Width?  "); screen.flush();
    widthOfPool = new Float(keyboard.readLine()).floatValue();

    screen.print("Depth?  "); screen.flush();
    depthOfPool = new Float(keyboard.readLine()).floatValue();

    // calculations

    volumeOfPool   = lengthOfPool * widthOfPool * depthOfPool;
    capacityOfPool = volumeOfPool * CAPACITY;
    timeToFillPool = capacityOfPool / (RATE_OF_FLOW * 60);

    // display information

    screen.println("\nStatistics of Swimming Pool\n");
    screen.println("Volume      \t" + volumeOfPool   + " cubic feet");
    screen.println("Capacity    \t" + capacityOfPool + " gallons");
    screen.println("Filling time\t" + timeToFillPool + " hours");
}
}
```

Test results

```
Input dimensions of Swimming Pool

Length? 50.0
Width?  20.0
Depth?  5.0

Statistics of Swimming Pool

Volume         5000.0 cubic feet
Capacity       37400.0 gallons
Filling time   12.466666 hours
```

2.6 Syntax Errors

The following case study is developed to find the average cost of three newspapers. Syntax errors have been deliberately introduced into the coding to show you the type of error messages the compiler will generate. It is your task to find the errors, correct them, and verify that the program does indeed function correctly.

Case Study: Cost of Newspapers

Problem. Write a program to input the name and cost in cents of three newspapers, calculate the total cost and average cost in cents, and display the results of the two computations.

Problem Analysis. By including the names of the newspapers in the prompts to input the price of the newspapers, the program becomes customized to the user's data. The total cost of the papers is obviously the sum of the three prices, and the average is calculated by dividing the total cost by 3. Since the price of the papers is assumed to be in cents and by default of integer type, the calculation for the average should produce an integer result.

In the implementation of this program there is only one class containing the `main` method.

Algorithm

First level of design

1. input data for newspapers
2. calculate costs
3. output results

Second level of design

1.1 input name of first newspaper
1.2 input price of the first newspaper
1.3 input name of the second newspaper
1.4 input price of the second newspaper
1.5 input name of the third newspaper
1.6 input price of the third newspaper

2.1 calculate the total cost of all three newspapers
2.2 calculate the average cost of the three newspapers

3.1 display the total cost
3.2 display the average cost

Data Dictionary The names of the three newspapers, the costs of the three newspapers, the total cost, and the average price are all items of data. The names of the newspapers are strings, and the prices, total cost, and average price are integer variables.

```
String    namePaper1, namePaper2, namePaper3;
int       pricePaper1, pricePaper2, pricePaper3;
int       totalPrice, averagePrice;
```

Desk Check The names of the newspapers are the Globe, Mercury, and the Courier, and their respective costs are 40 cents, 50 cents and 60 cents. By obeying each statement in the pseudocode design it is possible to assign data values to the variables and perform the appropriate arithmetic. The same data can then be used when the program is executed on the computer, and the results compared with those in the desk check.

variable	value
namePaper1	Globe
pricePaper1	40
namePaper2	Mercury
pricePaper2	50
namePaper3	Courier
pricePaper3	60
totalPrice	40+50+60 = 150
averagePrice	150/3 = 50

Screen Layout

```
                    Screen Layout Document

12345678901234567890123456789012345678901234567890

Input data on newspapers

Name of first paper? Globe
Price of Globe 40
Name of second paper? Mercury
Price of mercury 50
Name of third paper? Courier
Price of Courier 60


Statistics about newspapers

Total price 150 cents
Average price 50 cents
```

Coding - line numbers have been deliberately inserted into the listing of the program to help you find the syntax errors.

```
1:   // chap_2\Ex_5.java
2:   // program to input the names and prices of three newspapers,
3:   // calculate and display the total cost of the papers and the
4:   // average price
5:
6:   import java.io.*;
7:
8:   class Ex_5
9:   {
10:    static BufferedReader keyboard = new
11:            BufferedReader(new InputStreamReader(System.in));
12:    static PrintWriter screen      = new PrintWriter(System.out, true);
13:
14:    public static void main(String[] args)
15:    {
16:        String namePaper1, namePaper2, namePaper3;
17:        int pricePaper1, pricePaper2, pricePaper3;
18:        int totalPrice, averagePrice;
19:
20:        screen.println("Input data on newspapers\n");
21:        screen.print("Name of first paper? ") screen.flush();
22:        namePaper1 = keyboard.readLine();
23:        screen.print("Price of " + namePaper1 + " "); screen.flush();
24:        pricePaper1 = new Integer(keyboard.readLine()).intValue();
25:
26:        screen.print("Name of second paper? "); screen.flush();
27:        namePaper2 = keyboard.readLine();
28:        screen.print("Price of " + namePaper2 + " "); screen.flush();
29:        pricePaper2 = new Integer(keyboard.readLine()).intValue();
30:
31:        screen.print("Name of third paper? "); screen.flush();
32:        namePaper3 = keyboard.readLine();
33:        screen.print("Price of " + namePaper3 + " "); screen.flush();
34:        pricePaper3 = new Integer(keyboard.readLine()).intvalue();
35:
36:        totalrice = pricePaper1 + pricePaper2 + pricePaper3;
37:        averagePrice = totalPrice / 3;
38:
39:        screen.println("\nStatistics about newspapers\n");
40:        screen.println("Total price " + totalPrice + " cents");
41:        screen.println("Average price " + averagePrice + " cents");
42:    }
43:   }
```

The line numbers included in the following listing of syntax errors, indicate the line of text where the error has been detected. For example, `Ex_5.java:21:` refers to line 21.

Listing of Syntax Errors

```
Ex_5.java:21: Invalid type expression.
             screen.print("Name of first paper? ") screen.flush();
                         ^
Ex_5.java:21: Invalid declaration.
             screen.print("Name of first paper? ") screen.flush();
                                                                ^
Ex_5.java:22: Exception java.io.IOException must be caught, or it must be
declared in the throws clause of this method.
             namePaper1 = keyboard.readLine();
                                  ^
Ex_5.java:34: Method intvalue() not found in class java.lang.Integer.
             pricePaper3 = new Integer(keyboard.readLine()).intvalue();
                                                                     ^
Ex_5.java:36: Undefined variable: totalrice
             totalrice = pricePaper1 + pricePaper2 + pricePaper3;
             ^
Ex_5.java:37: Variable totalPrice may not have been initialized.
             averagePrice = totalPrice / 3;
                            ^
6 errors
```

When you have found all the sources of the errors and corrected the program, re-compile the program and run it using the same test data used in the desk check. The test results should be as follows.

```
Input data on newspapers

Name of first paper? Globe
Price of Globe 40
Name of second paper? Mercury
Price of Mercury 50
Name of third paper? Courier
Price of Courier 60

Statistics about newspapers

Total price 150 cents
Average price 50 cents
```

Re-run the program, however, this time try typing in the value of the Globe as **40c**. The remainder of the test data is unchanged. You should get the following test result.

```
Input data on newspapers

Name of first paper? Globe
Price of Globe 40c
java.lang.NumberFormatException: 40c
        at java.lang.Integer.parseInt(Integer.java:238)
        at java.lang.Integer.<init>(Integer.java:342)
        at Ex_5_modified.main(Ex_5_modified.java:24)
```

If you inspect the Java API documentation for the wrapper class `Integer` you will notice that the constructor throws a `NumberFormatException` if the argument is not a parsable integer.

> ⚠️ Later in the book you will be shown how to handle these exceptions in a program. For now accept the fact that the computer will stop the program from running if you type numerical data that is in the wrong format.

2.7 Logical Errors

The following case study has been developed to calculate the number of cans of paint necessary to cover the walls of a room. The case study contains a deliberate logical error.

Case Study: Determining Paint Quantity

Problem. A rectangular-shaped living room has a total window area of 40 square feet and a total door area of 20 square feet. Write a program to input the length, width, and height of the room and calculate the area of available wall space. If a ½ gallon can of paint will cover 200 square feet of wall, calculate and display the number of cans required to paint the walls of the room. Note - the window and door areas and floor and ceiling are not to be painted.

Problem Analysis. The arithmetic expressions required to calculate the number of cans required follows.

Wall area   = (2*height*length)+(2*height*width)-window area - door area
                    = 2*height*(length+width)-(window area + door area)
cans   = (wall area / paint cover);

In the implementation of this program there is only one class containing the `main` method.

Algorithm

First level of design

1. input dimensions of room
2. calculate number of cans
3. output result

Second level of design

1.1 input length
1.2 input width
1.3 input height

2.1 calculate wall area
2.2 calculate number of cans

3.1 display number of cans

Data Dictionary. The constants in this problem are the window and door areas and area of coverage of a can of paint. The dimensions of the room are to be input at the keyboard, and declared as variables of type float. Before the number of cans of paint can be calculated, it is useful for clarity, but not necessary, to calculate the area of the walls to be painted. This variable will again be of type float.

Three constants can be identified as:

```
final float PAINT_COVER = 200.0f;
final float WINDOW_AREA = 40.0f;
final float DOOR_AREA   = 20.0f;
```

The variables are:

```
float length, width, height;
float wallArea;
float cansOfPaint;
```

Desk Check. The test data for the length, width and height of the room are 30, 15 and 8 respectively.

variable	values
length	30
width	15
height	8
wallArea	2*8*(30+15)-(40+20)=(16*450)-60=660
cansOfPaint	660/200 =3.3

Screen Layout Document

```
12345678901234567890123456789012345678901234567890

Input dimensions of room

Length? 30.0
Width?  15.0
Height?  8.0

Number of cans to purchase = 3.3
```

Coding

```java
// chap_2\Ex_6.java
// program to calculate the amount of paint needed to paint the
// walls of a room

import java.io.*;

class Ex_6
{
    static BufferedReader keyboard = new
    BufferedReader(new InputStreamReader(System.in));
    static PrintWriter screen       = new PrintWriter(System.out, true);

    public static void main(String[] args) throws IOException
    {
        // constants
        final float PAINT_COVER = 200.0f;
        final float WINDOW_AREA = 40.0f;
        final float DOOR_AREA   = 20.0f;

        // variables
        float length, width, height;
        float wallArea;
        float cansOfPaint;

        // input room dimensions
        screen.println("Input dimensions of room\n");

        screen.print("Length? "); screen.flush();
        length = new Float(keyboard.readLine()).floatValue();

        screen.print("Width? "); screen.flush();
        width = new Float(keyboard.readLine()).floatValue();

        screen.print("Height? "); screen.flush();
        height = new Float(keyboard.readLine()).floatValue();

        // calculate wall are and number of cans of paint
        wallArea = 2*height*(length+width)-(WINDOW_AREA + DOOR_AREA);
        cansOfPaint = wallArea / PAINT_COVER;

        // output cans of paint
        screen.println("\nNumber of cans to purchase = " + cansOfPaint);
    }
}
```

Test results

```
Input dimensions of room

Length? 30.0
Width? 15.0
Height? 8.0

Number of cans to purchase = 3.3
```

The program has run correctly, but can you discover the logical error?

The problem stated that ½ gallon cans of paint would be purchased. How do you purchase 3.3, ½ gallon cans paint? You cannot buy 0.3 of a can of paint.

In calculating the number of cans to purchase, it will be necessary to adjust the result of dividing the wall area by paint coverage to give a whole number of cans; otherwise, as you have already discovered, the calculation will result in a partial can of paint.

Clearly if the number of cans is just in excess of 3, for example 3.001, then it is necessary to add a correction factor to increase the number to 4. But what if the number of cans is just below 4, for example 3.999, what factor do we add to increase the number of cans to 4?

The data type for the number of cans of paint is also wrong; it should have been stated as int and not float.

```
int cansOfPaint;
```

If we are only concerned in calculating the number of cans to an accuracy of 0.001 then a constant of 0.999 should be added to the theoretical number of cans before the result is truncated. Adding 0.999 to the result of the floating-point division, followed by a truncation by casting the expression to an integer number, will round any fractional left over amount to the next whole can.

```
cansOfPaint = (int)((wallArea / PAINT_COVER) + 0.999f);
```

With the modifications the test results for the program are as follows.

```
Input dimensions of room

Length? 30.0
Width? 15.0
Height? 8.0

Number of cans to purchase = 4
```

Summary

- A Java program is constructed from many classes. A class may contain any combination of data declarations, constructors, and class and instance methods. The implementation of methods within a class may reuse the methods defined in the Java API.

- To reuse any method defined by the Java API, it is necessary to import the appropriate class. A class can be imported by specifically stating the name of the package and class in an import statement. Alternatively, to make all the classes of a package available in a program, use only the package name followed by the wildcard symbol *.

- A program may contain just one class that contains the main method.

- Program implementation involves the following stages.

Using an editor to key a program into the computer.
Compiling the program into bytecodes.
Using an interpreter to execute or run the bytecode program.

- Java programs are portable. A compiler will produce the same bytecode program, regardless of the computer system being used. The bytecode program can be executed on any computer that has the appropriate interpreter for the computer being used.

- Software development consists of the stages of analysis, design, programming and maintenance. Because software development evolves through the experience gained at each stage, it is possible to go back to any of the stages and modify the solution to the problem. .

- Programming consists of analyzing the problem, designing an algorithm, coding the algorithm into a computer program, testing the computer program, and supplying sufficient documentation so that the program can easily by understood and modified by others.

- Program design can be organized into seven steps.

    Problem Analysis
    Algorithm
    Data Dictionary
    Desk Check
    Screen Layout
    Coding
    Test results

- To solve a problem, break it down into parts and attempt to solve the smaller problems, rather than tackle the problem as a whole. This approach to problem solving is known as stepwise refinement and uses pseudocode as a method of expressing the algorithm.

- Using a screen layout document to design the input of data and the output of results in an interactive computing environment will greatly facilitate the coding of the program.

- The program is coded from the algorithm, data dictionary, and screen layout document.

- As a means of checking program accuracy, a program should be run for the first time with the same test data used during the desk-check.

- Two distinct types of errors may occur in designing a program. The first is a syntax error, which may be inadvertently introduced at the coding stage, by not correctly following the grammatical rules of the language. The second is the logical error, which may be traced back to the algorithm when wrong assumptions may have been made about how to process the data.

Review Questions

1. True or false - a Java program may be constructed from several classes.

2. True or false - a class may contain declarations and methods.

3. What is the purpose of the import list?

4. True or false - the `main` method may be omitted from an application program.

5. Why is the `main` method declared as `void`?

6. True or false - you interpret a program before you compile it.

7. What does a compiler do?

8. True or false - a bytecode file may be used on a different computer to the one that produced the file.

9. Why are Java programs portable?

10. Name the four main activities associated with the software development life cycle.

11. List the activities involved in programming.

12. What is a desk check?

13. What is peer-group evaluation?

14. What is pseudocode?

15. True or false - pseudocode is written in Java.

16. What is a data dictionary?

17. True or false - a desk check is used after the program has been written.

18. What is the purpose of a screen layout document?

19. At what stages in programming would test data be used?

20. Distinguish between syntax and logical errors.

Exercises

You should develop working programs as answers to the following questions. Be sure to check that the computer output is correct.

21. Write a program to output a message of your choice on the screen.

22. Write a program to input your distance from a town, and the constant speed you are traveling towards that town. Calculate and output the time it will take you to arrive at the town.

23. Modify question 22, to input the name of the town and use this name in displaying the time it will take you to reach your destination.

24. Write a program to convert and display a temperature, input in degrees Fahrenheit, to a temperature in degrees Celsius. The equation for conversion is *Celsius = (Fahrenheit-32)*5/9*.

25. Write a program to input the elapsed time in seconds since midnight. Calculate and output the number of hours, minutes, and seconds since midnight.

26. Write a program to input the radius of a sphere and calculate and display the surface area and volume of the sphere. The formula for the *surface area* is $4\pi\ r^2$, and the volume is r/3 * *surface area*.

Programming Problems

You should document complete program designs, and compile and run each program, as answers to the following questions.

27. We all keep loose change in our pockets. Write a program to calculate the total value of your loose change. You will need to input the number of half dollars, quarters, dimes, nickels, and pennies and then display the total value of the coinage in dollars and cents.

28. The interest payable on a loan is calculated according to the following equation:

$$interest = principal \frac{rate}{100} \frac{time}{365}$$

Write a program to input the principal amount borrowed, the rate of interest as a percentage, and the time of the loan in days. Calculate and output the value of the interest.

29. Write a program to input your name, height (in inches), and weight (in pounds); convert the height to centimeters and weight to kilograms and display the following results. Note - 1 inch = 2.54 centimeters and 1 pound = 0.4546 kilograms.

> Personal Details
> Name   Henry Smith
> Height 180 cm
> Weight 75 Kg

30. Write a program to input an amount of money as a whole number, for example $157, and display an analysis of the minimum number of $20, $10, $5 and $1 notes that make up this amount.

31. Write a program to input the length, width, and depths at the deepest and shallowest ends of a rectangular swimming pool that has a constant gradient between the opposite ends of the pool. Calculate the volume of water required to fill the pool.

32. Figure 2.6 illustrates the price of food and drinks at Ben's Breakfast Bar. Ben gives a discount of 25% on the cost of any three items of food or drink purchased. Write a program to input the names and prices of three items chosen from the menu and output a fully itemized bill, including local tax at 5%.

Ben's Breakfast Bar

MENU

Eggs	$2.75
Blueberry Pancakes	$4.00
Bagel with cream cheese	$1.50
English Muffin	$0.95
Yogurt	$1.00
Corned Beef Hash	$1.75
Toast	$0.75
Fries	$1.00
Tea or Coffee	$0.75
Hot Chocolate	$0.95

Figure 2.6

33. A person is paid a gross weekly wage based upon the number of hours worked per week and the hourly rate of pay. Calculate the net pay for an employee after the following deductions:

Federal Income Tax at 15% of gross pay;
Social Security Tax at 6.2% of gross pay;
Payroll Savings at 3% of gross pay;
Retirement Pension at 8.5% of gross pay;
Health Insurance at $5.75 per employee.

Design a suitable layout for an employee's pay check. Write a program to input the hourly rate of pay, the number of hours worked in a week, calculate the deductions, and display the pay check.

34. A quotation for framing a photograph is based upon the following information.

The outside edge of the wooden frame is 6 inches longer and 6 inches wider than the photograph. The cost of the wood to make the frame is $2.50 per foot.

Two backing cards are required to be mounted with the photograph. Each card is 5.5 inches longer and 5.5 inches wider than the photograph. The cost of the backing card is $1.50 per square foot.

The photograph is to be protected under glass. The size of the glass is the same as a backing card. The cost of the glass is $5.50 per square foot.

Computerize the process of supplying a fully itemized quotation for framing a photograph.

Chapter 3
Selection

All the programs in the previous chapter were constructed from a sequence of statements. Each time a program was run, the computer would execute the same statements in the same order. How do you write a program that will allow different statements to be executed depending upon the result of a condition?

This chapter introduces the techniques of coding conditions and branching on the result of a condition to alternative statements in a program. By the end of the chapter you should have an understanding of the following topics.

- The syntax and use of the two-way branch statement - `if..else`.

- The construction and evaluation of a conditional expression.

- The use of nested, or embedded selection statements.

- The use of logical operators in the construction of conditional expressions.

- The syntax and use of the multi-way branch statement - `switch`.

3.1 If..else Statement

Consider the following problem.

Write a program to calculate the gross weekly wage for an hourly-paid employee. Input to the program the hourly rate of pay, and the number of hours worked in a week. If an employee works for more than 40 hours in a week, the employee is paid overtime for the hours worked in excess of 40 hours, at the rate of 1 ½ times the hourly rate.

The solution to the problem can be expressed as follows.

1. input rate of pay
2. input number of hours worked
3. if hours is greater than 40
4.   calculate gross wage with overtime
5. else
6.   calculate gross wage (without overtime)
7. display gross weekly wage

The algorithm after statement (2) splits into two paths. This split is depicted in Figure 3.1. If the answer to the condition *hours > 40* is true one path is taken and the gross wage is calculated <u>with</u> overtime, however, if the answer is false then a different path is taken and the gross wage is calculated without overtime.

After the calculations have been made, the algorithm resumes along one path and displays the gross weekly wage.

Note the symbol > implies *is greater than*.

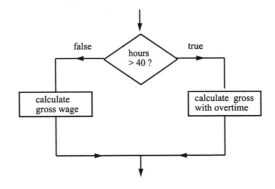

Figure 3.1 Selection based on numbers

Program Example 3.1 demonstrates that the split into two paths can be coded by using the if ..
else statement.

Program Example 3.1: Calculate Gross Weekly Wage

```java
// chap_3\Ex_1.java
// program to calculate a gross weekly wage

import java.io.*;

class Ex_1
{
    static BufferedReader keyboard = new
            BufferedReader(new InputStreamReader(System.in));
    static PrintWriter screen       = new PrintWriter(System.out, true);

    public static void main(String[] args) throws IOException
    {
        float rateOfPay;
        float hoursWorked;
        float grossWage;

        // input rate of pay

        screen.print("Rate of pay? "); screen.flush();
        rateOfPay = new Float(keyboard.readLine()).floatValue();

        // input hours worked

        screen.print("Hours worked? "); screen.flush();
        hoursWorked = new Float(keyboard.readLine()).floatValue();

        // calculate gross wage

        if (hoursWorked > 40.0)
            grossWage = 1.5f*rateOfPay*(hoursWorked-40.0f) + 40.0f*rateOfPay;
        else
            grossWage = hoursWorked * rateOfPay;

        // output gross wage

        screen.println("Gross wage $" + grossWage);
    }
}
```

In tracing through the program the following operations take place. After the values for the
rateOfPay and hoursWorked have been input, the computer tests the condition
hoursWorked > 40.0. If this condition is true, the statement to calculate the gross wage with
overtime is executed; however, if this condition is false, the statement after the keyword else to
calculate the gross wage at the normal rate of pay is executed. After the calculation is performed, and
regardless of the path taken, the computer continues the execution of the remainder of the program.

The syntax of the if..else statement follows:

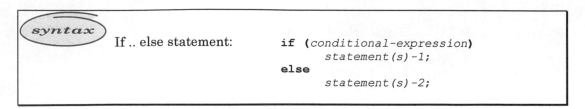

where the conditional-expression will equate to either true or false. If the conditional-expression is true then statement(s)-1 will be executed; if the conditional expression is false then statement(s)-2 will be executed. After either statement has been executed, the computer will continue with the execution of the next statement after statement(s)-2. The following output shows the results of running the program twice with two different values for hoursWorked.

Test results from program being run twice

```
Rate of pay? 10
Hours worked? 35
Gross wage $350.0

Rate of pay? 10
Hours worked? 50
Gross wage $550.0
```

The relational operator > is not the only operator that can be used in a conditional-expression. Figure 3.2 lists the six relational operators that can be used with primitive data types in a conditional-expression. If you need to compare strings then you must use the appropriate method in the String class.

operator	meaning
>	greater than
<	less than
==	equal to
>=	greater than or equal to
<=	less than or equal to
!=	not equal to

Figure 3.2

⚠ Notice that the test for equality is a double equals sign ==. Be careful not to use the single equals sign when testing for equality, remember = is reserved for assignment.

⚠️ The storage of real numbers in the memory of a computer may not always be done precisely. For example, the storage of 0.33 in binary can only be an approximation to the true value of the number. For this reason you should exercise extreme caution when comparing two real numbers for equality.

Consider the following program that, depending on the weather, tells the user which garment to wear.

Program Example 3.2: String Comparison

```java
// chap_3\Ex_2.java
// program to demonstrate the if..else statement

import java.io.*;

class Ex_2
{
    static BufferedReader keyboard = new
            BufferedReader(new InputStreamReader(System.in));
    static PrintWriter screen       = new PrintWriter(System.out, true);

    public static void main(String[] args) throws IOException
    {
        String reply;
        String garment;

        screen.print("Is it raining outside? "); screen.flush();
        reply = keyboard.readLine();
        reply = reply.toUpperCase();

        if (reply.equals("YES"))
            garment = "raincoat";
        else
            garment = "overcoat";

        screen.println("Before you go out today take your " + garment);
    }
}
```

Test results from program being run twice

```
Is it raining outside? yes
Before you go out today take your raincoat

Is it raining outside? no
Before you go out today take your overcoat
```

In tracing through the program, the following operations will take place. The user is asked if it is raining, to which an expected response is either yes or no. The response is changed to upper case letters to enable the comparison to be made with the string "YES". The selection in the program is depicted in Figure 3.3.

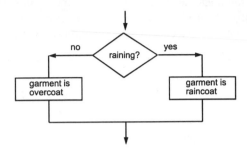

Figure 3.3 Selection based on strings

The coding for this selection is:

```
if (reply.equals("YES"))
    garment = "raincoat";
else
    garment = "overcoat";
```

If the reply is "YES" then the string "raincoat" is assigned to the string object garment. If the reply is any other string other than "YES" (possibly "NO") then the string "overcoat" is assigned to the string object garment. In either situation the computer executes the next statement after the selection and informs the user what garment to wear before venturing outdoors.

Notice that it has not been possible to make a direct comparison of the reply with "YES" in the conditional expression. You might have been tempted to code (reply == "YES"), but this would be wrong, since you would be comparing the references to the strings and not the values of the strings (refer back to Figure 1.18). Instead you need to use the method equals from the String class. The method returns either true or false depending upon the result of the comparison.

⚠ You must use the instance methods compareTo, equals and equalsIgnoreCase defined in the String class, if you need to compare the values of strings.

You should adopt the habit of indenting code within an `if` statement. Indentation clarifies which statements are associated with the conditional expression being true and which statements are associated with it being false (after the `else`). Indentation of the statements after the `else` also indicates to the reader where the `if` statement finishes, since the next statement after the `if` statement will be indented the same distance from the left-hand margin as the keywords `if` and `else`. Indentation is ignored by the compiler.

In the previous two program examples, only one statement was executed regardless of whether the conditional expression evaluated to true or false. What if more than one statement is to be executed? The answer is to treat the group of statements as a **block** by introducing braces {}; for example,

```
if (alpha == beta)
{
    A = B;
    C = D;
}
else
{
    A = D;
    C = B;
}
```

If only one statement is executed in a selection statement, the use of braces can improve the clarity of the code, even though the braces are themselves redundant. In program Example 3.3, braces have been included in the selection statement purely to improve the readability of the code.

3.2 Nested if Statements

The statement that follows the conditional expression or the keyword `else`, can also be an `if` statement. In program Example 3.2, if the weather had been warm then wearing either a raincoat or an overcoat could prove to be very uncomfortable. If a second item of data is included about the temperature then it is possible to more accurately specify what to wear whether it is raining or not. Let us therefore consider the following embellishments to the problem scenario.

Program Example 3.3: Nested Ifs

If it is raining and the temperature is less than 60 degrees Fahrenheit, then wear a raincoat; otherwise, if it is warmer, then take an umbrella. However, if it is not raining and the temperature is less than 60 degrees Fahrenheit, then wear an overcoat; otherwise, if it is warmer, then wear a jacket. The program has been reconstructed in Program Example 3.3 to take these new facts into account. The outer if statement is used to determine which path to take depending upon whether it is raining. The inner if statements are used to determine which path to take depending upon the temperature.

Figure 3.4 shows you the different paths that can be taken when the program runs.

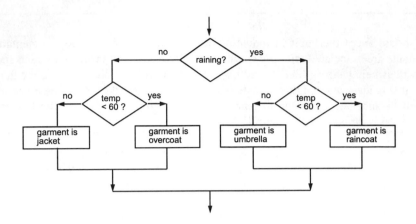

Figure 3.4 Nested selections

```java
// chap_3\Ex_3.java
// program to demonstrate the if..else statement

import java.io.*;

class Ex_3
{

    static BufferedReader keyboard = new
            BufferedReader(new InputStreamReader(System.in));
    static PrintWriter screen      = new PrintWriter(System.out, true);

    public static void main(String[] args) throws IOException
    {
        String reply;
        String garment;
        int    temperature;

        screen.print("What is the temperature outside today? ");
        screen.flush();
        temperature = new Integer(keyboard.readLine()).intValue();

        screen.print("Is it raining outside? ");
        screen.flush();
        reply = keyboard.readLine();
        reply = reply.toUpperCase();

        if (reply.equals("YES"))
        {
            if (temperature < 60)
                garment = "raincoat";
            else
                garment = "umbrella";
        }
        else
```

```
        {
            if (temperature < 60)
                garment = "overcoat";
            else
                garment = "jacket";
        }

        screen.println("Before you go out today take your " + garment);
    }
}
```

Test results from program being run four times

```
What is the temperature outside today? 50
Is it raining outside? yes
Before you go out today take your raincoat

What is the temperature outside today? 50
Is it raining outside? no
Before you go out today take your overcoat

What is the temperature outside today? 60
Is it raining outside? yes
Before you go out today take your umbrella

What is the temperature outside today? 60
Is it raining outside? no
Before you go out today take your jacket
```

In this program, after both the temperature and reply have been input, if the conditional expression `reply.equals("YES")` is true, then the statement after the conditional expression will be obeyed by another if statement! If the conditional expression `temperature < 60` is true, then the statement `garment = "raincoat"` will be executed; however, if the conditional expression `temperature < 60` is false, then the statement `garment = "umbrella"` will be executed. In either case the computer will then branch to the next executable statement after the last statement in the outer if statement.

If the conditional expression `reply.equals("YES")` is false, then the statement after the else (in the outer if statement) will be obeyed, and if the conditional expression `temperature < 60` is true, then the statement `garment = "overcoat"` will be executed; however, if the conditional expression `temperature < 60` is false, then the statement `garment = "jacket"` will be executed.

To divert from the theme of nested if statements, consider the illustration in Figure 3.5. How do we code the `if` statement when there is only one statement to execute when the condition is true?

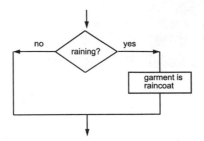

Figure 3.5 A one-way selection

The answer is simply to omit the keyword else. For example, the illustration in Figure 3.5 would be coded as:

```
if (reply.equals("YES"))
    garment = "raincoat";
```

The statement after the condition can be either a single statement or a block (many statements contained between braces {}).

Returning to the theme of nested if statements. If statements can be nested to any depth; however, you should pay particular attention to the use of indentation and the grouping of the else keywords. In the following example, to which if statement does the single else statement belong?

```
if (alpha == 3)
    if (beta == 4)
        screen.println("alpha 3\tbeta 4");
else
    screen.println("alpha beta not valid");
```

The indentation suggests that the else belongs to if (alpha == 3), however, as you might expect this is wrong. The rule in Java regarding which else belongs to which if is simple. An else clause belongs to the nearest if statement that has not already been paired with an else. This example can be rewritten taking into account the correct indentation.

```
if (alpha == 3)
    if (beta == 4)
        screen.println("alpha 3\tbeta 4");
    else
        screen.println("alpha beta not valid");
```

If the else clause did belong to if (alpha == 3), then braces would be introduced into the coding as follows:

```
if (alpha == 3)
{
   if (beta == 4)
      screen.println("alpha 3\tbeta 4");
}
else
   screen.println("alpha beta not valid");
```

3.3 Boolean Data Type

The boolean primitive data type was given a brief mention in Chapter 1. To recapitulate, a variable of type **boolean** is permitted to have only one of two values, either **true** or **false**. A boolean variable is initialized by Java to be `false`.

The conditional expression in an `if` statement must evaluate to a `boolean` value, that is either true or false.

A variable may be declared as `boolean`, and initialized at its point of declaration to either `true` or `false`. This variable may be reassigned either of the boolean values at a later stage in the program.

In Program Example 3.3, how would the computer respond to data being input that did not match either yes or no in response to a reply? Under these circumstances the conditional statement `(reply.equals.("YES"))` would be false and the computer would assign "overcoat" to the string object `garment` if the temperature was less than sixty degrees, or would assign "jacket" to the string object `garment` if the temperature was warmer. This is clearly a logical error in the program. It is the responsibility of the programmer to trap any invalid data and report the exceptional circumstances to the user of the program.

Program Example 3.4: Boolean Data Type.

The next program traps and reports on data being input that does not conform to the reply yes or no. The program introduces a boolean variable `error`, which means that the values `true` or `false` can be assigned to it. In the program the variable `error` is initialized to `false` on the assumption that no invalid data will be input. However, as soon as invalid data is recognized , the value of error is changed to `true`. Since `error` is of type boolean it may be used in the conditional expression of an `if` statement. Notice in the last segment of the program code that if there has been an error, the message of what garment to take is suppressed and replaced by a data error message.

```java
// chap_3\Ex_4.java
// program to demonstrate the if..else statement

import java.io.*;

class Ex_4
{
    static BufferedReader keyboard = new
            BufferedReader(new InputStreamReader(System.in));
    static PrintWriter screen       = new PrintWriter(System.out, true);

    public static void main(String[] args) throws IOException
    {
        String  reply;
        String  garment = new String();
        int     temperature;
        boolean error = false;

        screen.print("What is the temperature outside today? ");
        screen.flush();
        temperature = new Integer(keyboard.readLine()).intValue();

        screen.print("Is it raining outside? ");
        screen.flush();
        reply = keyboard.readLine();
        reply = reply.toUpperCase();

        if (reply.equals("YES"))
        {
            if (temperature < 60)
                garment = "raincoat";
            else
                garment = "umbrella";
        }
        else
        {
            if (reply.equals("NO"))
            {
                if (temperature < 60)
                    garment = "overcoat";
                else
                    garment = "jacket";
            }
            else
                error = true;
        }

        if (error)
            screen.println("DATA ERROR - reply not in correct format");
        else
            screen.println("Before you go out today take your " + garment);
    }
}
```

Test results from program being run twice

```
What is the temperature outside today? 65
Is it raining outside? yes
Before you go out today take your umbrella

What is the temperature outside today? 65
Is it raining outside? I don't know
DATA ERROR - reply not in correct format
```

3.4 Conditional Expressions

From the discussions so far, it should be clear to you that the conditional expressions can equate to one of two values, either true or false. Examples of conditional expressions given so far are (hoursWorked > 40), (reply.equals("YES")), (reply.equals("NO")), (temperature < 60), and (error).

Program Example 3.5: Logical AND

Program Example 3.5 will input the name of a person and decide whether he or she is a suspect to a crime. We believe that the crime was committed by a person between 20 and 25 years of age, and between 66 and 70 inches tall. The program displays the name of the suspect if the person fits this description.

```java
// chap_3\Ex_5.java
// program to display the name of a suspect to a crime who is aged
// between 20 and 25 years and between 66 and 70 inches tall

import java.io.*;

class Ex_5
{
    static BufferedReader keyboard = new
            BufferedReader(new InputStreamReader(System.in));
    static PrintWriter screen      = new PrintWriter(System.out, true);

    public static void main(String[] args) throws IOException
    {
        String name;
        int    age;
        int    height;

        screen.print("Input name of suspect "); screen.flush();
        name = keyboard.readLine();

        screen.print("Age? "); screen.flush();
        age = new Integer(keyboard.readLine()).intValue();

        screen.print("Height? "); screen.flush();
        height = new Integer(keyboard.readLine()).intValue();
```

```
    if (age >= 20 && age <= 25)
    {
        if (height >= 66 && height <= 70)
            screen.println(name + " is a suspect and should be
                                    interrogated");
    }
  }
}
```

Test results

```
Input name of suspect Artful Dodger
Age? 23
Height? 69
Artful Dodger is a suspect and should be interrogated
```

In Program Example 3.5, there was no output if a person is not a suspect.

The conditions used in this program are (age >= 20), (age <= 25), (height >= 66), and (height <= 70). It has been possible to combine these conditions into (age >= 20 && age <= 25) and (height >=66 & height <= 70) by using the logical operator && (AND). A truth table for logical AND is given in Figure 3.6. This table may be interpreted as follows.

condition X	condition Y	X && Y
false	false	false
false	true	false
true	false	false
true	true	true

Figure 3.6 Truth Table for Logical AND

If (age >= 20) is condition X and (age <= 25) is condition Y, then X && Y can only be true if both condition X is true and condition Y is true. In other words, both conditions (age >= 20) and (age <= 25) must be true for the expression to be true. Therefore, if either condition X or condition Y or both happen to be false, the complete expression given by X && Y is false.

Similarly, both conditions in the expression (height >= 66 && height <= 70) must be true for the conditional expression to be true. If either one condition or both conditions are false, then the conditional expression is false.

In the program if the age is between 20 and 25 years, then the computer executes the next if statement, and if the height is between 66 and 70 inches, then the name of the suspect is printed.

The program can be reconstructed, by omitting the second if statement, and combining the conditions for age and height as follows:

```
if (age >= 20 && age <= 25 && height >= 66 && height <= 70)
    screen.println(name + " is a suspect and should be interrogated");
```

The same program can be reconstructed yet again using different conditions and the logical operator
|| (OR). By considering the age and height to lie outside the ranges, it is possible to construct the
following conditional expressions:

```
(age < 20 || age > 25)
(height < 66 || height > 70)
```

From the truth table for logical OR, given in Figure 3.7, if (age < 20) is condition X and (age >
25) is condition Y, then X||Y is true if X is true or Y is true or both are true. Clearly both conditions
cannot be true in this example.

condition X	condition Y	X || Y
false	false	false
false	true	true
true	false	true
true	true	true

Figure 3.7 Truth Table for Logical OR

Similarly, if (height < 66) is condition X and (height > 70) is condition Y, then X||Y is
true if X is true or Y is true or both are true. Once again both conditions cannot be true in this
example.

The conditions for age and height can also be combined into

```
(age < 20 || age > 25 || height < 66 || height > 70)
```

Thus, if any one of the conditions is true, the entire conditional expression is true and the suspect is
released. However, if all the conditions are false, then the entire conditional expression must be false,
the suspect is between 20 and 25 years of age and between 66 and 70 inches tall, and is held for
interrogation, as depicted in Program Example 3.6.

By examining the truth tables for logical AND and logical OR, Figures 3.6 and 3.7
respectively, it is clear there are occasions when only the condition X need be evaluated. For
example, when using logical AND, if condition X is false there is no need for the computer to
evaluate condition Y. Similarly, when using logical OR, if condition X is true there is no need for the
computer to evaluate condition Y. The evaluation of only the first condition in a logical expression is
known as **short-circuit evaluation**. Both logical operators && and || use short-circuit evaluation. If
you need to avoid short-circuit evaluation then you may use the corresponding logical operators &
and |.

> When using the logical operators **&&** and **||**, be careful which condition to write as the first condition in a logical expression. Using short-circuit evaluation, the condition(s) in the remainder of a logical expression may not be evaluated, and as a result your program may not run as predicted!

Program Example 3.6: Logical OR

```java
// chap_3\Ex_6.java
// program to display the name of a suspect to a crime who is aged
// between 20 and 25 years and between 66 and 70 inches tall

import java.io.*;

class Ex_6
{
    static BufferedReader keyboard = new
            BufferedReader(new InputStreamReader(System.in));
    static PrintWriter screen      = new PrintWriter(System.out, true);

    public static void main(String[] args) throws IOException
    {
        String name;
        int    age;
        int    height;

        screen.print("Input name of suspect "); screen.flush();
        name = keyboard.readLine();

        screen.print("Age? "); screen.flush();
        age = new Integer(keyboard.readLine()).intValue();

        screen.print("Height? "); screen.flush();
        height = new Integer(keyboard.readLine()).intValue();

        screen.print(name);

        if (age < 20 || age > 25 || height < 66 || height > 70)
            screen.println(" is not a suspect and should be released");
        else
            screen.println(" is a suspect and should be interrogated");
    }
}
```

Test results from program being run twice

```
Input name of suspect Bill Sykes
Age? 44
Height? 68
Bill Sykes is not a suspect and should be released

Input name of suspect Artful Dodger
Age? 23
Height? 69
Artful Dodger is a suspect and should be interrogated
```

3.5 Else If Statements

The complexity of nested if statements can be reduced by combining conditions and using logical AND. For example, the following part of the nested selection in Program Example 3.4.

```java
if (reply.equals("YES"))
{
   if (temperature < 60)
      garment = "raincoat";
   else
      garment = "umbrella";
}
else
{
   if (reply.equals("NO"))
   {
      if (temperature < 60)
         garment = "overcoat";
      else
         garment = "jacket";
   }
   else
      error = true;
```

can be re-coded as

```java
if       (reply.equals("YES") && temperature < 60)
         garment = "raincoat";
else if (reply.equals("YES") && temperature >= 60)
         garment = "umbrella";
else if (reply.equals("NO") && temperature < 60)
         garment = "overcoat";
else if (reply.equals("NO") && temperature >= 60)
         garment = "jacket";
else
         error = true;
```

An `else` keyword followed by an `if` keyword is very common in programming. In fact, in many computer languages, except for Java, there is an *elseif* statement. In Java we can write the `else` keyword on the same line as the `if` keyword as if it is one keyword, *elseif*. It is not, but indentation produces a very clear multibranch structure that is actually made of multiple two-branch `if else` statements.

3.6 Switch

An ordinal variable has a value that belongs to an ordered set of items. For example, integers are ordinal types since they belong to the set of values from -2,147,483,648 to +2,147,483,647. A character is an ordinal type since it belongs to the Unicode character set. Real numbers and strings are not ordinal types.

If selection is to be based upon an ordinal type then a switch statement can be used in preference to multiple if statements.

The syntax of the **switch** statement follows.

---

syntax

Switch statement: **switch** (*expression*)
                         {
                                   case *c1*: *statement(s)*;
                                   case *c2*: *statement(s)*;
                                      .
                                      .
                                 default: *statement(s)*;
                         }

The expression must evaluate to an ordinal value. Each possible ordinal value is represented as a case label, which indicates the statement to be executed corresponding to the value of the expression. Those values that are not represented by case labels will result in the statement after the optional default being executed. For example,

```
number = Integer(keyboard.readLine()).intValue();
switch (number)
{
   case 1:  screen.println("one"); break;
   case 2:  screen.println("two"); break;
   case 3:  screen.println("three"); break;
   default: screen.println("number not in the range 1..3");
}
```

In the example a number is input at the keyboard. If this number is 1, then the string `one` will be output; if it is 2 then the string `two` will be output; if it is 3 then the string `three` will be output. If the number is not 1, 2 or 3, then the string `number not in range 1..3` will be output.

It is necessary to include a way of exiting from the `switch` statement at the end of every `case`. Failure to exit from the `switch` will result in the execution of all the `case` statements following the chosen `case`. One method of exiting from a `switch` statement is through the use of a **break** statement at the end of every `case` list. The keyword `break` causes the `switch` to terminate, and execution resumes with the next statement (if any) following the end of the `switch` statement.

If the optional `default` statement was not present and the value of number had not been in the range 1 to 3, then the computer would branch to the end of the `switch` statement.

In Program Example 3.7, a user is invited to input a value for an exit number on Highway 6 at Cape Cod. Depending upon the value, from 1 to 12, of the exit number, the names, numbers, or both of the adjoining roads at that exit are displayed. If the value input is not in the range 1 to 12, the statement after the default will warn the user of the data error. The multiple selection in this problem can be highlighted by the illustration in Figure 3.8.

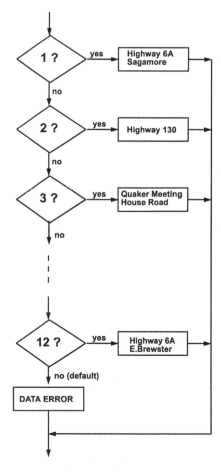

Figure 3.8 Multiple Selection

Program Example 3.7: Switch Statement

```java
// chap_3\Ex_7.java
// program to demonstrate the switch and break statements

import java.io.*;

class Ex_7
{
    static BufferedReader keyboard = new
            BufferedReader(new InputStreamReader(System.in));
    static PrintWriter screen      = new PrintWriter(System.out, true);

    public static void main(String[] args) throws IOException
    {
        int exitNumber;

        screen.print("Input exit number on Highway 6 "); screen.flush();
        exitNumber = new Integer(keyboard.readLine()).intValue();

        switch (exitNumber)
        {
        case 1:  screen.println("Highway 6A/ Sagamore Bridge");break;
        case 2:  screen.println("Highway 130");break;
        case 3:  screen.println("Quaker Meeting House Road");break;
        case 4:  screen.println("Chase Road/ Scorten Road");break;
        case 5:  screen.println("Highway 149/ Martons Mills");break;
        case 6:  screen.println("Highway 132/ Hyannis");break;
        case 7:  screen.println("Willow Street/ Higgins Crowell Road");break;
        case 8:  screen.println("Union Street/ Station Avenue");break;
        case 9:  screen.println("Highway 134/ S.Dennis");break;
        case 10: screen.println("Highway 124/ harwich Port");break;
        case 11: screen.println("Highway 137/ S.Chatham");break;
        case 12: screen.println("Highay 6A/ E.Brewster");break;
        default: screen.println("DATA ERROR - incorrect exit number");
        }
    }
}
```

Test results from the program being run three times

```
Input exit number on Highway 6 8
Union Street/ Station Avenue

Input exit number on Highway 6 2
Highway 130

Input exit number on Highway 6 13
DATA ERROR - incorrect exit number
```

By comparing the switch statement in the program with the syntax notation, you should note the following points.

An expression is any expression that will evaluate to an ordinal type. In this example the expression consists of a single variable `exit_number` of type integer, which is expected to evaluate to an integer in the range 1..12.

A case label is any value that corresponds to the ordinal type in the expression. Case labels in this example represent the junctions numbers 1,2,3,4,5,6,7,8,9,10,11, and 12. Case labels must be unique.

The optional default traps any values of the expression that are not represented as case labels. Without this option, no action would occur when a value was out of range.

In program Example 3.7, only one case value was associated with a set of statements. What if more than one case value may be used for the same set of statements?

For example, if the requirement was to compute the number of days in a particular month in the year, a switch statement could be used. The variable month is an integer in the range 1..12, indicating the months January..December. Different case labels, separated by a colon, are used for each month of the year, for the month containing 31 days, 30 days and 28 days (assuming a non leap year).

```
switch (month)
{
   case 1: case 3: case 5: case 7: case 8: case 10: case 12:
                           daysInMonth = 31; break;
   case 4: case 6: case 9: case 11:
                           daysInMonth = 30; break;
   case 2:                 daysInMonth = 28;
}
```

Case Study: Price of Food and Drink

Problem. Write a program to find the price of food at Ben's Breakfast Bar (see Figure 2.6 in Chapter 2). You are required to display the items of food and drink available, input the name of a single item of food or drink, and display the price.

Problem Analysis. The name of the single item of food or drink is compared with each item of food or drink in the menu using a series of nested if statements. If there is a match between the input item and the menu item then a numerical value representing the cost of the food or drink is assigned to the price of the item.

In the implementation of this program there is only one class containing the `main` method.

Algorithm

First level of design

1. display menu
2. input item of food or drink
3. obtain price of food or drink
4. output price of item

Second level design

3.1 if item is eggs price is 2.75
3.2 else if item is pancakes price is 4.00
3.3 else if item is bagel price is 1.50
3.4 else if item is muffin or chocolate price is 0.95
3.5 else if item is yogurt or fries price is 1.00
3.6 else if item is hash price is 1.75
3.7 else if item is toast or tea or coffee price is 0.75
3.8 else error in item

4.1 if error
4.2   display item not listed in menu
4.3 else
4.4   display price of item

Data Dictionary. There are just three variables. A string object describing the item of food; a floating-point real for the price of the food and a boolean flag to show whether the wrong data was input.

```
String  food;
float   price = 0f;
boolean inputError = false;
```

Desk Check. The algorithm can be checked with the following test data - pancakes, eggs, chocolate, water.

food	price	inputError
		false
pancakes	4.00	false
eggs	2.75	false
chocolate	0.95	false
water		true

```
                    ┌─────────────────────────────────────────────────────────┐
                    │                 Screen Layout Document                  │
                    ├─────────────────────────────────────────────────────────┤
                    │ 1234567890123456789012345678901234567890123456789 0      │
                    ├─────────────────────────────────────────────────────────┤
                    │ Input an item of food from the following menu           │
                    │                                                         │
                    │ eggs        pancakes    bagel      muffin               │
                    │ yogurt      hash        toast      fries                │
                    │ tea         coffee      chocolate                       │
                    │                                                         │
                    │ ? pancakes                                              │
                    │                                                         │
                    │ The price of pancakes is $4.0                           │
                    └─────────────────────────────────────────────────────────┘
```

Coding

```java
// chap_3\Ex_8.java
// program to display the price of a chosen item of food

import java.io.*;

class Ex_8
{
    static BufferedReader keyboard = new
            BufferedReader(new InputStreamReader(System.in));
    static PrintWriter screen      = new PrintWriter(System.out, true);

    public static void main(String[] args) throws IOException
    {
        String  food;
        float   price=0f;
        boolean inputError = false;

        // display menu and input item of food

        screen.println("Input an item of food from the menu\n");
        screen.println("eggs      pancakes    bagel      muffin");
        screen.println("yogurt    hash        toast      fries");
        screen.println("tea       coffee      chocolate\n\n");

        screen.print("? "); screen.flush();
        food = keyboard.readLine();

        if      (food.equals("eggs"))
                    price = 2.75f;
        else if (food.equals("pancakes"))
                price = 4.00f;
        else if (food.equals("bagel"))
                price = 1.50f;
        else if (food.equals("muffin") || food.equals ("chocolate"))
                    price = 0.95f;
        else if (food.equals("yogurt") || food.equals ("fries"))
```

```
                    price = 1.00f;
      else if (food.equals("hash"))
                    price = 1.75f;
      else if (food.equals("toast") || food.equals ("tea")
                                    || food.equals ("coffee"))
                    price = 0.75f;
      else
         inputError = true;

      if (inputError)
         screen.println("\nFood not listed in menu\n");
      else
         screen.println("\nThe price of a " + food + " is $" + price);
   }
}
```

Test results

```
Input an item of food from the menu

eggs      pancakes   bagel      muffin
yogurt    hash       toast      fries
tea       coffee     chocolate


? pancakes

The price of a pancakes is $4.0
```

Case Study: Validation of Dates including Leap Years

Problem. The final program in this chapter validates a date. The format of the date MMDDYYYY is a single integer representing month, day and year. The single integer is split into individual integers representing MM, DD and YYYY. The program checks that the number of months in a year should not exceed 12, and that the number of days in each month has not been exceeded. The program also reports on leap years.

Problem Analysis. The validation of the date has a three-part solution.

The first part is to validate a month as an integer in the range 1 to 12. If the month is treated as an ordinal value of a switch expression, with case labels occurring for each of the twelve months, then should a month not be in the range 1 to 12, the error can be trapped as the default value. The second part involves the calculation of a leap year, and clearly will only be considered if the month happens to be February. The calculation of a leap year uses the following rule:

if the year is evenly divisible by 4 and the year is not a century
or the year is a century that is divisible by 400
then the year is a leap year

This rule can be expressed as the following conditional expression:

```
if ((((year%4 == 0) && (year%100 != 0)) || (year%400 == 0))
    screen.println(year + " is a leap year");
```

The expression may be evaluated using the years 1992, 1993, 1900, and 2000 as test data.

(1992%4 == 0)&&(1992%100 !=0)) || (1992%400 ==0) is true

(1993%4 == 0)&&(1993%100 !=0)) || (1993%400 ==0) is false

(1900%4 == 0)&&(1900%100 !=0)) || (1900%400 ==0) is false

(2000%4 == 0)&&(2000%100 !=0)) || (2000%400 ==0) is true

The third part of the solution involves the calculation of the number of days in a month. Since a switch statement is being used to select the appropriate month, the number of days in the month can be assigned according to the appropriate case label. For example, if the case label is either 1,3,5,7,8,10 or 12, then there are 31 days in the month; if the case label is 4,6,9, or 11, then there are 30 days in the month; however, if the case label is 2 and the year is a leap year then there are 29 days; otherwise, there are 28 days in the month.

Algorithm

First level design

1. input date
2. split date into month, day and year
3. calculate number of days in the month
4. output results

Second level design

3.1 switch month
3.2   1,3,5,7,8,10,12   : number of days in month is 31
3.3   4,6,9,11   : number of days in month is 30
3.4   2   : if leap year then
3.5   number of days in month is 29
3.6   else
3.7   number of days in month is 28
3.8   default   : error in month number

4.1 if month is February and the number of days is 29 then
4.2   report leap year
4.3 if day > number of days in month or error then
4.4   report error
4.5 else
4.6   report date is valid

Data Dictionary. The date is input as an integer, which must be split into the component parts month, day and year. The number of days in a month needs to be calculated. If the month or day is out of range then this must be flagged as an error. The six variables are declared as follows.

```
int     date;
int     month, day, year;
int     numberOfDays;
boolean error = false;
```

Desk Check. Dates should be chosen that fully test the algorithm. For example, a valid date (3 18 1987), leap years (2 12 1992), (2 29 2000) and either a month or a day that is out of range (2 30 1987).

variables	value(s)			
date	03181987	02121992	02292000	02301987
month	3	2	2	2
day	18	12	29	30
year	1987	1992	2000	1987
numberOfDays	31	29	29	28
error	false	false	false	true

Screen Layout Document

```
12345678901234567890123456789012345678901234567890

Input a date in the format MMDDYYYY
02121992
1992 is a Leap Year
Date checked and is valid
```

Coding

```java
// chap_3\Ex_9.java
// program to validate a date in the format MMDDYYYY

import java.io.*;

class Ex_9
{
    static BufferedReader keyboard = new
            BufferedReader(new InputStreamReader(System.in));
    static PrintWriter screen      = new PrintWriter(System.out, true);

    public static void main(String[] args) throws IOException
```

```
{
    int date;
    int month, day, year;
    int numberOfDays = 0;
    boolean error = false;

    // input date in format MMDDYYYY
    screen.println("Input a date in the format MMDDYYYY");
    date = new Integer(keyboard.readLine()).intValue();

    // split up date into MM DD and YYYY
    month = date / 1000000;
    day   = (date % 1000000) / 10000;
    year  = (date % 10000);

    // calculate number of days in month
    switch(month)
    {
        // test for Jan, Mar, May, Jul, Aug, Oct, Dec
        case 1:
        case 3:
        case 5:
        case 7:
        case 8:
        case 10:
        case 12: numberOfDays = 31; break;

        // test for Apr, Jun, Sep, Nov
        case 4:
        case 6:
        case 9:
        case 11: numberOfDays = 30; break;

        // test for Feb being a Leap Year
        case 2:if (((year%4 == 0) && (year%100 != 0)) || (year%400 == 0))
                    numberOfDays = 29;
            else
                    numberOfDays = 28;
              break;

        default: error = true;
    }

    // output results

    if (month == 2 && numberOfDays == 29)
        screen.println(year + " is a Leap Year");

    if (day > numberOfDays || error)
        screen.println("DATA ERROR - check day or month");
    else
        screen.println("Date checked and is valid");
}
}
```

Test results from program being run four times

```
Input a date in the format MMDDYYYY
03181987
Date checked and is valid

Input a date in the format MMDDYYYY
02121992
1992 is a Leap Year
Date checked and is valid

Input a date in the format MMDDYYYY
02292000
2000 is a Leap Year
Date checked and is valid

Input a date in the format MMDDYYYY
02301987
DATA ERROR - check day or month
```

Summary

- A conditional expression evaluates to either true or false.

- Depending upon the result of the conditional expression, it is possible for the computer to select different statements in an `if` statement.

- Comparison of real numbers for equality should be avoided, since real numbers are not always accurately stored by the computer.

- Conditional expressions can be combined into one expression by using the logical operators `&&` (AND) and `||` (OR).

- Short-circuit evaluation will result in conditions not being evaluated in a conditional expression.

- Both `&&` and `||` use sort-circuit evaluation. If long evaluation is required use `&` and `|` respectively.

- `If` statements may be nested within each other.

- In nested `if` statements an `else` keyword belongs to the nearest `if` keyword that has not already been paired with an `else`.

- When selection is based upon an ordinal type, a `switch` statement may be used.

- All case labels must be unique and of the ordinal type compatible with the selector type.

Review Questions

1. What is the syntax of an if statement?

2. Distinguish between the operators = and ==.

3. How many statements are allowed after the if keyword?

4. How many statements are allowed after the else keyword?

5. What is a conditional expression?

6. What symbols are used for the logical operators AND and OR?

7. What is short-circuit evaluation?

8. Why do we indent statements in an if statement?

9. What are nested if statements?

10. Explain the purpose of the switch statement.

11. Why should a break statement be used within a switch statement?

12. What are case labels?

13. When is the default label used in a switch statement?

14. If a statement corresponds to many case labels in a switch statement, how are the case labels organized?

Exercises

15. If A=1, B=-2, C=3, D=4, E='S', and F='J', state whether the following conditions are true or false.

(a) A==B
(b) A>B
(c) (A<C && B<D)
(d) (A<C && B>D)
(e) (A>B || C<D)
(f) E>F
(g) ((A+C)>(B-D)) && ((B+C)<(D-A))

16. Code the following conditions in Java.

(a) X is equal to Y

(b) X is not equal to Y
(c) A is less than or equal to B
(d) Q is not greater than T
(e) X is greater than or equal to Y
(f) X is less than or equal to Y and A is not equal to B
(g) A is greater than 18 and H is greater than 68 and W is greater than 75
(h) G is less than 100 and greater than 50
(i) H is less than 50 or greater than 100.

17. Trace through the following segment of code for each of A, B, and C and state the output in each case.

(a) A=16, B=16, C=32
(b) A=16, B=-18, C=32
(c) A=-2, B=-4, C=16

```
if (A>0)
{
    if (B<0)
        screen.println("x");
    else
        if (C>20)
            screen.println("y");
}
else
    screen.println("z");
```

18. Trace through the following segment of code for each new value of the variable character and state the output.

(a) character = 'B';
(b) character = '4';
(c) character = 'a';

```
switch (character)
{
    case 'a': case 'b': case 'c': screen.println("small letter"); break;
    case 'A': case 'B': case 'C': screen.println("capitalletters"); break;
    case '1': case '2': case '3': screen.println("digits"); break;
    default                     : screen.println("error in data");
}
```

19. Correct the syntax in this program segment.

```
if y > 25
    x == 16;
    screen.println("x = " + x);
else
    y = 20
```

20. The lengths of the four sides of a quadrilateral and one internal angle are input into a computer. Design an algorithm using pseudocode, to categorize the shape of the quadrilateral as a square, rhombus, rectangle, parallelogram, or irregular quadrilateral. Remember to give your algorithm a desk check using suitably chosen data.

The rules for determining the shape of the quadrilateral follow.

Name	All sides equal?	Opposite sides equal?	Internal angle is a right angle
square	true	true	true
rectangle	false	true	true
rhombus	true	true	false
parallelogram	false	true	false
irregular	false	false	-

Programming Problems

21. Modify Program Example 3.6 to cater for both sexes, and to eliminate all women from the list of suspects.

22. A worker is paid at the hourly rate of $8 per hour for the first 35 hours worked. Overtime is paid at 1½ times the hourly rate for the next 25 hours worked and 2 times the hourly rate for additional hours worked. Write a program to input the number of hours worked per week and then calculate and output the overtime paid.

23. A student traveling to Florida for Spring break will consider a particular airline if the round trip ticket costs less than $200 and has a layover of no longer than 4 hours; or if the ticket costs between $200 and $300 and has no layover. Write a program to input the name of an airline, cost if ticket, and layover time; output the name of the airline only if it meets the student's criteria.

24. A student choosing among payment plans for a college loan wants to keep the monthly payments to less than $200. If the initial amount of the loan is $5000 then write a program to calculate which plans are acceptable given different loan length and simple interest rates.

25. A researcher needs to screen individuals for certain characteristics before admitting them to a medical research study. The criteria for admittance are:

gender: females only
age: 18 to 40 years
weight: no greater than 180 pounds
blood group: O only

Write a program to input the name of a person, together with his or her gender, age, weight, and blood group; display only the names of those individuals who meet the specified criteria.

26. Write a program to implement the algorithm that you designed and tested in question 20.

27. A salesperson earns commission on the value of sales. Figure 3.9 shows the scale of the commission. Write a program to input a figure for the value of the sales, and then calculate and output the commission.

value of sales	commission
$1 - $999	1%
$1000 - $9999	5%
$10000 - $99999	10%

Figure 3.9 Scale of commission

28. A barometer dial is calibrated into the following climatic conditions: STORM, RAIN, CHANGE, FAIR, and DRY. Write a program that will input one of these readings, and output clothing suggestions from the following rules.

STORM	wear overcoat and hat
RAIN	wear raincoat and take umbrella
CHANGE	behave as for FAIR if it rained yesterday and for RAIN if it did not
FAIR	wear jacket and take umbrella
DRY	wear jacket

29. Write a program to mimic a calculator. Input two real numbers and state whether the numbers are to be added, subtracted, multiplied, or divided. Cater for the possibility of a denominator being zero in the division of two numbers.

30. A bicycle shop in Hyannis rents bicycles by the day at different rates throughout the year, according to the season (see Figure 3.10). The proprietor also gives a 25% discount if the rental period is greater than 7 days. Renters must also pay a $50 returnable deposit for each bicycle rented. Write a program to input the season and the number of days of rental and then calculate and display a total charge that includes the deposit.

season	charge
Spring	$5.00
Summer	$7.50
Autumn	$3.75
Winter	$2.50

Figure 3.10 Rental rates

Chapter 4
Repetition

In the previous chapter it was necessary to run some programs several times to demonstrate the effect that different items of input data would have on the results. At the time you might have thought this approach was a little cumbersome. How much better it would be if we had a structure in the program that would allow statements to be repeated.

The purpose of this chapter is to introduce you to three methods for repeating statements that are based on the control structures known as *while*, *do..while*, and *for*. The chapter also contains information on an alternative means of data input and screen output. By the end of the chapter, you should have an understanding of the following topics.

- The concept of a loop.

- The syntax and appropriate use of `while`, `do.while`, and `for` loop statements.

- The use of postfix increment and decrement operators.

- Input and output streams that allow reading from and writing to files.

- Splitting strings into individual tokens.

4.1 Loops

In writing computer programs it is often necessary to repeat part of a program a number of times. One way to achieve repetition is to write out that part of the program as many times as it is needed. This method is very impractical, since it produces a very lengthy computer program and the number of repetitions is not always known in advance.

A better way to repeat part of a program a number of times is to introduce a loop into the code. The illustration in Figure 4.1 shows one mechanism for setting up a loop.

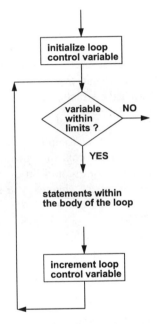

Figure 4.1 Loop variable controlled by a counter

In this example a counter is used as a loop control variable to record the number of times part of the program is repeated. The following operations take place on the loop control variable.

1. The loop control variable must be initialized before the computer enters the loop.
2. The value of the loop control variable is tested to see whether it is within specified limits for looping to continue. - if the loop control variable is not within these limits, then the computer must exit from the loop.
3. The statements within the body of the loop are executed.
4. The value of the loop control variable is incremented by one to indicate that the statements have been performed once.
5. Go back to step 2, thereby completing the loop.

Notice from Figure 4.1, if the loop control variable is initialized to a value that is outside of the limits, then the loop will never be entered and the statements within the body of the loop will never be executed.

The loop control variable does not have to be assigned values from within the program. The initialization and incremental increase of this variable can be replaced by reading data from an input device such as a keyboard. The illustration in Figure 4.2 shows reading values of the loop control variable in place of assigning values from within a program. Notice that a certain value input from the keyboard will trigger the exit from the loop. This value is known as a **sentinel** value.

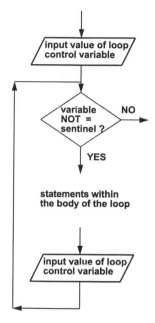

Figure 4.2 Loop variable controlled by data

4.2 While

A while loop will allow a statement to be repeated zero or more times and behaves in the same manner as depicted by the illustrations in Figures 4.1 and 4.2. The syntax of the while loop follows.

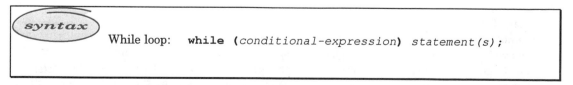

Notice that many statements may follow the conditional expression. If more than one statement is to be repeated, it is necessary to enclose the statements within braces { } so the computer treats the statements as a block.

Loop Controlled by a Counter

The following segment of code uses a `while` loop and a loop variable controlled by a counter, as illustrated in Figure 4.1.

```
counter = 1;                          // initialize loop control variable
while (counter <= 5)                  // test if variable is within limits
{
    screen.print(counter + "\t");
    screen.flush();
    counter = counter + 1;            // increment loop control variable
}
```

The value of counter is initialized to 1; the condition (counter<=5) is true; therefore, the value of the counter is output. The counter is incremented by 1 to the value 2; the condition (counter<=5) is true, so the value of counter is output again. The process continues while the condition (counter<=5) remains true. When counter is incremented to the value 6, the condition (counter<=5) becomes false and the computer exits from the `while` loop.

Loop Controlled by Data

Consider the use of a `while` loop to display numbers on a screen while the numbers are not zero. The numbers are input from a keyboard, and the value 0 (zero) is the sentinel value. The following segment of code uses a `while` loop and a loop variable controlled by data, as illustrated in Figure 4.2.

```
// input value of loop control variable
number = new Integer(keyboard.readLine()).intValue();

while (number != 0)                   // test if variable is a sentinel value
{
    screen.print(number + "\t");
    screen.flush();

    // input value of loop control variable
    number = new Integer(keyboard.readLine()).intValue();
}
```

If the first number to be read is zero, then the conditional expression (number!=0) will be false. The computer will not enter the loop but branch to the next executable statement after the end of the compound statement delimited by the braces { }. Since the loop was not entered, the loop is repeated zero times.

However, if the first number to be read was nonzero, the conditional expression would be true and the computer would execute the statements contained within the loop. To this end the number would be displayed on the screen, and the next number input at the keyboard. The computer then returns to the line containing the conditional expression, which is re-evaluated to test whether the new number is not zero. If the condition is true, the computer continues to execute the statements in the loop. If the condition is false, the computer will branch to the next executable statement after the end of the compound statement.

To restate the behavior of the `while` loop: if the first number read is zero, then the loop is not entered, and the statements within the loop have been repeated zero times. If the second number to be read is zero, the statements in the loop will have been repeated once. If the third number to be read is zero, the statements in the loop will have been repeated twice, and so on. Therefore, if the hundredth number to be read is zero, the statements inside the loop will have been repeated ninety-nine times.

Note that for clarity, the body of the `while` loop is indented. Therefore, when other kinds of loops are introduced in this chapter, we will follow the same pattern of indentation. In addition, we will utilize indentation in writing the algorithm for such code. Getting into the habit of identifying the structure of a loop at the algorithm stage of program design will facilitate the eventual coding of the loop.

The outline program given in the second example has been developed into the following Java program.

Program Example 4.1: While Loop with Numeric Sentinel

```java
// chap_4\Ex_1.java
// program to demonstrate a while loop

import java.io.*;

class Ex_1
{
    static BufferedReader keyboard = new
            BufferedReader(new InputStreamReader(System.in));
    static PrintWriter screen       = new PrintWriter(System.out, true);

    public static void main(String[] args) throws IOException
    {
        int number;

        screen.print("input an integer - terminate with 0 ");
        screen.flush();
        number = new Integer(keyboard.readLine()).intValue();

        while (number != 0)
        {
            screen.println(number);

            screen.print("input an integer - terminate with 0 ");
            screen.flush();
            number = new Integer(keyboard.readLine()).intValue();
        }
    }
}
```

The specimen results from the program show (a) the statements within the loop being repeated twice and (b) the statements within the loop not being repeated at all.

(a) Test results

```
input an integer - terminate with 0 36
36
input an integer - terminate with 0 18
18
input an integer - terminate with 0 0
```

(b) Test results

```
input an integer - terminate with 0 0
```

Program Example 3.5 allowed us to input the age and height of an individual to determine whether he or she fitted a description of a criminal. We will revise that program to include a while loop to allow the program to be repeated many times without rerunning the program. Before the while loop is entered the user is requested to input the name of a suspect. If the word EXIT is input, this is taken as the sentinel value to allow an exit from the while loop.

Remember in Java you compare strings by using the method equals from the String class. For our revised program example, the equals method becomes part of the conditional expression in the while statement. If the contents of the string object name equals the string literal "EXIT" then the result of the conditional expression is true. But we want to repeat the statements when this comparison is false, in other words name is not equal to the sentinel value "EXIT". Therefore, the conditional statement is negated using the logical operator !, which represents **logical NOT**. For example, the conditional expression found in the while statement is coded as !name.equals("EXIT").

The while loop will be exited only when the conditional expression is false, in other words when the string literal "EXIT" has been input. As long as the string "EXIT" is not input in response to the prompt to input the name of a suspect, the computer will continue to process the details of all suspects to the crime.

Program Example 4.2: While Loop with String Sentinel

```java
// chap_4\Ex_2.java
// program to display the name of a suspect to a crime who is aged
// between 20 and 25 years and between 66 and 70 inches tall
import java.io.*;

class Ex_2
{
    static BufferedReader keyboard = new
            BufferedReader(new InputStreamReader(System.in));
    static PrintWriter screen      = new PrintWriter(System.out, true);

    public static void main(String[] args) throws IOException
    {
        String name;
        int    age;
```

```
int     height;

screen.print("Input name of suspect - terminate with EXIT ");
screen.flush();
name = keyboard.readLine();

while (!name.equals("EXIT"))
{
    screen.print("Age? "); screen.flush();
    age = new Integer(keyboard.readLine()).intValue();

    screen.print("Height? "); screen.flush();
    height = new Integer(keyboard.readLine()).intValue();

    if (age < 20 || age > 25 || height < 66 || height > 70)
        screen.println(name + " is not a suspect and should be
                                released\n");
    else
        screen.println(name + " is a suspect and should be
                                interrogated\n");

    screen.print("Input name of suspect - terminate with EXIT ");
    screen.flush();
    name = keyboard.readLine();
}
    }
}
```

Test results

```
Input name of suspect - terminate with EXIT Smith
Age? 20
Height? 68
Smith is a suspect and should be interrogated

Input name of suspect - terminate with EXIT Jones
Age? 26
Height? 68
Jones is not a suspect and should be released

Input name of suspect - terminate with EXIT Evans
Age? 25
Height? 69
Evans is a suspect and should be interrogated

Input name of suspect - terminate with EXIT EXIT
```

4.3 Do..While

The illustration in Figure 4.3 shows another method for repeating statements within a program. Notice the absence of a decision symbol from the beginning of the loop, which implies that it is possible to execute the statements within the loop at least once. The decision symbol appears at the end of the loop. Thus the computer will exit from the loop only when the condition associated with this symbol is false.

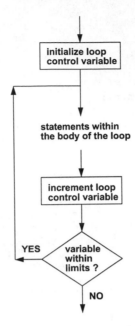

Figure 4.3 A loop that is executed at least once

Unlike a `while` loop a `do..while` loop always permits the statements within the loop to be executed at least once by the computer. The syntax of the `do..while` loop follows.

syntax

do .. while Statement:

do *statements(s)* **while** *(conditional-expression)*;

For example,

```
counter = 1;                          // initialize loop control variable
do
{
    screen.print(counter + "\t");
    screen.flush();
    counter = counter + 1;            // increment loop control variable
} while (counter <= 5);               // test if variable is within limits
```

The value of counter is initialized to 1; the `do..while` loop is entered and the value of counter is output. The counter is incremented by 1 to the value 2; the condition (counter<=5) is true, so the value of counter is output again. The process continues while the condition (counter<=5) remains true. When the counter is incremented to the value 6, the condition (`counter<=5`) becomes false and the computer exits from the `do..while` loop.

Notice that the computer enters the loop without any test for entry being made. Hence the contents of a `do..while` loop will always be executed at least once. There can be either a single statement or a compound statement between the keywords do and while.

Like the `while` loop the `do..while` loop may also use a loop variable controlled by data as illustrated in Figure 4.4.

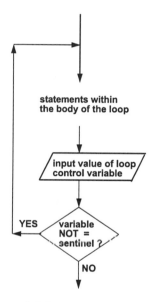

Figure 4.4 Loop controlled by data

Extend Program Example 3.1, to calculate and display the gross weekly wages for five workers all employed at the same hourly rate. The algorithm given in Program Example 3.1 can be modified so that the steps to input the hours worked, calculate the gross wage with or without overtime, and output the gross wage are repeated for each employee. If a counter is increased by 1 every time the gross wage is calculated and output for an employee, when the counter reaches the value of 5, the steps will not need to be repeated again and the algorithm can stop.

Program Example 4.3 illustrates how a `do..while` loop may be used with a counter to repeat the statements necessary to input the hours worked for an employee, and calculate and display the gross wage for an employee.

Program Example 4.3: Do..While Loop

```java
// chap_4\Ex_3.java
// program to calculate a gross weekly wage

import java.io.*;

class Ex_3
{
    static BufferedReader keyboard = new
            BufferedReader(new InputStreamReader(System.in));
    static PrintWriter screen      = new PrintWriter(System.out, true);

    public static void main(String[] args) throws IOException
    {
        final int NUMBER_OF_EMPLOYEES = 5;

        float rateOfPay;
        float hoursWorked;
        float grossWage;
        int   counter;

        // input rate of pay
        screen.print("Rate of pay? "); screen.flush();
        rateOfPay = new Float(keyboard.readLine()).floatValue();

        counter = 0;

        do
        {
            // input hours worked
            screen.print("Hours worked? "); screen.flush();
            hoursWorked = new Float(keyboard.readLine()).floatValue();

            // calculate gross wage
            if (hoursWorked > 40.0)
               grossWage = 1.5f*rateOfPay*(hoursWorked-40.0f) +
                           40.0f*rateOfPay;
            else
               grossWage = hoursWorked * rateOfPay;

            // output gross wage
            screen.println("Gross wage $" + grossWage);

            counter = counter + 1;

        } while (counter != NUMBER_OF_EMPLOYEES);
    }
}
```

Test results

```
Rate of pay? 10
Hours worked? 35
Gross wage $350.0
Hours worked? 50
Gross wage $550.0
Hours worked? 40
Gross wage $400.0
Hours worked? 45
Gross wage $475.0
Hours worked? 38
Gross wage $380.0
```

4.4 Increment/ Decrement Operators

At this point in the chapter it is worth digressing to the topic of incrementing and decrementing values, in particular in the context of control variables found in loops.

If you want to increase the value of an integer variable counter by one, then you write

```
counter = counter + 1
```

The same result can be achieved by writing

```
counter++
```

Similarly, if you wanted to decrease the value of counter by one, then you would write

```
counter = counter - 1
```

the same result can be achieved by writing

```
counter--
```

These new operators are known as increment and decrement postfix operators; they are written after the variables as **++** and **--** respectively and can be used to increase or decrease an integer numeric variable or a character variable by <u>one</u>. The increment and decrement postfix operators are useful within loops as the next program illustrates. The Java language also has increment and decrement prefix operators, but they are not used in this book.

Program Example 4.4 illustrates how the increment and decrement postfix operators may be used within loops to change the values of the loop control variables. The program illustrates a simple counting exercise to count down from 10 to 0, and also to display the alphabet from A to Z.

Program Example 4.4: Increment and Decrement Postfix Operators

```java
// chap_4\Ex_4
// program to demonstrate the use of increment and decrement postfix
// operators within while loops

import java.io.*;

class Ex_4
{
    static PrintWriter screen = new PrintWriter(System.out, true);

    public static void main(String[] args) throws IOException
    {
        final char ASCII_CODE_Z = 'Z';

        int  counter   = 10;
        char asciiCode = 'A';

        // count down from 10 to 0

        screen.print("countdown .. "); screen.flush();
        while (counter >= 0)
        {
            screen.print(counter + " "); screen.flush();
            counter--;  // same as counter = counter - 1
        }
        screen.println("blast off!!\n");

        // code to display the alphabet

        screen.print("alphabet .. "); screen.flush();
        while (asciiCode <= ASCII_CODE_Z)
        {
            screen.print(asciiCode); screen.flush();
            asciiCode++;
        }
    }
}
```

Test results

```
countdown .. 10 9 8 7 6 5 4 3 2 1 0 blast off!!

alphabet .. ABCDEFGHIJKLMNOPQRSTUVWXYZ
```

4.5 For Loop

The syntax of a `for` statement in Java follows:

---
syntax

for loop:

for (*expression1 ; expression2 ; expression3* **)** *statements(s)*

---

where expression1 represents the declaration (if necessary) and initialization of the loop control variable; expression2 is a condition under which repetition will continue, and expression3 is a statement to increment or decrement the loop control variable. For example

```
for (int counter = 1; counter <= 5; counter++)
{
    screen.print(counter + "\t");
    screen.flush();
}
```

The output from this code is

```
1    2    3    4    5
```

The `for` statement can be regarded as a shorthand version of the following while loop.

```
expression1;
while (expression2)
{
    statements(s);
    expression3;
}
```

The `while` loop and the `for` loop are interchangeable in that both types of loops can be used for counting. The following code produces exactly the same output as the for loop example.

```
int counter = 1;
while (counter <= 5)
{
    screen.print(counter + "\t");
    screen.flush();
    counter++;
}
```

The following program illustrates the use of the `for` loop.

The expressions in a `for` loop are optional.

(1) If expression1 is omitted, the initialization (and declaration) of the loop control variable must take place before entry into the loop.

(2) If expression2 is omitted, then the loop does not terminate unless it contains a break statement.

(3) If expression3 is omitted, then increasing or decreasing the loop variable must take place within the body of the loop.

Program Example 4.5: The for Loop

```
// chap_4\Ex_5
// program to demonstrate the use of the for loop

import java.io.*;

class Ex_5
{
    static PrintWriter screen = new PrintWriter(System.out, true);

    public static void main(String[] args) throws IOException
    {
        for (int counter = 1; counter < 4; counter++)
        {
            screen.print(counter + "\t");
            screen.flush();
        }
        screen.println();

        int counter = 1;                    // (1) initialization
        for (; counter < 4; counter++)
        {
            screen.print(counter + "\t");
            screen.flush();
        }
        screen.println();

        for (counter = 1;; counter++)
        {
            screen.print(counter + "\t");
            screen.flush();
            if (counter == 3) break;        // (2) condition to exit
        }
        screen.println();

        for (counter = 1; counter < 4;)
        {
            screen.print(counter++ + "\t");  // (3) increment loop control
            screen.flush();
        }
        screen.println();
    }
}
```

Test results

```
1          2          3
1          2          3
1          2          3
1          2          3
```

By omitting all three expressions in a `for` loop, it is possible to set up an infinite loop - one that repeats without ending! Unless you deliberately want your program to run forever, such programming practice should be avoided.

For example, the following segment of code continues to print the message until the user interrupts the running program.

```
for ( ; ; )
{
    screen.println("forever and ever … ");
}
```

Notice that even when the expressions are omitted in for loops, the semicolon separators must be present.

4.6 Which Loop?

You should by now understand the syntax and semantics of the three loop structures - `while`, `do..while`, and `for`. However, knowing which loop to use in a program requires more explanation.

While

The first statement in a `while` loop contains a condition to exit from the loop. This condition guards entry into the loop. If the guarding condition is false, then entry into the loop will be denied. Whenever there is the possibility that you do not want the program to execute the statements within the loop, you should use a `while` loop.

In this example input data is used to control entry into the loop.

```
inputData = keyboard.readLine();
while (! inputData.equals(sentinal))
{
    .
    .
    .
    inputData = keyboard.readLine();
}
```

Notice that when data is used to control entry into a loop, it is necessary to read ahead for a datum in order to test the guarding conditional statement. It is also necessary to include a second read statement within the body of the loop to supply data for testing the conditional statement.

Do..While

The feature of this loop is that it is not guarded by any condition, and the computer will always execute the statements within the loop at least once. This feature can be useful when validating data. In the following example, the body of the loop will continue to be executed until a number is input that lies within the range 0..10.

```
do
{
    screen.print("input a number in the range 0..100 ");
    screen.flush();
    number = new Integer(keyboard.readLine()).intValue();
} while (number < 0 || number > 100);
```

For

A `for` loop is normally used for counting. However, since it behaves in a manner similar to a `while` loop, it can be used if the body of the loop needs to be guarded against initial entry. The following example illustrates the use of a `for` loop to control a counter to display the alphabet.

```
for (char asciiChar = 'A'; asciiChar <= 'Z'; asciiChar++)
{
    screen.print(asciiChar + "\t" + (int)asciiChar + "\t");
    screen.flush();
    if (asciiChar % 2 == 0) screen.println();
}
```

In this example the `char` variable `asciiChar` acts as a counter from 'A' to 'Z'. To display the ASCII code for each character it is necessary to cast the variable as an integer. The `if` statement is used to generate a new line when two pairs of results have been output.

4.7 Streams Revisited

In this and previous chapters input was confined to entering data through a keyboard and output to displaying information on a screen. When there is a requirement to permanently store data, there is a need to create files. Data can be written to or read from files held on magnetic media. Common media that you are likely to use for storing your files will be floppy disks that you carry around or hard disks that are part of the computer.

You are already familiar with text files. All the source program files created using an editor have been text files.

Up to now all input has been as strings through the keyboard and output as strings to the screen of a monitor. This does suffer from the disadvantages of slow input speed when there is a considerable amount of data to input, and not enough screen area when there are copious results to output. If the `System.in` and `System.out` values are replaced by new values that relate to computer files, then it will be possible to read input from a file in place of the keyboard and write output to a file in place of the screen.

A file must be **opened** before we can gain access to the device for reading or writing. In Java, when a file is opened, an object is created and a stream is associated with the object.

The class **FileReader** contains a constructor that requires the pathname (path and filename) of an input file. In the example that follows the pathname is given as `a:\\chap_4\\data.txt`. Note - the double backslash `\\` is necessary to avoid any confusion with an escape character in the string. If you are using a SUN Solaris system, the path names use `/` in place of `\`.

```
FileReader file = new FileReader("a:\\chap_4\\data.txt");
```

To provide the same method that was used with keyboard input (`readLine`) it is necessary to use the object `file` in the constructor of the `BufferedReader`; thus creating a stream object `inputFile` that is associated with reading from the disk file with the pathname `a:\\chap_4\\data.txt`. Note - **a:** implies reading a file from floppy-disk drive a.

```
BufferedReader inputFile = new BufferedReader(file);
```

When a file is no longer required it must be closed. The method defined in the class `BufferedReader` is **close()**.

The following information is used in Program Example 4.6. A text file contains data that relate to the insured values of several domestic appliances. For example, a television is insured for $395.95, a music center is insured for $550.00, a desk-top computer is insured for $995.95, and so on.

Note - this file has been created and stored on disk using an editor, in the same way as you would create and store a program source file.

```
395.95
television
550.00
music center
995.95
desk-top computer
199.95
microwave oven
299.99
washing machine
149.95
freezer
0
```

The data appears in the file in lines, where each line of text corresponds to a single line of data that would have been input at the keyboard. The last value in the file is 0 (zero), to act as a sentinel value.

Program Example 4.6: Reading and Displaying the Contents of a Text File

The program demonstrates how to open the file data.txt and read and display the contents line by line. If the file cannot be opened this will automatically generate a FileNotFoundException and the program will automatically be abandoned (exceptions will be covered later in the book).

```
// chap_4\Ex_6
// program to read data from a file and display the information
// on the screen

import java.io.*;

class Ex_6
{
    static BufferedReader keyboard = new
            BufferedReader(new InputStreamReader(System.in));
    static PrintWriter screen       = new PrintWriter(System.out, true);

    public static void main(String[] args) throws IOException
    {
        FileReader file             = new FileReader("a:\\chap_4\\data.txt");
        BufferedReader inputFile = new BufferedReader(file);

        String name;
        float price;

        price = new Float(inputFile.readLine()).floatValue();
        while (price != 0)
        {
            name = inputFile.readLine();
            screen.println(price + "\t"+ name);
            price = new Float(inputFile.readLine()).floatValue();
        }

        inputFile.close();
    }
}
```

Test results

```
395.95   television
550.0    music center
995.95   desk-top computer
199.95   microwave oven
299.99   washing machine
149.95   freezer
```

The class **FileWriter** contains a constructor that requires the pathname (path and filename) of an output file. In the example that follows the pathname is given as a:\\chap_4\\results.txt.

```
FileWriter file2 = new FileWriter("a:\\chap_4\\results.txt");
```

To provide the same methods that were used with screen output (print, println, flush) it is necessary to use the object file2 in the constructor of the PrintWriter; thus creating a stream object outputFile that is associated with writing to the disk file with the pathname a:\\chap_4\\results.txt.

```
PrintWriter outputFile = new PrintWriter(file2);
```

Program Example 4.7: Reading and Writing Text Files

When using files, output does not necessarily need to be directed to a screen. Output can also be directed to another text file. Program Example 4.7 modifies the contents of the file used in the previous program so that the price of each appliance is increased by the rate of inflation; the new price and the name of the appliance are written to a text file.

```java
// chap_4\Ex_7
// program to read data from a file, modify the information
// and write the information back to a different text file

import java.io.*;

class Ex_7
{
    public static void main(String[] args) throws IOException
    {
        final float RATE_OF_INFLATION = 0.025f;

        FileReader file1        = new FileReader("a:\\chap_4\\data.txt");
        BufferedReader inputFile = new BufferedReader(file1);

        FileWriter file2        = new FileWriter("a:\\chap_4\\results.txt");
        PrintWriter outputFile  = new PrintWriter(file2);

        String name;
        float price;

        price = new Float(inputFile.readLine()).floatValue();
        while (price != 0)
        {
            price = price + (price * RATE_OF_INFLATION);
            name = inputFile.readLine();
            outputFile.println(price + " " + name);
            price = new Float(inputFile.readLine()).floatValue();
        }

        inputFile.close();
        outputFile.close();
    }
}
```

(handwritten margin note: Read in)
(handwritten margin note: Write out)

Test results - contents of `a:\\chap_4\\results.txt`

```
405.84875 television
563.75 music center
1020.84875 desk-top computer
204.94875 microwave oven
307.48975 washing machine
153.69875 freezer
```

4.8 Tokenizing

The practice of creating a text file with one item of data per line does not always convey what a group of items represents. For example, it would be clearer to create a text file containing data that was grouped together in lines

```
395.95 television
550.00 music center
995.95 desk-top computer
.
```

rather than having single items per line

```
395.95
television
550.00
music center
995.95
desk-top computer
.
```

Similarly a passage of text is clearer to both read and enter at the keyboard as

```
To be or not to be,
that is the question;
whether it is nobler in the mind,
to take arms against a sea of trouble,
or by opposing, end them
.
```

rather than single words per line

```
To
be
or
not
to
be
.
```

Given that the grouping of items of data or words on one line is a more natural way of creating a text file, how can we program the computer to split up a string into the individual items (tokens) of data on a line? The answer is to use methods from the class **StringTokenizer** found in the package **util** (utilities). A listing of the constructors and methods of this class follow. The constructors and instance methods written in bold type will be used in this chapter.

```
public class StringTokenizer implements Enumeration
{
    public StringTokenizer(String str, String delim,
                            boolean returnTokens);
    public StringTokenizer(String str, String delim);
    public StringTokenizer(String str);
    public boolean hasMoreTokens();
    public String nextToken();
    public String nextToken(String delim);
    public boolean hasMoreElements();
    public Object nextElement();
    public int countTokens();
}
```

Before a line of text can be split up an object of type StringTokenizer must be instantiated from the input string. For example:

```
StringTokenizer data = new StringTokenizer(inputFile.readLine());
```

A line of text can only be split into tokens if we know what the delimiting character is for each token. For example in a line of text where items of data are separated by a space and the end of the line from the next line by a return character, both the space and return characters are token delimiters. If the token delimiter is not specified then the delimiter is assumed to be any white space character. A **white space** character is generally regarded as either a space '\u0020', horizontal tabulation '\u0009', new line '\u000A', vertical tabulation '\u000B' or form feed character '\u000C'.

Both nextToken methods return a token of type String. The method nextToken() will return a token delimited by any white space character, and nextToken(String delim) will return a token specifically delimited by the character delim. For example,

String token = data.nextToken(), will return a token delimited by any white space character, and
String token = data.nextToken("\u000A") will return a token specifically delimited by a new line character only.

⚠ Notice that the second nextToken instance method requires a string argument and not a character argument.

The method countTokens() will return the number of tokens in a string that are delimited by any white space character.

Program Example 4.8: Count the Number of Words in a Text File.

In the program that follows a line of text is read from a text file. The line is tokenized into words, and the number of tokens in the line is also calculated. The program displays each word on the screen and keeps a count on the number of words in the line of text. The process is repeated for further lines of text while there are tokens in a line. The end of the file has been delimited by two return characters. hence upon reading the first return the, the number of tokens in that line will be zero.

```java
// chap_4\Ex_8.java
// program to demonstrate how a string of text can be tokenized
// into single words that are separated by white space characters

import java.io.*;
import java.util.*;

class Ex_8
{
    static PrintWriter screen = new PrintWriter(System.out, true);

    public static void main(String[] args) throws IOException
    {
        FileReader file              = new FileReader("a:\\chap_4\\passage.txt");
        BufferedReader inputFile = new BufferedReader(file);

        StringTokenizer data;
        int             numberOfTokens;
        int             numberOfWords = 0;

        data = new StringTokenizer(inputFile.readLine());
        numberOfTokens = data.countTokens();

        while (numberOfTokens !=0)
        {
            for (int words=1; words <= numberOfTokens; words++)
            {
                screen.print(data.nextToken() + " ");
                screen.flush();
            }
            screen.println();

            numberOfWords = numberOfWords + numberOfTokens;

            data = new StringTokenizer(inputFile.readLine());
            numberOfTokens = data.countTokens();
        }

        screen.println("\nThere are "+numberOfWords+" words in the text.");
    }
}
```

Test results

```
To be or not to be,
that is the question;
whether it is nobler in the mind,
to take arms against a sea of trouble,
or by opposing, end them.

There are 30 words in the text.
```

Before we leave the topic of tokenizing, it is worth mentioning that there is a class in the java.io package called StreamTokenizer. A StreamTokenizer takes an input stream and divides it into tokens, allowing the tokens to be read one at a time. When you have learnt more about classes and methods we will explore this class further.

Case Study: Savings Account Interest

Problem. You open a savings account with a specified amount of money; the bank will pay 1.5% interest each quarter. You plan to make no deposits or withdrawals, but you want to see what each quarterly balance, including interest, will be over a period of time.

Problem Analysis. Calculating the interest for one quarter of a year is the product of the balance and the quarterly rate *interest = balance * quarterlyRate*. Before you can calculate the interest for the next quarter, it is necessary to increase the balance by the interest for the first quarter *balance = balance + interest*. This calculation of interest and balance continues for all the quarter years within the investment period.

Algorithm

1. input balance and term
2. output headings
3. calculate length of term in quarter years
4. for every quarter year in term
5.   calculate interest
6.   calculate balance
7.   output quarter year, interest, and balance

Data Dictionary. The quarterly rate can be declared in the program as a constant of value 0.015f. The balance and interest are both quantities of money, and therefore, are declared as type float. The variable term, the length of the term in quarterly years, and the last quarter year are all declared as type integer.

```
final float QUARTERLY_RATE = 0.015f;
float balance;
float interest;
int   term;
int   lastQuarter;
```

Desk Check - The initial balance is 2000 and the term 1 year

balance	term	lastQuarter	quarterYears	interest	(quarterYears<=lastQuarter)
2000	1	4	1		
2030			2	30.00	true
2060.45			3	30.45	true
2091.36			4	30.91	true
2122.73			5	31.37	false

```
                  Screen Layout Document

12345678901234567890123456789012345678901234567890

Input initial balance 2000
Input length of investment in years 1
quarter      interest      balance
1            30.00         2030.00
2            30.45         2060.45
3            30.91         2091.36
4            31.37         2122.73
```

Coding

```java
// chap_4\Ex_9.java
// program to calculate the accumulated interest payable on a savings
// account

import java.io.*;

class Ex_9
{
    static BufferedReader keyboard = new
            BufferedReader(new InputStreamReader(System.in));
    static PrintWriter screen       = new PrintWriter(System.out, true);
```

```
public static void main(String[] args) throws IOException
{
    final float QUARTERLY_RATE = 0.015f;

    float balance;
    float interest;
    int term;
    int lastQuarter;

    screen.print("Input initial balance ");
    screen.flush();
    balance = new Float(keyboard.readLine()).floatValue();

    screen.print("Input length of investment in years ");
    screen.flush();
    term = new Integer(keyboard.readLine()).intValue();

    screen.println("\nquarter\tinterest\tbalance\n");

    lastQuarter = 4 * term;

    for (int quarterYears = 1; quarterYears <= lastQuarter;
            quarterYears++)
    {
        interest = balance * QUARTERLY_RATE;
        balance = balance + interest;
        screen.println(quarterYears + "\t" + interest + "\t" + balance);
    }
}
}
```

Test results

```
Input initial balance 2000
Input length of investment in years 2

quarter interest         balance

1       30.0             2030.0
2       30.449999        2060.45
3       30.906748        2091.3567
4       31.37035         2122.727
5       31.840904        2154.5679
6       32.318516        2186.8865
7       32.803295        2219.6897
8       33.295345        2252.985
```

Case Study: Stock Control of Books

Problem. The following listing of a text file has been created using an editor and stored under the name `books.txt`. Each line in the file represent the quantity in stock, the price of a book, and the title of the book. For example there is 1 copy, priced at $8.95 of Art in Athens. There is a sentinel value of two new line characters at the end of the file.

```
1 8.95 Art in Athens
2 3.75 Birds of Prey
1 7.55 Eagles in the USA
3 5.25 Gone with the Wind
2 3.75 Hate, Lust and Love
3 5.95 Maths for Adults
3 3.75 Modern Farming
3 5.25 Raiders of Planet X
1 8.95 Splitting the Atom
1 3.75 The Invisible Man
2 3.75 The Otter
4 5.95 The Tempest
2 5.95 The Trojan Wars
2 3.75 Under the Seas
2 7.55 Vampire Bats
```

Write a program to read each line of the file and produce a text file of a report similar to that illustrated in the Report Layout Document below.

```
┌─────────────────────────────────────────────────────────────┐
│              Report Layout Document                           │
├─────────────────────────────────────────────────────────────┤
│ 12345678901234567890123456789012345678901234567890            │
│                                                               │
│                  STOCK REPORT ON BOOKS                        │
│                                                               │
│ quantity      price         title                             │
│ 1             8.95          Art in Athens -> REORDER          │
│ 2             3.75          Birds of Prey                      │
│ 1             7.50          Eagles in the USA -> REORDER       │
│ 3             5.20          Gone with the Wind                 │
│ .             .             .                                  │
│ .             .             .                                  │
│                                                               │
│ Number of books in stock 32                                   │
│ Value of books in stock $170.15                               │
└─────────────────────────────────────────────────────────────┘
```

Notice from the design of the document that when the stock level falls to one item, the report indicates that the stock should be replenished. Notice also that totals are calculated for the number of books and for the value of all the books in stock and printed at the end of the report.

Problem Analysis. The text file is processed in a similar manner to the file described in Program Example 4.8. A complete line of text is read and then tokenized and assigned to an object of type StringTokenizer. The number of tokens in each line of text is also calculated. Since each token in a line is represented as a string it is a matter of using the wrapper classes `Integer` and `Float` to convert the tokens for the quantity and price to `int` and `float` primitive types respectively. To prevent the title of each book being tokenized as individual words, it is necessary to change the delimiter to a new line character that is present at the end of each title string.

The solution to the problem has two parts. The first part requires reading the text file and writing the same information to the report file. When the stock level falls to one book per title, the message to reorder that book title should also be written to the file. The second part calculates the cumulative totals for the number of books in stock and the total value of the books, every time the quantity and price is read from the file. When the number of tokens in a line is zero the end of the input file will have been reached, and the information on the cumulative totals is written to the report. Note - the value of books of a specific title is the product of the quantity and the price.

Algorithm

First level of design

1 open input file for reading
2 open output file for writing
3 process files
4 close input file
5 close output file

Second level refinement

3 process files
3.1 write headings to output file
3.2 read line of file
3.3 calculate number of tokens in line
3.4 while number of tokens is not zero
3.5   read quantity from input file
3.6   read price of book from input file
3.7   read title of book from input file
3.8   write quantity, price and title of book to output file
3.9   if quantity <= reorder level
3.10   write reorder to output file
3.11   increase total quantity of books by quantity
3.12   increase total price of books by price
3.13   read line of file
3.14   calculate number of tokens in line
3.15 write total quantity of books to output file
3.16 write total price of books to output file

Data Dictionary. For each different line in the text file a variable for quantity, price and title must be declared. Since the algorithm keeps cumulative totals on the total number of books and total value of the books, it is necessary to include to further variables for the total quantity and total price. Each line of text that is read is tokenized into an object of type `StringTokenizer`, and the number of tokens in a line is also recorded.

```
int             quantity;
int             totalQuantity = 0;
float           price;
float           totalPrice = 0.0f;
int             numberOfTokens;
String          title;
StringTokenizer data;
```

Desk Check. For test data the values of the prices, quantities and titles shown in the data file for the first three books are used. For the purpose of this check assume these are the only items in the file.

reorder level	1				
numberOfTokens		5	5	6	0
(numberOfTokens != 0)		true	true	true	false
quantity		1	2	1	
price		8.95	3.75	7.50	
title		Art in Athens	Birds of Prey	Eagles in the USA	
(quantity<=reorder level)?		true	false	true	
totalQuantity	0	1	3	4	
totalPrice	0	8.95	16.45	23.95	

Coding

```
// chap_4\Ex_10
// program to read a file containing a stock list of books and write the
// contents of the file, showing which books to reorder, and the total
// number of books together with the total value of the stock to another
// file

import java.io.*;
import java.util.*;

class Ex_10
{
    public static void main(String[] args) throws IOException
    {
        final int    REORDER_LEVEL = 1;
        final String NEW_LINE = new String(\u000A);

        FileReader file1           = new FileReader("a:\\chap_4\\books.txt");
        BufferedReader inputFile = new BufferedReader(file1);

        FileWriter file2           = new FileWriter("a:\\chap_4\\report.txt");
        PrintWriter outputFile = new PrintWriter(file2);
```

```
int             quantity;
int             totalQuantity = 0;
float           price;
float           totalPrice = 0.0f;
int             numberOfTokens;
String          title;
StringTokenizer data;

outputFile.println("              STOCK REPORT ON BOOKS\n");
outputFile.println("quantity\tprice\t\ttitle\n");

// tokenize a line from file
data = new StringTokenizer(inputFile.readLine());
numberOfTokens = data.countTokens();

while (numberOfTokens != 0)
{
   quantity = new Integer(data.nextToken()).intValue();
   price = new Float(data.nextToken()).floatValue();
   title = data.nextToken(NEW_LINE);

   outputFile.print(quantity + "\t\t\t" + price + "\t" + title);
   outputFile.flush();

   if (quantity <= REORDER_LEVEL)
      outputFile.println(" -> REORDER");
   else
      outputFile.println();

   totalQuantity = totalQuantity + quantity;
   totalPrice = totalPrice + (price * quantity);

   // tokenize the next line from file
   data = new StringTokenizer(inputFile.readLine());
   numberOfTokens = data.countTokens();
}

outputFile.println("\nNumber of books in stock " + totalQuantity);
outputFile.println("Value of books in stock $" + totalPrice);

inputFile.close();
outputFile.close();
   }
}
```

Test results from file report.txt

```
           STOCK REPORT ON BOOKS

quantity price      title

1         8.95    Art in Athens -> REORDER
2         3.75    Birds of Prey
1         7.55    Eagles in the USA -> REORDER
3         5.25    Gone with the Wind
2         3.75    Hate, Lust and Love
3         5.95    Maths for Adults
3         3.75    Modern Farming
3         5.25    Raiders of Planet X
1         8.95    Splitting the Atom -> REORDER
1         3.75    The Invisible Man -> REORDER
2         3.75    The Otter
4         5.95    The Tempest
2         5.95    The Trojan Wars
2         3.75    Under the Seas
2         7.55    Vampire Bats

Number of books in stock 32
Value of books in stock $170.6
```

Summary

- The statements within a `while` loop can be executed zero or more times.

- The statements within a `do..while` loop are executed at least once.

- Both loops use conditional expressions to control the number of repetitions.

- All statements within a `while` loop and a `do..while` loop will be executed while the conditional expression is true.

- Counter variables may be increased or decreased by one by using the postfix increment **++** and the postfix decrement **−** operators.

- A `for` loop is a specialization of a `while` loop. You can always replace a `while` loop with a `for` loop. However, you cannot always replace a `for` loop with a `while` loop.

- If the first expression in a `for` loop is omitted, then the initialization (and declaration) of the loop control variable must take place outside of the loop.

- If the second expression in a `for` loop is omitted, then the loop does not terminate unless it contains a `break` statement.

- If the third expression in a `for` loop is omitted, then the loop control variable must be incremented or decremented within the body of the loop.

- By omitting all three expressions from within a `for` loop, it is possible to set up an infinite loop.

- A keyboard may be replaced by a file for the input of data to a program.

- A screen may be replaced by a file for the output of the results from a program.

- Files must be opened before they can be used and closed when no longer needed in a program.

- A line of text may be divided into individual tokens, where each token represents an item of data.

Review Questions

1. What is the purpose of a loop?

2. Is the conditional expression true or false upon exiting from a `while` loop?

3. What is the minimum number of times a `do..while` loop can be repeated?

4. How is a sentinel value used to control a `while` loop?

5. State the fundamental operations associated with using a `while` loop as a counter.

6. At what point in the loop does each expression in a `for` statement execute?

7. True or false - the statement `counter=counter-1` is the same as the expression `counter--`.

8. What does the statement x++ do?

9. What is an infinite loop?

10. What is a text file?

11. What is a token?

Exercises

12. Desk check the following `while` loop. What is output from the program segment?

```
int counter = 1;
while (counter < 10)
{
   screen.print("\t" + counter);
   screen.flush();
   counter = counter + 2;
}
```

13. Desk check the following `do..while` loop using the test data 10, -1 and 9. What is the purpose of the loop?

```
do
{
   digit = new Integer(keyboard.readLine()).intValue();
} while (digit < 0 || digit > 9);
```

14. Desk check the following `for` loop. What is output?

```
for (int counter = 0x61; counter <= 0x7A; counter++)
{
   screen.print((char)counter);
   screen.flush();
}
```

15. Discover the errors in the following segments of code.

(a)

```
int i = 10;
while (i > 0);
{
   screen.println("T minus " + i + " and counting");
   i--;
}
```

(b)

```
for (int i=10; i > 0; i--);
   screen.println("T minus " + i + " and counting");
```

16. Use a `for` loop to rewrite the following segment of code.

```
int x = 30;
while (x >= 3)
{
   screen.println(x);
   x--;
}
```

17. Figure 4.5 illustrates the steps required to convert the decimal number 3947 to the hexadecimal number F6B.

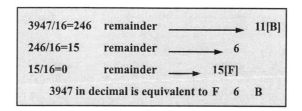

Figure 4.5 *Conversion of a decimal to a hexadecimal*

Design an algorithm using pseudocode, to convert a decimal number to a hexadecimal number. Desk check your answer with the data shown in Figure 4.5.

Programming Problems

18. Write a program that uses a loop to display the message - Hello World - ten times on the screen.

19. Write a program to input a message of your choice and the number of times you want to repeat it; then display the message repeatedly.

20. Write a program to output a table of conversion from miles to kilometers. The table should contain column headings for miles and kilometers. Miles should be output as integer values between 1 and 50, in steps of 1 mile. new headings should be printed at the beginning of the table and after 20 and 40 miles, respectively. Note 1 mile = 1.609344 kilometers.

21. Write a program using `while` loops to output the following:

(a) The odd integers in the range 1 to 29.

(b) The squares of even integers in the range 2 to 20.

(c) The sum of the squares of the odd integers between 1 and 13.

(d) The alphabet in lower case - without using the `toLowerCase` method.

22. Repeat question 21 using `for` loops.

23. Repeat question 21 using `do..while` loops.

24. Write a program to find and print the arithmetic mean of a list of nonzero numbers. The number of numbers is not known in advance. Terminate the sequence of numbers with zero.

25. Write a program to find and print the largest integer from twenty integers stored in a text file. Assume that the numbers are stored one per line.

26. Return your answer to question 17. Write a program to input a positive integer number and convert the value to a hexadecimal number. Hint - Since the solution will require you to display a number starting with the least significant digit through to the most significant digit, you will need to use the escape sequence \r (carriage return) to move the cursor to the beginning of a line without advancing to a new line.

27. A diamond merchant has recently received a consignment of stones. The diamonds are to be categorized into the weight classes given in Figure 4.6. At the end of the weighing the merchant requires a print out of the total number of stones in each category and the percentage weight of each category. Assume that the electric balance the merchant uses is calibrated in milligrams. Write a program to input the weights of the diamonds and output the required statistics. Note - 200 mg is equivalent to 1 carat (SI).

class	carats
A	>100
B	>65
C	>35
D	>15
E	>5
F	<=5

Figure 4.6

28. You plan to take a walking holiday in the Canadian Rockies. The trip is expected to last five days (unless the bears get you!). From your map of the area, you measure the distances you want to walk each day. The Canadian map is metric, with 1 centimeter equivalent to 0.78 kilometers. You estimate that because of the mountainous terrain your average speed of walking will be 1.5 miles per hour (you think in miles per hour, not kilometers per hour!).

You task is to estimate how many miles you will walk each day and how long it will take you. Calculate the total distance you will have traveled by the end of the holiday and the total time you will spend walking between daily destinations. Note 1 kilometer is equivalent to 0.625 miles.

Computerize the process of estimating the distances and times.

Write a program to input the map distances traveled on each leg of the journey and calculate the actual distances in miles and the time to walk between destinations.

29. Use an editor to create a file booze.txt that contains the details of items of stock in a bar. Each line in the file contains the data: stock quantity, unit price, and description; for example, a line of text might contain: 3 30.00 Brandy, which represents 3 bottles of Brandy at $30.00 per bottle.

Write a program to read each line from the text file booze.txt and create a report stock.txt similar in layout and content to that illustrated in Figure 4.7, where the value of the stock is the product of the respective quantity and price.

<table>
<tr><td colspan="4" align="center">**Report Layout Document**</td></tr>
<tr><td colspan="4">123456789012345678901234567890123456789012345678901234567890</td></tr>
<tr><td colspan="4" align="center">BAR STOCK REPORT</td></tr>
<tr><td>QUANTITY</td><td>PRICE</td><td>VALUE</td><td>DESCRIPTION</td></tr>
<tr><td>3</td><td>30.00</td><td>90.00</td><td>Brandy</td></tr>
<tr><td>5</td><td>18.50</td><td>92.50</td><td>Gin</td></tr>
<tr><td>5</td><td>17.00</td><td>85.00</td><td>Rum</td></tr>
<tr><td>10</td><td>15.50</td><td>155.00</td><td>Vodka</td></tr>
<tr><td>8</td><td>25.00</td><td>200.00</td><td>Whiskey</td></tr>
<tr><td>TOTAL</td><td></td><td>$622.50</td><td></td></tr>
</table>

Figure 4.7

30. A text file viewers.txt contains the following three items per line:

category code of program
estimated size of viewing audience (millions)
name of television program

The category of program is coded using a single character as follows.

D - drama
L - light entertainment
M - music
S - science fiction

A typical record from the file might contain the following data:

D 5.25 NYPD Blue

The data indicate that 5.25 million viewers watched the television program NYPD Blue, and that the show is a drama.

Use an editor to create the text file with programs of your own choice so that the contents of your file are ordered on the category code as the key. Group all the drama programs together, all the light-entertainment programs together, and so on.

Write a computer program to input a category code and generate output similar to that shown in Figure 4.8. This output lists the names of all the programs in the chosen category, the audience viewing figures, and the total number of viewers who watched programs in that category.

Screen Layout Document

```
12345678901234567890123456789012345678901234567890

CATEGORY - DRAMA

audience         program

5.25             NYPD Blue
7.45             Murder She Wrote
7.50             L.A.Law

20.20 millions total audience
```

Figure 4.8

Chapter 5
Arrays

Up to now all variables have been associated with either primitive types or objects, and little importance has been attached to the organization of data in the memory of a computer. This chapter introduces the array, which is the commonest of the data structures, is available in most computer languages, and uses techniques for accessing data that can lead to simple and more effective programming solutions. By the end of the chapter, you should have an understanding of the following topics.

- Concept of a one dimensional array.

- The declaration of an array.

- Input and output of data stored in an array.

- Arrays of primitive types and arrays of objects.

- Multidimensional arrays.

- Vectors.

5.1 One-dimensional Array

Consider for a moment how you would store five integer values in the memory of the computer. The obvious answer is to create five variable names and assign a value to each variable. For example,

```
int number1 = 54;
int number2 = 26;
int number3 = 99;
int number4 = -25;
int number5 = 13;
```

If you adopted the same approach to storing fifty integer values, then the coding would become quite tedious. Clearly, we need a better data structure to store data of the same type, a data structure that reduces the amount of coding to a minimum.

Well, such a data structure is available and it is called an array. An **array** is a named collection of one or more items of data of the same type. Each individual element of data can be accessed by the name of the array and a numbered index indicating its position within the array. Arrays come in various dimensions, however, for the moment we will only consider a one-dimensional array.

Before an array can be used it must be declared. Figure 5.1 illustrates the declaration of an array called numbers. Notice that int[] numbers has created only one memory location to represent the identifier numbers. This location is automatically initialized to the value null indicated by a slash in the memory location for numbers. In order to allocate space for storing integers it is necessary to use the new keyword and specify an amount of memory to allocate for the storage of, in this example, five integers. In Figure 5.1 each allocated memory cell is indexed with a value from 0 to 4, and the contents of the five cells have automatically been initialized to zero. Notice from Figure 5.1 that the five cells are pointed at or referenced by the identifier numbers.

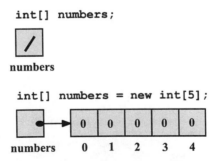

Figure 5.1 Declaration of an array of integers

The syntax for the declaration of a one-dimensional array follows.

One-dimensional array declaration:
```
type-specifier [] array-name =
new type-specifier[ number-of-cells ];
```

For example, the array depicted in Figure 5.1 is declared as:

```
int[] numbers = new int[5];
```

This states that the name of the array is `numbers`. It is an array containing 5 cells, having subscripts numbered 0 through to 4 respectively. The contents of the array is of type `int`.

5.2 Storing Numbers in an Array

There are two techniques for storing numbers in an array. The first is by initialization at the point of declaration, and the second by assigning the numbers to cells directly.

If the first technique is used, the way in which the array is declared will change from that described in the previous section. The syntax for the declaration of a one-dimensional array is modified as follows.

One-dimensional array declaration and initialization:
```
type-specifier [] array-name = { list of numbers };
```

For example,

```
int[] numbers = {54,26,99,-25,13}
```

Since the compiler can count the number of items of data in the list, there is no need to explicitly state how much memory to allocate in order to store the numbers. Figure 5.2 illustrates how to conceptualize the storage of the five numbers in the array.

Figure 5.2 Conceptual representation of numbers in an array

Access to numbers in the array is through the name of the array, followed by the index, in square brackets, of where the number is stored. For example, the contents of numbers[0] is 54; the contents of numbers[1] is 26, and so on.

In Program Example 5.1 that follows, the array numbers is declared and initialized. The contents of the array is then displayed on the screen.

Program Example 5.1: Array Initialization

```
// chap_5\Ex_1.java
// program to assign numbers directly to the cells of an array
// and display the contents of the cells

import java.io.*;

class Ex_1
{
    static PrintWriter screen = new PrintWriter(System.out, true);

    static public void main(String[] args) throws IOException
    {
        int[] numbers = {54,26,99,-25,13};

        screen.println("Contents of Array\n");
        screen.println("cell 0 " + numbers[0]);
        screen.println("cell 1 " + numbers[1]);
        screen.println("cell 2 " + numbers[2]);
        screen.println("cell 3 " + numbers[3]);
        screen.println("cell 4 " + numbers[4]);
    }
}
```

Test results

```
Contents of Array

cell 0 54
cell 1 26
cell 2 99
cell 3 -25
cell 4 13
```

The original idea of introducing an array to store integers was to reduce the amount of coding required to assign numbers to memory and output the numbers from memory. Program Example 5.1 hardly inspires confidence that the original idea can be implemented! All it proves is that the same name numbers, using a different index value from 0 through to 4, can be used in place of the five different names. The program was introduced only to show you that it is possible to explicitly access any cell in the array.

To reduce the amount of coding, it is necessary to replace the explicit use of the index by a control variable identifier. Instead of explicitly coding `numbers[0]`, `numbers[1]`, `numbers[2]`, `numbers[3]` and `numbers[4]`, it is far easier to use `numbers[index]` and embed this statement in a `for` loop that changes the value of `index` from 0 to 4. For example, integers can be input from a keyboard and stored in an array using

```
for (int index=0; index != 5; index++)
{
    numbers[index] = new Integer(keyboard.readLine()).intValue();
}
```

and the contents of each cell of the array can be displayed on the screen using

```
for (int index=0; index != 5; index++)
{
    screen.println("cell " + index + "\t" + numbers[index]);
}
```

where the array `numbers` was declared in Figure 5.1. In this declaration the number of cells in the array was explicitly coded as 5.

> **ℹ** A good programming practice is to replace the numeric literal that defines the number of cells in the array with a constant. Consequently, if the size of the array changes, the only statement in the program that needs to be modified is the declaration of the constant.

The declaration should be modified to include

```
// size of array
static final int SIZE = 5;

// declaration of the array
int[] numbers = new int[SIZE];
```

The next program demonstrates both ideas, of using a constant `SIZE` to define the size of the array, and a loop control variable `index` to refer to position of the individual cells within the array. Notice in this program that the constant `SIZE` is also used in the `for` loops to detect when the loop control variable `index` is about to go out of range.

Program Example 5.2: Input and Output of Data to an Array

```
// chap_5\Ex_2.java
// program to input numbers into a one-dimensional array
// and display the contents of the array

import java.io.*;
```

```java
class Ex_2
{
    static BufferedReader keyboard = new
            BufferedReader(new InputStreamReader(System.in));
    static PrintWriter screen      = new PrintWriter(System.out, true);

    static public void main(String[] args) throws IOException
    {
        // size of array
        final int SIZE = 5;
        int[] numbers = new int[SIZE];

        // input numbers into the array
        screen.println("Input " + SIZE + " integers, one per line\n");
        for (int index=0; index != SIZE; index++)
        {
            screen.print("cell " + index + " "); screen.flush();
            numbers[index] = new Integer(keyboard.readLine()).intValue();
        }

        // display numbers held in the array
        screen.println("\n\nContents of Array\n");
        for (int index=0; index != SIZE; index++)
            screen.println("cell " + index + "\t" + numbers[index]);
    }
}
```

Test results

```
Input 5 integers, one per line

cell 0 54
cell 1 26
cell 2 99
cell 3 -25
cell 4 13


Contents of Array

cell 0   54
cell 1   26
cell 2   99
cell 3   -25
cell 4   13
```

The use of a `for` statement to control the index to an array is not confined to input and output but can also be used to compare data between cells. In this next program five numbers are stored in an array, and the contents of the array are inspected to find the largest number.

The `for` loop controls the index so that it is possible to gain access to consecutive items of data and compare each item with the largest number found so far.

```
largest = numbers[0];
```

```
for (int index=1; index != SIZE; index++)
   if (numbers[index] > largest) largest = numbers[index];
```

The variable `largest` is assigned the first value in the array. The control variable identifier is then set to access the remaining cells in the array. If a number in one of these cells is greater than the current value of the variable `largest`, then `largest` is assigned this value.

Program Example 5.3: Finding the Largest Number in an Array

```
// chap_5\Ex_3.java
// program to input numbers into a one-dimensional array
// and display the largest number in the array

import java.io.*;

class Ex_3
{
    static BufferedReader keyboard = new
            BufferedReader(new InputStreamReader(System.in));
    static PrintWriter screen      = new PrintWriter(System.out, true);

    static public void main(String[] args) throws IOException
    {
        // size of array
        final int SIZE = 5;

        int[] numbers = new int[SIZE];
        int largest;

        // input numbers into the array
        screen.println("Input " + SIZE + " integers, one per line\n");
        for (int index=0; index != SIZE; index++)
        {
            screen.print("cell " + index + " "); screen.flush();
            numbers[index] = new Integer(keyboard.readLine()).intValue();
        }
        // find and output the largest number in the array
        largest = numbers[0];
        for (int index=1; index != SIZE; index++)
            if (numbers[index] > largest) largest = numbers[index];

        screen.println("\nLargest number in the array is " + largest);
    }
}
```

Results

```
Input 5 integers, one per line

cell 0 54
cell 1 26
cell 2 99
cell 3 -25
cell 4 13


Largest number in the array is 99
```

In the previous examples the size of the array was stated at the time of writing the program. This need not always be the case. In Java it is possible to postpone assigning a value for the size of an array until program execution. By doing this you create a **dynamic array**, and hence tailor the storage requirements to the amount of data available.

Program Example 5.4: A Dynamic Array

```java
// chap_5\Ex_4.java
// program to input the size of a one-dimensional array;
// input numbers into the into the array and calculate
// and display the mean of the numbers

import java.io.*;

class Ex_4
{
    static BufferedReader keyboard = new
            BufferedReader(new InputStreamReader(System.in));
    static PrintWriter screen      = new PrintWriter(System.out, true);

    static public void main(String[] args) throws IOException
    {
        int    sizeOfArray;
        int    sum = 0;
        float mean;

        screen.print("How many numbers do you want to input? ");
        screen.flush();
        sizeOfArray = new Integer(keyboard.readLine()).intValue();

        // declare the array
        int[] numbers = new int[sizeOfArray];

        // input numbers into the array
        screen.println("\nInput " + sizeOfArray + " integers, one per
                        line\n");
        for (int index=0; index != sizeOfArray; index++)
        {
            screen.print("cell " + index + " "); screen.flush();
            numbers[index] = new Integer(keyboard.readLine()).intValue();
        }
```

```
   // calculate the sum of the numbers in the array
   for (int index=0; index != sizeOfArray; index++)
      sum = sum + numbers[index];

   // calculate the arithmetic mean of the numbers
   mean = (float)sum/(float)sizeOfArray;

   screen.println("\nMean of numbers in the array is " + mean);
   }
}
```

Test results

```
How many numbers do you want to input? 5

Input 5 integers, one per line

cell 0 54
cell 1 26
cell 2 99
cell 3 -25
cell 4 13

Mean of numbers in the array is 33.4
```

Before continuing with the next section, it is important to recapitulate on the following points regarding one-dimensional arrays.

- The contents of the array must be of the same data type. In other words, an array can contain all integers or all reals or all characters or all strings, but not a mixture of types.

- Each item in the array is stored in a separate cell. If an array contained five integers, then each integer would occupy a single cell.

- Each cell has a unique location value that shows the cell's position within the array. This location is known as an index and starts at value 0.

- The array is given one name, irrespective of the number of items it contains.

- Before an array can be used, it must be declared like any other variable.

- An item of data within a cell is accessed by using the name of the array followed by the position, index or subscript, within square brackets.

Case Study: Simulation of Rolling a Die

Problem. In rolling a die (singular of dice), one of the six sides will appear uppermost. If the die is rolled many thousands of times, each of the six sides should have an equal probability of appearing uppermost, provided the die was not biased (loaded!). Write a program that counts the number of times each of the six sides appears uppermost when rolled many number of times. At the end of the trial, display the number of times each of the six sides of the die appeared uppermost.

Problem Analysis. The solution to this problem uses a one-dimensional array that contains the frequency of occurrences of the spots on the sides of the die. An array containing seven cells is declared with indexes 0 through 6. Cells 1 through 6 are used to store the frequency of occurrence of each side of the die. This strategy makes programming the final solution considerably clearer to read and understand than using array indexes 0 through 5 to represent each side of the die. The first cell (index 0) is not used. Figure 5.3 illustrates the contents of the cells after 6000 trials (rolling the die 6000 times).

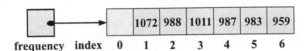

Figure 5.3Representation of frequency of spots on a die

How can we simulate rolling a die? What technique is available to produce the digits 1 through 6 at random in the same way that the uppermost side of a die appears at random? The answer is to use a random number generator from the class **Random**, in package **util** (utilities). An object of type Random is instantiated using

```
Random value = new Random(); // random number
```

The instance method `nextInt()` returns an integer random number that lies in the range of all integer numbers. Therefore, `value.nextInt()` will return a pseudo-random integer anywhere in the permissible range of integers, which also includes negative values as well as positive values.

Change the pseudo-random number into a number between 0 and 5, by using modulo arithmetic. For example, `value.nextInt() % SIDES`, where SIDES is an integer constant initialized to 6. Since the pseudo-random number may be negative it is necessary to change this value to positive by taking the absolute (positive) value of the pseudo-random number using the method **abs** from the class **Math**. Math is a class that does not require objects to be instantiated. You will understand why this is so, later in the book. Math is part of the `java.lang` package and is imported by default. The expression for the pseudo-random number has now evolved to

```
Math.abs(value.nextInt % SIDES).
```

However, because of the modulo arithmetic this will only return a number in the range 0 through 5. To simulate the rolling of a die it will be necessary to add the value 1 to the expression, resulting in the assignment

```
spots = Math.abs(value.nextInt() % SIDES) + 1;
```

The assignment `spots = 6` implies that the side of the die with six spots appears uppermost. If the value from this expression is used as a subscript to the array `frequency`, then the statement `frequency[spots]++` will increase the contents of the cell 6 in the array by 1.

Algorithm

First level

1. input the number of trials
2. while number of trials is positive
3.   initialize the frequency of occurrences to zero
4.   roll the die for the number of trials
5.   display the frequency of occurrence of the spots
6.   input the number of trials

Second level refinement

4. roll the die for the number of trials
4.1 for every trial
4.2   calculate a random number in the range 1 through 6 to represent the spot number
4.3   increase the frequency by 1 for the calculated spot number

Data Dictionary. The number of cells in the array frequency should be expressed by the integer constant that defines the number of sides of a die. There will be a need to record the number of trials and the number of spots that appear uppermost at each roll of the die. An object of type Random is needed to generate a pseudo-random number.

```
static final int SIDES = 6;

int trials; // number of times you roll the die
int spots;  // faces on the die
int[] frequency   = new int[SIDES+1];
Random value = new Random();
```

Desk Check. The test data will be the number of trials, which can be kept at a minimum of 6 and 0.

Initialization of the array

SIDES	6						
trials	6						
(trials > 0)?	true						
spots	1	2	3	4	5	6	7
spots <= SIDES	true	true	true	true	true	true	false
frequency[spots]	0	0	0	0	0	0	

Rolling the die for a set number of trials

SIDES	6						
trials	6						0
(trials > 0)?	true						false
roll	1	2	3	4	5	6	
(roll <= trials)?	true	true	true	true	true	true	
spots	3	5	2	3	3	4	
frequency[spots]	1	1	1	2	3	1	

The desk check reveals that after six rolls of the die there were 0 ones, 1 two, 3 threes, 1 four, 1 five and 0 sixes. To determine which spots appear on each roll simply choose any number between 1 and 6.

Screen Layout Document
12345678901234567890123456789012345678901234567890
Input number of trials (0 to exit) 6000 number of spots 1   2   3   4   5   6 frequency   1072   988   1011   987   983   959

Coding

```
// chap_5\Ex_5.java
// program to simulate throwing a die for different numbers of trials
// and record the frequency that each side of the die (spots) appears
// in each trial

import java.io.*;
import java.util.Random;

class Ex_5
{
    static BufferedReader keyboard = new
            BufferedReader(new InputStreamReader(System.in));
    static PrintWriter screen       = new PrintWriter(System.out, true);

    static public void main(String[] args) throws IOException
    {
        final int SIDES = 6; // number of faces on die
        int trials;          // number of times you roll the die
        int spots;           // faces on the die
        int[] frequency = new int[SIDES+1];
        Random value    = new Random(); // random number

        screen.print("Input the number of trials (0 to exit) ");
        screen.flush();
        trials = new Integer(keyboard.readLine()).intValue();

        while (trials > 0)
        {
            // initialize frequency of occurrencies to zero
            for (spots=1; spots <= SIDES; spots++)
                frequency[spots] = 0;

            // simulate rolling a die for a given numbe of trials
            for (int roll=1; roll <= trials; roll++)
            {
                spots = Math.abs(value.nextInt() % SIDES) + 1;
                frequency[spots]++;
            }

            // display frequency of occurrences of spots
            screen.println("number of spots\t1\t2\t3\t4\t5\t6");
            screen.print("frequency       \t"); screen.flush();
            for (spots=1; spots <= SIDES; spots++)
                screen.print(frequency[spots] + "\t");

            screen.println("\n");

            screen.print("Input the number of trials (0 to exit) ");
            screen.flush();
            trials = new Integer(keyboard.readLine()).intValue();
        }
    }
}
```

Test results

```
Input the number of trials (0 to exit) 6000
number of spots 1       2       3       4       5       6
frequency       994     973     1033    997     974     1029

Input the number of trials (0 to exit) 60000
number of spots 1       2       3       4       5       6
frequency       9918    10028   10095   10026   9994    9939

Input the number of trials (0 to exit) 600000
number of spots 1       2       3       4       5       6
frequency       100126  99551   99950   100625  99920   99828

Input the number of trials (0 to exit) 0
```

Case Study: Is a Word a Palindrome?

Problem. Write a program to test for a word being a palindrome, that is a word spelled the same way backwards as forwards.

Problem Analysis. The first question to ask in trying to solve this problem, is how do we analyze individual characters in a string? Java classes are very comprehensive, and it should come as no surprise that there is a method in the String class that will convert a string to individual characters stored in separate cells of a one-dimensional array. The method is **toCharArray()**. To convert a string contained in the object word, to individual characters stored in the one-dimensional array characterArray the following code is required.

```
char[] characterArray = word.toCharArray();
```

In testing a word for being a palindrome, is the word Radar equivalent to the word RADAR? If it meant to be the same then all characters in the word must be converted to upper case. The statement to store a word as single characters in each cell of an array can be modified to capitalize all alphabetic characters, thus

```
char[] characterArray = word.toUpperCase().toCharArray();
```

The method used to test the word is to inspect the characters at either end of the word. If these characters are the same, then the next two characters at either end of the word are compared. The comparisons continue until there is no match between the characters or there are no further comparisons possible. The movement of the indexes is shown in Figure 5.4.

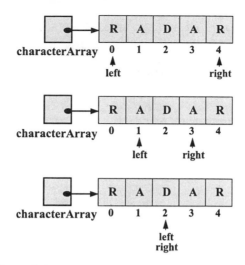

Figure 5.4 Comparison of characters in the array

In assigning `left` and `right` to the first and last indexes in the array, it is necessary to know the length of the array. Fortunately, there is a variable in Java that allows you to find the length of any array specified in a program. Not surprisingly the variable is called **length**. In the this example the expression `characterArray.length` will return the value 5, since there are five cells in the array. Assigning values to `left` and `right` becomes

```
left = 0;
right = characterArray.length-1;
```

Since the array is indexed from 0 (zero) it is necessary to deduct 1 from the length of the array in calculating a value for the `right` index.

Algorithm

First level

1 do
2   input a single word
3   convert word string to single characters in an array
4   initialize left and right indexes
5   compare characters in the word
6   output result
7 while palindrome

Second level refinement

5 compare characters in the word
5.1 while left and right indexes have not crossed over and characters match
5.2   if left character equals right character
5.3   move left index one cell to the right
5.4   move right index one cell to the left
5.5   else
5.6   characters do not match

6 output result
6.1 if characters match
6.2   display word is a palindrome
6.3 else
6.4   display word is not a palindrome

Data Dictionary. The word is represented as an object of type String. This word is also stored as single characters in a one-dimensional array - characterArray. There are left and right indexes and a boolean variable charactersMatch which will be set to false as soon as there is no match detected between single characters.

```
String word;
int left, right;
boolean charactersMatch;
char[] characterArray;
```

Desk Check. Test data used are *radar* and *mouse*.

charactersMatch	true			true	false
word	radar			mouse	
characterArray	RADAR			MOUSE	
left	0	1	2	0	
right	4	3	2	4	
(left<=right && charactersMatch)?	true	true	true	true	
characterArray[left]	R	A	D	M	
characterArray[right]	R	A	D	E	
(characterArray[left] == characterArray[right])?	true	true	true	false	

In the first test, the word *radar* is a palindrome, and the characters match; in the second test, the word *mouse* is not a palindrome, since the characters do not match.

```
                        ┌─────────────────────────────────────────────┐
                        │          Screen Layout Document             │
                        ├─────────────────────────────────────────────┤
                        │ 12345678901234567890123456789012345678901234567890 │
                        │                                             │
                        │ Input a word radar                          │
                        │ radar is a palindrome                       │
                        │                                             │
                        │ Input a word mouse                          │
                        │ mouse is not a palindrome                   │
                        └─────────────────────────────────────────────┘
```

Coding

```java
// chap_5\Ex_6.java
// program to input a word and test whether it is a palindrome

import java.io.*;

class Ex_6
{
    static BufferedReader keyboard = new
            BufferedReader(new InputStreamReader(System.in));
    static PrintWriter screen      = new PrintWriter(System.out, true);

    static public void main(String[] args) throws IOException
    {
        String word;
        int left, right;
        boolean charactersMatch;

        do
        {
            charactersMatch = true;

            screen.print("Input a word "); screen.flush();
            word = keyboard.readLine();

            char[] characterArray = word.toUpperCase().toCharArray();

            left = 0;
            right = characterArray.length-1;

            // compare characters in the word
            while (left <= right && charactersMatch)
            {
                if (characterArray[left] == characterArray[right])
                {
                    left++;
                    right--;
                }
                else
                    charactersMatch = false;
            }
```

```
        // display word if palindrome otherwise exit
        if (charactersMatch)
            screen.println(word + " is a palindrome\n");
        else
            screen.println(word + " is not a palindrome\n");

    } while (charactersMatch);
  }
}
```

Test results

```
Input a word radar
radar is a palindrome

Input a word rotator
rotator is a palindrome

Input a word poop
poop is a palindrome

Input a word mouse
mouse is not a palindrome
```

Case Study: Count the Number of Vowels in a Sentence

Problem. Write a program to input a phrase and inspect each character. Keep a count of the number of different vowels that appear in the phrase and display these values when the end of the phrase is reached.

Problem Analysis. The solution to this problem is similar to that of the case study to simulate rolling a die. An array is used to store a count of the frequency of occurrences of vowels in a phrase, rather than spots on a die. The array illustrated in Figure 5.5 indicates the frequency of occurrences of vowels in a phrase.

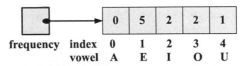

frequency	index	0	1	2	3	4
		0	5	2	2	1
	vowel	A	E	I	O	U

Figure 5.5 Frequency count of vowels

The technique used to input a string of text and store the individual characters of the text in a one-dimensional array is similar to the previous case study on finding whether a word was a palindrome or not.

Algorithm

First level

1 input a phrase
2 calculate the length of the phrase
3 convert the phrase to individual characters in an array
4 count the number of vowels in the array
5 output the values of the vowel count

Second level refinement

4 count the number of vowels in the array
4.1 for each character in the character array
4.2   switch on value of character
4.3   'A' : increase frequency[0] by 1
4.4   'E': increase frequency[1] by 1
4.5   'I': increase frequency[2] by 1
4.6   'O': increase frequency [3] by 1
4.7   'U': increase frequency[4] by 1

5 output the values of the vowel count
5.1 for each cell in the frequency array
5.2   display contents of frequency array

Data Dictionary. Two one-dimensional arrays are used, one to store the frequency of the vowels, and the second to store the individual characters from the phrase. An object of type String is required to store the phrase. Rather than keep evaluating the length of the phrase within a for loop it is good practice to perform this calculation just once, hence the need for an identifier to store the length of a phrase. Further good practice is to declare an integer constant that represents the number of vowels, rather than making reference to the string literal 5, that has no clear meaning.

Since access will be made to the individual cell positions of both arrays within for loops, there will be a need to declare an index. However, this can be declared within each for loop.

```
static final int NUMBER_OF_VOWELS = 5;

int[]   frequency;
char[]  characterArray;
String  phrase;
int     phraseLength;
int     index;
```

Desk Check. The test data is the phrase *Counter*.

frequency[0]	0							
frequency[1]	0					1		
frequency[2]	0							
frequency[3]	0	1						
frequency[4]	0		1					
phrase	Counter							
phraseLength	7							
characterArray	COUNTER							
index	0	1	2	3	4	5	6	7
(index != phraseLength)?	true	true	true	true	true	true	true	false
characterArray[index]	C	O	U	N	T	E	R	

The contents of the array frequency illustrates that frequency[1] was 1, frequency[3] was 1 and frequency[4] was 1, illustrating that there was 1 E, 1 O and 1 U in the word counter.

Screen Layout Document

```
12345678901234567890123456789012345678901234567890

Input a phrase - Count the vowels in this sentence.

A    E    I    O    U
0    5    2    2    1
```

Coding

```java
// chap_5\Ex_7.java
// program to count the number of vowels in a phrase

import java.io.*;

class Ex_7
{
    static BufferedReader keyboard = new
            BufferedReader(new InputStreamReader(System.in));
    static PrintWriter screen      = new PrintWriter(System.out, true);

    static public void main(String[] args) throws IOException
    {
        final int NUMBER_OF_VOWELS = 5;
        int[]  frequency = {0,0,0,0,0};
        String phrase;
```

[handwritten: Char [] Charray= phrase. to UperCase (). toChar. Array ();]
[handwritten: ← string input sentence.]

```
int      phraseLength;

    screen.print("Input a phrase - "); screen.flush();
    phrase = keyboard.readLine();
    phraseLength = phrase.length();

    char[] characterArray = phrase.toUpperCase().toCharArray();

    // examine contents of characterArray for vowels
    for (int index=0; index != phraseLength; index++)
        switch (characterArray[index])
        {
            case 'A': frequency[0]++; break;
            case 'E': frequency[1]++; break;
            case 'I': frequency[2]++; break;
            case 'O': frequency[3]++; break;
            case 'U': frequency[4]++;
        }

    // display number of vowels in phrase
    screen.println("\nA\tE\tI\tO\tU");
    for (int index=0; index != NUMBER_OF_VOWELS; index++)
    {
        screen.print(frequency[index] + "\t");
        screen.flush();
    }
  }
}
```

[handwritten: "\n" = new line.]

Test results

```
Input a phrase - Count the vowels in this sentence.

A        E       I        O        U
0        5       2        2        1
```

5.3 Arrays of Objects

So far in this chapter we have dealt with one-dimensional arrays that contain primitive data types, for example arrays of integers and arrays of characters. But what if we wanted to store an array of strings. A string is an object, therefore, it will be necessary to store an array of objects. Figure 5.6 illustrates how we would store an array of the following names - Gomez, Jackson, Smythe, Quayle.

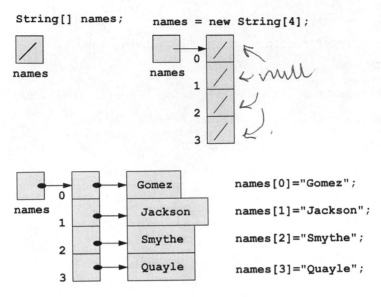

Figure 5.6 An array of strings

We can declare a variable `names` that references an array of strings as

`String[] names;`

This is a single reference variable that is initialized to a `null` value.

To allocate enough memory for storing the four names we need to use the `new` keyword and specify how many cells are required for storing string data.

`names = new String[4];`

Since the data are objects of type `String`, they cannot be stored in these cells. Remember from Chapter 1 that all strings are stored by reference. Instead, each cell contains a reference to the string data. Initially all references in this array will automatically be set at `null`.

When a string is assigned to any of these cells the compiler will automatically generate more storage space for the string. The contents of the cell then points or makes reference to this new storage space. The following assignments will create references from each cell to the strings specified.

```
names[0] = "Gomez";
names[1] = "Jackson";
names[2] = "Smythe";
names[3] = "Quayle";
```

An alternative and much simpler way to initialize the array `names` is to use the following declaration.

```
String[] names = {"Gomez","Jackson","Smythe","Quayle"};
```

The contents of the array can be accessed using an index. The following code indicates how the contents of the array may be displayed on a screen.

```
for (int index=0; index != 4; index++)
{
   screen.println(names[index]);
}
```

get used to using this format instead of <=4.

5.4 Multidimensional Arrays

An array is not confined to one dimension (one index). In fact, an array can be extended to two dimensions and beyond in order to provide a flexible data structure for the solution to a problem. A two-dimensional array is a repetition of one-dimensional arrays. The structure can be thought of as matrix or grid. In Figure 5.7 the two-dimensional array represents the monthly rainfall over four regions of an island and is composed from four one-dimensional arrays, where each one-dimensional array is represented by a row.

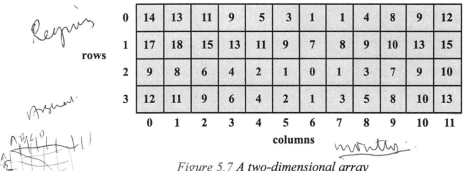

Figure 5.7 A two-dimensional array

The array may be initialized at its point of declaration as follows.

```
int[][] rainfall = {{14,13,11,9,5,3,1,1,4,8,9,12},
                    {17,18,15,13,11,9,7,8,9,10,13,15},
                    {9,8,6,4,2,1,0,1,3,7,9,10},
                    {12,11,9,6,4,2,1,3,5,8,10,13}};
```

Alternatively the array may be declared

```
float[][] rainfall = new float[REGIONS][MONTHS];
```

where there are 4 regions and 12 months and the data for the rainfall can be stored in the array from stream input.

Access to all the cells within the two-dimensional array is possible using two for loops. An outer `for` loop is used to process each row, and an inner `for` loop processes each cell within the one-dimensional array depicted by the row. For example the contents of the two-dimensional array illustrated in Figure 5.7 can be output using the following code.

```
for (int row=0; row != REGIONS; row++)
{
    for (int column=0; column != MONTHS; column++)
    {
        screen.print(rainfall[row][column] + " ");
        screen.flush();
    }

    screen.println();
}
```

If you perform a desk check on this code you will end up with the following values.

row	0												
(row != 4)?	true												
column	0	1	2	3	4	5	6	7	8	9	10	11	12
(column != 12)?	true	true	true	true	true	true	true	true	true	true	true	true	false
rainfall[row][column]	14	13	11	9	5	3	1	1	4	8	9	12	

row	1												
(row != 4)?	true												
column	0	1	2	3	4	5	6	7	8	9	10	11	12
(column != 12)?	true	true	true	true	true	true	true	true	true	true	true	true	false
rainfall[row][column]	17	18	15	13	11	9	7	8	9	10	13	15	

row	2												
(row != 4)?	true												
column	0	1	2	3	4	5	6	7	8	9	10	11	12
(column != 12)?	true	true	true	true	true	true	true	true	true	true	true	true	false
rainfall[row][column]	9	8	6	4	2	1	0	1	3	7	9	10	
row	3												
(row != 4)?	true												
column	0	1	2	3	4	5	6	7	8	9	10	11	12
(column != 12)?	true	true	true	true	true	true	true	true	true	true	true	true	false
rainfall[row][column]	12	11	9	6	4	2	1	3	5	8	10	13	

row	4
(row != 4)?	false

Case Study: Calculate Rainfall over an Island

Problem. The annual rainfall is recorded on a monthly basis over four regions of an island: North, South, East and West. Write a program to read rainfall data from a text file and store the data in a two-dimensional array. Calculate and output the average rainfall for each region over the year. Your output should be similar to that shown in the Screen Layout Document.

```
Screen Layout Document

123456789012345678901234567890123456789012345678901234567890

Rainfall Statistics

region      total   average

North         90    7
South        145    12
East          60    5
West          84    7
```

Problem Analysis. It is evident from the Screen Layout Document that the names of the four regions need to be displayed. These can either be displayed as string literals coded into the program, or as the contents of a one dimensional array. The latter option will lead to succinct programming. If a one-dimensional array is declared as

```
String[] nameOfRegion = {"North","South","East","West"};
```

then `nameOfRegion[0]` contains North, `nameOfRegion[1]` contains South, and so on. If an index represents a region in the range 0 through 3, then the array can be used as a look-up table for the name of the region.

The data for the annual rainfall is given in the two-dimensional array illustrated Figure 5.7, where each row represents the monthly rainfall for a region on the island. The first row (index 0) represents the North, the second row (index 1) represents the South, the third row (index 2) represents the East, and the fourth row (index 3) represents the West. The twelve cells in each row represent the monthly rainfall for a region.

To calculate the total and average rainfall for a region is a matter of summing the monthly rainfall over the year for a particular region to give the total, and dividing this figure by 12 to give the average. This process is repeated for each of the four regions.

You may recall that in Chapter 4, the technique of tokenizing a line of text from a text file was introduced. This method will be used for reading rainfall data from the file and storing it into the two-dimensional array. You may assume that one line of text contains twelve numbers, separated by spaces, that represent the monthly rainfall for a year. There are four lines of text in the file, representing the rainfall over the four regions of the island. The file of data is shown here for your convenience.

```
14  13  11  9  5  3  1  1  4  8  9  12
17  18  15  13  11  9  7  8  9  10  13  15
9  8  6  4  2  1  0  1  3  7  9  10
12  11  9  6  4  2  1  3  5  8  10  13
```

Algorithm

First level

1 read and store data from text file into two-dimensional array
2 output headings
3 calculate and output total and average rainfall for each region

Second level refinement

1 read and store data from text file into two-dimensional array
1.1 for each region
1.2   tokenize line of text from file
1.3   for each month
1.4   assign monthly rainfall to two-dimensional array

3 calculate and output total and average rainfall for each region
3.1 for each region
3.2   output name of region
3.3   initialize total to zero
3.4   for each month
3.5   increase total by rainfall for that month
3.6   divide total by 12 to give average rainfall for region
3.7   output average rainfall

Data Dictionary. There are two arrays, a one-dimensional array to store the names of the regions, and a two-dimensional array to store the rainfall. Variables will be needed to store the total and average. After these values have been output they will be overwritten by new values for the next region. An object of type `StringTokenizer` must be declared to store a line of text from the file. Indexes to access the arrays will be declared within their respective for loops. Two constants are defined to represent the 4 regions and 12 months of a year.

```
static final int REGIONS = 4;
static final int MONTHS  = 12;
String[] nameOfRegion = {"North","South","East","West"};
float[][] rainfall    = new float[REGIONS][MONTHS];
float          total;
float          average;
StringTokenizer data;
```

Desk Check. The test data is already given in Figure 5.7. This check will calculate the total and average rainfall for the first region.

region	0												
(region!=4)?	true												
nameOfRegion[region]	North												
month	0	1	2	3	4	5	6	7	8	9	10	11	12
(month!=12)?	true	true	true	true	true	true	true	true	true	true	true	true	false
rainfall[region][month]	14	13	11	9	5	3	1	1	4	8	9	12	
total	0	14	27	38	47	52	55	56	57	61	69	78	90
average	7.5												

Perform your own desk check on the algorithm for the next region, and calculate the total and average rainfall.

Coding

```
// chap_5\Ex_8
// program to calculate the average rainfall over the
// four regions of an island

import java.io.*;
import java.util.*;

class Ex_8
{
    static PrintWriter screen = new PrintWriter(System.out, true);

    public static void main(String[] args) throws IOException
    {
        final int REGIONS = 4;
        final int MONTHS = 12;

        FileReader file =
        new FileReader("a:\\chap_5\\rainfall.txt");
        BufferedReader inputFile = new BufferedReader(file);

        StringTokenizer data;
        float          total;
        float          average;

        String[] nameOfRegion = {"North","South","East","West"};
        float[][] rainfall = new float[REGIONS][MONTHS];
        // read monthly rainfall figures per region from a file
        // and store this data in a two-dimensional array

        for (int region=0; region != REGIONS; region++)
        {
            data = new StringTokenizer(inputFile.readLine());

            for (int month=0; month != MONTHS; month++)
```

```
            {
                rainfall[region][month] = new
                Float(data.nextToken()).floatValue();
            }
        }

        screen.println("Rainfall Statistics\n");
        screen.println("region\ttotal\taverage\n");

        for (int region=0; region != REGIONS; region++)
        {
            screen.print(nameOfRegion[region] + "\t");
            screen.flush();

            total = 0;

            for (int month=0; month != MONTHS; month++)
            {
                total = total + rainfall[region][month];
            }

            average = total / MONTHS;

            screen.println(total + "\t" + average);
        }
    }
}
```

Test results

```
Rainfall Statistics

region   total    average

North    90.0     7.5
South    145.0    12.083333
East     60.0     5.0
West     84.0     7.0
```

It is possible to create an array with more than two dimensions. A three-dimensional array is a repetition of two-dimensional arrays; a four dimensional array is a repetition of three-dimensional arrays, and so on.

Figure 5.8 illustrates a three-dimensional array that consists of 4 two-dimensional arrays; each two-dimensional array consists of 2 one-dimensional arrays; each one-dimensional array contains 4 cells.

The three-dimensional array is used to store the votes cast for the election of a union representative. There are four regions in a city where voting takes place; these are designated regions 0, 1, 2, and 3 corresponding to the 4 two-dimensional arrays.

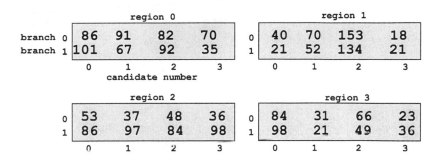

Figure 5.8 A three-dimensional array

There are two union branches in every region; these are designated branches 0 and 1 corresponding to the two-dimensional arrays in each region.

Finally, there are four candidates in the election; these are designated candidate numbers 0, 1, 2, and 3 corresponding to the 4 cells in each one-dimensional array.

The array may be initialized at its point of declaration as follows.

```
int[][][] votes = {{{86,91,82,70},{101,67,92,35}},
                   {{40,70,153,18},{21,52,134,21}},
                   {{53,37,48,36},{86,97,84,98}},
                   {{84,31,66,23},{98,21,49,36}}};
```
Alternatively, the declaration for this array may be coded as follows.

```
int[][][] votes = new int[REGIONS][BRANCHES][CANDIDATES];
```

where there are 4 regions, 2 branches and 4 candidates, and the data stored in the array from an input stream.

Access to any cell within the three-dimensional array is possible using three `for` loops. An outer `for` loop is used to process each two-dimensional array; a middle `for` loop is used to process each row of the two-dimensional array; and an inner `for` loop processes each column within the two-dimensional array. For example the contents of the three-dimensional array illustrated in Figure 5.8 can be output using the following code.

```
for (int region=0; region != REGIONS; region++)
{
   for (int branch=0; branch != BRANCHES; branch++)
   {
      for (int candidate=0; candidate != CANDIDATES; candidate++)
      {
            screen.print(votes[region][branch][candidate] + " ");
            screen.flush();
      }
   }
   screen.println();
}
```

Complete the following desk check on the code for region 2 and region 3. What is the value of the region that will cause the code to terminate?

region	0									
(region != REGIONS)?	true									
branch	0					1				2
(branch != BRANCHES)?	true					true				false
candidate	0	1	2	3	4	0	1	2	3	4
(candidate != CANDIDATES)?	true	true	true	true	false	true	true	true	true	false
votes[region][branch][candidate]	86	91	82	70		101	67	92	35	

region	1									
(region != REGIONS)?	true									
branch	0					1				2
(branch != BRANCHES)?	true					true				false
candidate	0	1	2	3	4	0	1	2	3	4
(candidate != CANDIDATES)?	true	true	true	true	false	true	true	true	true	false
votes[region][branch][candidate]	40	70	153	18		21	52	134	21	

Case Study: Votes Cast in an Election

Problem. Write a program to create the three-dimensional array illustrated in Figure 5.8. Initialize the contents of this array from data stored in a text file, and display the percentage of the total vote cast for each candidate. The output from the program is illustrated in the Screen layout Document.

```
               Screen Layout Document

12345678901234567890123456789012345678901234567890

Election Results

Candidate         Percentage Vote

Gomez             27.4
Jackson           22.4
Smythe            34.0
Quayle            16.2
```

Problem Analysis. The technique of reading the text file and storing the data in the array is the same as the previous case study. The only difference is that we need to cater for the extra dimension of the array. At the same time as storing the data it would be prudent to keep a running total of the number of votes cast for all the candidates. This total is needed to calculate the percentage total vote for each candidate. The contents of the text file follows.

```
86  91  82  70  101  67  92  35
40  70  153  18  21  52  134  21
53  37  48  36  86  97  84  98
84  31  66  23  98  21  49  36
```

Inspecting the Screen Layout Document it is clear that the names of the candidates are to be displayed. The names are stored in a one-dimensional array and the index for a name is used to look-up the name in the array. This technique was also used in the previous case study.

To calculate the percentage of the total vote for each candidate, it is necessary to sum for each candidate, all the votes cast in the branches of each region. This figure is then divided by the total number of votes cast, and multiplied by 100 to bring it to a percentage. The expression is written as

```
percentageVote = 100.0f * (float)candidateVote / (float)totalVotes;
```

Algorithm

First level

1 read and store data from text file into the three-dimensional array and compute total vote
2 output headings
3 calculate and output percentage of the total vote for each region

Second level refinement

1 read and store data from text file into two-dimensional array
1.1 for each region
1.2   tokenize line of text from file
1.3   for each branch
1.4   for each candidate
1.5   assign votes to three-dimensional array
1.6   increase total vote

3 calculate and output percentage of the total vote for each region
3.1 for each candidate
3.2   initialize candidate vote to zero
3.3   for each region
3.4   for each branch
3.5   increase candidate vote
3.6   calculate percentage of total vote by candidate
3.7   output candidate name and percentage vote for candidate

Data Dictionary. There are two arrays, a one-dimensional array for storing the names of the candidates, and a three-dimensional array for storing the votes cast. Variables are needed to store the total votes cast for all candidates, and the votes cast for individual candidates as well as the percentage of the total vote cast for a candidate. An object of type StringTokenizer must be declared to store a line of text from the file. Indexes to access the arrays will be declared within their respective for loops. Three constants are defined to represent the 4 regions, 2 branches and 4 candidates.

```
final int REGIONS    = 4;
final int BRANCHES   = 2;
final int CANDIDATES = 4;

StringTokenizer data;
int             totalVotes = 0;
int             candidateVote;
float           percentageVote;
String[] nameOfCandidate = {"Gomez","Jackson","Smythe","Quayle"};
int[][][] votes = new int[REGIONS][BRANCHES][CANDIDATES];
```

Desk Check. A check is made for one candidate. The test data is taken from the array illustrated in Figure 5.8.

totalVotes	2080										
candidate	0										
(candidate != 4)?	true										
candidateVote	0	86	187	227	248	301	387	471	569		
region	0		1		2		3		4		
(region != 4)?	true		true		true		true		false		
branch	0	1	2	0	1	2	0	1	2	0	1	2
(branch != 2)?	true	true	false	true	true	false	true	true	false	true	true	false
votes[region] [branch] [candidate]	86	101		40	21		53	86		84	98	

nameOfCandidate[candidate]	Gomez
percentageVote	27.35

Coding

```
// chap_5\Ex_9
// program to calculate the percentage of votes cast for
// candidates in an election

import java.io.*;
import java.util.*;

class Ex_9
{
    static PrintWriter screen = new PrintWriter(System.out, true);

    public static void main(String[] args) throws IOException
    {
        final int REGIONS    = 4;
```

```
final int BRANCHES   = 2;
final int CANDIDATES = 4;

FileReader file = new FileReader("a:\\chap_5\\votes.txt");
BufferedReader inputFile = new BufferedReader(file);

StringTokenizer data;
int             totalVotes = 0;
int             candidateVote;
float           percentageVote;

String[] nameOfCandidate = {"Gomez","Jackson","Smythe","Quayle"};
int[][][] votes = new int[REGIONS][BRANCHES][CANDIDATES];

// read votes cast per region per branch per candidate
// from a file, and store this data in a three-dimensional array
// calculate the total number of votes cast
for (int region=0; region != REGIONS; region++)
{
    data = new StringTokenizer(inputFile.readLine());

    for (int branch=0; branch != BRANCHES; branch++)
    {
        for (int candidate=0; candidate != CANDIDATES; candidate++)
        {
            votes[region][branch][candidate] =
            new Integer(data.nextToken()).intValue();
            totalVotes = totalVotes + votes[region][branch][candidate];
        }
    }
}

// calculate and output the percentage votes cast per candidate
screen.println("Election Results\n");
screen.println("Candidate\tPercentage Vote\n");

for (int candidate=0; candidate != CANDIDATES; candidate++)
{
    candidateVote = 0;
    for (int region=0; region != REGIONS; region++)
    {
        for (int branch=0; branch != BRANCHES; branch++)
        {
            candidateVote = candidateVote +
                            votes[region][branch][candidate];
        }
    }

    percentageVote = 100.0f * (float)candidateVote /
                            (float)totalVotes;
    screen.println(nameOfCandidate[candidate] + "\t\t" +
                percentageVote);
}
}
}
```

Test results

```
Election Results

Candidate         Percentage Vote

Gomez             27.35577
Jackson           22.403847
Smythe            34.03846
Quayle            16.201923
```

When defining a multidimensional array, you do not need to specify the number of cells that are contained in each dimension. The first N dimensions, where N is at least 1, must have the number of cells specified. The N dimensions may be followed by additional dimensions with no dimension size specified.

For example, the following declarations are legal.

```
int[][][] threeD = new int[20][][];
String[][][][] spaghetti = new String[10][20][][];
```

However, the following declaration is illegal since the number of cells being specified in each dimension is not continuous.

```
float[][][] data = new float[100][][3];
```

5.5 Vectors

Although the declaration of the size of an array, may be performed at run-time, the size of the array is then fixed for the duration of the executing program. An object instantiated as a **Vector**, however, will allow for the storage of objects in an array, when the size of the array is not known. A partial listing for the class Vector follows.

```
public class Vector extends Object implements Cloneable
{
    // Constructor(s)
    public Vector(int initialCapacity);

    // Methods
    public final void addElement(Object obj);
    public final int capacity();
    public final Object elementAt(int index);
    public final Object firstElement();
    public final int indexOf(Object elem);
    public final Object lastElement();
    public final int size();
    public final void trimToSize();

}
```

Notice that a constructor will allow you to specify the initial capacity of the vector. However, when the vector cannot store any more data, then provided there is enough computer memory available, the vector automatically doubles in size to accommodate further data storage. The partial listing of the class's methods, indicates that there are methods which allow you to perform the following functions.

`addElement(Object obj)` - insert an object into the next free location in the vector.
`capacity()` - return the capacity of the Vector.
`elementAt(int index)` - return the object stored in the vector at the position index
`firstElement()` - return the object stored at index position 0 (zero).
`indexOf(Object elem)` - return the index of the object element stored in the Vector.
`lastElement()` - return the object element stored at the position size-1.
`size()` - return the number of object elements stored in the Vector.
`trimToSize()` - reduce the capacity of the Vector to the number of elements stored in the Vector.

Program Example 5.5 allows a user to input as many single words into a vector as necessary, and display a list of the words. The program demonstrates some of the methods defined in the `Vector` class and shows that a vector may be indexed in the same manner as a one-dimensional array.

Program Example 5.5 Using a Vector to Store Data

```java
// chap_5\Ex_10.java
// program to demonstrate storing and retrieving data from a Vector

import java.io.*;
import java.util.*;

class Ex_10
{
    static BufferedReader keyboard = new
            BufferedReader(new InputStreamReader(System.in));
    static PrintWriter screen = new PrintWriter(System.out, true);

    static public void main(String[] args) throws IOException
    {
        final int INITIAL_SIZE = 4;
        Vector dataStore = new Vector(INITIAL_SIZE);
        int     sizeOfVector;
        String word;

        screen.println("Input single words, one per line, "+
                    type EXIT to quit\n");

        screen.print("Word? "); screen.flush();
        word = keyboard.readLine();
        while (! word.equals("EXIT"))
        {
            dataStore.addElement(word);
            screen.println("index "+dataStore.indexOf(word)+
                        "\tcontents "+word+
                        "\tcapacity of vector "+dataStore.capacity());
            screen.print("Word? "); screen.flush();
            word = keyboard.readLine();
        }
}
```

```
        }
      screen.println("\nsize of vector " + dataStore.size());
      screen.println("capacity of vector " + dataStore.capacity());
      screen.println("first element " + dataStore.firstElement());
      screen.println("last element " + dataStore.lastElement());
      screen.println("element at index 5 " + dataStore.elementAt(5));
      dataStore.trimToSize();
      sizeOfVector = dataStore.capacity();
      screen.println("\ntrimmed size capacity "+sizeOfVector);

      screen.println("Contents of Vector\n");
      for (int index=0; index != sizeOfVector; index++)
      {
          screen.print(dataStore.elementAt(index) + " "); screen.flush();
      }
    }
}
```

Test results

```
Input single words, one per line, type EXIT to quit

Word? apple
index 0 contents apple  capacity of vector 4
Word? banana
index 1 contents banana capacity of vector 4
Word? grape
index 2 contents grape  capacity of vector 4
Word? melon
index 3 contents melon  capacity of vector 4
Word? fig
index 4 contents fig     capacity of vector 8
Word? lycee
index 5 contents lycee   capacity of vector 8
Word? orange
index 6 contents orange capacity of vector 8
Word? lemon
index 7 contents lemon   capacity of vector 8
Word? quince
index 8 contents quince capacity of vector 16
Word? EXIT

size of vector 9
capacity of vector 16
first element apple
last element quince
element at index 5 lycee

trimmed size capacity 9
Contents of Vector

apple banana grape melon fig lycee orange lemon quince
```

Notice the capacity of the vector was initially set at 4 by the constructor. After four items of data had been input the capacity of the vector was automatically increased to eight. After eight items of data had been input the capacity of the vector was doubled again to sixteen.

By specifying the name of an object in the method `indexOf`, it is possible to obtain the index of the cell containing the object.

The `size` of the vector indicates the number of items of data stored, whereas the `capacity` of the vector indicates the total number of cells, whether occupied by data or not.

It is possible to access any cell within the vector by using the appropriate class methods. In this example, the methods `firstElement`, `lastElement` and `elementAt` have been used to find the elements at index 0, 8 and the range 0..8 respectively.

Once a vector has been filled with data, and there are wasted cells not being used, it is possible to trim the vector to the size of the array by using the method `trimToSize`.

5.6 Non-rectangular arrays

If you look back at the figures that depict one, two and three dimensional arrays (Figures 5.2, 5.7 and 5.8 respectively), each figure has been illustrated as a rectangular array. But multidimensional arrays are represented as arrays of arrays. Therefore, it is quite feasible to declare and initialize a two dimensional array as follows.

```
int[][] twoD = {{1},{2,3},{4,5,6},{7,8,9,10}};
```

The shape of the array twoD is triangular, having the data arranged as:

```
1
2    3
4    5    6
7    8    9    10
```

where `twoD[0][0]` is the value 1; `twoD[1][0]` is the value 2; `twoD[1][1]` is the value 3, and so on.

Program Example 5.6: Initialization and output from a triangular array.

```
// chap_5\Ex_11.java
// program to illustrate a triangular array

import java.io.*;

class Ex_11
{
    static PrintWriter screen = new PrintWriter(System.out, true);
```

```
public static void main(String[] args) throws IOException
{
    final int MAX_CELLS = 4;

    int[][] twoD = {{1},{2,3},{4,5,6},{7,8,9,10}};

    // display contents of the triangular array

    int cells = 1;

    for (int row=0; row != cells; row++)
    {
        for (int column=0; column != cells; column++)
        {
            screen.print(twoD[row][column]+"\t");
        }

        screen.println();

        if (cells < MAX_CELLS)
            cells++;
        else
            break;
    }

    screen.println();
}
}
```

Test results

```
1
2       3
4       5       6
7       8       9       10
```

In Program Example 5.11 care was taken not to increment the number of cells beyond the maximum number of cells in the triangular array. In this example if the variable `cells` had increased to 5, then the system would have generated an `ArrayIndexOutOfBoundsException`.

In all Java array references, the index is checked to make sure that it within the limits of the array. The index is checked that it is not below zero, and not greater than or equal to the length of the array. If the index goes out of bounds (not within the limits of the array) then an `ArrayIndexOutOfBoundsException` is thrown.

Summary

- An array stores its data by reference, the same as an object.

- Storage space is allocated to an array using the keyword new.

- The length of an array can be determined through the class variable length.

- A one-dimensional array is a data structure that can be used to store data of one type.

- An array is subdivided into cells. Each cell has a unique index value, and the first cell has an index of 0 (zero).

- If the array is static it is a good practice to declare the number of cells of an array as a constant.

- Access to any item of data in the array is through the name of the array, followed by the position of the data in the array, that is, the index of the cell that contains the data.

- A loop control variable in a for statement is a useful way of representing the index of an array. By varying the value of the loop control variable, it is possible to access any cell within the array.

- An array can have more than one dimension.

- An N-dimensional array can be thought of as a repetition of (N-1)-dimensional arrays.

- Arrays of any dimension may be initialized at the point of declaration.

- The declaration of an array may omit the lower-order dimensions, provided those dimensions that are declared are continuously described.

- A Vector is a class that will allow a one-dimensional array to be instantiated that does not require the size of the array to be specified.

- The Vector class contains many instance methods that permit information to be obtained about the vector and data stored in the vector.

- An array may be initialized with data so that it becomes non-rectangular in shape.

Review Questions

1. True or false - an array stores data of different types.

2. What is an index to an array?

3. Is the index of the first cell in an array always 0?

4. Declare an array `realNumbers` to contain five floating-point numbers.

5. Modify the declaration in question (4) to initialize the contents of respective cells to the real values 1.0, 2.0, 3.0, 4.0 and 5.0.

6. State an alternative method to that described in question (5) for the initialization of the array.

7. Write a statement to show how you would display a number in the third cell of the array declared in question 4.

8. What method in the `String` class is used to store a string as an array of characters?

9. What is the order, in terms of rows and columns, when indexing a two-dimensional array?

10. Define a two-dimensional array.

11. How does a three-dimensional array differ from a two-dimensional array.

12. Illustrate how you might visualize an array declared as `char[][][] data = new char[3][2][10]`.

13. Is the following declaration legal?

```
String[][][] words = new String[10][][2];
```

14. Draw the shape of the following two-dimensional array.

```
char[][] letters = {{'a','b','c','d'},{'e','f'},{'g','h','i'},{'j'}};
```

15. Is the array reference `letters[1][2]` legal? If not, then what exception will be generated?

16. How does a vector differ from an array?

17. True or false - data stored in a vector may be accessed as a data stored in a multidimensional array.

18. Distinguish between the instance methods `size` and `capacity` in the class Vector.

Exercises

19. Desk check the following segment of code. What is the final value of the identifier value?

```
int[] alpha = {-10,16,19,-15,20};
int value = 0;

for (int index=0; index != 5; index++)
   value = value + alpha[index];
```

20. What is the result of `alpha[3]-alpha[1]` in the array declared in question 19?

21. What is the error in the following segment of code?

```
char[] string = "abracadabra";
```

22. Given the declaration

```
String data = "Ten green bottles standing on the wall.";
```

Describe the functionality of the following statement.

```
char [] string = data.toCharArray();
```

23. What is the value of `string.length` for the string declared in question 22.

24. Desk check the following code and determine the final contents of the array.

```
int[] numbers = {5,2,8,7,0,3};
int left = 0;
int right = numbers.length()-1;

while (left <= right)
{
   numbers[right] = numbers[left];
   left++;
   right--;
}
```

25. Use the data from Figure 5.7 to determine the values of the following expressions.

```
rainfall[3][8]; rainfall[0][11]; rainfall[1][5].
```

26. Use Figure 5.7 to determine the value of sum after the following code is executed

```
int sum = 0;
for (int column=0; column != 3; column++)
{
   for (int row=0; row != 4; row ++)
      sum = sum + rainfall[row][column];
}
```

27. Use Figure 5.8 to determine the values printed with the following code

```
for (int branch=0; branch != 2; branch++)
{
   for (int region=0; region != 4; region++)
   {
      screen.print(votes[region][branch][3]+"\t");
      screen.flush();
   }
   screen.println();
}
```

28. Desk check the following program segment; explain the meaning of each statement, and display the contents of the array.

```
int[][] array = new int[4][];

for (int i=0; i < array.length; i++)
{
    array[i] = new int[i+1];

    for (int j=0; j<i+1; j++)
    {
        array[i][j] = i+j;
    }
}
```

29. Using the Java documentation for the class Vector, describe the functions of the following methods.

(a) public final boolean contains(Object elem);
(b) public final synchronized void copyInto(Object[] anArray);
(c) public final boolean isEmpty();
(d) public final int lastIndexOf(Object elem);

30. Desk check the following program segment; explain the meaning of the statements, and draw the contents of the vector dataStore after the execution of each statement.

```
Vector dataStore = new Vector(1);
dataStore.addElement("Sybil");
dataStore.addElement("Basil");
dataStore.addElement("Polly");
```

Programming Problems

31. Write a program to store the alphabet as characters in an array. The program should display

(a) The entire alphabet.
(b) The first six characters of the alphabet.
(c) The last ten characters of the alphabet.
(d) The tenth character of the alphabet.

32. Write a program to input ten integers in numerical ascending order into a one-dimensional array X; copy the numbers from array X to another one-dimensional array Y, such that array Y contains the numbers in descending order. Output the contents of array Y.

33. The monthly sunshine record for a holiday resort follows.

Month	Jan	Feb	Mar	Apr	May	Jun	Jul	Aug	Sep	Oct	Nov	Dec
Hours of Sunshine	100	90	120	150	210	250	300	310	280	230	160	120

Write a program to

(a) Store the names of the months and the hours of sunshine in two one-dimensional arrays.
(b) Calculate and display the average number of hours of sunshine over the year.
(c) calculate and display the names of the months with the highest and lowest number of hours of sunshine.

34. Return to Chapter 2, and Figure 2.6. Write a program to

(a) Store the names of the food and drink sold at Ben's Breakfast Bar as strings in a one-dimensional array named `foodAndDrink`. Store the corresponding prices of the food and drink as real numbers in another one-dimensional array named `prices`, such that the index for the price in one cell can be used to match the corresponding food or drink in the array `foodAndDrink`.

(b) Input the name of an item of food or drink, and search the array `foodAndDrink` for a match between the strings. If a match is possible then use the index to the matched food to display the price of the food from the array `prices`. Repeat this routine until an item of food is input that does not exist in the array `foodAndDrink`.

35. Write a program to input a phrase and display the Unicode, in hexadecimal, for each character of the phrase.

36. Write a program to input a phrase that is guaranteed to contain an opening parenthesis and a closing parenthesis, in that order, and possibly repeated. For example, such a phrase might be

```
for (int index=0; index != 5; index++) screen.println(index);
```

(a) Scan each character in the phrase and output only those characters that are contained between the opening and closing parentheses.
(b) Re-scan the phrase and output only those characters that are outside of the opening and closing parentheses.

37. The dictionary definition of a palindrome is "a word or <u>phrase</u> that reads the same backwards as forwards (e.g. rotator, <u>nurses run</u>). Modify the Case Study: Is a Word a Palindrome? to cater for phrases as well as individual words being read from a text file.

38. Modify the Case Study: Calculate Rainfall over an Island to

(a) Calculate and display by month, the average rainfall in all regions.
(b) The names of the wettest and driest months.

39. Modify the Case Study: Votes Cast in an Election to

(a) Initialize a one-dimensional array with the names of the four regions which are Bay View, Metropolis, Parkside, and Suburbia.

(b) Calculate and display the total vote in each named region, for each of the four named candidates.

(c) Display the name of the winner of the election, together with the total number of votes cast for that candidate.

40. The following information represents the major divisions of geological time.

Era	Period	Epoch	Millions of years ago
Cenozoic	Quaternary	Holocene	0.01
		Pleistocene	2
	Tertiary	Pliocene	5
		Miocene	24
		Oligocene	38
		Eocene	55
		Paleocene	65
Mesozoic	Cretaceous		144
	Jurassic		213
	Triassic		248
Paleozoic	Permian		286
	Carboniferous		360
	Devonian		408
	Silurian		438
	Ordovician		505
	Cambrian		590

Organize the above data into a data structure containing arrays and write a menu-driven program to allow a user to specify an era, period or epoch and display the geological time.

Chapter 6
Classes and Methods

In Chapter 2 you were introduced to the idea that a Java program is constructed from many classes, where a class typically may contain data, class methods, constructors and instance methods. However, up to now we have only used one class containing the `main` method in the construction of a program. All that is about to change!

In this chapter you will be shown how to create class methods, constructors and instance methods; and you will begin to write programs using the techniques of object-oriented programming.

By the end of this chapter you should have an understanding of the following topics.

- Creating class and instance methods.

- Returning a value from a method.

- Passing data as arguments in a method call.

- The scope and life of identifiers.

- Creating a constructor.

- Designing and writing object-oriented programs that contain more than one class.

6.1 Introduction

By now you have enough information to write small programs. However, at this stage it is important to explain how specific programmed activities can be formed into building blocks known as methods. A **method** is a group of self-contained declarations and executable statements that perform an activity. The methods themselves may represent activities associated with a particular classification or data type. For example, the `Math` class contains a number of methods that represents the classification of various mathematical functions; and the `String` class contains a number of methods that allow information to obtained from, and operations to be performed on, objects of type `String`.

From using the Java API, you are already familiar with the organization of methods grouped into classes, and classes grouped into packages. In constructing computer programs we will adopt the same organization. In this chapter you will be shown how to construct your own methods, and incorporate these methods into your own classes. In the next chapter you will be shown how to encapsulate your classes into a package.

Writing a program as a collection of methods within classes, has the following advantages over writing just one long `main` method.

- The program becomes easier to design, since you separate out many different activities that form the methods of a class. Designing algorithms for individual methods is easier than attempting to design an algorithm for one large `main` method.

- A program that is divided into many specific methods is easier to code and test, since you tend to concentrate on developing individual methods and not the whole program at once.

- The layout of the code is normally clearer to follow, and hence easier to maintain in the future.

In chapter 1, you were shown how to call both class methods and instance methods. These methods often required you to pass an argument of the same type as the formal parameter list to the method, or use a value returned by the method. For example:

`int limit = Math.abs(-3);` is a call to the class method `abs`, passing the argument -3, and assigning the returned value to the variable `limit`.

`screen.println("Hello World");` is a call to the instance method `println`, passing the String argument "Hello Word" so that it may be displayed on the `screen` object.

When we call a method it is common practice to send the method data via the formal parameter list. The method may perform calculations on that data and return the result of the calculation to the calling statement. In constructing your own methods, it necessary for you to understand how to construct and use a formal parameter list, and how to return a value from a method. In the following sections you will be shown how to construct methods, return values from the methods and write formal parameter lists to accept arguments from a method call.

6.2 Programmer-defined Class Methods

A Java application consists of at least one class method, the `main` method. In Program Example 6.1 a second class method has been introduced to display a message. The program illustrates how to define a method within a class; how to call the method; and how the computer returns to the `main` method after the method has been executed.

Program Example 6.1: Calling and Returning from a Class Method

```
// chap_6\Ex 1.java
// program to demonstrate how to call a programmer-defined method

import java.io.*;

class Ex_1
{
    static PrintWriter screen = new PrintWriter(System.out, true);

    public static void main(String[] args) throws IOException
    {
        screen.println("Program execution starts at the [main] method;");
        display();
        screen.println("returned to the [main] method.");
    }

    // method to display a message
    static void display()
    {
        screen.println("method [display] has been called;");
    }
}
```

Test results

```
Program execution starts at the [main] method;
method [display] has been called;
returned to the [main] method.
```

The `main` method is executed before any other method. In this example the message `Program execution starts at the [main] method;` is displayed. The next line in the `main` method is `display()` and is the method call. A method call is simply the name of a method that signals the computer to branch to the actual method and perform the tasks it defines. The parenthesis contain any arguments to be passed to the method from the caller. Such arguments form the actual-parameter list (in this example, there are no arguments). After executing the method call `display()` in the `main` method, the computer branches to the following method:

```
static void display()
// method to display a message
{
    screen.println("method [display] has been called;");
}
```

This syntax is the method definition. This particular method displays on the screen the message `method [display] has been called;`. After completing the method, the computer branches back to the next executable statement after the method call and the message `returned to the [main] method.` is displayed. Execution of the remaining statements in the `main` function continues.

Now that we have taken a first look at methods within the context of a Java application, we must pause to understand the generic syntax of this very important component. The syntax of a method definition follows.

Method:
```
modifier(s) return-type method-name ( formal-parameter-list )
{
        declarations
        statements
}
```

The modifier used in the example is `static`. A **static** method is one that cannot be invoked by an object, in the same way as the methods discussed in the previous chapters have been used. Over the next two chapters you will become familiar with a list of other modifiers, of which `static` is just one example.

The return-type identifies the type of value that the method will return. This can be a primitive type or a class. If no data is returned to the caller, the keyword `void` is used for the return-type.

The formal-parameter-list indicates the data types for any arguments the function expects to receive from the caller. Each individual argument passed to the method must have its own corresponding parameter. If no arguments are being passed to the method, then the parenthesis remains empty.

Declarations refer to constant and variable declarations for use within the method, and statements refer to the executable instructions within the method.

6.3 The return Keyword

Program Example 6.2 illustrates how the method `sum` returns the sum of two numbers to the `main` method. The return-type identifies the type of the value that the method will return to the caller. The syntax of the return statement is:

Return statement: **return** *expression;*

where the expression may be omitted depending upon the use of the statement. Program Example 6.2 specifies the statement being used as `return first+second`.

In Program Example 6.2 the return type for `sum` has been declared as `int`. The function `sum` invites the user to type in two numbers `first` and `second`. It is this value `first+second` that is returned by the function sum using the `return` statement. The `return` statement has a dual purpose; it assigns a value to the method and also marks the position in the method where the computer must return to the calling method, in this case the `main` method.

Program Example 6.2: Returning a Value from a Class Method

```java
// chap_6\Ex_2.java
// program to demonstrate calling a method that returns a value

import java.io.*;

class Ex_2
{
    static BufferedReader keyboard = new
            BufferedReader(new InputStreamReader(System.in));
    static PrintWriter screen = new PrintWriter(System.out, true);

    //-----------------------------------------------------------

    public static void main(String[] args) throws IOException
    {
        screen.println("Sum of numbers is " + sum());
    }

    //-----------------------------------------------------------

    // method to return the sum of two values
    static int sum() throws IOException
    {
        int first, second; // numbers to input

        screen.print("First number? "); screen.flush();
        first = new Integer(keyboard.readLine()).intValue();

        screen.print("Second number? "); screen.flush();
        second = new Integer(keyboard.readLine()).intValue();

        return first+second;
    }

    //-----------------------------------------------------------
}
```

Test results

```
First number? 34
Second number? 46
Sum of numbers is 80
```

Notice from Program Example 6.2 that it is quite acceptable to call a class method from within the `println` statement. For example, in `screen.println("Sum of numbers is " + sum());` the method `sum()` is called before the `println` statement can be executed. The method `sum()` returns an integer value that is then displayed on the screen.

If a method type is `void`, it is acceptable to use a `return` statement without an expression to force the computer to return to the caller. However, if the method type is `void` and the `return` statement is omitted, the computer will automatically return at the end of the method, as demonstrated in Program Example 6.1.

A class method may contain several `return` statements when there are places in a class method that logically allow for the termination of the execution of the method.

6.4 Value Parameters

There are two techniques for passing arguments in Java. The first technique evaluates the argument and creates a local copy of the value, assigning it to the corresponding parameter in the called method. Arguments of primitive data type are passed in this way. In program Example 6.3, the method `pieces` is used to return the number of pieces of wood that may be cut to a set size from a length of wood. The method call is made using the statement `pieces(length,size)` that contains two arguments `length` and `size`, both declared as `float` in the `main` method. The formal-parameter list is coded as `(float length, float size)`.

> ⚠️ Both the actual-parameter list and the formal-parameter list must contain the same number of arguments, in the same order and of the same data type.

Figure 6.1 illustrates that computer memory is allocated to storing the variables `length` and `size` in the `main` method, and to storing the parameters `length` and `size` in the method `pieces`. Any change to the parameters `length` and `size` would be localized to the function `pieces` and would not change the values of `length` and `size` in the `main` method.

method:	main	
arguments	pre-call values	post-call values
length	10.0	10.0
size	1.5	1.5

method:	pieces	
returned value: 6		
parameters	initial values	final values
length	10.0	1.0
size	1.5	1.5

Figure 6.1 Passing parameters by value

Program Example 6.3: Parameters Passed by Value

```
// chap_6\Ex_3.java
// program to demonstrate value parameters

import java.io.*;

class Ex_3
{
    static BufferedReader keyboard = new
            BufferedReader(new InputStreamReader(System.in));
    static PrintWriter screen = new PrintWriter(System.out, true);

    //-----------------------------------------------------------------

    public static void main(String[] args) throws IOException
    {
        float length, size;

        screen.print("Length of wood? "); screen.flush();
        length = new Float(keyboard.readLine()).floatValue();

        screen.print("Size of pieces? "); screen.flush();
        size = new Float(keyboard.readLine()).floatValue();

        screen.print(pieces(length,size) + " pieces of size " + size);
        screen.println(" cut from wood of length " + length);
    }

    //-----------------------------------------------------------------

    // method to calculate the number of pieces of wood that can
    // be cut to a set size from a length of wood
    static int pieces(float length, float size)
    {
        int numberOfPieces;

        numberOfPieces = (int) (length / size);
        length = length - (numberOfPieces * size);
        screen.println("Length of wood remaining " + length);

        return numberOfPieces;
    }

    //-----------------------------------------------------------------

}
```

(handwritten annotation: "Kall method." with circle around `pieces(length,size)`; handwritten boxes numbered 1 2 2 4 5 6 to the right)

Test results

```
Length of wood? 10.0
Size of pieces? 1.5
Length of wood remaining 1.0
6 pieces of size 1.5 cut from wood of length 10.0
```

6.5 Reference Parameters

The second method of passing arguments to a called method relates to all those items of data that are stored by reference. I refer to objects and arrays (refer back to Figure 1.17 Class types stored by reference and Figure 5.1 Declaration of an array of integers). In such circumstances it is the reference to the object or array that is passed and not the specific values of the object or array. The implication of this technique being that any changes made to the values of the parameters in the called method will result in changes being made to the values of the corresponding arguments in the calling method. These facts are illustrated in Figure 6.2, where a reference to an array (the arrowed line) is passed as an argument to the method convert. The method convert changes some of the values in this array. Consequently the original values in the array associated with the main method have changed.

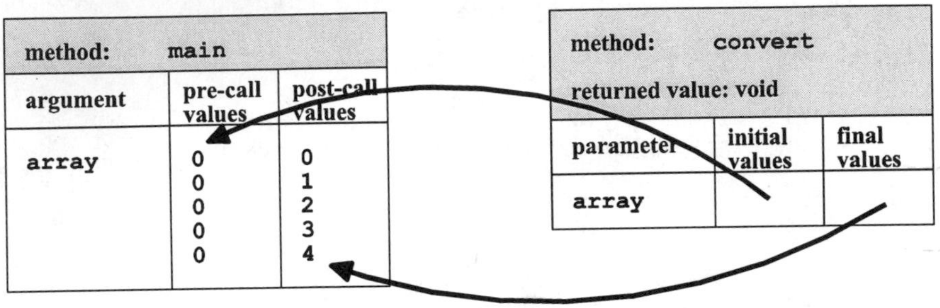

Figure 6.2 Passing an array by reference

Program Example 6.4 illustrates how an array is passed by reference. Notice in this program that the values of the array have been displayed before and after the call to the method convert. Notice also that another class method has been used to display the contents of the array. The reasoning behind using a method for displaying the data was to reduce the amount of repeated coding that would otherwise be necessary.

Program Example 6.4: Passing an Array by Reference

```
// chap_6\Ex_4.java
// program to demonstrate reference parameters for an array

import java.io.*;

class Ex_4
{
    static PrintWriter screen = new PrintWriter(System.out, true);

    //-------------------------------------------------------------

    public static void main(String[] args) throws IOException
    {
        int[] array = {0,0,0,0,0};

        screen.print("Array before call "); screen.flush();
        display(array);
```

Method

```
    convert(array);
    screen.print("Array after call "); screen.flush();
    display(array);
}

//----------------------------------------------------------------

// method to add the value of the index to the contents
// of each cell in the array
static void convert(int[] array)
{
    int lengthOfArray = array.length;

    for (int index=0; index != lengthOfArray; index++)
    {
        array[index] = array[index] + index;
    }
}

//----------------------------------------------------------------

// method to display the contents of an array
static void display(int[] array)
{
    int lengthOfArray = array.length;

    for (int index=0; index != lengthOfArray; index++)
    {
        screen.print(array[index] + " ");
        screen.flush();
    }

    screen.println();
}

//----------------------------------------------------------------

}
```

Results

```
Array before call 0 0 0 0 0
Array after call 0 1 2 3 4
```

String objects are immutable. That is to say the contents of the string cannot be changed. A call to the instance methods toLowerCase() and toUpperCase() on a string object will return a new string object, and will not modify the original string.

If you intend to pass a string object as an argument, with the intention of changing the values of the string object then use the class StringBuffer to instantiate a object that represents a string of characters. The characters in a StringBuffer object can be changed allowing the object to grow or shrink in length as necessary.

Program Example 6.5 illustrates how a `StringBuffer` object may be passed as an argument in a method call, with the intention of changing the contents of the object.

Program Example 6.5: Passing Strings by Reference using the StringBuffer Class

```java
// chap_6\Ex_5.java
// program to demonstrate reference parameters

import java.io.*;

class Ex_5
{
    static PrintWriter screen = new PrintWriter(System.out, true);

    //-------------------------------------------------------------------

    public static void main(String[] args) throws IOException
    {
        StringBuffer data = new StringBuffer("abracadabra");

        screen.println("Data before call " + data);
        convert(data);
        screen.println("Data after call " + data);
    }

    //-------------------------------------------------------------------

    // method to change every character in the array to upper case
    static void convert(StringBuffer data)
    {
        int lengthOfString = data.length();

        for (int index=0; index != lengthOfString; index++)
        {
            data.setCharAt(index, (char)(index+65));
        }
    }

    //-------------------------------------------------------------------

}
```

Test results

```
Data before call abracadabra
Data after call ABCDEFGHIJK
```

Notice that it is necessary to instantiate the object `data` in the normal way. There is no short cut instantiation as with objects of type `String`.

6.6 Command Line Arguments

It is possible to pass arguments to the `main` method. The parameter list for the `main` method is defined as an array `args` of `String` objects. The arguments that are passed are stored as strings in the array `args`. The first parameter is stored at `args[0]`, the second at `args[1]`, the third at `args[2]`, and so on. Since the parameters are stored in an array, the number of cells in the array, is calculated as `args.length`.

In Program Example 6.6 a sentence is passed to the `main` method as a series of command line arguments. Each word in the sentence is stored as a separate string in the array `args`. The program then displays on the screen the contents of each cell in the array. Notice that the number of arguments in the array is only calculated once, before the computer enters the `for` loop.

The programming environment that you are using will dictate the manner in which you are allowed to pass arguments to the `main` method. If you are using Java on a Sun or equivalent Solaris-based computer, you will typically enter the parameters after the name of the executable program file, for example:

```
java Ex_6 This text has been passed as command line arguments!
```

However, if you are using a fully integrated program development environment, such as Microsoft's Visual J++™, then you will need to enter the parameters in a separate window before executing the program; open project settings and in the stand-alone interpreter mode input the program arguments.

Program Example 6.6 Passing Arguments to the main Method

```
// chap_6\ex_6.java
// program to demonstrate how to pass arguments to the main method

import java.io.*;

class Ex_6
{
    static PrintWriter screen = new PrintWriter(System.out, true);

    public static void main(String[] args) throws IOException
    {
        int numberOfArgs = args.length;

        for (int index=0; index != numberOfArgs; index++)
            screen.println(args[index]);
    }
}
```

Test results

The command line was:

```
java Ex_6 This text has been passed as command line arguments!
```

```
This
text
has
been
passed
as
command
line
arguments!
```

6.7 Scope and Lifetime of Identifiers

The **scope** of an identifier refers to the region of a program in which an identifier can be used. An identifier can have either class scope or block scope. An identifier with **class scope** is accessible from its point of declaration throughout the entire class. Program Example 6.7 illustrates that the object screen and the constant PI may be used by any method declared within the class. The arrowed line drawn along the left-hand side of the code indicates the scope of the two identifiers screen and PI within the class.

Program Example 6.7. Identifiers with Class Scope.

```java
// chap_6\Ex_7.java
// program to demonstrate identifiers with class scope

import java.io.*;

class Ex_7
{
    static final float PI = 3.14159f;
    static PrintWriter screen = new PrintWriter(System.out, true);

    public static void main(String[] args) throws IOException
    {
        float radiusOfCircle;
        radiusOfCircle = new Float(args[0]).floatValue();
        screen.println("Circumference " + circumference(radiusOfCircle));
        screen.println("Area " + area(radiusOfCircle));
    }

    //------------------------------------------------------------

    static float circumference(float radius)
    {
        return 2*PI*radius;
    }

    //------------------------------------------------------------

    static float area(float radius)
    {
        return PI*radius*radius;
    }
}
```

Test results

The command line was:

```
java Ex_7 10.0
```

```
Circumference 62.831802
Area 314.159
```

However, an identifier with **block scope** is only accessible from the point of declaration to the end of the block. A **block** begins with an open brace { and ends with a close brace } and contains declarations and executable statements. Program Example 6.8 illustrates the block scope of the object data. The identifier data has been declared and the object data instantiated with keyboard input within the method callMethod. The identifier data is also used within the method to return the value of the string input. The identifier data is not accessible outside of the method, however, the value of data has been returned.

Program Example 6.8. Identifiers with Block Scope.

```java
// chap_6\Ex_8.java
// program to demonstrate block scope

import java.io.*;

class Ex_8
{
    static BufferedReader keyboard = new
            BufferedReader(new InputStreamReader(System.in));
    static PrintWriter screen = new PrintWriter(System.out, true);

    //-------------------------------------------------------------

    public static void main(String[] args) throws IOException
    {
        screen.println("Input lines of text - enter EXIT to terminate");
        while (! callMethod().equals("EXIT"));
    }

    //-------------------------------------------------------------

    static String callMethod() throws IOException
    {
        String data = new String(keyboard.readLine());
        return data;
    }

    //-------------------------------------------------------------

}
```

Test results

```
Input lines of text - enter EXIT to terminate
Paris
in the
Spring!
EXIT
```

The identifiers of a formal parameter list may also be regarded as having block scope. In Program Example 6.7, the value of the radius of the circle is passed as a command line parameter, to the formal parameter list `args` of the main method. The floating-point value of the parameter `args[0]` is assigned to the identifier `radiusOfCircle`. Both identifiers `arg` and `radiusOfCircle` have block scope and are not accessible outside of the `main` method. However, the value of `radiusOfCircle` can be passed as an argument in a call to the methods `circumference` and `area`. Similarly, in both of the methods `circumference` and `area`, the parameter `radius` only has block scope within each method.

> ⚠️ Block scope is not always recognized by the use of braces { }. In a `for` loop with a single statement braces are not mandatory, yet any variable defined by the `for` loop is visible in the statement that follows the `for` definition.

The **lifetime** of an identifier is the period during which the value of the identifier exists in computer memory. The lifetime of an identifier will vary according to the nature of the identifier. Identifiers declared as being `static` exist for the life of the program, such as the object `screen`, and the constant `PI` in Program Example 6.7. Whereas parameters and identifiers having block scope only exist during the execution of the method. For example, in Program Example 6.7 the value of the parameter `radius` will be destroyed when the method is not being executed. Similarly, in Program Example 6.8 the value of the local variable `data` will be destroyed when the method is not being executed. In the latter example, the destroying of the `String` object is of great significance.

Consider what would happen if the object `data` was not destroyed. Every time the method was called memory would be allocated to storing a new string. If the method was called very many times then it is feasible that you would run out of memory for storing any more strings!

When an object goes out of scope, the amount of memory allocated to storing that object is returned back to the heap for future use by other objects. The **heap** is an area of memory set aside for the dynamic allocation of computer memory to objects during run time.

The Java system automatically returns memory to the heap when it is no longer required. This process is known as **garbage collection**.

NOW DO THIS   Before continuing with this chapter you are recommended to turn to the Exercises at the end of the chapter and answer questions 34, 35, 36 and 37.

6.8 Constructors

The instantiation of an object is understood to be the allocation of memory for storing the object's data and the initialization of this memory space with appropriate values.

> A class may contain a number of **instance variables** that represent the data for a particular object. Each object will have its <u>own set</u> of instance variables, which represent the state of an object.

Instantiation is made possible by the use of a constructor which serves several purposes.

- A constructor is given the same name as the class to allow for the data type of objects to be declared.

- A constructor is normally used in conjunction with the keyword new which allocates memory space from the heap.

- A constructor provides the storage in memory and the initialization of the instance variables allocated to the object.

- For each separate invocation of the constructor a new object will become instantiated.

Consider rewriting the Case Study: Time taken to fill a Swimming Pool described in Chapter 2, using the techniques of object-oriented programming.

You may recall that the swimming pool was specified by its dimensions; and the program displayed the volume, capacity and time to fill the swimming pool.

We can create a class SwimmingPool that contains a constructor to define the type and initialize the variables of the class.

```
// constructor
public SwimmingPool(float length, float width, float depth)
{
    lengthOfPool = length;
    widthOfPool  = width;
    depthOfPool  = depth;
}
```

where the instance variables lengthOfPool, widthOfPool and depthOfPool are declared within the class SwimmingPool. An object largePool can be declared using the following statement:

```
SwimmingPool largePool = new SwimmingPool(50.0f, 20.0f, 5.0f);
```

which initializes the instance variables `lengthOfPool`, `widthOfPool` and `depthOfPool` to the values 50.0, 20.0 and 5.0 respectively.

6.9 Instance Methods

As you are well aware, instance methods relate to some aspect of the instantiated object. For example, the `length` of a string, the conversion of a string `toUpperCase` characters, and so on. In the class `SwimmingPool` suitable instance methods might be:

```
public float volumeOfPool();
public float capacityOfPool();
public float timeToFillPool();
```

that return the volume of the pool, the capacity of water in the pool and the time taken to fill the pool with water. Notice that these methods return single values and do not require formal parameters. Remember from Chapter 1, that a public method is used anywhere its class is used.

Instance methods are invoked by using the object, and not called directly, as with class methods. Therefore, we can find the volume, capacity and time to fill the pool by invoking the instance methods as follows.

```
largePool.volumeOfPool();
largePool.capacityOfPool();
largePool.timeToFillPool();
```

> **i** Instance methods may be constructed using the same techniques for returning a value and passing parameters as described for class methods.

An instance method may have modifiers, a return type, a name and a formal parameter list. For example, the three instance methods of the `SwimmingPool` class are constructed as follows

```
public float volumeOfPool()
{
    return lengthOfPool*widthOfPool*depthOfPool;
}

public float capacityOfPool()
{
    return lengthOfPool*widthOfPool*depthOfPool*CAPACITY;
}

public float timeToFillPool()
{
    return
    (lengthOfPool*widthOfPool*depthOfPool*CAPACITY)/(RATE_OF_FLOW*60);
}
```

where the constants CAPACITY and RATE_OF_FLOW are declared as class constants within the class SwimmingPool.

There will be data for which it is not necessary to keep sets of values for each object of the class type. For example, the constants RATE_OF_FLOW and CAPACITY are the same for every object of the class SwimmingPool. This data is known as **class data**, and is qualified by the modifier static.

```
static final float RATE_OF_FLOW = 50.0f;
static final float CAPACITY = 7.48f;
```

Program Example 6.9: Time Taken to Fill Swimming Pool.

A Java program may be constructed from more than one class. In this example we will construct the program using two classes - the class SwimmingPool and a class Ex_9 that instantiates objects of type SwimmingPool and tests the instance methods of these objects.

Notice that in the class Ex_9, there are two class methods, the main method and the method displayStatistics. You may notice that the main method instantiates two objects, smallPool and largePool. Since we need to display the volume, capacity and time to fill each pool, it is good programming practice to create a method that can be called from the main method whenever the statistics of the pool are to be displayed, rather than repeating the same code twice in the main method.

```
// chap_6\Ex_9.java
// program to display the statistics of a swimming pool

import java.io.*;

class SwimmingPool
{
    // rate of water flow into pool is 50 US gallons per minute
    static final float RATE_OF_FLOW = 50.0f;

    // cubic foot of water has a capacity of 7.48 US gallons
    static final float CAPACITY = 7.48f;

    // instance variables
    float lengthOfPool;
    float widthOfPool;
    float depthOfPool;

    //-------------------------------------------------------------

    // constructor
    public SwimmingPool(float length, float width, float depth)
    {
        lengthOfPool = length;
        widthOfPool  = width;
        depthOfPool  = depth;
    }
```

```java
    //-------------------------------------------------------------

    // instance methods
    public float volumeOfPool()
    {
        return lengthOfPool*widthOfPool*depthOfPool;
    }

    //-------------------------------------------------------------

    public float capacityOfPool()
    {
        return lengthOfPool*widthOfPool*depthOfPool*CAPACITY;
    }

    //-------------------------------------------------------------

    public float timeToFillPool()
    {
        return
        (lengthOfPool*widthOfPool*depthOfPool*CAPACITY)/(RATE_OF_FLOW*60);
    }
}

class Ex_9
{
    static PrintWriter screen       = new PrintWriter(System.out, true);

    // class methods
    //-------------------------------------------------------------------

    static void displayStatistics(float volume, float capacity, float time)
    {
        screen.println("\nStatistics of Swimming Pool\n");
        screen.println("Volume       \t" + volume   + " cubic feet");
        screen.println("Capacity     \t" + capacity + " gallons");
        screen.println("Filling time\t" + time      + " hours");
    }

    //-------------------------------------------------------------------

    public static void main(String[] args) throws IOException
    {
        SwimmingPool smallPool = new SwimmingPool(10.0f, 6.0f, 4.0f);
        SwimmingPool largePool = new SwimmingPool(50.0f, 20.0f, 5.0f);

        displayStatistics(smallPool.volumeOfPool(),
                    smallPool.capacityOfPool(),
                    smallPool.timeToFillPool());

        displayStatistics(largePool.volumeOfPool(),
                    largePool.capacityOfPool(),
                    largePool.timeToFillPool());
    }
}
```

Test results

```
Statistics of Swimming Pool

Volume          240.0 cubic feet
Capacity        1795.2 gallons
Filling time    0.5984 hours

Statistics of Swimming Pool

Volume          5000.0 cubic feet
Capacity        37400.0 gallons
Filling time    12.466666 hours
```

(handwritten note: — write problem list nouns.)

6.10 Object-oriented Program Design

Program design features prominently throughout the book. The design method uses pseudocode to describe the major steps that the program must perform. Each step is then refined into smaller steps until each step can be translated into statements in Java. This approach to program design means that you analyze a problem in terms of top-down decomposition, starting with an abstract view of the program and ending with a detailed view.

In object-oriented programming we tend to focus upon the production of classes at an early stage in the design. We identify the data used in the problem, and analyze which methods should operate upon data of this type. Once the business of identifying the classes and methods has been performed, there is no reason why the development of the algorithm for each method should not follow the same design approach as we have already used.

To our prescriptive approach of program design we supplement the Problem Analysis stage with an **Analysis of Classes**. The class and instance methods of each class, may then be developed using pseudocode, into Java methods. The design for each method is tested and documented in the normal way before being coded.

In attempting to analyze classes you should perform the following stages.

Identify classes and objects

The identification of classes and objects is the hardest part of object-oriented design. One simple technique for identifying classes is to write a description of the problem, list all the nouns that appear in the description, and then choose your possible classes from the list.

For example, "Write a program to input the dimensions of a swimming pool and calculate and display the volume, capacity and time to fill the pool". From the list of possible nouns only swimming pool can be considered as a viable class. We can visualize a swimming pool as an object, and instantiate many swimming pool objects of different dimensions.

The nouns dimensions, volume, capacity and time (to fill) all represent attributes of a swimming pool, and can hardly be visualized as objects.

Identify data and methods

Once you have identified a class, the next step is to determine the operations that an object can perform or can have performed upon itself, and also the information an object of a class must maintain.

If we identify all the <u>verbs</u> in the description of the problem, we can choose a list of possible actions that an object may perform or have performed upon itself. For example, "<u>Write</u> a program to <u>input</u> the dimensions of a swimming pool and <u>calculate</u> and <u>display</u> the volume, capacity and time to <u>fill</u> the pool". From the list of verbs, input, calculate and display are possible candidate methods for an object of type SwimmingPool.

Data representing the dimensions of the swimming pool will be input to the object using the class constructor. In the SwimmingPool class the dimensions of the pool represent the instance data of the class. The attributes of lengthOfPool, widthOfPool and depthOfPool describe the data of the SwimmingPool class.

The verb calculate applies to calculating the volume, capacity and time to fill the pool, therefore, volumeOfPool, capacityOfPool and timeToFillPool are all methods that return further attributes of a swimming pool. The verbs display and fill may be dismissed since the three methods incorporate all the functionality required to acquire information about the pool.

> ⚠️ The technique of identifying the nouns and verbs in a description to the problem is by no means a rigorous approach, and it definitely does not scale well to anything beyond fairly trivial problems.

Although the third and fourth stages of analyzing classes are briefly discussed in this chapter, you are not expected to use these techniques until later in the book.

Finding relationships between classes

This stage looks for any relationships that may exist between classes. Classes can build upon and cooperate with other classes. Often one class depends upon another class, because it cannot be used unless the other class exists.

Arranging the classes into hierarchies

Creating class hierarchies is an extension of the first step, identifying classes, but it requires information gained during the second and third steps. By assigning attributes and behavior to classes, you have a clearer idea of their similarities and differences; by identifying the relationships between classes you see which classes need to incorporate the functionality of others.

Case Study: Reporting on the Statistics of a Sentence.

Problem. Write a program to read single sentences from text files, and display the statistics of each sentence. The statistics include the sentence itself; the number of vowels the sentence contains; the classified frequency of the vowels; the number of consonants, and the number of words in the sentence.

Problem Analysis. The solution to the problem reuses ideas and techniques taken from Chapter 4 - Program Example 4.8: Count the Number of Words in a Text File; and Chapter 5 - Case Study: Count the Number of Vowels in a Sentence. You are advised to reread these programs before continuing with this case study.

Analysis of Classes.

Identify classes and objects. A statement that summarizes the purpose of the program follows. "Write a program to read a <u>sentence</u> and return, the <u>sentence</u>, the number of <u>vowels</u>, the <u>classification</u> of the <u>vowels</u>, the number of <u>consonants</u> and the number of <u>words</u> in the <u>sentence</u>."

The list of nouns that might qualify as suitable classes is sentence, vowels, classification, consonants, and words. However, Sentence may be considered as a suitable class, since we can visualize a sentence as an object, and instantiate many objects from many sentences. You may argue that words is also a suitable class. However, a group of words may be thought of as a sentence.

Identify data and methods. If we examine the verbs in the description of the problem, then it is clear that <u>read</u> and <u>return</u> may offer suitable candidate methods. The class constructor will enable sentences to be read from files. The methods of the class must return the sentence, return the number of vowels, return the classification of the frequency of vowels, return the number of consonants and return the number of words. The constructor and methods for class Sentence follows.

```
class Sentence
{
   // class constructor
   public Sentence(String nameOfFile) throws FileNotFoundException,
                                        IOException;
   // instance methods
   // method to return the string that has been read from the file
   public String sentenceRead();
   // method to return as a reference parameter the classification of the
   // frequency of the vowels; a - vowels[0]; e - vowels[1]; etc.
   public void frequency(int[] vowels);
   // method to return the number of vowels in a sentence
   public int vowelCount();
   // method to return the number of consonants in a sentence
   public int consonantCount();
   // method to return the number of words in a sentence
   public int wordCount();
}
```

The parameter of the constructor is the name of the text file storing a sentence. Since this file needs to be opened and read by the constructor, the `FileReader` constructor might throw an exception if the file cannot be found, and the `BufferedReader` constructor might throw an exception when reading a line from the file. These exceptions are not handled by the constructor `Sentence`, therefore, should either exception occur, the constructor throws a `FileNotFoundException` and an `IOException`.

Data Dictionary for the Sentence class. The class contains a number of instance variables that can be accessed by the other methods in the class. A listing of the variables follows.

```
// data stream of the text file
FileReader file;
// data stream of the input file
BufferedReader inputFile;
// tokenized stream
StringTokenizer data;
// text read from file
StringBuffer text = new StringBuffer();
int numberOfWords = 0;
int numberOfConsonants = 0;
int numberOfVowels = 0;
// array to store frequency of vowels for each sentence
// a - vowelFrequency[0]; e -  vowelfrequency[1]; etc
int[] vowelFrequency = new int[NUMBER_OF_VOWELS];
```

Algorithm for the constructor

1. open input stream
2. read line from stream and split line into tokens
3. while number of tokens not zero
4.   for each token
5.   get word from line
6.   append word and space separator to string buffer
7.   increase word count by 1
8.   count vowels in word
9.   count consonants in word
10.   read line from stream and split line into tokens

ⓘ   Good programming practice dictates that if an activity can be separated out from the normal flow of the algorithm and represented as a separate method, then it leads to a more structured and clearer approach to programming.

There are two such activities in the pseudocode of the constructor that can be refined further and implemented as two separate methods. These are the activities of counting the vowels in a word and counting the consonants in a word.

Data Dictionary for the constructor. The constructor uses instance variables that are defined in the body of the class. However, there are two variables that are local to the constructor - one to store a count of the number of tokens, and another to store the value of a word.

```
int    numberOfTokens = 0;
String word;
```

Desk check of the constructor. The test data is be the sentence - Java is an object oriented language.

data			Java is an object oriented language.			
text			Java	Java is	Java is an	Java is an object
numberOfWords		0	1	2	3	4
numberOfConsonants		0	2	3	4	8
numberOfVowels		0	2	3	4	6
vowelFrequency	a	0	2	2	3	3
	e	0	0	0	0	1
	i	0	0	1	1	1
	o	0	0	0	0	1
	u	0	0	0	0	0
numberOfTokens		0	6			
word			Java	is	an	object

text		Java is an object oriented	Java is an object oriented language.
numberOfWords		5	6
numberOfConsonants		12	16
numberOfVowels		10	14
vowelFrequency	a	3	5
	e	3	4
	i	2	2
	o	2	2
	u	0	1
numberOfTokens		6	
word		oriented	language.

Algorithm for the method to count the vowels in a word

8. count vowels in a word
8.1   for each character in the word
8.2   switch on value of character
8.3   'a' :   increase frequency[0] by 1
8.4   'e' :   increase frequency[1] by 1
8.5   'i' :   increase frequency[2] by 1
8.6   'o' :   increase frequency[3] by 1
8.7   'u' :   increase frequency[4] by 1

Data Dictionary for method countVowels. The method has one formal parameter, the `String` word whose vowels are to be classified. The method contains a `for` loop, so an `index` will be required to count each character in the word. The array frequency that is updated refers to the instance variable `vowelFrequency`. The signature of the method is:

```
void countVowels(String word);
```

Algorithm for the method to count the consonants in a word

9. count consonants in a word
9.1   for each character in the word
9.2   switch on value of character
9.3   'b': 'c': 'd': 'f': 'g': 'h': 'j':
9.4   'k': 'l': 'm': 'n': 'p': 'q': 'r':
9.5   's': 't': 'v': 'w': 'x': 'y': 'z': increase number of consonants by 1

Data Dictionary for the method countConsonants. The method has one formal parameter, the `String word` whose consonants are to be counted. The method contains a `for` loop, so an `index` will be required to count each character in the word. The variable consonants that is updated refers to the instance variable `numberOfConsonants`. The signature for the method is:

```
void countConsonants(String word);
```

The constructor would have appeared to have done most of the work in solving the problem. The amount of work involved in coding the instance methods is trivial, since these methods need only return the respective values of the instance variables. For example, the instance method `sentenceRead` returns the value of the text in the string buffer; the instance method `frequency` assigns to the formal parameter `vowels` the values of the frequencies in the array `vowelFrequency`; the instance method `vowelCount` returns the sum of the frequencies of the array `vowelFrequency`; the instance method `consonantCount` returns the value of the instance variable `numberOfConsonants`, and the instance method `wordCount` returns the instance variable `numberOfWords`.

To write code to test the methods of the class `Sentence`, it is necessary to include another class `Ex_10`, in the program. The class `Ex_10` contains two class methods, the `main` method and a method `processLines`. The method `processLines` displays the statistics of a sentence as illustrated in the screen layout document. Without the inclusion of the class method `processLines` it would have been necessary to repeat the code to display the statistics of a sentence in the `main` method.

Screen Layout Document

```
12345678901234567890123456789012345678901234567890

Sentence: Java is an object oriented language.
Number of vowels: 14
Frequency of vowels in sentence
A     E     I     O     U
5     4     2     2     1
Number of consonants: 16
Number of words: 6
```

Algorithm for the method `processLines`.

1. display sentence
2. display number of vowels
3. display frequency of vowels in sentence
4. display number of consonants
5. display number of words

Data Dictionary for `processLines`. The method declares a formal parameter of type `Sentence` for an object passed to the method. The method `processLines` uses a local constant to represent the number of vowels, and a local array variable for storing the frequency of the vowels. The signature of the method is:

```
static void processLines(Sentence lines);
```

and the local data declarations for the method are:

```
final int NUMBER_OF_VOWELS = 5;
int[] vowels = new int[NUMBER_OF_VOWELS];
```

If you use the test data and results of the previous desk check, then the output from this program is depicted in the screen layout document.

Coding

```
// chap_6\Ex_10.java
// class to analyze sentences

import java.io.*;
import java.util.*;

class Sentence
{
    // class constant
    static final int  NUMBER_OF_VOWELS = 5;

    // instance variables
    FileReader file;
    BufferedReader inputFile;
    StringTokenizer data;
    StringBuffer text = new StringBuffer();
    int numberOfWords = 0;
    int numberOfConsonants = 0;
    int numberOfVowels = 0;
    int[] vowelFrequency = new int[NUMBER_OF_VOWELS];

    //----------------------------------------------------------------

    // method to classify the vowels in a word
    void countVowels(String word)
    {
        for (int index=0; index != word.length(); index++)
        {
            switch (word.charAt(index))
            {
            case 'a': vowelFrequency[0]++; break;
            case 'e': vowelFrequency[1]++; break;
            case 'i': vowelFrequency[2]++; break;
            case 'o': vowelFrequency[3]++; break;
            case 'u': vowelFrequency[4]++; break;
            }
        }
    }

    //----------------------------------------------------------------

    // method to count the consonants in a word
    void countConsonants(String word)
    {
        for (int index=0; index != word.length(); index++)
        {
            switch (word.charAt(index))
            {
            case 'b':case 'c':case 'd':case 'f':case 'g':case 'h':case 'j':
            case 'k':case 'l':case 'm':case 'n':case 'p':case 'q':case 'r':
            case 's':case 't':case 'v':case 'w':case 'x':case 'y':case 'z':
            numberOfConsonants++;
            }
        }
    }
```

```java
//-------------------------------------------------------------------

// class constructor
public Sentence(String nameOfFile) throws FileNotFoundException,
                                           IOException
{
    final String SPACE = "\u0020";

    int numberOfTokens = 0;
    String word;

    // open input stream
    file = new FileReader(nameOfFile);
    inputFile = new BufferedReader(file);
    // read line from stream and split into tokens
    data = new StringTokenizer(inputFile.readLine());
    numberOfTokens = data.countTokens();

    while (numberOfTokens != 0)
    {
        for (int token=1; token <= numberOfTokens; token++)
        {
            // get word from line
            word = new String(data.nextToken());
            // append word to string buffer text
            text.append(word+SPACE);

            numberOfWords++;
            countVowels(word.toLowerCase());
            countConsonants(word.toLowerCase());
        }

        // read next line from stream and split into tokens
        data = new StringTokenizer(inputFile.readLine());
        numberOfTokens = data.countTokens();
    }
}

//-------------------------------------------------------------------

// instance method to return the Sentence read from the file
public String sentenceRead()
{
    return text.toString();
}

//-------------------------------------------------------------------

// instance method to pass the classified frequency of vowels
public void frequency(int[] vowels)
{
    for (int index=0; index != NUMBER_OF_VOWELS; index++)
    {
        vowels[index] = vowelFrequency[index];
    }
}
```

```java
    //------------------------------------------------------------------

    // instance method to return the total number of vowels
    public int vowelCount()
    {
        int totalNumberOfVowels = 0;

        for (int index=0; index != NUMBER_OF_VOWELS; index++)
        {
            totalNumberOfVowels = totalNumberOfVowels + vowelFrequency[index];
        }

        return totalNumberOfVowels;
    }

    //------------------------------------------------------------------

    // instance method to return the number of consonants in the sentence
    public int consonantCount()
    {
        return numberOfConsonants;
    }

    //------------------------------------------------------------------

    // instance method to return the total number of words in the sentence
    public int wordCount()
    {
        return numberOfWords;
    }

    //------------------------------------------------------------------
}

class Ex_10
{
    static PrintWriter screen = new PrintWriter(System.out, true);

    // class method to display the statistics of a sentence
    static void processLines(Sentence lines)
    {
        final int NUMBER_OF_VOWELS = 5;
        int[] vowels = new int[NUMBER_OF_VOWELS];

        screen.println("Sentence: " + lines.sentenceRead());
        screen.println("Number of vowels: " + lines.vowelCount());

        lines.frequency(vowels);
        screen.println("Frequency of vowels in sentence");
        screen.println("A\tE\tI\tO\tU");
        for (int index=0; index != vowels.length; index++)
        {
            screen.print(vowels[index]+"\t");
            screen.flush();
        }
        screen.println();
```

```
        screen.println("Number of consonants: " + lines.consonantCount());
        screen.println("Number of words: " + lines.wordCount() + "\n");
    }

    //------------------------------------------------------------------

    public static void main(String[] args)throws IOException
    {
        // instantiate objects
        Sentence lines1 = new Sentence("a:\\chap_6\\lines1.txt");
        Sentence lines2 = new Sentence("a:\\chap_6\\lines2.txt");

        // process objects
        processLines(lines1);
        processLines(lines2);
    }

    //------------------------------------------------------------------

}
```

Results

```
Sentence: A Java bytecode program may be ported to different computers.
Number of vowels: 19
Frequency of vowels in sentence
A        E        I        O        U
5        7        1        5        1
Number of consonants: 32
Number of words: 10

Sentence: To be or not to be, that is the question; whether it is nobler in
the mind, to take arms against a sea of trouble, or by opposing, end them.
Number of vowels: 42
Frequency of vowels in sentence
A        E        I        O        U
7        13       8        12       2
Number of consonants: 63
Number of words: 30
```

Summary

- A program should be constructed from a number of classes, where each class contains a set of methods. This approach helps to improve program design, coding, testing and maintenance.

- A method should be written as a self-contained unit that represents a single programmed activity.

- When calling a method, the list of literals or variables, enclosed in parenthesis after the method name, is known as the actual parameter list.

- When declaring a method, the list of declarations, enclosed in parenthesis after the method name, is known as the formal parameter list.

- The number of actual parameters must be the same as the number of corresponding formal parameters.

- The order of the actual parameters and the formal parameters must be the same.

- The data types of the corresponding actual parameters and formal parameters must be the same.

- The names of the identifiers in the actual parameter list and the formal parameter list can be the same or different.

- After executing a method, the computer will return to the next executable statement after the method call.

- The computer will return to the calling method by either executing a return statement or by reaching the physical end of the method.

- The return statement may assign a value to the method and exit from the method.

- A method may contain parameters and local variables.

- Constants and variables may have either block scope or class scope.

- A constructor is used to initialize the instance variables of a class.

- For each invocation of a constructor a new object, with its own set of instance variables, is instantiated.

- Instance methods and class methods are constructed using the same techniques for returning a value and passing parameters.

- An instance method should be declared as `public` so that it is accessible from outside of its class.

- In designing object-oriented programs it is important to analyze classes at an early stage in the development of the software. The analysis of classes can be divided into the activities of identifying classes; identifying class data and methods; finding relationships between classes; and arranging classes into hierarchies.

- Once the classes and methods have been discovered, the designing and coding of the methods can follow the stages of algorithm design, data dictionary construction, testing, and coding used in the previous chapters.

Review Questions

1. Comment upon how instance methods and class methods are invoked.

2. State the names of at least two predefined classes that contain class methods.

3. What is the syntax of a programmer-defined method?

4. Does every method return a value?

5. What is a formal parameter list?

6. True or false - every method has a formal parameter list.

7. What is an actual parameter list?

8. True or false - a method may have many `return` statements.

9. True or false - a method may have no `return` statements.

10. Where does the computer return to upon exiting a method?

11. What is the scope of an identifier?

12. What is a block?

13. Distinguish between block scope and class scope.

14. Give an example of a parameter passed by value.

15. How is a value parameter represented in the memory allocated to a method?

16. True or false - an object is passed by value.

17. What is a reference parameter?

18. What is the lifetime of an identifier?

19. True or false - a `static` identifier has life for the duration of the program in which it is declared.

20. What do you understand by garbage collection?

21. What is a constructor?

22. Why should instance methods be defined as public?

23. True or false - an instance variable is `static`.

24. True or false - the arguments passed to a `main` method from a command line are stored as strings in a one-dimensional array.

25. What is the meaning of `args.length`, where `args` is the formal parameter in the main method?

Exercises

26. Desk check the following code. What is output from the `main` method?

```
public static void main(String[] args)
{
    screen.println(sum());
}

static int sum()
{
    int A = 12;
    int B = 13;

    return A+B;
}
```

27. Desk check the following code. What is output from the method `display`?

```
public static void main(String[] args)
{
    display("Hello World");
}

static void display(String message)
{
    screen.println(message);
}
```

28. Desk check the following code. What is output from method `display`?

```
public static void main(String[] args)
{
    display(25,13);
}

static void display(int A, int B)
{
    int C = A+B;

    screen.println(C);
}
```

29. Desk check the following code. What is output from the methods `valueOnly` and `main`?

```java
public static void main(String[] args)
{
    int A=41;
    int B=29;

    valueOnly(A,B);
    screen.println("A=" + A + " B=" + B);
}

static void valueOnly(int A, int B)
{
    A--;
    B++;
    screen.println("A=" + A + " B=" + B);
}
```

30. Desk check the following code. What is output from the `main` method?

```java
public static void main(String[] args)
{
    int[] data = {41,29};

    referenceOnly(data);
    screen.println(data[0] + "\t" + data[1]);
}

static void referenceOnly(int[] parameter)
{
    parameter[0]--;
    parameter[1]++;
}
```

31. State the errors in the following method calls and method signatures.

	class method call	class method signature
(a)	`alpha;`	`static void alpha();`
(b)	`beta(A,B,C);`	`static void beta();`
(c)	`delta(18,'*');`	`static void delta(char X, int Y);`
(d)	`gamma(X,Y);`	`static void gamma(int[] data);`

32. What is the error in the following method?

```java
static void alpha(int number)
{
    return 2*number;
}
```

33. In the following code, what is the value of `global` inside the method `overRide`?

```
class example
{
    static final int global = 29;     // constant with class scope

    static void overRide()
    {
        int global = 56;              // variable with block scope
        .
        .
        .
}
```

Programming Problems

In questions 34 to 37 you should devise just one class that contains static method(s) and a main method as your answer to each question.

34. Devise and test a class method that will take as parameters a message of your choice and the number of times you want the message displayed on the screen.

35. Devise and test a class method that will take as a parameter a four-digit account number and return a Modulus-11 check digit.

The modulus 11 check digit for a code number is calculated as follows. Using the code number 9118 as an example: multiply each digit by its associated weight and calculate the sum of the partial products - (5x9)+(4x1)+(3x1)+(2x8) = 68. Note the respective weights of each digit are 5,4,3,2, starting at the most significant digit.

The sum 68 is then divided by 11, and the remainder 2 is then subtracted from 11, the result 9 is the check digit. The complete code number, including the check digit as the least significant digit is 91189. If the value of the check digit is computed to be 10, this number is replaced by X.

36. Devise and test a class method to validate the time of day, input as a four character string parameter, using the 24-hour clock representation, e.g. 1436. Return a boolean value to indicate the validity of the time.

37. Devise and test a class method to calculate and return the number of ways of selecting a team of R players from N players. The mathematical solution to this problem is found by using the expression N!/(R!*(N-R)!) where ! means factorial (e.g. 4! = 4x3x2x1).

Since three factorial values for N, R and N-R have to be calculated, one class method for calculating the factorial value of a number should be incorporated into your program.

38. Write a program to calculate income tax, in an unspecified country, according to the following rules.

A tax allowance is given according to marital status: a single person is allowed $3,000; a married person $5,000, which is allowed only against one salary if both partners are working.

The pension contribution is 6% of the gross salary. Taxable income is the sum of the single/married allowance and the pension contribution, subtracted from the gross annual salary. Income tax is based upon taxable income and is levied at the following rates:

Tax Band 0   The first $5,000 of taxable income attracts tax at 0%

Tax band 1   A taxable income of up to $20,000 attracts tax at the rate of 20% for any amount over $5000.

Tax Band 2   A taxable income of up to $30,000 attracts tax at the rate of 30% for any amount over $20,000.

Tax band 3   A taxable income of up to $40,000 attracts tax at the rate of 40% for any amount over $30,000

Tax Band 4   A taxable income in excess of $40,000 attracts tax at the rate of 50%

Devise a class `PersonTax` that contains a constructor to input the name of a person, their gross annual salary and whether the person is married or single; and instance methods to return the tax allowance, pension contribution, taxable income, income tax and net salary for that person. Your program should display the tax statistics for several people.

39. Write a program to convert numbers represented in Roman numerals to decimal and hexadecimal numbers. For example MDCLXIV = 1664 in decimal and 680 in hexadecimal. Figure 6.3 indicates the size of each Roman numeral. Devise a class `Roman` that has methods to return the decimal and hexadecimal values of the Roman numbers.

Roman	Decimal
M	1000
D	500
C	100
L	50
X	10
V	5
I	1

Figure 6.3 Decimal values of Roman numerals

40. A carpenter has a supply of various lengths of wood. The carpenter wants to cut from them as many 5 meter lengths as possible, and where a 5 meter length cannot be cut, the carpenter will cut 2 meter lengths.

Write a program to input a length of wood and calculate and output the number of 5 meter, and 2 meter lengths and the amount of wasted wood. Repeat the program for different lengths of wood being input and keep a running total of the number of 5 meter and 2 meter pieces and the cumulative length of wasted word. At the end of the data, output the total number of 5 meter and 2 meter pieces and the cumulative length of wasted wood.

Devise a class LengthOfWood that contains methods to return the number of 5 meter and 2 meter pieces that may be cut from a single length of wood, and the amount of wasted wood. This class will also contain methods to return the total number of pieces of wood cut to 5 meter and 2 meter lengths, and the total wastage of wood.

41. Return to Chapter 5 and the section on Programming Problems. Rewrite your solution to question 39 by incorporating suitable classes and methods.

42. The letters of the alphabet A through Z can be represented in Morse code. Each letter is represented by a combination of up to four dots and/or dashes as illustrated in Figure 6.4.

```
A  .-        H  ....      O  ---       V  ...-
B  -...      I  ..        P  .--.      W  .--
C  -.-.      J  .---      Q  --.-      X  -..-
D  -..       K  -.-       R  .-.       Y  -.--
E  .         L  .-..      S  ...       Z  --..
F  ..-.      M  --        T  -
G  --.       N  -.        U  ..-
```

Figure 6.4 Morse Code Alphabet

Devise and test a class MorseCode that will allow you to return the Morse Code for a phrase written in English, and return in English a phrase written in Morse Code.

Chapter 7
Encapsulation

Encapsulation is an approach to program development that attempts to hide much of the implementation details of a class. The interface of each class is defined in such a way as to reveal as little as possible about its inner workings.

This approach leads to programs that are easy to change, with many changes requiring modification of only the inner workings of a single class and not the interface of the class.

Since the implementation details are hidden from the user, it is not possible for a user of the class to change well engineered code.

This approach to program development leads to classes that maintain their integrity, are readily understood, may be clearly documented and can be developed independently of each other.

By the end of this chapter you should have an understanding of the following topics.

- The creation of an abstract data type (ADT).

- Object instantiation and finalization.

- Properties of objects.

- The use of appropriate class, method and data modifiers.

- Use of classes to create records.

- Categorizing classes into a package.

7.1 Abstract Data Type

The key behind creating an abstract data type (ADT) is encapsulation. **Encapsulation** is the grouping together of data and a set of methods to perform actions on the data. Encapsulation is illustrated in Figure 7.1. Access to the data is allowed only via specific instance methods. The implementation of the data, constructors, instance methods and class methods may be hidden from the user. An encapsulated group, consisting of a data and its associated methods, is called an **abstract data type**.

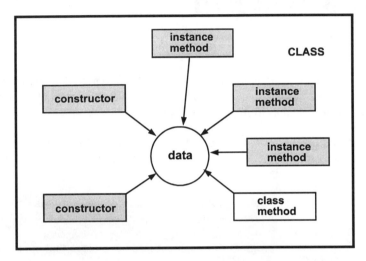

Figure 7.1 Encapsulation of data and methods within a class

Why should we want to hide the implementation details of a class? By denying programmers access to the implementation details, you can safely modify the implementation without worrying that you may inadvertently introduce errors into code that uses the class.

Another reason for encapsulation is to preserve the integrity of the data in your class. Direct access to the class data can result in variables not being correctly updated. Access to the data must be though trusted methods of the class.

In documenting the interface to an encapsulated class, there is no need to reveal the constants, variables and methods that users cannot access. The appearance of the interface becomes uncluttered and helps to improve the documentation of the class.

The concept of an abstract data type is not new. Consider for a moment the data type String. A variable of type String can apply the String constructors to build objects; these objects can invoke many predefined instance methods such as length(), toLowerCase(), and so on, and the programmer may use predefined class methods such as valueOf to convert any of the primitive types to data of type String.

The method of implementing the data type `String` is hidden from the user. Without consulting with the author of the class `String`, there is no way of knowing the internal format of a `String`. We can of course guess, that it might be stored as an array of characters! However, even if it is represented in this manner, we are precluded from accessing the array directly and must rely upon access through only those instance methods that are supplied for the class.

Similarly, the implementations of the constructors and instance methods are hidden from the user. As a user there is no way of inspecting how these operations are carried out, since the class will be stored as Java byte codes. Only the implementers of the classes should have access to the Java source code to prevent users from changing well-engineered software.

A user may declare variables of type `String` and apply any of the set of instance methods to objects of this type.

The `String` example demonstrates the following features that embody the requirements of the abstract data type.

- The abstraction has created a data type, for example `String`.

- It is possible to declare variables of a specific type, for example `String magic;`

- The type contains a set of instance methods for the access and manipulation of data of the said type.

- The implementation of the type, behind the scenes, uses whatever data and methods are necessary.

- User access to the type is through a restricted interface with the implementation details being hidden from the user of the type.

A **private** variable or method is only visible within its own class. Classes may not be `private`. A `public` class is visible anywhere. A `public` variable or method is visible anywhere its class is visible.

In creating classes, we will be creating abstract data types that conform to the above requirements. In the construction of an abstract data type, the data should be kept `private` to prevent access and hence changes to the values from outside of the class. The constructors and instance methods that are to be accessed from outside the class should be defined as `public`. Those instance methods that are part of the class, yet are not accessed from outside of the class, but used to help a public method achieve its goal should be `private`. Class methods should be defined as `static` and `public` if they are to be accessed from outside of the class, otherwise they should be labeled as `static` and `private`.

7.2 Constructors Revisited

You have already learned that a constructor is given the same name as the class; and you have probably observed that a class may contain more than one constructor. For example, if you inspect the constructors for the `String` class, you will notice there are nine constructors all with the same name `String`. Using the same name for methods, either constructors, instance methods or class methods, but not a mixture of all three, is known as **method overloading**.

You may wonder how the compiler can distinguish between methods of the same name? If you inspect the constructors for the `String` class, the only part of the constructor that distinguishes it from the other constructors is the formal parameter list. The number and type of parameters in the formal parameter list is the only way in which the compiler can distinguish overloaded methods.

Upon inspection of the `String` constructors, it would appear that none of the constructors return values; although it is rather curious that the `void` keyword has not been used to reflect this fact. So what's going on?

Despite no return type being specified in the constructor declarations, nor the `void` keyword used, an object is returned!

> The `this` object is implicitly returned. The keyword **this** refers to the current object, which is the object being instantiated in the case of the constructor.

Consider creating a class for a rational number (fraction). The class would contain two instance variables that represent a fraction, a `numerator` and a `denominator`. Both instance variables are declared as `private` since access to the variables must be restricted to only methods within the class.

At least two constructors may be provided for this class. The first is a default constructor that takes no parameters, yet initializes the `numerator` to zero and the `denominator` to 1. A more useful constructor has parameters, that represent values for the `numerator` and `denominator` of the instantiated object. The initial steps towards the creation of the class `Rational` follows, it contains two instance variables and two constructors:

```
class Rational
{
   private int numerator;                  // instance variables
   private int denominator;

   public Rational()                       // default constructor
   {
      numerator = 0;
      denominator = 1;
   }

   public Rational(int num, int denom)     // specific constructor
   {
      numerator = num;
```

```
        denominator = denom;
        makeRational();
    }

    .
    .
    .
```

where the class method `makeRational()` is used to reduce the fraction to its simplest rational form, for example, the fraction 6/8 would be represented as ¾.

Either constructor could have been written to include:

```
this.numerator = num;
this.denominator = denom;
```

where `this` refers to the object being instantiated. However, such a modification is not strictly necessary. The benefit of being able to refer to the object that invoked the instance method will be covered in the next section.

7.3 Instance Methods Revisited

To continue building the class `Rational` it will be necessary to include methods that can be applied to objects of type `Rational`. The mathematics of fractions should include such operations as addition, subtraction, multiplication and division.

> ⓘ Java does not allow operator overloading, so it is not possible to use the operators +, -, * and / in the context of rational numbers. The only exception to this rule is the overloading of the + operator for string concatenation.

The instantiation and invocation of the method to add two fractions together will be of the form:

```
Rational a = new Rational(1,2);
Rational b = new Rational(3,4);
Rational c;

c.add(a,b);
```

Notice that the rational numbers a and b are input as parameters in the method call, and the result is returned to the rational number or object c. Since c invoked the call to add the rational numbers a and b, any reference to the `this` keyword in the method, refers to the data of object c.

The instance method for the addition of two rational numbers follows.

```
class Rational
{
    .
    .

    public Rational add(Rational x, Rational y)
    {
        numerator = x.numerator * y.denominator +
                    y.numerator * x.denominator;
        denominator = x.denominator * y.denominator;
        makeRational();
        return this;
    }

    .
    .
```

If you had to add the fractions $xn/xd + yn/yd$ the result of the addition would take the form of $(xn.yd+xd.yn)/(xd.yd)$. Note - xn and yn refer to the numerator of the rational numbers x an y; and xd and yd refer to the denominator of the rational numbers x and y. In the method the instance variables `numerator` and `denominator` refer to the instance variables of the object C that invoked the method. These could also be expressed as `this.numerator` and `this.denominator` respectively. Access to the corresponding `numerator` and `denominator` instance variables for the rational parameters x and y is via the dot (.) notation. Thus `x.numerator` refers to the `numerator` instance variable for object x and `x.denominator` refers to the `denominator` instance variable for object y.

The value for the addition of the two fractions must be converted to a minimal form using the class method `makeRational()`. This method may of course alter the values for `this.numerator` and `this.denominator`. Since the method must return a value of type `Rational` it is necessary to return the object referred to by the `this` keyword. This of course is the object C.

Can you write instance methods to subtract, multiply and divide pairs of rational numbers? The answer is given in a program listing later in the chapter.

There are alternative definitions for the arithmetic methods of fractions. You could define an `add` instance method with only one parameter that returns the sum of the numbers, for example `a.add(b)`; or you could define an `add` class (static) method with two parameters that returns the sum of the numbers, for example **Rational.add(a,b)**. Which approach you choose will depend upon the problem set being used. For example, you may want to use the `add` instance method that takes just one parameter, in a problem set that contains complex expressions such as `a.add(b.add(c))`. In the programming problems at the end of this chapter you are given the opportunity to rewrite the Rational class using these alternative definitions.

7.4 Object Properties

You may recall that in Chapter 1 it was stated that class types are stored by reference, unlike primitive data types that are stored by value. Whenever an object is instantiated, all the non-static class variables for that object are allocated memory and initialized with data. Figure 7.2 illustrates that for the declaration of the two Rational objects a and b, separate memory is allocated for storing the values of the two objects, and references point at the two areas of memory.

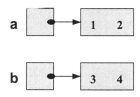

Figure 7.2 Storage of Objects

If we want to compare the two objects a and b for equality, the statement a==b will only compare the values of the references (arrowed lines in Figure 7.2) and not the contents of what is being referenced.

> The values of the references are the values of memory addresses taken from the heap. Therefore, the comparison of a==b is a comparison of whether a and b are the same memory addresses, in other words do they refer to the same area of memory for storing the object's data.

To compare the two objects for equality it is necessary to invent a new instance method that compares the values of the numerator and denominator for each object.

```
public boolean equals(Rational x)
{
    return ((this.numerator == x.numerator) &&
            (this.denominator == x.denominator));
}
```

The instance method equals is invoked using the statement a.equals(b), and returns a boolean value of either true or false. In the implementation of the method the this keyword refers to the object a that invoked the method. The object b is taken as the parameter x in the method. If the statement

```
((this.numerator == x.numerator) && (this.denominator == x.denominator));
```

evaluates to true then the value true is returned and the contents of the two objects are the same, otherwise if the statement evaluates to false then the value false is returned indicating that the contents of the two objects differ.

In chapter 1, it was stated that an assignment of one object to another does not produce a copy of the object, but only a reference to the object. For example, referring to the rational numbers, the statement c = a, will only cause object c to refer to object a, as illustrated in the top diagram in Figure 7.3. Thus if the value of object a changed, then object c would no longer make reference to the original values of object a.

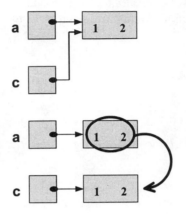

Figure 7.3 Reference vs Copy (clone)

If we want to make a copy of object a and assign this to object c, it is necessary to include a new instance method copy (the same as clone in the class Object) in the class Rational.

```
public Rational copy()
{
    Rational temporary = new Rational(this.numerator, this.denominator);
    return temporary;
}
```

The instance method would be invoked using the statement c = a.copy().

The object that invoked the method is a, therefore, any reference to the keyword this in the implementation of the method, refers to the object a. Notice from the implementation that a new object temporary is instantiated, and initialized with the data values associated with object a. This has copied the data values of the object a to the object temporary.

The object temporary is then returned from the instance method and assigned to the object c. Object c now has its own copy of object a. Any subsequent changes made to the value of object a will not alter the value of object c.

 Chapter 8 covers further work on the equals and clone methods.

Case Study: Arithmetic of Rational Numbers

Problem. Devise a class for the addition, subtraction, multiplication and division of rational numbers (fractions). The class should also contain methods to print a rational number and compare rational numbers for equality as well as copy one rational number to another.

Write a test program to test all the methods of the class `Rational`.

Problem Analysis. The arithmetic associated with rational numbers can be represented by the following expressions.

addition $xn/_{xd} + yn/_{yd} = (xn.yd+xd.yn)/_{(xd.yd)}$

subtraction $xn/_{xd} - yn/_{yd} = (xn.yd-xd.yn)/_{(xd.yd)}$

multiplication $xn/_{xd} . yn/_{yd} = (xn.yn) /_{(xd.yd)}$

division $xn/_{xd} / yn/_{yd} = (xn.yd) /_{(xd.yn)}$

These expressions are used in the instance methods that provide the arithmetic operations on the rational numbers.

Rational numbers must always be expressed in their minimal form. For example, the fraction $12/_{96}$ would need to be converted to $1/_8$, by finding the greatest common divisor (gcd) between the numerator and denominator and dividing both the numerator and denominator by this value. The gcd in the fraction $12/_{96}$ is 12, thus by dividing both the numerator and denominator by 12, the fraction is reduced to its minimal form of $1/_8$.

In calculating the minimal form for a fraction it is necessary to use two new methods; the first implements Euclid's algorithm for calculating the greatest common divisor (gcd); and the second is an algorithm known as `makeRational()` to divide both the numerator and denominator by the greatest common divisor, taking notice of the signs of the numerator and/or denominator.

Analysis of Classes. The definition of the class `Rational` follows. Notice that it contains the two constructors, together with instance methods to perform arithmetic, comparisons for equality and object assignment discussed earlier in the chapter and printing the value of a rational number. This is the public face of the class `Rational`. Access to the instance variables `numerator` and `denominator` and to the `private` methods `greatestCommonDivisor` and `makeRational` is denied.

```
class Rational
{
    // constructors
    public Rational();
    public Rational(int num, int denom);

    // instance methods
    public Rational add(Rational x, Rational y);
    public Rational subtract(Rational x, Rational y);
```

```
    public Rational multiply(Rational x, Rational y);
    public Rational divide(Rational x, Rational y);
    public void printFraction();
    public boolean equals(Rational x);
    public Rational copy();
}
```

Algorithm for the method greatestCommonDivisor

divide n by d and find the remainder
while remainder is not zero
        assign d to n
        assign remainder to d
        divide n by d and find remainder
assign d to gcd

Data Dictionary for greatestCommonDivisor. The method's signature is:

```
private int greatestCommonDivisor(int n, int d);
```

where the two integer formal parameters represent the numerator n and denominator d respectively. The method returns the greatest common divisor between the numerator and denominator. There is a local integer variable to represent the remainder.

Desk Check for greatestCommonDivisor.

n	d	remainder	(remainder==0)?	gcd
12	96	12	false	
96	12	0	true	
				12

Algorithm for the method makeRational()

Euclid's algorithm is used in a `private` method `makeRational()` that converts a numerator and denominator into a rational number by dividing by the greatest common denominator and adjusting the sign of the fraction according to the signs of the numerator and denominator. The purpose of the code is to remove the negative signs if the numerator and denominator are both negative, and to move the negative sign to the numerator if the denominator is negative and the numerator isn't negative.

The algorithm for the method `makeRational()` follows.

calculate the greatest common divisor for a given numerator and denominator
divide the numerator by the gcd
divide the denominator by the gcd
if either the numerator or denominator is zero the
       set the denominator to its absolute value
else
       calculate the divisor for absolute values of numerator and denominator
       if denominator positive
              divide the numerator by the divisor
              divide the denominator by the divisor
       else
              divide the numerator by the negative divisor
              divide the denominator by the negative divisor

Data Dictionary for makeRational()

The method's signature is:

```
private void makeRational();
```

The method has two local integer variables `gcd` and `divisor`. The `numerator` and `denominator` are `private` instance variables.

Desk Check for makeRational.

numerator	denominator	gcd	divisor	(denominator > 0)?
-12	-96	-12		
-1	-8		1	
				false
1	8			

The implementation of the class `Rational` follows. Notice that a separate class `IO`, has been defined for declaring the static variables `keyboard` and `screen`. Both objects will not only be used in the class `Rational`, but also used in the class that tests the methods of the `Rational` class.

Coding

```
// chap_7\Ex_1.java
// program to test the methods of the rational class

import java.io.*;

class IO
{
    static PrintWriter screen = new PrintWriter(System.out, true);
}
```

```
class Rational
{
    private int numerator;
    private int denominator;

    private int greatestCommonDivisor(int n, int d)
    {
        int remainder = n % d;

        while (remainder != 0)
        {
            n = d;
            d = remainder;
            remainder = n % d;
        }
        return d;
    }

    //------------------------------------------------------------

    private void makeRational()
    {
        int gcd;
        int divisor = 0;

        gcd = greatestCommonDivisor(numerator, denominator);
        numerator = numerator / gcd;
        denominator = denominator/ gcd;

        if (numerator == 0 || denominator == 0)
            denominator = Math.abs(denominator);
        else
        {
            divisor = greatestCommonDivisor(Math.abs(numerator),
                                            Math.abs(denominator));
            if (denominator > 0)
            {
                numerator = numerator / divisor;
                denominator = denominator / divisor;
            }
            else
            {
                numerator = numerator / (-divisor);
                denominator = denominator / (-divisor);
            }
        }
    }

    //------------------------------------------------------------
    // constructors

    public Rational()
    {
        numerator = 0;
        denominator = 1;
        makeRational();
    }
```

```
    //-------------------------------------------------------------------

    public Rational(int num, int denom)
    {
        numerator = num;
        denominator = denom;
        makeRational();
    }

    //-------------------------------------------------------------------
    // instance methods

    public Rational add(Rational x, Rational y)
    {

        numerator = x.numerator * y.denominator +
                    y.numerator * x.denominator;
        denominator = x.denominator * y.denominator;
        makeRational();
        return this;
    }
    //-------------------------------------------------------------------

    public Rational subtract(Rational x, Rational y)
    {
        numerator = x.numerator * y.denominator -
                    y.numerator * x.denominator;
        denominator = x.denominator * y.denominator;
        makeRational();
        return this;
    }

    //-------------------------------------------------------------------

    public Rational multiply(Rational x, Rational y)
    {
        numerator = x.numerator * y.numerator;
        denominator = x.denominator * y.denominator;
        makeRational();
        return this;
    }

    //-------------------------------------------------------------------

    public Rational divide(Rational x, Rational y)
    {
        numerator = x.numerator * y.denominator;
        denominator = x.denominator * y.numerator;
        makeRational();
        return this;
    }

    //-------------------------------------------------------------------
```

```
    public void printFraction()
    {
        if (denominator == 1)
            IO.screen.println(numerator);
        else
            IO.screen.println(numerator + "/" + denominator);
    }

    //------------------------------------------------------------------

    public boolean equals(Rational x)
    {
        return ((this.numerator == x.numerator) &&
                (this.denominator == x.denominator));
    }

    //------------------------------------------------------------------


    public Rational copy()
    {
        Rational temporary = new Rational(this.numerator, this.denominator);

        return temporary;
    }
    //------------------------------------------------------------------

}

class Ex_1
{
    public static void main(String[] args) throws IOException
    {
        Rational a = new Rational(-8,3);
        Rational b = new Rational(9,4);
        Rational c = new Rational();
        Rational d;

        IO.screen.print("a="); a.printFraction();
        IO.screen.print("b="); b.printFraction();

        IO.screen.print("a+b="); c.add(a,b).printFraction();
        IO.screen.print("a-b="); c.subtract(a,b).printFraction();
        IO.screen.print("a*b="); c.multiply(a,b).printFraction();
        IO.screen.print("a/b="); c.divide(a,b).printFraction();

        d=a.copy();
        IO.screen.print("d="); d.printFraction();

        if (d.equals(a)) IO.screen.println("Both d and a are equal");
    }
}
```

Test results

```
a=-8/3
b=9/4
a+b=-5/12
a-b=-59/12
a*b=-6
a/b=-32/27
d=-8/3
Both d and a are equal
```

7.5 Garbage Collection and Object Finalization

Java contains an automatic garbage collector, consequently there are no special methods set aside for the destruction of objects and reclamation of memory to the heap when the objects are no longer required.

The Java interpreter knows which objects it has allocated and which objects it can return to the heap. When you instantiate an object you not only get an allocation of memory from the heap, but a hidden reference counter. The counter is automatically incremented every time the object is assigned a reference. Whenever a reference to an object goes out of scope the counter is automatically decremented. Any object with a reference count of zero is a candidate for being destroyed and it's memory returned to the heap.

Java performs garbage collection as follows.

- When the amount of memory remaining in the heap falls below a predetermined level.

- When you specifically ask for garbage collection by calling **System.gc()**.

- Whenever the Java system has time. Generally, the garbage collector is executed when the system is idle waiting for user input.

Although garbage collection automatically frees up the memory resources used by objects it cannot free up other resources that an object may hold, for example closing an input stream.

Java provides a special instance method to deal with this situation. The method must be named **finalize()**, it takes no arguments and returns no value, and is automatically called before an object is returned to the heap.

The following points should be kept in mind when dealing with finalizers.

- A method finalizer is automatically invoked before garbage collection of the object. There is no requirement to explicitly invoke the finalizer.

- There is no guarantee that a finalizer will be invoked (if the program terminates prematurely), or what order finalizers will be invoked (if there are several).

7.6 Using Classes to Mimic Record Structures

In order to treat a collection of different data types as a single entity, we need to introduce the concept of a record. A **record** is a collection of one or more members, which may be of different types, grouped together under a single name. Each member is known as a **field** within the record.

Figure 7.4 illustrates the concept of a record containing four fields representing the name of a person, and the birthday of that person as month, day and year.

Jane	10	11	1953
name	month	day	year

Figure 7.4 A record containing four fields

Java does not support the concept of a record structure. However, it is possible to mimic a record, since a class structure may only contain class variables. The record illustrated in figure 7.4 may be represented by the following class.

```
class Record
{
    String    name;
    int       month;
    int       day;
    int       year;
}
```

An object of type `Record` can be instantiated as follows, and is depicted in figure 7.5.

```
Record birthday = new Record();
```

Note the constructor is taken to be the **default** constructor supplied by Java. This will initialize strings to `null`, and numbers to zero.

> ℹ️ If you do not define a constructor for a class, Java defines a default constructor for you. The default constructor takes no arguments and initializes the class's variables. Primitive type numeric variables are initialized to 0, boolean variables to `false` and references to `null`.

Data may be assigned to the individual fields of the record using the dot notation to access the field.

```
birthday.name  = "Jane";
birthday.month = 10;
birthday.day   = 11;
birthday.year  = 1953;
```

The assignment of data to fields of the record is also depicted in figure 7.5.

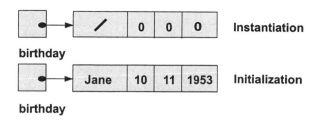

Figure 7.5 Instantiation of a record and assignment of fields

Similarly the contents of any field can be displayed by using the name of the record object, followed by the name of the field, separated by a dot.

For example, `screen.println(birthday.name);` will display the name **Jane**.

In Chapter 5 we noted that the contents of all the cells in a one-dimensional array must be of the same data type. In other words, an array can contain all integers, all reals, all characters, or all the same object references, but not a mixture of each type. This statement is perfectly true; however, it does not preclude a mixture of data types being stored in each cell of an array provided the types come under the umbrella of a record. Strictly speaking, since the records are treated as objects, the array must contain references in each cell to the record objects. Figure 7.6 illustrates five references to records being stored in a one-dimensional array, where each record is an object and has the format described earlier in this section.

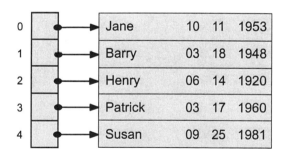

Figure 7.6 An array of records

Program Example 7.1 will allow a user to input the name and date of birth of a person at the keyboard. This information is then stored as a record in a one-dimensional array. When all the data has been input, the program displays the records from the array.

Encapsulation has not been used in Program Example 7.1, or Program Example 7.2 since the examples only serve to demonstrate how to create an array of records. Encapsulation, however, will be used in the Case Study: Student Examination Results.

Program Example 7.1: Storing Records in an Array

```java
// chap_7\Ex_2.java
// program to input fields of records at a keyboard
// and store the records in an array

import java.io.*;

class Record
{
    String name;
    int    month;
    int    day;
    int    year;
}

class Ex_2
{
    static BufferedReader keyboard = new
            BufferedReader(new InputStreamReader(System.in));
    static PrintWriter screen = new PrintWriter(System.out, true);

    // class method to create records and store the records in an array
    // and return the number of records stored
    static int createRecords(Record[] array) throws IOException
    {
        int index=0;
        String quit;
        do
        {
            Record birthday = new Record();
            screen.print("Name? "); screen.flush();
            birthday.name = keyboard.readLine();
            screen.print("Birthday month? "); screen.flush();
            birthday.month = new Integer(keyboard.readLine()).intValue();
            screen.print("         day? "); screen.flush();
            birthday.day = new Integer(keyboard.readLine()).intValue();
            screen.print("        year? "); screen.flush();
            birthday.year = new Integer(keyboard.readLine()).intValue();

            array[index] = birthday;
            index++;
            screen.print("Quit? - answer yes or no "); screen.flush();
            quit = keyboard.readLine().toUpperCase();
        } while (quit.equals("NO"));

        return index;
    }

    static public void main(String[] args) throws IOException
    {
        final int SIZE_OF_ARRAY = 50; // default size of array

        Record[] birthday = new Record[SIZE_OF_ARRAY];
        int numberOfRecords = createRecords(birthday);
```

```
for (int index=0; index != numberOfRecords; index++)
{
    screen.println(birthday[index].name + "\t " +
            birthday[index].month + " " +
            birthday[index].day + " " +
            birthday[index].year);
    }
  }
}
```

Test results

```
Name? Jane
Birthday month? 10
        day? 11
        year? 1953
Quit? - answer yes or no no
Name? Barry
Birthday month? 3
        day? 18
        year? 1948
Quit? - answer yes or no no
Name? Henry
Birthday month? 6
        day? 14
        year? 1920
Quit? - answer yes or no no
Name? Patrick
Birthday month? 3
        day? 17
        year? 1960
Quit? - answer yes or no no
Name? Susan
Birthday month? 9
        day? 25
        year? 1981
Quit? - answer yes or no yes
Jane      10 11 1953
Barry      3 18 1948
Henry      6 14 1920
Patrick    3 17 1960
Susan      9 25 1981
```

7.7 Stream Tokenizing

Tokenizing was first introduced in Chapter 4, as a method of splitting up a line of text from a file into tokens. With stream tokenizing we read the contents of the entire stream token-by token, not individual lines token-by-token, until the end of the stream file is reached.

A `StreamTokenizer` takes an input stream and parses it into tokens, allowing the tokens to be read one at a time. In this example a token will be delimited by any white space character, however, the `StreamTokenizer` class will allow you to specify any characters as a token delimiters. You are advised to inspect the contents of the class `StreamTokenizer`, for your convenience an abridged version follows.

```
public class StreamTokenizer
{
    public static final int TT_EOF = -1;
    public static final int TT_EOL = '\n';
    public static final int TT_NUMBER = -2;
    public static final int TT_WORD = -3;
    public int ttype;
    public String sval;
    public double nval;
    public StreamTokenizer (InputStream in);
    public int nextToken() throws IOException;
    .
    .
    .
}
```

Basically the constructor for this class uses the character input stream Reader as an argument. This can be the keyboard stream or any defined file stream. For example,

```
FileReader file = new FileReader ("data.txt");
StreamTokenizer inputStream = new StreamTokenizer(file);
```

A token's type `ttype` is either `TT_EOF`, `TT_EOL`, `TT_NUMBER`, `TT_WORD`, or a nonnegative byte value that was the first byte of the token.

If the value of `ttype` is `TT_NUMBER`, then the value of `nval` is the numerical value of the number.

If the value of `ttype` is `TT_WORD` or a string quote character, then the value of `sval` is a string.

If the value of `ttype` is `TT_EOF`, then the end of the file (stream) has been reached.

A token from the `inputStream` is made available by using the instance method `nextToken()`, for example `inputStream.nextToken();`

The following code may be used to count the total number of tokens in a stream.

```
        numberOfTokens = 0;
        tokenType = inputStream.nextToken();
        while (tokenType != StreamTokenizer.TT_EOF)
        {
            numberOfTokens++;
            tokenType = inputStream.nextToken();
        }
```

A token is made available from the input stream; while the token is not the end of the stream file, the variable `numberOfTokens` is increased by 1, and another token is made available from the input stream. The process of increasing the number of token continues until the end of the stream is detected.

The contents of a stream may be split into the fields of a record and records written to a one-dimensional array. However, it is quite likely that we will not know the number of tokens in the stream file in advance, and therefore, we cannot specify the size of the array for storing the records.

You have two choices. You can either read the stream twice and use an array to store the records; or read the stream once and use a vector to store the records. If you make the first choice it will be necessary to count the number of tokens in the stream on the first reading. The one dimensional array can then be declared, knowing the number of tokens that exist in the stream and the number of tokens in a record. On the second reading you will build records from the tokens, and write the records to consecutive cells in the one-dimensional array.

If you make the second choice you will read the stream once, building records, and writing the records to consecutive cells in the vector. At the end of the file, to avoid wasting memory space, you could trim the size of the vector to the number of records stored.

The second choice is more appealing, since it offers an elegant and faster solution compared with the first choice. The code used to implement the second choice would be as follows.

```
// create a vector
Vector recordStore = new Vector();

tokenType = inputStream.nextToken();
while (tokenType != StreamTokenizer.TT_EOF)
{
   // create a birthday record to store in the vector
   birthday = new Record();

   // assign four tokens to the respective fields of a record
   birthday.name = inputStream.sval;       inputStream.nextToken();
   birthday.month=(int)inputStream.nval; inputStream.nextToken();
   birthday.day  =(int)inputStream.nval; inputStream.nextToken();
   birthday.year =(int)inputStream.nval;

   // write a record to the vector
   recordStore.addElement(birthday);
   tokenType = inputStream.nextToken();
}
```

Notice that within the while loop it is necessary to call the default constructor of the Record class for every record that is to be stored in the vector. This is to create an instance of the record prior to assigning the data to the fields of the record object. Also after each token has been assigned to a field of the record it is necessary to read the next token from the stream.

Program Example 7.2 reads data from a text file, stores the data as records in a vector, and displays the contents of the vector on the screen.

The contents of the text file used in this program is:

```
Jane 10 11 1953
Barry 3 18 1948
Henry 6 14 1920
Patrick 3 17 1960
Susan 9 25 1981
```

Program Example 7.2: Storing Records from a File in a Vector

```java
// chap_7\Ex_3.java
// program to read lines of text from a file and store the respective
// tokens on each line as fields of records in a vector

import java.io.*;
import java.util.*;

class Record
{
   String name;
   int    month;
   int    day;
   int    year;
}

class Ex_3
{
   static PrintWriter screen = new PrintWriter(System.out, true);

   static public void main(String[] args) throws IOException,
                                    FileNotFoundException
   {
      FileReader file = new FileReader ("a:\\chap_7\\birthday.txt");
      StreamTokenizer inputStream = new StreamTokenizer(file);

      Record birthday;
      int    tokenType;
      Vector recordStore = new Vector();

      tokenType = inputStream.nextToken();
      while (tokenType != StreamTokenizer.TT_EOF)
      {
         birthday = new Record();
         birthday.name = inputStream.sval;      inputStream.nextToken();
         birthday.month=(int)inputStream.nval; inputStream.nextToken();
         birthday.day  =(int)inputStream.nval; inputStream.nextToken();
         birthday.year =(int)inputStream.nval;
         recordStore.addElement(birthday);
         tokenType = inputStream.nextToken();
      }

      recordStore.trimToSize();
      int sizeOfVector = recordStore.size();

      // display fields of records stored in the vector
      for (int index=0; index != sizeOfVector; index++)
      {
         birthday = (Record) recordStore.elementAt(index);
```

```
        screen.println(birthday.name + "\t " +
                       birthday.month + " " +
                       birthday.day + " " +
                       birthday.year);
      }
    }
}
```

Test results

```
Jane      10 11 1953
Barry      3 18 1948
Henry      6 14 1920
Patrick    3 17 1960
Susan      9 25 1981
```

7.8 Inner Classes

Java will allow one class to be nested within another class. This feature is useful in encapsulation, since it allows you to incorporate a class definition of a record within the class that makes specific reference to the record type. A **member class** is just another class component, in the same way that both constants, variables and methods are also class components. The code within a member class can implicitly refer to any of the constants, variables and methods of its enclosing class. For example, a Birthday class may contain the Record class nested as a member class, together with an instance variables, a constructor and other methods of the Birthday class.

```
class Birthday
{
    class Record
    {
        private String name;
        private int    month;
        private int    day;
        private int    year;
    }

    // instance variable of the Birthday class initialized as an
    // object of the inner class Record, using the default constructor
    // of the class
    private Record person = new Record();

    // constructor of the Birthday class
    public Birthday(String firstName, int mm, int dd, int yy)
    {
        person.name  = firstName;
        person.month = mm;
        person.day   = dd;
        person.year  = yy;
    }
    .
    .
    .
}
```

Notice that in order to access the fields of the member class, it has been necessary to create an instance of the class `Record`. The instance of the member class may then be used in the enclosing class.

To create an object of type `Birthday`, is simply a matter of instantiating the appropriate variable. For example:

```
Birthday jane = new Birthday("Jane",10,11,1953);
```

> Every instance of a member class is internally associated with an instance of the class that defines or contains the member class. For example, within the instance of the class `Birthday`, we have an instance of the class `Record`.
>
> The methods of a member class may implicitly refer to the constants and variables defined within the member class, as well as those defined by any enclosing class, including private constants and variables of the enclosing classes.

Case Study: Student Examination Results

Problem. The results of students taking four examinations are stored as records in a text file. Each record in the file contains the following fields.

> id - a unique student number in the range 100 to 999;
> name - the name of a student (there could be other students with the same name in other records);
> results - the percentage marks in the four examinations.

Write a program to search for the record of a student using either the student id or student name as the key to the record; list the record for which the search was successful; and list all the student records.

Problem Analysis. The contents of the text file used in this problem is listed below.

```
100 Rankin.W 45 55 65 75
150 Jones.D 60 80 90 75
250 Smith.P 90 80 45 60
300 Davies.J 70 65 55 40
400 Smith.P 40 50 60 55
450 Adams.C 25 40 35 40
455 Collins.Z 55 87 43 20
501 Evans.M 65 75 70 95
525 Jones.D 45 80 75 55
550 Owens.H 45 55 65 70
```

The contents of the file is read and transferred to the vector illustrated in Figure 7.7. Since each record is an instantiation of the class `Record`, the array will contain references to the record objects.

The technique of reading the file using stream tokenizing, and storing the records in a vector is identical to the technique explained in section 7.7 and used in Program Example 7.2.

The results from each of the four examinations will be stored in a one-dimensional array within the `results` field of the record.

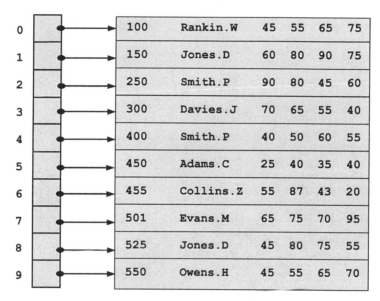

0	100	Rankin.W	45	55	65	75
1	150	Jones.D	60	80	90	75
2	250	Smith.P	90	80	45	60
3	300	Davies.J	70	65	55	40
4	400	Smith.P	40	50	60	55
5	450	Adams.C	25	40	35	40
6	455	Collins.Z	55	87	43	20
7	501	Evans.M	65	75	70	95
8	525	Jones.D	45	80	75	55
9	550	Owens.H	45	55	65	70

Figure 7.7 The contents of the vector

Analysis of Classes. A student record may be represented by the following class.

```
class Record
{
   int     id;              // unique student number
   String  name;            // student name
   int[]   results;         // examination results
}
```

A class is required that encapsulates the class `Record`, and contains methods to read the text file and build a vector of records; search the vector on either the id or the name of a student; display a student record and display all the records in the array. The public face of this class follows. Don't be fooled into thinking that the class only contains a constructor and four methods; there are other methods included in the implementation of the class `StudentRecords`. These other methods are out of sight of the user, since they assist only the visible methods and cannot be called directly from within a user's program.

Although the class `Record` will be nested as part of the `StudentRecords` class, it is not shown in the public face of the `StudentRecords` class.

```
class StudentRecords
{
    // constructor
    public StudentRecords(String filename) throws IOException;

    // instance methods
    public boolean searchId(int id);
    public boolean searchName(String name);
    public void displayAllRecords();
    public void displayStudentRecord();
}
```

where the methods have the following functionality.

`public StudentRecords(String filename)` - This is the only class constructor. The constructor will read all the records from the text file - `filename`; and store these records as objects being referenced from the vector.

`public boolean searchId(int id)` - will search the vector for a student record that matches the value of the student `id` passed as a formal parameter. If a match is found the method will assign the index value of the vector to the instance variable `positionInVector`, and return `true`; otherwise the method will reset the instance variable `positionInVector` to zero and return `false`.

`public boolean searchName(String name)` - will search the vector for a student record that matches the value of a student `name` passed as a formal parameter. If a match is found the method will assign the index value of the vector to the instance variable `positionInVector`, and assign the value index+1 to another instance variable `positionToSearch` and return `true`; otherwise the method will reset the instance variables `positionInVector` and `positionToSearch` to zero and return `false`. Since the name of a student is not guaranteed to be unique, it may be necessary to return to the `searchName` method after a name has been found, and continue to search the vector from the index position after the position of the previous match. This position is stored in the instance variable `positionToSearch`.

`public void displayAllRecords()` - will display all the records referenced by the vector, and display the average mark for each student record.

`public void displayStudentRecord()` - will display the individual record and average mark of a single student whose `id` or `name` has been searched for prior to this method being used.

The class constant and instance variables for the class `StudentRecords` follow.

```
// class constants
static final int NUMBER_OF_SUBJECTS = 4;

// instance variables
private int      positionInVector;
private int      positionToSearch = 0;
private int      sizeOfVector;
private Vector   recordStore = new Vector();
private Record   student;
```

Algorithm for the Constructor StudentRecords.

open file
get token
while token type is not end of file
       instantiate student record
       assign token to id field of record
       get next token
       assign token to name field of record
       allocate memory for results array
       for every subject
              get next token
              assign token to results array in field of record
       add record to vector
       get next token
trim vector to size
get size of vector
close file

Data Dictionary for Constructor StudentRecords. The constructor has one formal parameter, the name of the file. There are two local objects the `file` and the `inputStream`. There is a local `for` loop control variable `subject` to access the local array `results`, and a local integer variable `tokenType` for recording the data type of the token. There are three instance variables `sizeOfVector`, `recordStore` and `student` that are visible in this constructor. The signature of the method is:

```
public StudentRecords(String filename) throws IOException;
```

Desk Check of the constructor StudentRecords.   The test data will be the first two lines of the file.

```
100 Rankin.W 45 55 65 75
150 Jones.D 60 80 90 75
```

next token	100	Rankin.W	45	55	65	75
(token type not end of file)?	true					
student.id	100					
student.name		Rankin.W				
subject		0	1	2	3	4
(subject != NUMBER_OF_SUBJECTS)?		true	true	true	true	false
student.results[subject]		45	55	65	75	

next token	150	Jones.D	60	80	90	75
(token type not end of file)?	true					
student.id	150					
student.name		Jones.D				
subject		0	1	2	3	4
(subject != NUMBER_OF_SUBJECTS)?		true	true	true	true	false
student.results[subject]		60	80	90	75	

next token	TT_EOF
(token type not end of file)?	false

Algorithm for the Method searchId

for every record in the vector
  if id matches record id then
    assign index of record to position in vector
    return true
record not found - assign zero to position in vector and return false

Data Dictionary for Method searchId. The method has one formal parameter, the student `id` on which to search the vector. Since the instance variables `student` and `positionInVector` are both visible within any method in the class `StudentRecords`, there is no need to specifically pass these variables as parameters. There is a local variable `index` used to gain access to the vector. The signature for the method is:

```
public boolean searchId(int id);
```

Desk check of searchId. The test data for this desk check will be the vector depicted in Figure 7.7 and a student `id` of 400.

id	400				
index	0	1	2	3	4
student.id	100	150	250	300	400
(id==student.id)?	false	false	false	false	true
(index != sizeOfVector)?	true	true	true	true	
positionInVector					4

The method returns the value `true`. The instance variable `positionInVector` which is visible to all instance methods in the class `StudentRecords` indicates the position in the vector where the match of the `id` was found.

Algorithm for the method searchName

for every record in the vector starting at index value positionToSearch
        if name matches record name then
                assign index of record to position in vector
                assign index+1 to next positionToSearch
                return true
record not found - assign zero to position in vector and to positionToSearch, and return false

Data Dictionary for Method searchName. The method has one formal parameter, the name of a student on which to search the vector. The instance variables `student`, `positionInVector` and `positionToSearch` are all visible within this method. There is a local variable `index` used to gain access to the vector. The signature for the method is:

```
public boolean searchName(String name);
```

Desk Check of searchName. The test data for this desk check will be the vector illustrated in Figure 7.7 and the name Smith.P.

name	Smith.P		
index	0	1	2
student.name	Rankin.W	Jones.D	Smith.P
(name.equals(student.name))?	false	false	true
(index != sizeOfVector)?	true	true	
positionInVector			2
positionToSearch	0		3

The method returns the value `true`. The instance variable `positionInVector`, which is visible to all instance methods in the class `StudentRecords`, indicates the position in the vector where the match of the `name` was found.

Since there may be more than one entry in the vector for Smith.P the method should be repeatedly called until the end of the vector is encountered. The new position to start the search is given by the instance variable `positionToSearch`.

name	Smith.P	
index	3	4
student.name	Davies.J	Smith.P
(name.equals(student.name))?	false	true
(index != sizeOfVector)?	true	
positionInVector		4
positionToSearch	3	5

In the problem description it was stated that the average mark for a student would be output in addition to the details of a student record. Since the average mark will be displayed when either the method `displayAllRecords` or `displayStudentRecord` is called, it makes sense to introduce a method into the class to calculate and return the average mark for a particular student.

Algorithm for the method average.

set sum to zero
for every subject
        increase sum by result for particular student
return sum/number of subjects

Data Dictionary for the Method average. The method returns the average mark over the four examinations taken by a particular student. The method has one formal parameter, the `index` to the vector, that will enable access to be made to a particular record for a student. The vector is an instance variable, and is therefore visible within this method. The method contains a local variable `subject`, used as a `for` loop control variable to gain access the array `results`. The signature for the method is:

```
private int average(int index);
```

Desk Check for the method average. The value of the formal parameter is 3. This is the index to the array `students`. Refer to Figure 7.7 for the marks.

index	3				
sum	0	70	135	190	230
subject	0	1	2	3	4
(subject != NUMBER_OF_SUBJECTS)?	true	true	true	true	false
students[index].results[subject]	70	65	55	40	
sum/NUMBER_OF_SUBJECTS					57

The method returns the average of the marks as 57.

Algorithm for the method displayAllRecords

for every record in the array
        print the student id and student name
        for every subject
                print the marks awarded
        print average mark for student

Data Dictionary for the method displayAllRecords. This method does not have a formal parameter list. The method has access to the vector. There are two local variable `index` and `subject` used to gain access to the vector and array `results` respectively. The signature for the method is:

```
public void displayAllRecords();
```

Partial Desk Check of displayAllRecords. Desk check on the first two records in the vector, to show how access is made to the fields of a student record. Note average(index) is a call to the method `average`.

index	0				
student.id	100				
student.name	Rankin.W				
(index != sizeOfVector)?	true				
subject	0	1	2	3	4
student.results[subject]	45	55	65	75	
(subject != NUMBER_OF_SUBJECTS)?	true	true	true	true	false
average(index)				60	

index	1				
student.id	150				
student.name	Jones.D				
(index != sizeOfVector)?	true				
subject	0	1	2	3	4
student.results[subject]	60	80	90	75	
(subject != NUMBER_OF_SUBJECTS)?	true	true	true	true	false
average(index)				76	

Algorithm for the method displayStudentRecord.

print the student id and student name for a student specified by positionInVector
for every subject
        print the marks awarded for a student specified by positionInVector
print average mark for student

Data Dictionary for the method displayStudentRecord. This method does not have a formal parameter list. The method has access to the vector. There is one local variable `subject` used to gain access to the `results` for a student record specified by the index value `positionInVector`. The signature for the method is:

```
public void displayStudentRecord();
```

Desk Check of displayStudentRecord. Desk check on the record indexed by the value of `positionInVector` being 1. Note average(index) is a call to the method `average`.

positionInVector	1				
student.id	150				
student.name	Jones.D				
subject	0	1	2	3	4
student.results[subject]	60	80	90	75	

```
(subject !=
NUMBER_OF_SUBJECTS)?   true      true      true      true      false
average(index)                                                           76
```

Coding of the class StudentRecords

Note - the class IO has been included since the objects `keyboard` and `screen` are required by the class `StudentRecords`.

```java
class IO
{
   static BufferedReader keyboard = new
           BufferedReader(new InputStreamReader(System.in));
   static PrintWriter screen = new PrintWriter(System.out, true);
}

//-------------------------------------------------------------------

class StudentRecords
{
   class Record
   {
      private int    id;          // unique student number
      private String name;        // student name
      private int[]  results;     // examination results
   }

   // class constants
   static final int NUMBER_OF_SUBJECTS = 4;

   // instance variables
   private int    positionInVector;
   private int    positionToSearch = 0;
   private int    sizeOfVector;
   private Vector recordStore = new Vector();
   private Record student;

   //-------------------------------------------------------------------
   // method to return the average mark of a student
   private int average(int index)
   {
      int sum = 0;

      student = (Record) recordStore.elementAt(index);

      for (int subject=0; subject != NUMBER_OF_SUBJECTS; subject++)
      {
         sum = sum + student.results[subject];
      }

      return sum / NUMBER_OF_SUBJECTS;
   }
```

```
//-----------------------------------------------------------------
// constructor
public StudentRecords(String filename) throws IOException
{
    FileReader file = new FileReader (filename);
    StreamTokenizer inputStream = new StreamTokenizer(file);

    int tokenType;

    tokenType = inputStream.nextToken();
    while (tokenType != StreamTokenizer.TT_EOF)
    {
        student       = new Record();
        student.id    = (int)inputStream.nval;
        inputStream.nextToken();
        student.name  = inputStream.sval;
        student.results = new int[4];

        for (int subject=0; subject != NUMBER_OF_SUBJECTS; subject++)
        {
            inputStream.nextToken();
            student.results[subject]=(int)inputStream.nval;
        }

        recordStore.addElement(student);
        tokenType = inputStream.nextToken();
    }

    recordStore.trimToSize();
    sizeOfVector = recordStore.size();
    file.close();
}

//-----------------------------------------------------------------
// method to search the vector for a unique student id
// if found set positionInVector to the value of the index
// and return true, otherwise reset positionInVector to zero
// and return false
public boolean searchId(int id)

{
    for (int index=0; index != sizeOfVector; index++)
    {
        student =    (Record) recordStore.elementAt(index);

        if (id == student.id)
        {
            positionInVector = index;
            return true;
        }
    }

    positionInVector = 0;
    return false;
}
```

```
// method to search the Vector for a student name, if found set
// positionInVector and return true, if not found reset
// positionInVector to zero and return false
public boolean searchName(String name)

{
    for (int index=positionToSearch; index != sizeOfVector; index++)
    {
        student =    (Record) recordStore.elementAt(index);

        if (name.equals(student.name))
        {
            positionInVector = index;
            positionToSearch = index+1;
            return true;
        }
    }

    positionInVector = 0;
    positionToSearch = 0;
    return false;
}

//-------------------------------------------------------------------
// display every record in the vector
public void displayAllRecords()
{
    for (int index=0; index != sizeOfVector; index++)
    {
        student =    (Record) recordStore.elementAt(index);

        IO.screen.print(student.id + " " + student.name + " " + "\t");
        for (int subscript=0; subscript != 4; subscript++)
        {
            IO.screen.print(student.results[subscript] + " ");
        }

        IO.screen.println("\taverage " + average(index));
    }
}

//-------------------------------------------------------------------
// display details about a particular student whose position in
// the vector has been located
public void displayStudentRecord()
{
    student =    (Record) recordStore.elementAt(positionInVector);

    IO.screen.print(student.id + " " + student.name + " " + "\t");
    for (int subject=0; subject != 4; subject++)
    {
        IO.screen.print(student.results[subject] + " ");
    }

    IO.screen.println("\taverage " + average(positionInVector));
}
}
```

The Screen Layout Document illustrates the functionality of the program used to test the methods of the class `StudentRecords`.

As you can see from the Screen Layout Document the test program is a menu-driven program offering the user the option to list the contents of the vector of records; search the vector of records using a student id of your choice; search the vector of records using a student name of your choice or quit the system.

```
                    Screen Layout Document

12345678901234567890123456789012345678901234567890

Do you want to
[list] all the students
[id]   search on student id
[name] search on student name
[quit]
choose word? list
100 Rankin.W    45   55   65   75   average 60
150 Jones.D     60   80   90   75   average 76
250 Smith.P     90   80   45   60   average 68
300 Davies.J    70   65   55   40   average 57
525 Jones.D     45   80   75   55   average 63

Do you want to
[list] all the students
[id]   search on student id
[name] search on student name
[quit]
choose word? id
id? 300
300   Davies.J   70   65   55   40   average 57

Do you want to
[list] all the students
[id]   search on student id
[name] search on student name
[quit]
choose word? name
name? Jones.D
150   Jones.D    60   80   90   75   average 76
525   Jones.D    45   80   75   55   average 63
```

Algorithm for the test program main

1. initialize class StudentRecords
2. do
3.   get menu choice
4.   if choice equals list
5.   print all records in array
6.   else if choice equals id
7.   input id
8.   if id found
9.   display student details
10.   else if choice equals name
11.   input name
12.   while name found
13.   display student details
14. while choice not to quit

Data Dictionary for the test program main. This method takes one formal parameter, the name of the text file. There is one object of type `StudentRecords` - classOf1998. There are three local variables the menu choice, a student's id and a student's name.

Algorithm for the class method menu.

3. get menu choice
3.1 display a menu of the list of options available
3.2 do
3.3   input an option
3.3 while option not in menu
3.4 return menu choice

Data Dictionary for the method menu. The method requests the user to input a choice from the menu and returns the value of the choice made. The method contains one local string variable `choice`. The signature of the method is:

```
static String menu() throws IOException;
```

The reader is left to desk check the functionality of the `main` and `menu` methods in order to gain fuller understanding of this case study.

Coding for the test program.

```
// chap_7\Ex_4.java
// program to test the validity of the methods in the class StudentRecords

import java.io.*;
import java.util.*;
```

```
class IO {..}

class StudentRecords
{
   class Record {..}
}

class Ex_4
{
   static String menu() throws IOException
   {
      String choice;

      IO.screen.println("\nDo you want to");
      IO.screen.println("[list] all the students");
      IO.screen.println("[id]   search on student id");
      IO.screen.println("[name] search on student name");
      IO.screen.println("[quit]");

      do
      {
         IO.screen.print("choose word? "); IO.screen.flush();
         choice = IO.keyboard.readLine().toLowerCase();
      } while (! choice.equals("list") &&
               ! choice.equals("id") &&
               ! choice.equals("name") &&
               ! choice.equals("quit"));
      return choice;
   }

   //--------------------------------------------------------------

   public static void main(String[] args) throws IOException
   {
      String menuChoice;
      String name;
      int    id;

      // initialize class
      StudentRecords classOf1998 = new StudentRecords(args[0]);

      do
      {
         menuChoice = menu();
         if (menuChoice.equals("list"))
         {
            classOf1998.displayAllRecords();
         }
         else if (menuChoice.equals("id"))
         {
            IO.screen.print("id? "); IO.screen.flush();
            id = new Integer(IO.keyboard.readLine()).intValue();
            if (classOf1998.searchId(id))
               classOf1998.displayStudentRecord();
         }
         else if (menuChoice.equals("name"))
         {
```

```
        IO.screen.print("name? "); IO.screen.flush();
        name = IO.keyboard.readLine();
        while (classOf1998.searchName(name))
          classOf1998.displayStudentRecord();
    }
  } while (! menuChoice.equals("quit"));
  }
}
```

Test results - the command line parameter was: `java Ex_4 a:\\chap_7\\marks.txt`

```
Do you want to
[list] all the students
[id]   search on student id
[name] search on student name
[quit]
choose word? list
100 Rankin.W     45 55 65 75      average 60
150 Jones.D      60 80 90 75      average 76
250 Smith.P      90 80 45 60      average 68
300 Davies.J     70 65 55 40      average 57
400 Smith.P      40 50 60 55      average 51
450 Adams.C      25 40 35 40      average 35
455 Collins.Z    55 87 43 20      average 51
501 Evans.M      65 75 70 95      average 76
525 Jones.D      45 80 75 55      average 63
550 Owens.H      45 55 65 70      average 58

Do you want to
[list] all the students
[id]   search on student id
[name] search on student name
[quit]
choose word? id
id? 300
300 Davies.J     70 65 55 40      average 57

Do you want to
[list] all the students
[id]   search on student id
[name] search on student name
[quit]
choose word? name
name? Jones.D
150 Jones.D      60 80 90 75      average 76
525 Jones.D      45 80 75 55      average 63

Do you want to
[list] all the students
[id]   search on student id
[name] search on student name
[quit]
choose word? quit
```

ⓘ   The test program illustrates how the student records for a group of students are accessed. However, it is possible to redesign the test program to cater for many different groups of student records without the need to change any of the methods in the class `StudentRecords`.

7.9 Static Initializers

The initialization of instance variables is taken care of through the appropriate class constructor. However, what about the initialization of class variables and constants? The initialization of class variables and constants has already been dealt with. For example, within a class it would be permissible to use the following simple initializers.

```
class example
{
    static final int sizeOfArray = 10;

    static final String[] rainbow =
    {"red","orange","yellow","green","blue","indigo","violet"};
    .
    .
    .
}
```

But how do we initialize class variables, such as an array, when the values are not known in advance? The answer is to use a static initializer. A **static initializer** is a block of code preceded by the word keyword `static`. A static initializer is not like a class method. It does not have a name; it does not have a formal parameter list; it does not return a value and it is not called from another part of the program.

You may wonder how the static initializer can be executed if it cannot be called! When a class is loaded the static initializer is automatically executed by the system before the `main` method is executed.

A class may have a series of static initializers, one following the next in a sequence. In which case the system will execute all the static initializers in sequence before executing the `main` method.

Program Example 7.3 illustrates the use of a static initializer to initialize an array with random numbers prior to the `main` method being executed.

Program Example 7.3: Use of a Static Initializer.

```
// chap_7\Ex_5.java
// program to demonstrate a static initializer

import java.io.*;
```

```
class Ex_5
{
    static PrintWriter screen = new PrintWriter(System.out, true);

    static final int sizeOfArray = 10;
    static double[] array = new double[sizeOfArray];

    // static initializer
    static
    {
        for (int index=0; index != sizeOfArray; index++)
        {
            array[index] = Math.random();
        }
    }

    static public void main(String[] args) throws IOException
    {
        screen.println("Table of Random Numbers");
        for (int index=0; index != sizeOfArray; index++)
        {
            screen.println(array[index]);
        }
    }
}
```

Test results

```
Table of Random Numbers
0.4082992730307996
0.7329400147928526
0.1950353653382787
0.42112857304718987
0.6016363109271804
0.20688575170941825
0.2916584667878587
0.31193821758571394
0.6347151974075128
0.0837258206621444
```

7.10 Packages

You are already familiar with importing Java's standard API packages into a program, and using the classes defined in the packages. Java also permits the inclusion of user-defined packages. Therefore, it is possible to define a package containing the implementation of your own classes.

You must admit, the coding to input any data of a primitive type at the keyboard or display information on a screen, is far from straightforward when using the standard Java API. How better it would have been to have access to a class of methods that simplified keyboard input and screen output. The following definition of the class SimpleInput contains a number of methods to simplify the input of characters, integers, floating-point numbers and double precision numbers at the keyboard. The methods are defined using their respective signatures.

```
public class SimpleInput
{
    // method to input non white-space character at the keyboard
    public static char readChar() throws IOException;
    // method to input an integer at the keyboard
    public static int readInt() throws IOException;
    // method to input a floating point real at the keyboard
    public static float readFloat() throws IOException;
    // method to input a double precision real at the keyboard
    public static double readDouble() throws IOException;
}
```

The following definition of the class SimpleOutput contains a number of methods to simplify the output of strings, with and without a new line, and the output of a new line.

```
public class SimpleOutput
{
    // method to display a string
    public static void print(String parameter);
    // method to display a string followed by a new line
    public static void printLine(String parameter);
    // method to display a new line
    public static void newLine();
}
```

To include the implementation of the classes SimpleInput and SimpleOutput as part of the package simpleIO, it is necessary to use a **package** statement at the beginning of each file containing the implementation of the classes. The package statement must appear as the first non-comment, non-blank line in a Java source code file.

Java places each package in its own directory. The name of the directory is the same name as the package. Thus the simpleIO package is placed in the simpleIO directory. For example, when you reference the SimpleInput class, the Java system knows to look in the file simpleIO\SimpleInput.class for the byte code file.

Since Java is designed to be independent from any one environment, a CLASSPATH environmental variable is used to determine where to start looking for user-defined classes. CLASSPATH consists of a set of directory names.

> ⚠ Setting the CLASSPATH environmental variable will differ between a Windows environment and a UNIX environment, so you are recommended to consult the appropriate manual for the system you are using.

The implementation of the classes SimpleInput and SimpleOutput follow. Note the inclusion of package simpleIO at the beginning of each java source code file.

```java
// class SimpleInput contains the methods
// readChar
// readInt
// readFloat
// readDouble

package simpleIO;

import java.io.*;
import java.util.*;

public class SimpleInput
{
    static BufferedReader keyboard = new
            BufferedReader(new InputStreamReader(System.in));

    static final char NUL = '\u0000';

    // method to input a non white-space character at the keyboard
    public static char readChar() throws IOException
    {
        String data;

        StringTokenizer input = new StringTokenizer(keyboard.readLine());

        data = input.nextToken();

        if (data.length() == 1)
            return data.charAt(0);
        else
            return NUL;
    }

    //-----------------------------------------------------------------
    // method to input an integer at the keyboard
    public static int readInt() throws IOException
    {
        return new Integer(keyboard.readLine()).intValue();
    }

    //-----------------------------------------------------------------
    // method to input a floating point real at the keyboard
    public static float readFloat() throws IOException
    {
        return new Float(keyboard.readLine()).floatValue();
    }

    //-----------------------------------------------------------------
    // method to input a double precision real at the keyboard
    public static double readDouble() throws IOException

    {
        return new Double(keyboard.readLine()).doubleValue();
    }
}
```

```
// class SimpleOuput contains methods
// print
// printLine
// newLine

package simpleIO;

import java.io.*;

public class SimpleOutput
{
    static PrintWriter screen = new PrintWriter(System.out, true);

    // method to display a string
    public static void print(String parameter)
    {
        screen.print(parameter);
        screen.flush();
    }

    //------------------------------------------------------------------
    // method to display a string followed by a new line
    public static void printLine(String parameter)
    {
        screen.println(parameter);
    }

    //------------------------------------------------------------------
    // method to display a new line
    public static void newLine()
    {
        screen.println();
    }
}
```

Both java source files, `SimpleInput.java` and `SimpleOutput.java` are compiled in the normal way. Each compilation will produce a respective java byte class file that is stored in the subdirectory `simpleIO`.

Program Example 7.4 imports the classes `SimpleInput` and `SimpleOutput` from the package `simpleIO`, and uses the methods defined therein.

Program Example 7.4: Importing from the User-defined Package simpleIO

```java
// chap_7\Ex_6.java
// program to demonstrate the use of a user defined package

import java.io.*;
import simpleIO.*;

class Ex_6
{
    public static void main(String[] arg) throws IOException
    {
        char    character;
        int     wholeNumber;
        float   realNumber;
        double bigRealNumber;

        SimpleOutput.print("Character? ");
        character = SimpleInput.readChar();

        SimpleOutput.print("Integer number? ");
        wholeNumber = SimpleInput.readInt();

        SimpleOutput.print("Real number? ");
        realNumber = SimpleInput.readFloat();

        SimpleOutput.print("Double precision number? ");
        bigRealNumber = SimpleInput.readDouble();

        SimpleOutput.printLine("\n\nSummary of Input Data\n");
        SimpleOutput.printLine("Character = " + character);
        SimpleOutput.printLine("Integer number = " + wholeNumber);
        SimpleOutput.printLine("Real number = " + realNumber);
        SimpleOutput.printLine("Double precision number = " + bigRealNumber);
    }
}
```

Test results

```
Character? a
Integer number? 1234
Real number? 56.93
Double precision number? -1.2345E-45


Summary of Input Data

Character = a
Integer number = 1234
Real number = 56.93
Double precision number = -1.2345E-45
```

Summary

- Encapsulation is the grouping together of data and a set of methods to perform actions on data of that class type. An encapsulated group is called an abstract data type.

- Modifiers are used to alter the behavior of a class, method or variable. A `public` class is visible anywhere. A `public` method or variable is visible anywhere its class is visible. A `private` method or variable is only visible within its own class. Classes may not be `private`.

- A constructor is used to initialize an object with data. Every instance of a class is an object of the class. Every object has its own data set.

- Java supplies a default constructor that initializes the instance variables for every class.

- A programmer may write as many constructors for a class as necessary. This implies that the name of the constructor must be overloaded (the same name used again).

- The compiler distinguishes between different overloaded constructors and methods by the number and type of parameters in the formal parameter list.

- Java does not allow operator overloading except for the use of **+** for both numeric addition and string concatenation.

- The `this` keyword refers to the current object for which the instance method or constructor is called.

- If two objects are to be compared for equality, then a separate method must be created. The use of the **==** operator will only compare the references to the objects and not the instance variables of the objects.

- Similarly, if the instance variables of one object are to be assigned to another object, then a separate method must be created. The use of the = operator will only assign the value of the reference and not allocate extra memory for the instance variables to be replicated and assigned to an object.

- When an object has gone out of scope the automatic garbage collector will release the memory occupied by an object's data to the heap.

- A class may contain a finalizer method for the purpose of releasing other resources used by an object that are not dealt with by automatic garbage collection.

- A record is a collection of one or more fields, which may be of different types, grouped together under a single name. Java does not specify a record type, however, it may be simulated as a class containing no methods, only instance variables. The record must be instantiated as an object, normally by using a default constructor.

- Classes may be nested. Every instance of a member class is internally associated with an instance of the class that defines or contains the member class.

- The methods of a member class can implicitly refer to the fields defined within the member class, as well as those defined by any enclosing class, including private fields of the enclosing class.

- A static initializer is used to initialize a static variable in a class when simple initialization is not appropriate.

- The source code for a class may be headed by the keyword `package`. The `package` describes the subdirectory that is used to group classes that share a particular commonality.

Review Questions

1. What is an abstract data type?

2. True or false - data abstraction permits users to access data using their own methods.

3. True or false - a class may be defined as being `private`.

4. True or false - a `private` method or variable is only visible within its own class.

5. Why should instance methods be defined as `public`?

6. What is the purpose of the keyword `this`?

7. How many constructors may be defined in a class?

8. Can Java automatically define its own constructor for a class if one is not present?

9. How and when is the memory allocated to an object's data released to the heap?

10. True or false - constructors and methods may be overloaded.

11. True or false - all operators in Java may be overloaded.

12. True or false - the operator `==` is used to compare the instance data of two objects.

13. Why is it better to write a method to assign one object to another?

14. What is the purpose of the statement `System.gc()`?

15. True or false - all classes contain a `finalizer` method.

16. True or false - a finalizer method must be called from within an application program for it to be invoked.

17. What purpose does a default constructor serve?

18. Describe the meaning of three values of a token type, in the `StreamTokenizer` class.

19. What is the value and type of a numeric token, in the `StreamTokenizer` class?

20. What is a field?

21. True or false - a record is a recognized data type in Java.

22. True or false - a record may be represented as a class.

23. True or false - a static initializer will initialize all the instance variables of a class.

24. Can an inner class gain access to the constants and variables of the outer class?

25. How do you include your own classes in a package?

Exercises

26. Desk check the following program and determine what values are output for x.

```
class StaticTest
{
    private static int x = 0;

    public void increaseX() {x++;}

    public void printX() {screen.println("value of x is " + x);}
}
class Question_26
{
    public static void main(String[] args) throws IOException
    {
        StaticTest objectA = new StaticTest();
        StaticTest objectB = new StaticTest();

        objectA.printX();
        objectA.increaseX();
        objectA.printX();
        objectB.increaseX();
        objectB.printX();

    }
}
```

27. If the code in question 26 is changed, by deleting the modifier `static` in the declaration of the variable x; desk check the code again and determine what values of x are output.

28. Devise a method to test whether a rational number is greater than another rational number.

29. The following code is designed to set each cell in a five-element array to the date 1/1/2000 . Desk check the code. Will this code compile? What is the logical error?

```
class Date
{
    int month;
    int day;
    int year;
}

class Question_29
{
    {
        Date[] array = new Date[5];
        for (int index=0; index != 5; index++)
        {
            array[index].month = 1;
            array[index].day   = 1;
            array[index].year   = 2000;
        }
    }
}
```

30. Rewrite the code to question 29 so that it contains no errors, and represents a static initializer.

Programming Problems

31. Create a class `Circle` that contains the following methods.

```
class Circle
{
    // constructor
    public Circle(int radius);

    // instance methods
    // returns the circumference of a circle
    public float circumference();
    // returns the area of a circle
    public float area();
    // returns the volume of a sphere whose cross-section is a great circle
    public float sphericalVolume();
}
```

Write a program to test all the methods of the class.

32. Complete the `Birthday` class defined in section 7.8. Include a method to calculate and return the age of a person.

You will need to use the class `java.util.Calendar` to complete this question. The class method `getInstance()` will return an object containing the current date. The year, month and day may be obtained from the corresponding date field constants of the class `Calendar`.

33. Rewrite the add, subtract, multiply and divide methods of the class `Rational`, such that each method only takes one parameter. For example, the instance method add, is invoked using the syntax `a.add(b)`, where a and b are objects of type `Rational`. The `add` method adds together the rational numbers a and b and returns the sum. Use more complex expressions, such as `a.add(b.add(c))` when testing the newly written methods of the class `Rational`.

34. Create a class `VeryLargeInteger` class that contains the following methods.

```
class VeryLargeInteger
{
    // constructor
    public VeryLargeInteger(String value);

    // instance methods
    public VeryLargeInteger add(VeryLargeInteger A,VeryLargeInteger B);
    public VeryLargeInteger subtract(VeryLargeInteger A,VeryLargeInteger B);
    public boolean equals(VeryLargeIntegerA);
    public boolean isGreaterThan(VeryLargeInteger A);
    public boolean islessThan(VeryLargeInteger A);
    public boolean isNotZero();
    public displayNumber();
}
```

Write a program to create `VeryLargeInteger` variables, and demonstrate the instance methods of the class are correct.

35. A stack is a data structure that allows data to be inserted and removed from one end of the structure only. The stack is known as a Last In First Out (LIFO) structure. Create a `Stack` class that stores strings in the structure and contains the following methods.

```
class Stack
{
    // constructor
    public Stack(int sizeOfStack);

    // instance methods
    // insert an item at the top of the stack
    public void push(String item);
    // remove and return an item from the top of the stack
    public String pop();
    // return the item from the top of the stack but do not remove the item
    public String peek();
    // return the maximum number of items the stack can hold
    public int capacity();
    // return the number of items stored in the stack
    public int numberOfItems();
    // return true if the stack is empty, else return false
    public boolean isEmpty();
}
```

Use a one-dimensional array and a stack-top index as two instance variables of the stack (there could be others!). Write a program to test the instance methods of the class `Stack`.

Write a second program to input a sentence; push each word of the sentence on to a stack; remove each word from the stack and display the word until the stack is empty. The sentence should be displayed in reverse order.

36. Devise a class for the addition, subtraction, multiplication, and division of complex numbers. The class should also contain a method to display complex numbers.

A complex number has two parts (A, iB) where A is the real part, B is the imaginary part, and i = $\sqrt{-1}$. The following expressions show how arithmetic can be performed on two complex numbers, so that a real part R, and an imaginary I are evaluated.

addition
R = A.real + B.real
I = A.imaginary + B.imaginary

subtraction
R = A.real - B.real
I = A.imaginary - B.imaginary

multiplication
R = (A.real * B.real) - (A.imaginary * B.imaginary)
I = (A.real * B.imaginary) + (A.imaginary * B.real)

division
T = A * (B.real - B.imaginary)
N = (B.real)^2 - (B.imaginary)^2
R = T.real / N
I = T.imaginary / N

Write a program to test the instance methods in the class.

37. If floating-point computations are performed on amounts of money, inaccuracies can occur in the results. Devise a class `Money` that will cater for the addition, subtraction, multiplication and division of money. Include methods that replace the operations of ==, > and < on items of money. Also include a method to display an amount of money.

Write a program to test all the methods of the class `Money`.

38. Devise a class `CharacterString` that has the following methods.

```
class CharacterString
{
    // constructor
    public CharacterString(char[] value);

    // instance methods
    // return the length of a CharacterString
    public int length();
    // delete N characters from this string starting at the Ith character
    public CharacterString delete(int N, int I);
```

```
    // insert CharacterString A into this string, starting at position I
    public CharacterString insert(CharacterString A, int I);
    // remove substring A from this string
    public CharacterString remove(CharacterString A);
    // duplicate this string
    public CharacterString duplicate();
    // test this string with string A for equality
    public boolean equals(CharacterString A);
    // display this string
    public void display();
}
```

Write a program to test all the methods of the class CharacterString.

39. A computerized address book may be regarded as an object. Create a class AddressBook, that will allow for the initialization of the data in the book from a text file. The class must contain methods to allow the insertion and deletion of entries in the book; search the book on the name of a person; display the address of a person; and display the names and details of all those people whose surnames fall in the range of specified letters in the alphabet (e.g. names in the range B to H). Prior to the address book being closed, the contents of the data structure holding the names and addresses should be written back to the original file.

Write a program to create an address book object, and test all the methods of the class AddressBook.

40. Create a class Horologic that contains the following methods.

```
class Horologic
{
    // constructor
    public Horologic(); // initialize with the current time of day

    // instance methods
    // display the current time in a 24-hour format as hh:mm:ss
    public void display24();
    // display the current time in a 12-hour format as hh:mm followed by
    // either am or pm
    public void display12();
    // return the number of elapsed seconds since Midnight
    public int elapsedTime();
}
```

Write a program to test every method in the class Horologic. You will need to use the class java.util.Calendar to complete this question. The class method getInstance() will return an object containing the current time of day. The hours, minutes and seconds may be obtained from the corresponding time field constants of the class Calendar.

41. Figure 7.8 illustrates a data structure comprising two vectors; the first vector for storing references to the names of children in a school class and the second vector for storing references to the addresses of where the children live. The name of the first child, Lisa, is referenced at cell 0 of

the first vector. Lisa's address, 125 River View, is also referenced at the cell 0 of the second vector. Some children in the class have brothers and/or sisters in the same class. The data structure indicates that the siblings live at the same address. Lisa has a brother Eric, who also lives at 125 River View.

The class `SchoolChildren` uses a data structure of the type shown in Figure 7.8 for any school class.

```
class SchoolChildren
{
    // constructor to build the data structure from the contents of a file
    public SchoolChildren(String filename);
    // instance method to return the number of children in a school class
    public int numberOfChildren();
    // return true if childName has a sibling, else return false
    public boolean hasSibling(String childName);
    // display all the siblings for childName
    public void displaySiblings(String childName);
}
```

The class constructor should read pairs of strings containing the name of a child and the address of that child from a text file. All the names of the children will be stored in the child vector. An address that is read will be compared with the address strings that are already stored. If the address already exits in the structure, then the corresponding cell for that child must make reference to the cell that contains the address; otherwise, the new address string is stored in the structure.

Write a program to demonstrate the functionality of the constructor and instance methods for different school classes.

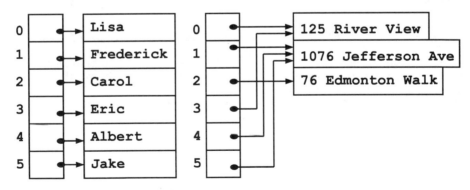

Figure 7.8 Structure of String objects

Chapter 8
Class Hierarchy

In the previous two chapters you were taught how to create your own classes. This chapter extends your knowledge of object-oriented programming by showing you how one class can inherit the characteristics of another class to build a hierarchical relationship between classes.

By the end of the chapter you should have an understanding of the following topics.

- The concepts of inheritance.

- Defining hierarchies of subclasses and superclasses.

- Using methods appropriate to a class through polymorphism.

- Using an abstract class to create a clearly defined and documented hierarchy.

- The creation and use of interfaces.

8.1 Inheritance

Figure 8.1 illustrates how different car models are derived from a fundamental concept of a vehicle. The concept of the vehicle is a blueprint of the generic car and specifies such features as four wheels, an engine, a transmission unit, and a saloon body shell. Different models of motor car can be derived from this concept of a vehicle, and each derivation incorporates a plan for a specific car such as a VW Beetle, Jaguar, or Rolls Royce. All three vehicles have inherited the characteristics of the generic car; that is to say, they all have four wheels, they all contain engines and transmission units, and they are all built with a saloon body shell. However, each particular model has a different set of four wheels, a different engine and transmission unit, and a different shape of body shell.

The concept or blueprint of the vehicle is the base class. The VW Beetle, Jaguar, and Rolls Royce all inherit characteristics from the base class and represent derived classes.

The cars themselves are the objects, since they are instances, created in the factory, of a particular model or class of car.

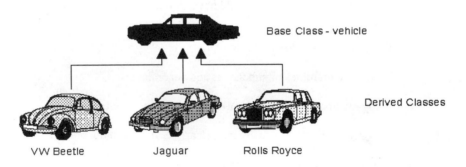

Figure 8.1 Base and derived classes

Figure 8.1 illustrates the class hierarchy between the base class vehicle and the derived classes VW Beetle, Jaguar, and Rolls Royce. By convention, the arrows in the figure always point from the derived class to the base class.

This example illustrates some of the fundamental features of inheritance.

Inheritance is the process by which one class receives the characteristics of another class.

The initial class is called the base or parent class; in Java this is known as the **superclass**. The receiving class is called the derived or child class; in Java this is known as the **subclass**.

What are the benefits of using inheritance?

- Inheritance increases the level of abstraction in a program.

- Inheritance improves the clarity in the design of classes, by allowing the implementation of methods to be postponed in superclasses and appear in subclasses.

- Inheritance increases your ability to reuse classes. Software can be extended by reusing many previously defined classes and adding new methods to the subclasses.

8.2 Example of Inheritance

Consider a class that describes a worker. The class should, at the very least, contain some form of reference to an individual worker. In the example to follow this will be the name of a person. As the example becomes more elaborated the class will contain such information as the number of hours per week the person worked, and the rate of pay of the person.

```
class Worker
{
    // instance variables
    protected String nameOfWorker;

    // constructor
    public Worker(String name)
    {
        nameOfWorker = name;
    }

    // instance method
    public String getName()
    {
        return nameOfWorker;
    }
}
```

Notice that the instance variable `nameOfWorker` is not declared as `private` but declared as `protected`. Normally variables are declared as `private` to prevent access from outside of the class. However, although `private` variables are inherited by subclass objects (in that each such object has its own copy of that variable with its own value), such variables cannot be accessed directly by the object itself, and can only be accessed through any protected or public access method of the superclass. A **protected** variable can be accessed from any method of any class in the same package.

The class is given a constructor for initializing the name of the worker, and an instance method to return the name of the worker. Another class, `Executive` may be defined that inherits all the characteristics of the class `Worker`.

The Java syntax for achieving inheritance follows.

 Inheritance: **class** *subclass-name* **extends** *superclass-name*

For example, the statement

```
class Executive extends Worker
```

permits all the variables and methods of the class `Worker` to be inherited by the class `Executive`. Failure to use inheritance would mean that all the variables and methods that are common to both a `Worker` and an `Executive` would need to be re-coded as part of the definition of the class `Executive`.

```
class Executive extends Worker
{
    public Executive(String name)
    {
        super(name);
    }
}
```

What has the class `Executive` inherited from the class `Worker`?

The answer is the variable `nameOfWorker` and the instance method `getName()`. Inheritance allows both the variable and the instance method to be used for objects of type `Executive` despite both the variable and method not being explicitly defined in this class.

Notice that a new constructor has been defined for the class `Executive` that includes the initialization of the name of an executive. The coding of the `Executive` constructor, has made use of the `Worker` constructor, by making specific reference to the constructor of the superclass through the reserved word **super**.

The `super` keyword, if present in a constructor, must always be the first statement in a constructor body.

In the following program, notice that the instance method `getName` has been invoked by an object of type `Executive`, even though the instance method was defined in the class `Worker`.

Program Example 8.1: Demonstration of Inheritance Between Worker and Executive Classes.

```
// chap_8\Ex_1.java
// demonstration of inheritance between worker
// and executive staff

import java.io.*;

class Worker
{
    // instance variables
    protected String nameOfWorker;
```

```
    // constructor
    public Worker(String name)
    {
        nameOfWorker = name;
    }

    // instance method
    public String getName()
    {
        return nameOfWorker;
    }
}

class Executive extends Worker
{
    public Executive(String name)
    {
        super(name);
    }
}

class Ex_1
{
    static PrintWriter screen = new PrintWriter(System.out,true);

    public static void main(String[] args)
    {
        Worker storeman = new Worker("Fred");
        Executive director = new Executive("Clive");

        screen.println(storeman.getName());
        screen.println(director.getName());
    }
}
```

Test results

```
Fred
Clive
```

When you construct an object of a subclass, the constructor for the superclass also gets invoked. Should you omit a call to the superclass constructor from your subclass constructor, Java will automatically insert this call for you. If the superclass does not contain a default (no argument) constructor, this will result in a compilation error.

Constructor calls are automatically chained. A sequence of constructor methods are invoked from subclass to superclass and eventually to the Object class. Because a superclass constructor is always invoked before the subclass constructor, the body of the Object constructor is executed first, followed by the execution of the bodies of the constructors down through the class hierarchy, and finally to the execution of the subclass constructor body.

Java is a strictly typed language. This implies that the compiler would never allow you to assign an object or primitive of one type to an object or primitive of a different type unless casting was permitted.

What about the assignment of objects within a hierarchy? What will the compiler allow? You may recall when one class inherits from another, an object of the subclass is also a legal superclass object. Therefore, assignment of objects within a hierarchy is possible as follows.

- Any object of a subclass can be assigned to an object of its superclass.

- The only superclass objects that can be assigned to a subclass-typed variable, even with an appropriate cast, are those superclass objects that are actually subclass objects.

Program Example 8.2: Demonstration of Object Assignment Over a Hierarchy.

```
// chap_8\Ex_2.java
// demonstration of object assignment over a hierarchy

import java.io.*;

class Worker {..}

class Executive extends Worker {..}

class Ex_2
{
    static PrintWriter screen = new PrintWriter(System.out,true);

    public static void main(String[] args)
    {
        Worker storeman;
        Executive salesDirector = new Executive("Clive");
        Executive marketingDirector;

        // any object of a subclass can be assigned to a superclass
        storeman = salesDirector;
        screen.println("Name of storeman "+storeman.getName());

        // any object of a superclass can be assigned
        // to a subclass with an appropriate cast
        marketingDirector = (Executive)storeman;
        screen.println("Name of marketing director "+
                        marketingDirector.getName());
    }
}
```

Test results

```
Name of storeman Clive
Name of marketing director Clive
```

8.3 Overriding Superclass Methods

A subclass may replace an inherited method from a superclass. When a subclass defines a method with the same name, return type and argument list as a method in a superclass, the superclass method is said to be **overridden**.

When the overridden method is invoked for an object of the class, the new definition of the method is called and not the old definition from the superclass.

> Overriding a method is not the same as overloading a method as discussed in Chapter 7. Overloading involves providing several methods with the same name, but having different formal parameter lists. In overriding, not only are the names of the methods the same, but the formal parameter lists of the overridden methods are also the same.

In Program Example 8.3, the classes Worker and Executive have gained more functionality. The Worker class now contains instance methods to setHoursWorked, setRateOfPay and calculate grossWage. The Executive class gains instance methods to setAnnualSalary and calculate grossWage. Notice the inherited instance method grossWage has been overridden in the Executive class.

The test program listed in class Ex_3, calculates and displays the gross wages for a person in the Worker class and a person in the Executive class.

Program Example 8.3: Program to Demonstrate Overriding Superclass Methods

```
// chap_8\Ex_3.java
// demonstration of overriding a superclass method

import java.io.*;

class Worker
{
   // instance variables
   protected String nameOfWorker;

   protected float hoursWorked;
   protected float rateOfPay;

   // constructor
   public Worker(String name)
   {
      nameOfWorker = name;
   }

   // instance methods
   public String getName()
   {
      return nameOfWorker;
   }
```

```java
   public void setHoursWorked(float hours)
   {
      hoursWorked = hours;
   }

   public void setRateOfPay(float rate)
   {
      rateOfPay = rate;
   }

   public float grossWage()
   {
      return hoursWorked * rateOfPay;
   }
}

class Executive extends Worker
{
   public Executive(String name)
   {
      super(name);
   }

   // instance variable
   protected float annualSalary;
   // instance methods
   public void setAnnualSalary(float salary)
   {
      annualSalary = salary;
   }

   public float grossWage()
   {
      return annualSalary/12.0f;
   }
}

class Ex_3
{
   static PrintWriter screen = new PrintWriter(System.out,true);

   public static void main(String[] args)
   {
      Worker storeman = new Worker("Fred");
      storeman.setHoursWorked(40.0f);
      storeman.setRateOfPay(10.0f);
      screen.println(storeman.getName()+" earns  $"+storeman.grossWage());
      Executive director = new Executive("Clive");
      director.setAnnualSalary(12000.0f);
      screen.println(director.getName()+" earns  $"+director.grossWage());
   }
}
```

Test results

```
Fred earns  $400.0
Clive earns  $1000.0
```

In Program Example 8.3 it is clear which version of `grossWage` is to be invoked by the type of the object being used in the call to the instance method. Thus `storeman.grossWage()` and `director.grossWage()` will invoke the methods for returning the gross wage of a worker and an executive respectively.

It is possible to make reference to the inherited method from a superclass, even when the method has been overridden in the subclass. The inherited method from the superclass can be invoked by using the keyword `super`. For example, in the class `Executive`, the inherited method `grossWage`, represents the gross wage for a `Worker`. The inherited method `grossWage` can be accessed by the statement `super.grossWage()`.

---

i   In Java finalizer methods are <u>not</u> automatically chained. If you have defined a `finalize()` method in a subclass, this may override a `finalize()` method in a superclass, and as a consequence the `finalize()` method in the superclass will never get called. To avoid this problem always include the statement **`super.finalize();`** as the last statement in the finalizer of the subclass.

8.4 Polymorphism

In the previous example, consider what would happen if we modified `class Ex_3` to include a class method that displayed the gross wage of a superclass object.

Program Example 8.4: An Example of Polymorphism.

```
// chap_8\Ex_4.java
// demonstration of overriding a superclass method

import java.io.*;

class Worker {..}

class Executive extends Worker {..}

class Ex_4
{
    static PrintWriter screen = new PrintWriter(System.out,true);

    static void displayGrossWage(Worker person)
    {
        screen.println(person.getName()+" earns  $"+person.grossWage());
    }

    public static void main(String[] args)
    {
        Worker storeman = new Worker("Fred");
        storeman.setHoursWorked(40.0f);
        storeman.setRateOfPay(10.0f);
```

```
        displayGrossWage(storeman);

        Executive director = new Executive("Clive");
        director.setAnnualSalary(12000.0f);

        displayGrossWage(director);
    }
}
```

Test results

```
Fred earns   $400.0
Clive earns   $1000.0
```

The modification has given the same set of numerical results for the gross wages of a worker and an executive as the previous example. You may wonder how this is possible when you examine the class method `displayGrossWage`?

The method `displayGrossWage` expects a formal parameter of a `Worker` object. Within the method it will display the gross wage of a `Worker` object. However, this method is called using an `Executive` object. How does the compiler know to use the correct `grossWage` method for the appropriate object? The answer is that the compiler doesn't know, and the decision on which `grossWage` method to use is postponed until run-time! **Dynamic method lookup** is a technique where each object has a table of its methods, and Java searches for the correct versions of any overridden methods at run-time.

ⓘ Dynamic method lookup is not as fast as invoking a method directly. Dynamic method lookup is not required for `static` or `private` methods and those methods and classes declared as **final**. A `final` method cannot be overridden and a `final` class cannot be extended.

Java's ability to decide amongst methods based on the run-time class is known as **polymorphism**.

Polymorphism is a way of giving a method one name that is shared up and down an object hierarchy, with each object in the hierarchy implementing the method in a way appropriate to itself. Polymorphism applies only to a specific set of methods. To write polymorphic classes we require two things.

- The classes must be part of the same inheritance hierarchy.

- The classes must support the same set of required methods.

8.5 Shadowed Variables

In section 8.3 we noticed that when the overridden method is invoked for an object of the class, the new definition of the method is called and not the old definition from the superclass. What happens if an inherited variable has the same name as a variable of the subclass? The variable of the subclass is said to **shadow** the inherited variable with the same name. The variable is visible in the superclass, yet the inherited variable cannot be accessed by the same name in the superclass. But what if you needed to use the inherited variable in the superclass, how can it be accessed? The answer is to use the reserved word `super`. For example, if class B is a subclass of class A, and both contain a variable named `common`.

```
class A
{
    protected int common;
        .
}

class B extends A
{
    // shadow the inherited variable common from class A
    protected int common;
        .
}
```

Then in class B the variable `common` may be referred to by either `common` or `this.common`. However, the inherited variable `common` is referred to by `super.common` or by `((A)this).common`.

Notice that the keyword `this` may be cast to refer to the appropriate class, in this case class A. This technique is useful if you want to refer to a variable in a class beyond the immediate superclass higher up the class hierarchy.

Although you may refer to shadowed variables by casting an object to the appropriate type, this technique cannot be used to refer to overridden methods. In Program Example 8.5 `objectB` has been cast to an object of class A and assigned to `objectA`. Despite the method `function()` being overridden in class B, `objectA.function()` does not invoke the original method in superclass A.

Program Example 8.5: Overriding is not Overshadowing

```
// chap_8\Ex_5.java

import java.io.*;

class A
{
    protected int X=2;
    public A(){}
    public int function(){return 2*X;}
}

class B extends A
{
    protected int X=3;
    public B(){}
    public int function(){return 3*X;}
}
```

```
class Ex_5
{
    static PrintWriter screen = new PrintWriter(System.out, true);

    static public void main(String[] args) throws IOException
    {
        A objectA;
        B objectB = new B();

        screen.println("X from class B "+objectB.X);
        screen.println("Value of function from class B
                        ="+objectB.function());

        objectA = (A)objectB;   // cast objectB to an instance of class A

        screen.println("\nYou may refer to shadowed variables by casting ");
        screen.println("an object of the appropriate type.");
        screen.println("X from class A "+objectA.X);
        screen.println("\nYou cannot refer to overriden methods by casting");
        screen.println("an object to the appropriate type.");
        screen.println("Value of function is still from class B
                        ="+objectA.function());
    }
}
```

Results

```
X from class B 3
Value of function from class B =9

You may refer to shadowed variables by casting
an object of the appropriate type.
X from class A 2

You cannot refer to overriden methods by casting
an object to the appropriate type.
Value of function is still from class B =9
```

8.6 Abstract Methods and Classes

In constructing a hierarchy of relationships between various classes it is sometimes beneficial to include a class, normally at the top of the hierarchy, whose methods cannot be instantiated. The class acts as a blueprint for all subclasses, and as such can be extended to suit different classes within the taxonomy.

For example, in the java.io package, InputStream is an abstract class and the superclass of all input streams. The purpose of InputStream is to define the basic input methods that all input stream classes provide. InputStream is acting as a blueprint of all the basic input methods that should be inherited by input stream classes. These methods are then implemented in ways appropriate to each class. Figure 8.2 illustrates how the superclass InputStream extends to all the classes of the input streams.

An **abstract method** is defined by the method's signature and has no method body. An **abstract class** is a class that contains at least one abstract method. As a result, an abstract class <u>cannot</u> be instantiated since there would be no means of implementing the abstract method(s) within the class. When a class contains at least one abstract method the class is automatically taken to be abstract. However, not all the methods of an abstract class need be abstract. There can be a mixture of constructors, implemented methods and method signatures.

A subclass of an abstract class may be instantiated, provided the abstract methods of the abstract class are overridden and implemented in the subclass. If not all the abstract methods are implemented, the subclass must also remain abstract.

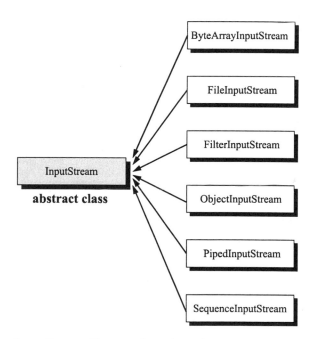

Figure 8.2 Input Stream Classes inherit from the InputStream Abstract Class

8.7 Is-a and has-a Relationships

With inheritance, you can describe **is-a** hierarchies representing many possible type variants.

We have seen from Figure 8.1 that a VW Beetle is-a vehicle; a Jaguar is-a vehicle and a Rolls Royce is-a vehicle. In Program Example 8.1 we can see that an Executive is-a Worker.

As a rule of thumb, in the is-a hierarchy we can say that inheritance is appropriate if every object of class Y may also be viewed as an object of class X. In Program Example 8.6, an abstract class RoundShape provides the superclass for the classes Circle and Sphere. We can say that a circle is-a round shape, and a sphere is-a round shape.

But the abstract class RoundShape contains an inner class Center. In considering the relationship between the class Center and the class RoundShape, it was <u>incorrect</u> to use an is-a relationship, since RoundShape is-not-a Center. For this reason class RoundShape did not inherit from class Center.

The **has-a** relationship describes that every object of a class X has-a set of attributes of type Y. In Program Example 8.6 it was correct to say that a RoundShape has-a Center, and therefore the class Center may be treated as an attribute of the class RoundShape.

The class RoundShape is an abstract class, and contains an abstract method to calculate the area of a round shape. This method is implemented in the class Circle as the area of a circle, and in class Sphere as the surface area of a sphere.

Program Example 8.6: Demonstration of Is-a and Has-a Relationships

```java
// chap_8\Ex_6.java
// program to demonstrate object assignment over a hierarchy

import java.io.*;

abstract class RoundShape
{
    // coordinates of center
    protected class Center
    {
        int x,y;
    }

    protected Center C = new Center();
    protected float radiusOfCircle;

    //-----------------------------------------------------------------
    // constructor
    public RoundShape(int xCenter, int yCenter, float radius)
    {
        C.x=xCenter;
        C.y=yCenter;
        radiusOfCircle = radius;
    }

    //-----------------------------------------------------------------
    // abstract method
    abstract public float area();
    //-----------------------------------------------------------------
}
```

```
class Circle extends RoundShape
{
    // constructor
    public Circle(int xCenter, int yCenter, float radius)
    {
        super(xCenter, yCenter, radius);
    }

    //-------------------------------------------------------------
    // return area of circle
    public float area()
    {
        return (float)(Math.PI*Math.pow((double)radiusOfCircle,2.0));
    }
    //-------------------------------------------------------------
}

class Sphere extends RoundShape
{
    // constructor
    public Sphere(int xCenter, int yCenter, float radius)
    {
        super(xCenter, yCenter, radius);
    }

    //-------------------------------------------------------------
    // return surface area of sphere
    public float area()
    {
        return (float)(4.0*Math.PI*Math.pow((double)radiusOfCircle,2.0));
    }
    //-------------------------------------------------------------
}

class Ex_6
{
    static PrintWriter screen = new PrintWriter(System.out,true);

    public static void main(String[] args)
    {
        Circle c = new Circle(5,5,2.5f);
        Sphere s = new Sphere(5,5,2.5f);

        // display details about the circles
        screen.println("Area of circle "+c.area());
        screen.println("Area of sphere "+s.area());
    }
}
```

Test results

```
Area of circle 19.634954
Area of sphere 78.53982
```

Case Study: Ships at Sea - An Example of Inheritance

Problem. A computer simulation is an imitation of the behavior of a system. This case study is a computer simulation of the movement of different types of ships at sea. In this example the course a ferry and a liner travel, over a predefined area, will be displayed. The information output when running the simulation will be the name, position, bearing and speed at a particular time in the simulation for each ship. To ascertain the movement of ships within a predefined area, the simulation time may be period of several hours. However, the time it takes the simulation program to run will be a second or two.

Problem Analysis. Figures 8.3 illustrates the properties of a ship, showing the common characteristics of the name, position [x,y], bearing, and current speed.

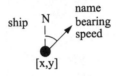

Figure 8.3 Representation of a ship

Figure 8.4 illustrates how a ship may be depicted within a predefined area. The figure shows the course sailed by the QEII (Queen Elizabeth II), on a bearing of 45 degrees, at a speed of 20 knots, over a time interval of one hour. The course plotted for the QEII, is from position [3,1] to position [17,15].

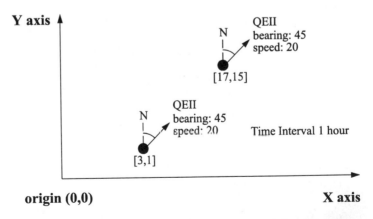

Figure 8.4 Movement of a ship over a predefined area

In simulating the course of a ship it is necessary to calculate the distance traveled by a ship over a set time. Figure 8.5 illustrates how the new position of a ship may be calculated knowing the distance traveled on a particular bearing. This calculation only returns the coordinates of the position as an integral value. The calculation does not take into account the effect of currents or winds.

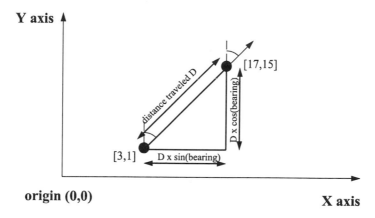

Figure 8.5 Calculation of the new position of a ship

From Figure 8.5, the distance traveled (in nautical miles) on a set bearing, is the product of the speed of the ship (in knots) and the time (in hours). The new coordinates of the position of the ship can then be calculated as $x_{new} = x_{old} + distance*sine(bearing)$; $y_{new} = y_{old} + distance*cosine(bearing)$.

Analysis of Classes. A generic ship may be modeled as an object that has a name, and properties of position, bearing and speed. In addition to the class constructors, this class will contain methods to retrieve the data associated with a ship, calculate the new position of the ship after a time period, alter course and change the speed of the ship. Apart from getting the maximum speed of a ship and changing the speed, which rely upon the particular properties of a specific type of ship, all the other methods are common to any ship. For this reason the methods changeSpeed and getMaxSpeed will be defined as an abstract method in the ship class, thus making the class ship abstract. Since the data and methods belonging to the ship class are common to all ships, the abstract ship class may be taken as the superclass of all vessels.

In the real world ferries and liners have vastly different properties - dimensions, tonnage, stopping distance, acceleration, maximum speed, turning area, and so on. In this simulation we will distinguish a ferry from a liner by different maximum speeds only. Both Ferry and Liner subclasses will inherit the characteristics of the abstract superclass Ship as depicted in Figure 8.6. However, both the Ferry and Liner classes must contain a method to implement the changeSpeed method defined as being abstract in the superclass.

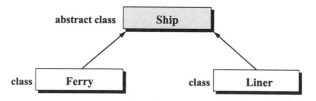

Figure 8.6 Class Hierarchy

A class `Ship` may be defined as follows.

```
abstract class Ship
{
    // constructors
    public Ship();
    public Ship(String id, int X, int Y, int direction, int initialSpeed);

    // instance methods
    public String getName();
    public int    getX();
    public int    getY();
    public int    getDirection();
    public int    getSpeed();
    public void   changeCourse(int newDirection);
    public void   calculateNewPosition(int timeInterval);

    // abstract methods
    abstract public void changeSpeed(int newSpeed);
    abstract public int  getMaxSpeed();
}
```

Since the coding of this class is a trivial exercise, the author has omitted the normal stages of algorithm development for the methods in the class.

```
abstract class Ship
{
    // declaration of variables

    protected String name;          // name of ship
    protected int    x,y;           // coordinates of position
    protected int    bearing;       // compass bearing from North
    protected int    speed;         // speed of ship

    // constructors
    public Ship()
    {
        name = ""; x=0; y=0; bearing=0; speed=0;
    }
    public Ship(String id, int X, int Y, int direction, int initialSpeed)
    {
        name = id;
        x = X;
        y = Y;
        bearing = direction;
        speed = initialSpeed;
    }

    // instance methods
    public String getName(){return name;}
    public int    getX(){return x;}
    public int    getY(){return y;}
    public int    getDirection(){return bearing;}
    public int    getSpeed(){return speed;}
```

```
public void    changeCourse(int newDirection)
{
   bearing = newDirection;
}

public void    calculateNewPosition(int timeInterval)
{
   double angle;
   double distance;

   // timeInterval is the number of elapsed minutes since
   // the previous distance was calculated
   distance = speed * timeInterval / 60;
   angle = ((double)bearing * Math.PI / 180.0);

   // calculate new position
   x = x + (int)(distance * Math.sin(angle));
   y = y + (int)(distance * Math.cos(angle));
}

// abstract methods
abstract public void changeSpeed(int newSpeed);
abstract public int  getMaxSpeed();
}
```

A new characteristic that distinguishes a `Ferry` from a `Liner` is the inclusion of the maximum speed of each vessel. In the implementation of the parametized constructor and abstract method `changeSpeed` in the classes `Ferry` and `Liner`, it is necessary to check that the maximum speed of the ship cannot be exceeded.

```
class Ferry extends Ship
{
   final static int maxSpeed = 25;

   public Ferry(){super();}
   public Ferry(String id, int X, int Y, int direction, int initialSpeed)
   {
      super(id, X, Y, direction, initialSpeed);
      if (initialSpeed > maxSpeed) this.speed = 0;
   }

   public void changeSpeed(int newSpeed)
   {
      if (newSpeed <= maxSpeed && newSpeed >= 0)
      {
         speed = newSpeed;
      }
   }

   public int getMaxSpeed(){return maxSpeed;}
}
```

```
class Liner extends Ship
{
    final static int maxSpeed = 45;

    public Liner(){super();}
    public Liner(String id, int X, int Y, int direction, int initialSpeed)
    {
        super(id, X, Y, direction, initialSpeed);
        if (initialSpeed > maxSpeed) this.speed = 0;
    }

    public void changeSpeed(int newSpeed)
    {
        if (newSpeed <= maxSpeed && newSpeed >= 0)
        {
            speed = newSpeed;
        }
    }

    public int getMaxSpeed(){return maxSpeed;}
}
```

The simulation is used to calculate the position, bearing and speed of a particular set of ships over a period of simulated time. Time is a suitable candidate for a class, and will contain the following constructors and methods.

```
class Time
{
    // constructor used to set the time interval between the movement
    // of the ships
    public Time(int interval);

    // instance methods
    // update increases the simulated time by the time interval
    public void update();

    // getHours will return the hour component of the simulated time
    public int getHours();

    // getMinutes will return the minute component of the simulated time
    public int getMinutes();

    // elapsedTime will return the number of simulated minutes since the
    // start of the simulation
    public int elapsedTime();
}
```

The class Time uses two instance variables to assist in recording the passing of time - a one-dimensional array to store the hours and minutes, and a primitive variable to store the time interval.

The implementation of the class `Time` follows. Once again the coding of this class is a trivial exercise, the author has omitted the normal stages of algorithm development for the methods in the class.

```
class Time
{
    // instance variables

    // the array time stores the hours in time[0] and the minutes in time[1]
    // both the hours and minutes are initialized to zero at the start of
    // the simulation
    private int[] time = {0,0};

    // the number of minutes the time must be updated, after the simulation
    // of a set of events, such as the ships moving to a new position
    private int    timeInterval;

    // constructor
    public Time(int interval)
    {
        timeInterval = interval;
    }

    // instance methods

    // increase the time by the time interval
    public void update()
    {
        time[1] = time[1]+timeInterval;
        if (time[1] >= 60)
        {
            time[0] = time[0] + (int)(time[1]/60);
            time[1] = time[1] % 60;
        }
    }

    // get the hours component of simulated time
    public int getHours()
    {
        return time[0];
    }

    // get the minutes component of simulated time
    public int getMinutes()
    {
        return time[1];
    }

    // return the number of minutes that have elapsed since the
    // start of the simulation
    public int elapsedTime()
    {
        return 60*time[0] + time[1];
    }
}
```

Algorithm for main method

1.	*do*
2.	*display data for ferry*
3.	*calculate new position of ferry*
4.	*display data for liner*
5.	*calculate new position for liner*
6.	*update simulation time*
7.	*while elapsed time less than or equal to half maximum simulation time*
8.	*change course of ferry*
9.	*change speed of liner*
10.	*do*
11.	*display data for ferry*
12.	*calculate new position of ferry*
13.	*display data for liner*
14.	*calculate new position for liner*
15.	*update simulation time*
16.	*while elapsed time less than or equal to maximum simulation time*

Data Dictionary for main method. The main method contains two constants; the maximum time the simulation is to run, and the time interval between the movement of the ships. In this implementation only two ships are represented, a ferry and a liner. A variable is also required to simulate the passing of time.

```
final int MAX_SIMULATION_TIME = 240;
final int TIME_INTERVAL = 30;

Ferry rollOnRollOff;
Liner queenElizabeth2;

Time simulationTime;
```

Desk Check for the main method.

Normally we would desk check the complete algorithm of the main method. However, this algorithm contains statements to display the data for the ferry and calculate the new position of the ferry. The same statements are also repeated for the liner. The desk check of the main method concentrates only on the calculation of the position of the ferry using the following test data.

The ship is a ferry named VIKING, at a current position of [40,50], on a bearing of 90º, at simulation time 2.00 and traveling at 20 knots. The maximum speed for a ferry is 25 knots. The bearing changes to 135º at the next time interval.

simulation time	2.00	2.30	3.00	3.30	4.00
name of ship	VIKING				
x	40	50	57	64	71
y	50	50	43	36	29
bearing	90	135			
speed	20				
max speed	25				
TIME_INTERVAL	30				
distance	10	10	10	10	10
angle	90.pi/180	135.pi/180	135.pi/180	135.pi/180	135.pi/180

Algorithm to display data for any ship.

1. display simulation time
2. display name of ship
3. display position
4. display bearing
5. display current speed and maximum speed

Data Dictionary for display data method. The method shipData requires two parameters, an object of type Ship and an object of type Time. Since Ship is a superclass, it is perfectly legal to pass subclass objects such as Ferry and Liner to this method. There are no local declarations in this method. The signature for the method is:

```
static void shipData(Ship object, Time time);
```

Screen Layout Document

```
12345678901234567890123456789012345678901234567890123456789 0

[2:0]    VIKING   Position: 40,50 Bearing:  90    Speed: 20[25]
[2:0]    QEII     Position: 32,32 Bearing:  45    Speed: 25[45]
[2:30]   VIKING   Position: 50,50 Bearing: 135    Speed: 20[25]
[2:30]   QEII     Position: 40,40 Bearing:  45    Speed: 40[45]
[3.0]    VIKING   Position: 57,43 Bearing: 135    Speed: 20[25]
[3.0]    QEII     Position: 54,54 Bearing:  45    Speed: 40[45]
```

Coding

```java
// chap_8\Ex_7.java

import java.io.*;

abstract class Ship {..}

class Ferry extends Ship {..}

class Liner extends Ship {..}

class Time {..}

class Ex_7
{
    static PrintWriter screen = new PrintWriter(System.out, true);

    static void shipData(Ship object, Time time)
    // method to display the data on any type of ship
    {
        screen.print("["+time.getHours()+":"+time.getMinutes()+"]");
        screen.print("\t"+object.getName());
        screen.print("\tPosition: "+object.getX()+","+object.getY());
        screen.print("\tBearing: "+object.getDirection());
        screen.print("\tSpeed: "+object.getSpeed());
        screen.print("["+object.getMaxSpeed()+"]\n");
        screen.flush();
    }

    static public void main(String[] args)
    {
        // simulation over 240 minutes
        final int MAX_SIMULATION_TIME = 240;
        // simulate movement every 30 minutes
        final int TIME_INTERVAL = 30;

        // instantiate ships
        // VIKING; x,y [0,50]; bearing 90; speed 20
        // QEII;   x,y [0,0];  bearing 45; speed 25
        Ferry rollOnRollOff = new Ferry("VIKING",0,50,90,20);
        Liner queenElizabeth2  = new Liner("QEII",0,0,45,25);

        // instantiate time
        Time simulationTime = new Time(TIME_INTERVAL);

        // display data on ships
        do
        {
            shipData(rollOnRollOff,simulationTime);
            rollOnRollOff.calculateNewPosition(TIME_INTERVAL);
            shipData(queenElizabeth2,simulationTime);
            queenElizabeth2.calculateNewPosition(TIME_INTERVAL);
            simulationTime.update();
        } while (simulationTime.elapsedTime() <= MAX_SIMULATION_TIME/2);

        // change course and speed of ships
```

```
        rollOnRollOff.changeCourse(135);
        queenElizabeth2.changeSpeed(40);

        // display data on ships
        do
        {
            shipData(rollOnRollOff,simulationTime);
            rollOnRollOff.calculateNewPosition(TIME_INTERVAL);
            shipData(queenElizabeth2,simulationTime);
            queenElizabeth2.calculateNewPosition(TIME_INTERVAL);
            simulationTime.update();
        } while (simulationTime.elapsedTime() <= MAX_SIMULATION_TIME);
    }
}
```

Test results

```
[0:0]    VIKING  Position: 0,50    Bearing: 90    Speed: 20[25]
[0:0]    QEII    Position: 0,0     Bearing: 45    Speed: 25[45]
[0:30]   VIKING  Position: 10,50   Bearing: 90    Speed: 20[25]
[0:30]   QEII    Position: 8,8     Bearing: 45    Speed: 25[45]
[1:0]    VIKING  Position: 20,50   Bearing: 90    Speed: 20[25]
[1:0]    QEII    Position: 16,16   Bearing: 45    Speed: 25[45]
[1:30]   VIKING  Position: 30,50   Bearing: 90    Speed: 20[25]
[1:30]   QEII    Position: 24,24   Bearing: 45    Speed: 25[45]
[2:0]    VIKING  Position: 40,50   Bearing: 90    Speed: 20[25]
[2:0]    QEII    Position: 32,32   Bearing: 45    Speed: 25[45]
[2:30]   VIKING  Position: 50,50   Bearing: 135   Speed: 20[25]
[2:30]   QEII    Position: 40,40   Bearing: 45    Speed: 40[45]
[3:0]    VIKING  Position: 57,43   Bearing: 135   Speed: 20[25]
[3:0]    QEII    Position: 54,54   Bearing: 45    Speed: 40[45]
[3:30]   VIKING  Position: 64,36   Bearing: 135   Speed: 20[25]
[3:30]   QEII    Position: 68,68   Bearing: 45    Speed: 40[45]
[4:0]    VIKING  Position: 71,29   Bearing: 135   Speed: 20[25]
[4:0]    QEII    Position: 82,82   Bearing: 45    Speed: 40[45]
```

Note. The notification of change in either the speed or direction of a ship is displayed in the next time interval. The effect of this change can only be monitored after the next time interval. For example, the ferry VIKING changed course on a bearing of 135 degrees at simulation time 2.30, however, the effect of this change on the position of the ferry is displayed at simulation time 3.0.

The previous example dealt with just two ships. However, it is possible to store Ship objects in an array, and process the contents of the array, as the following code illustrates. An array vessels has been created that points to objects of type Ship. The first cell vessels[0] points to a ferry; and the second and third cells vessels[1] and vessels[2] respectively, point to liners.

```
static public void main(String[] args)
{
    final int MAX_SIMULATION_TIME = 240;
    final int TIME_INTERVAL = 30;
    final int NUMBER_OF_SHIPS = 3;
```

```
// array to store ship objects
Ship[] vessels = new Ship[NUMBER_OF_SHIPS];

// instantiation of ship objects
vessels[0] = new Ferry("VIKING",0,50,90,20);
vessels[1] = new Liner("QEII",0,0,45,25);
vessels[2] = new Liner("Oriana",0,25,135,15);

// instantiate time
Time simulationTime = new Time(TIME_INTERVAL);

do
{
    for (int index=0; index != NUMBER_OF_SHIPS; index++)
    {
        shipData(vessels[index],simulationTime);
        vessels[index].calculateNewPosition(TIME_INTERVAL);
    }
    simulationTime.update();
} while (simulationTime.elapsedTime() <= MAX_SIMULATION_TIME/2);
}
```

Test results

```
[0:0]    VIKING   Position: 0,50    Bearing: 90     Speed: 20[25]
[0:0]    QEII     Position: 0,0     Bearing: 45     Speed: 25[45]
[0:0]    Oriana   Position: 0,25    Bearing: 135    Speed: 15[45]
[0:30]   VIKING   Position: 10,50   Bearing: 90     Speed: 20[25]
[0:30]   QEII     Position: 8,8     Bearing: 45     Speed: 25[45]
[0:30]   Oriana   Position: 4,21    Bearing: 135    Speed: 15[45]
[1:0]    VIKING   Position: 20,50   Bearing: 90     Speed: 20[25]
[1:0]    QEII     Position: 16,16   Bearing: 45     Speed: 25[45]
[1:0]    Oriana   Position: 8,17    Bearing: 135    Speed: 15[45]
[1:30]   VIKING   Position: 30,50   Bearing: 90     Speed: 20[25]
[1:30]   QEII     Position: 24,24   Bearing: 45     Speed: 25[45]
[1:30]   Oriana   Position: 12,13   Bearing: 135    Speed: 15[45]
[2:0]    VIKING   Position: 40,50   Bearing: 90     Speed: 20[25]
[2:0]    QEII     Position: 32,32   Bearing: 45     Speed: 25[45]
[2:0]    Oriana   Position: 16,9    Bearing: 135    Speed: 15[45]
```

8.8 Interfaces

Consider the following scenarios illustrated in Figure 8.7

Part (a) illustrates that several classes may inherit from a single class. Therefore, class B can extend A, and class C can extend A. However, part (b) reveals that a single class cannot inherit from more than one class. The ability of one class to inherit from more than one superclass is known as **multiple inheritance**, and is forbidden in Java. What if you have defined classes where you explicitly want to inherit the characteristics from more than one class?

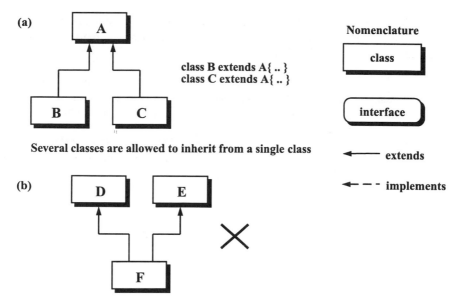

(a)

class B extends A{ .. }
class C extends A{ .. }

Several classes are allowed to inherit from a single class

Nomenclature

class

interface

◄─── extends

◄─ ─ ─ implements

(b)

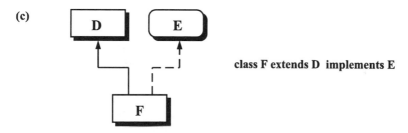

Multiple inhertiance of classes is FORBIDDEN in Java

(c)

class F extends D implements E

Class F is allowed to inherit from class D, and implement the abstract
methods defined in the interface E

(d)

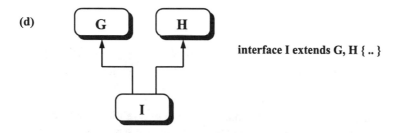

interface I extends G, H { .. }

Multiple inheritance of interfaces is allowed in Java

Figure 8.7 Inheritance - classes vs interfaces

The answer is to define an interface. An **interface** is a class that must contain only abstract methods and/or constants. The interface supplies a specification of methods and requires another class to implement the methods of the specification.

Part (c) illustrates that it is perfectly acceptable to extend class D (that is, inherit all the constants, variables, implemented constructors and implemented methods into class F), and inherit all the constants and abstract methods from class E with a view to implementing the methods from class E.

Java will permit multiple inheritance of interfaces, but not classes. In part (d) interface I has inherited all the abstract methods and constants from interfaces G and H. However, it is still necessary for a class to implement all the inherited abstract methods from G and H.

Note - it is possible for an interface not to contain any methods or constants.

All Java classes are ultimately derived from the `Object` class. A partial listing of the class `Object` follows.

```
public class Object
{
    // constructor
    public Object();

    // public instance methods
    public boolean equals(Object obj);

    // protected instance methods
    protected Object clone() throws CloneNotSuportedException,
                                    OutOfmemoryError;
}
```

All subclasses that implement a method to test whether two distinct objects contain the same values (`equals`), and all subclasses that implement a method to make a copy of an object (`clone`), should override these methods from the `Object` class. The method `clone()` may only be used where those subclasses have implemented the `Cloneable` interface. The `Cloneable` interface is a `public` interface found in the `java.lang` package and contains no methods.

```
public interface Cloneable{}
```

The interface simply indicates that the class that implements it may be cloned (copied) by calling the `Object` method `clone()`. Calling `clone()` for an object that does not implement this interface causes a `CloneNotSupportedException` to be thrown.

You may recall from the previous chapter, the implementation of a class `Rational`. This class contained methods for comparing two rational numbers for equality `equals(Rational x)`, and copying a rational number `clone()`.

The class `Rational` may be rewritten taking into account the inheritance of the methods `equals` and `clone` from the class `Object`. Both inherited methods are overridden, and the class must also implement the `Cloneable` interface.

```
class Rational extends Object implements Cloneable
{
    public boolean equals(Rational x)
    {
        return ((this.numerator == x.numerator) &&
                (this.denominator == x.denominator));
    }

    public Object clone()
    {
        Object temporary = new Rational(this.numerator, this.denominator);

        return temporary;
    }
}
```

> Since all classes are derived from the class `Object`, it is not strictly necessary to state that a subclass extends the `Object` class.

Notice the use of the keyword **implements** in the first line of the definition of the class Rational. The keyword `implements` is used to show which class intends to implement the `interface`.

Objects of type `Rational` can then be copied and compared for equality as follows.

```
Rational a = new Rational(1,2);
Rational b;

// copying an object
b = (Rational)a.clone();

// testing two objects for equality
if (a.equals(b))
```

Because `a.clone()` returns an object of type `Object`, it is necessary to cast the returned value before the assignment can be made.

> Interfaces are a data type, in the same way that classes are a data type. When a class implements an interface, instances of that class can be assigned to variables of the interface type.

Case Study: Sorting - An Example of the Use of an Interface

Problem. Often we have the need to order into sequence, sets of related data. For example, sets of names into alphabetic order, or sets of numbers into either ascending or descending numerical order. There are many algorithms used to sort data. Some algorithms are very efficient at sorting large quantities of data quickly; other algorithms are not so efficient, however, they are simple to write and understand, and can cope with sorting small amounts of data in a reasonable time.

Regardless of the algorithm being used, there will be a need to compare two items of data and determine which is the largest. The Java coding of this comparison will depend upon the type of data being sorted. For example, if two items of data A and B are numerical, then the comparison A>B will hold for all numerical types. However, if the two items of data are strings then a comparison using the > symbol is illegal and the instance method `compareTo` from the `String` class must be used. The need to use two different statements for comparing numerical data and string data implies that two different versions of the same algorithm must be coded.

This problem can be solved by introducing a general method to compare any data, and use this method in the sorting algorithm.

Problem Analysis. The `boolean` method `isGreaterThan`, used to compare data of any type, is specified in the interface `AnyType`. Classes `IntegerType` and `StringType` both inherit and implement the methods `isGreaterThan` in a way appropriate to the respective class. By specifying data of `AnyType` within the sorting algorithm, dynamic look-up will guarantee that the appropriate `isGreaterThan` method will be used when sorting data. Hence the sorting algorithm need only be coded once regardless of the type of data being sorted. The hierarchy diagram for the interface and supporting classes is illustrated in Figure 8.8.

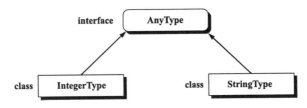

Figure 8.8 Hierarchy between interface and classes

The sorting algorithm being considered in this example is the Bubble Sort. This algorithm is inefficient and only applicable for sorting small quantities of data. However, the algorithm is easy to understand and program. Efficient sorting algorithms will be explained towards the end of this book, in Chapter 12, Data Structures.

The data to be sorted is stored in a one-dimensional array. In the first example the data are strings, therefore, the cells of the array store the references to the strings and not the actual strings.

Figure 8.9 illustrates five words stored in a one-dimensional array

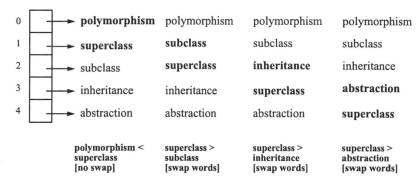

Figure 8.9 Illustration of the first pass in a Bubble Sort

On the first pass through the array, the word *polymorphism* is compared with *superclass*, since *polymorphism* is alphabetically less than *superclass* the two words are not exchanged. Next, *superclass* is compared with *subclass*, since *superclass* is alphabetically greater than *subclass* the two words are swapped over. The process is repeated again with *superclass* being compared with *inheritance*. Since *superclass* is alphabetically greater than *inheritance* the two words swap places in the array. Finally *superclass* is compared with *abstraction*. Once again *superclass* is alphabetically greater than *abstraction* and the two words are swapped. Alphabetically, the word *superclass* is now in its correct position in the array, with respect to the other words.

However, the words are not yet in the correct alphabetical order. The algorithm is repeated, but this time on the second pass through the array of words only four out of the five words need to be compared. We know that the word *superclass* is in its correct position, therefore, it is excluded from any further comparisons.

Figure 8.10 illustrates the movement of the words during the second, third and fourth passes through the array of words. Notice that on each subsequent pass through the array one word will appear in its correct position, therefore, the number of words to be compared must be reduced by one on the next pass. After four passes through the array of words, the words are sorted into alphabetical ascending order.

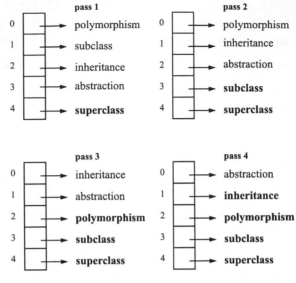

Figure 8.10 Subsequent passes in the Bubble Sort

Algorithm for the class method `bubbleSort`

for N-1 passes through the array (where N represents the number of items in the array)
    for each item in the array from cell 0 to cell N-number of passes
        if array element in current cell is greater than array element in next adjacent cell
            swap elements between adjacent cells

Data Dictionary for the class method `bubbleSort`. The method has one formal parameter the array to be sorted. The type for this array is defined by the interface as `AnyType`. Since items in the array may need to be swapped it is necessary to declare a local variable to temporarily store an item before it can be swapped. A local variable is also required to represent the number of items in the array. There will also be implicitly defined loop control variables `pass` and `index` to control the number of passes through the array and the position of each item in the array respectively. The method signature is:

```
public static void bubbleSort(AnyType[] array);
```

and local variables for the method

```
AnyType temporary;
int numberOfItems;
```

Desk Check of bubbleSort. The test data is identical to that shown in Figures 8.9. The desk check is performed on the first pass through the array.

temporary			superclass		superclass
numberOfItems	5				
pass	1				
index	0	1		2	
index != numberOfItems-pass?	true	true		true	
array[index]	polymorphism	superclass	subclass	superclass	inheritance
array[index+1]	superclass	subclass	superclass	inheritance	superclass
array[index] > array[index+1]?	false	true		true	

temporary		superclass	
numberOfItems	5		
pass	1		
index	3		4
index != numberOfItems-pass?	true		false
array[index]	superclass	abstraction	
array[index+1]	abstraction	superclass	
array[index] > array[index+1]?	true		

At the end of the desk check the largest item in the array, the word *superclass*, has been moved to the last cell (4). To continue the desk check, the value of the variable pass is increased to 2, and the desk check on the inner for loop is repeated. You are advised to continue the desk check to gain a fuller understanding of the algorithm.

Instance Methods.

Both classes IntegerType and StringType implement the method isGreaterThan from the interface AnyType. However, each class implements the method isGreaterThan on the assumption that the datum is either an integer or a string respectively. The coding of isGreaterThan from the class StringType follows.

```
public boolean isGreaterThan(AnyType object)
{
    return (this.word.compareTo(((StringType)object).word) > 0);
}
```

This is an instance method of the class StringType and is invoked in the Bubble Sort as follows.

```
if (array[index].isGreaterThan(array[index+1]))
```

where `array[index]` refers to an object of type `AnyType`. Notice that the method `isGreaterThan` has a single argument whose value is the adjacent object being compared `array[index+1]` and is also of type `AnyType`.

The object that invoked the method was `array[index]`, which, `this` refers to specifically. Therefore, `this.word` is the contents of `array[index]` and `object.word` is the contents of `array[index+1]`. Within the class `StringType` it is necessary to cast the parameter `object` to `StringType`. As mentioned earlier in the case study, strings can only be compared using the `compareTo` method from the class `String`.

Given the declaration `String a,b;` the statement `x=a.compareTo(b)` returns an integer value x. If x < 0, then string a is alphabetically less than string b; if x = 0, then strings a and b are identical; and if x > 0, then string a is alphabetically greater than b.

The statement `(this.word.compareTo(((StringType)object).word) > 0)` will equate to true if the contents of array[index] is greater than the contents of array[index+1], otherwise the statement will equate to false.

The class `PrintWriter` does not contain methods for printing objects of type `IntegerType` and `StringType`. If the values of the integer and string objects are to be printed, then it is also necessary to include methods to return an integer from an `IntegerType` and a string from a `StringType`.

Test Program.

To verify that the class method `bubbleSort` functions correctly for sorting both numbers and strings into ascending order it is necessary to include a program that initializes two arrays with appropriate test data, and displays the contents of the arrays before and after sorting. The program is straightforward to construct and is no more than a simple sequence of instructions.

A screen layout showing an example of the output from the test program follows.

Screen Layout Document

```
12345678901234567890123456789012345678901234567890

words before being sorted
polymorphism superclass subclass inheritance abstraction

words after being sorted
abstraction inheritance polymorphism subclass superclass
```

Coding

```
// chap_8\Ex_8.java
// program to illustrate a use for an interface
// when implementing a sorting algorithm

import java.io.*;

interface AnyType
{
    public boolean isGreaterThan(AnyType datum);
}

class IntegerType implements AnyType
{
    // this class implements an integer type
    private int number;

    // constructors
    IntegerType(){number = 0;}
    IntegerType(int i){number = i;}

    // implementation of isGreaterThan for integer comparison
    public boolean isGreaterThan(AnyType datum)
    {
        return (this.number > ((IntegerType)datum).number);
    }

    public int toInteger()
    {
        return number;
    }
}

class StringType implements AnyType
{
    // this class implements a string type
    private String word;

    // constructors
    StringType(){word = "";}
    StringType(String s){word = s;}

    // implementation of isGreaterThan for string comparison
    public boolean isGreaterThan(AnyType datum)
    {
        return (this.word.compareTo(((StringType)datum).word) > 0);
    }

    public String toString()
    {
        return word;
    }
}
```

```
class Sort
{
    public static void bubbleSort(AnyType[] array)
    {
        AnyType temporary;
        int numberOfItems = array.length;

        for (int pass=1; pass != numberOfItems; pass++)
        {
            for (int index=0; index != numberOfItems-pass; index++)
            {
                if (array[index].isGreaterThan(array[index+1]))
                {
                    temporary = array[index];
                    array[index] = array[index+1];
                    array[index+1] = temporary;
                }
            }
        }
    }
}

class Ex_8
{
    static final int ARRAY_SIZE = 5;
    static PrintWriter screen = new PrintWriter(System.out,true);

    public static void main(String[] args)
    {
        // initialize an array of five integers
        IntegerType[] numbers = new IntegerType[ARRAY_SIZE];

        numbers[0] = new IntegerType(70);
        numbers[1] = new IntegerType(91);
        numbers[2] = new IntegerType(-56);
        numbers[3] = new IntegerType(2);
        numbers[4] = new IntegerType(29);

        screen.println("numbers before being sorted");

        for (int index=0; index < ARRAY_SIZE; index++)
        {
            screen.print(numbers[index].toInteger()+"\t");
        }

        screen.println("\nnumbers after being sorted");

        Sort.bubbleSort(numbers);

        for (int index=0; index < ARRAY_SIZE; index++)
        {
            screen.print(numbers[index].toInteger()+"\t");
        }

        // initialize an array of five strings
        StringType[] words = new StringType[5];
```

```
words[0] = new StringType("polymorphism");
words[1] = new StringType("superclass");
words[2] = new StringType("subclass");
words[3] = new StringType("inheritance");
words[4] = new StringType("abstraction");

screen.println("\n\nwords before being sorted");

for (int index=0; index < ARRAY_SIZE; index++)
{
    screen.print(words[index].toString()+"\t");
}

screen.println("\nwords after being sorted");

Sort.bubbleSort(words);

for (int index=0; index < ARRAY_SIZE; index++)
{
    screen.print(words[index].toString()+"\t");
}
screen.println();
    }
}
```

Test results

```
numbers before being sorted
70        91        -56       2         29
numbers after being sorted
-56       2         29        70        91


words before being sorted
polymorphism      superclass        subclass          inheritance       abstraction

words after being sorted
abstraction       inheritance       polymorphism      subclass          superclass
```

Summary

- Inheritance is the process by which a subclass receives the data, class methods and instance methods from a superclass. In Java, a subclass may only inherit from one superclass; multiple class inheritance, where one subclass inherits from many superclasses, is forbidden.

- The keyword extends is used to define the subclass/ superclass relationship.

- Although private variables are inherited by subclass objects, such variables cannot be accessed directly by the object itself, and can only be accessed through any protected or public access method of the superclass.

- A `protected` variable can be accessed from any method of any class in the same package.

- The reserved word `super` may be used in different contexts.
     `super()` refers to the default, no argument constructor, of the superclass;
     `super` may also refer to parameterized constructors of the superclass;
     `super` may be used as a prefix to access inherited variables and inherited methods of a superclass in a subclass.

- Java will normally automatically call a superclass default constructor from a subclass constructor. If there is no explicit call to a default superclass constructor then Java will insert such a call. The absence of a superclass default constructor will result in a compilation error.

- Constructor calls within a class hierarchy are automatically chained. The sequence is always subclass to superclass to superclass .. object. The execution of the bodies of the constructors starts at the object constructor, followed by the superclass constructors, and finally the subclass constructor.

- An object of a subclass may be assigned to an object of its superclass.

- The only superclass objects that can be assigned to a subclass-typed variable, even with an appropriate cast, are those superclass objects that are actually subclass objects.

- A subclass may override an inherited method from a superclass. When the instance method is invoked by an object from the subclass, the overridden method is used and not the superclass method.

- Dynamic method lookup is a technique where each object has a table of its methods, and Java searches for the correct versions of any overridden methods at run-time.

- Java's ability to decide amongst methods based on the run-time class is known as polymorphism.

- Polymorphic methods must be part of the same inheritance hierarchy, and support the same set of required methods.

- An abstract class must contain at least one abstract method in addition to the declaration of variables, constructors, instance methods and class methods.

- An object cannot be instantiated from an abstract class. However, an object may be declared as being of abstract type.

- Abstract classes serve as a repository of variables and methods that are common to many classes lower down the class hierarchy.

- An interface may only contain constants and/or abstract methods. The interface supplies a specification that is inherited and implemented by a subclass. A subclass is allowed to inherit and implement from many interface classes.

Review Questions

1. In Figure 8.1 which class is the superclass?

2. True or false - a subclass inherits from a superclass.

3. Describe inheritance between classes.

4. True or false - a class can inherit a variable or method described as `private`.

5. Where can `protected` variables and methods be accessed?

6. Using the JDK API documentation what type of class is `OutputStream`?

7. Give two examples of the reserved word `super`.

8. When does Java insert a call to the default constructor of a superclass?

9. True or false - any object of a subclass can be assigned to a superclass.

10. True or false - any object of a superclass can be assigned to a subclass.

11. What do you call the existence of a method in a subclass with the same signature as a method in the superclass?

12. True or false - overloading and overriding a method is the same.

13. What is polymorphism?

14. Describe dynamic method lookup.

15. What methods do not use dynamic method lookup?

16. True or false - a final method may have a subclass.

17. True or false - a shadowed variable will prevent access to an inherited variable.

18. Describe how, in a subclass, you would refer to a variable that was defined far beyond the immediate superclass.

19. What is an abstract method?

20. True or false - an abstract class must contain at least one abstract method.

21. True or false - it is perfectly legal to instantiate an object of type abstract class.

22. In Figure 8.2 what is the reasoning behind defining `InputStream` as an abstract class?

23. True or false - several subclasses may inherit from one superclass.

24. True or false - a single subclass may inherit from several superclasses.

25. How does an interface differ from an abstract class?

26. What is the purpose of an interface? Give one example from the Java API where an interface is defined. State the rationale behind defining such an interface.

27. True or false - a single subclass may inherit from a single superclass, and also inherit from an interface.

28. True or false - a single subclass may inherit from any number of interfaces.

29. What is the Cloneable interface and why is it used?

30. True or false - when a class implements an interface, instances of that class can be assigned to variables of the interface type.

Exercises

Desk check the programs implemented in questions 31 through 35, stating the output in each case. Explain the principles why each program functions as it does.

31.

```
import java.io.*;

class A
{
    public A(){System.out.println("A");}
}

class B extends A
{
    public B(){System.out.println("B");}
}

class C extends B
{
    public C(){System.out.println("C");}
}
```

```
class Ans_31
{
    static public void main(String[] args)
    {
        C object = new C();
    }
}
```

32.

```
import java.io.*;

class A
{
    protected int X=25;

    public A(){}
}

class B extends A
{
    protected int X=35;

    public B(){}
}

class C extends B
{
    static PrintWriter screen = new PrintWriter(System.out,true);
    protected int X=45;

    public C(){}
    public void display()
    {
        screen.println("X in class C "+X);
        screen.println("X in class C "+this.X);
        screen.println("X in class B "+super.X);
        screen.println("X in class B "+((B)this).X);
        screen.println("X in class A "+((A)this).X);
    }
}

class Ans_32
{
    static public void main(String[] args)
    {
        C object = new C();
        object.display();
    }
}
```

33.

```java
import java.io.*;

class Output
{
    static PrintWriter screen = new PrintWriter(System.out,true);
}

class A
{
    protected int X=25;

    public A(){}
    public int getX(){return X;}
}

class B extends A
{
    protected int X=35;

    public B(){}
    public int getX()
    {
        Output.screen.println("value of X in class A "+super.getX());
        return X;
    }
}

class Ans_33
{
    static public void main(String[] args)
    {
        int X;
        B object = new B();

        X=object.getX();
        Output.screen.println("value of X in class B "+X);
    }
}
```

34.

```java
import java.io.*;

interface A
{
    static final int INTERFACE_CONSTANT = 65;
}

class B
{
    static final int CLASS_CONSTANT = 45;

    public B(){}
}
```

```
class C implements A
{
    static PrintWriter screen = new PrintWriter(System.out,true);

    public C(){}
    public void displayConstants()
    {
        screen.println("value of constant from interface A "+
                        INTERFACE_CONSTANT);
        screen.println("value of constant from class B "+
                    B.CLASS_CONSTANT);
    }
}

class Ans_34
{
    static public void main(String[] args)
    {
        C object = new C();

        object.displayConstants();
    }
}
```

35.

```
import java.io.*;

interface A
{
    static final int CONSTANT_A = 65;
}

interface B
{
    static final int CONSTANT_B = 75;
}


interface C extends A,B
{
    static final int CONSTANT_C = 85;
}

class D implements C
{
    static PrintWriter screen = new PrintWriter(System.out,true);

    public D(){}
    public void displayConstants()
    {

        screen.println("value of constant from interface A "+
                        CONSTANT_A);
        screen.println("value of constant from interface B "+
```

```
                        CONSTANT_B);
        screen.println("value of constant from interface C "+
                        CONSTANT_C);

    }
}

class Ans_35
{
    static public void main(String[] args)
    {
        D object = new D();

        object.displayConstants();
    }
}
```

Programming Problems

36. Devise a taxonomy of classes for two-dimensional shapes and three dimensional shapes. Implement your classes, and write a program to test each method within each class.

37. Employees in a company are divided into the classes `Employee`, `HourlyPaid`, `SalesCommissioned`, and `Executive` for the purpose of calculating their weekly wages or monthly salaries. The data to be maintained for each class may be summarized as follows:

`Employee` class	name of employee
`HourlyPaid` class	rate of pay
	total weekly hours worked
`SalesCommissioned` class	percentage commission on total sales
	total sales for month
`Executive` class	incremental point on annual salary scale

The methods used in each class may be summarized as follows.

`Employee` class	getName
	computePay - as an abstract method
`HourlyPaid` class	getRate
	getHours
	computePay
`SalesCommissioned` class	getPercentage
	getSales
	computePay
`Executive` class	getIncrement
	computePay

Note. To compute the monthly gross wage of an executive, it will be necessary to construct a one-dimensional array containing an increasing annual salary scale. each subscript to the array equates to an incremental point on the salary scale.

Implement the classes, and write a test program to verify that the classes function correctly.

38. Use the Case Study: Ships at Sea, as the basis to implementing the following scenario. Replace the ship by an airplane. In addition to the coordinates of the position of an airplane, include the height of the airplane. The characteristics of airplanes are shown in Figure 8.11

	Boeing 747	Concorde	LearJet	Tornado
Climb Rate	1400 fpm	3000 fpm	3000 fpm	2500 fpm
Cruising Speed*	490 knots	563 knots	440 knots	550 knots
Vortex Wake	heavy	heavy	light	small
Aircraft class	wide-bodied jet	super-sonic	jet	military jet

* Note this is only the subsonic cruising speed

Figure 8.11 Characteristics of Airplanes

In addition to the class airplane, include classes for a wide-bodied jet airliner, super-sonic airliner, light jet aircraft and a military jet.

Write a program that will simulate the movement of each type of airplane over a predefined airspace. Devise a display of the movement of each airplane in a similar manner to that used in the case study.

39. A city bank offers two different types of bank account. A savings account and a checking account. To distinguish a savings account from a checking account, the savings accounts are numbered from 000001, and checking accounts are numbered from 500000. Every time a new account is opened the system should generate a new unique account number.

Savings accounts charge no fee, provided the account contains a balance of more than $100, otherwise the account attracts an annual fee of $25.00. Savings accounts attract interest at the rate of 5% per annum.

Checking accounts pay no interest until the balance exceeds $2500. The interest is then 2.5% per annum. Checking accounts charge a fee of $1 for every transaction.

Devise appropriate classes for the different types of account. Include methods that you think appropriate for access and manipulation of data in an account.

Write a test program to verify that the classes have been implemented correctly.

40. A travel company arranges three different types of holidays - Cultural, Sports and Family. Each holiday can take place in one of many numerous global destinations staying at a range of popular-priced hotels or self-catering apartments.

Using the techniques of object-oriented programming you have learnt in this and previous chapters, devise a mini-system to allow clients to book holidays.

Chapter 9
Exception Handling

When designing computer programs it is necessary to cater for the possibility of the program failing owing to the occurrence of events at run-time.

Examples of such events might be attempting to open a file that does not exist; failure to detect the end of a file; trying to gain access to a cell of an array through a subscript that exceeds the permitted range; dividing a number by zero in an arithmetic computation; and so on. The list of events that can cause a program to malfunction is quite considerable!

The Java language incorporates the feature of exception handling, that when used, helps to reduce the probability of program malfunction and contributes towards the design and creation of safer computerized systems.

By the end of the chapter you should have an understanding of the following topics.

- The hierarchy of classes that support exception handling.

- Where in a program an exception is handled.

- The clauses `throw`, `try`, `catch` and `finally` used in exception handling.

- Multiple exceptions.

- Creating your own exception classes.

9.1 Introduction

An **exception** is an event occurring during the execution of a program that makes continuation impossible or undesirable. Examples of exceptions include division by zero, arithmetic overflow, array reference with index out of bounds and a fault condition on a peripheral. Many programming languages respond to an exception by aborting execution. However, one of the design goals of Java was to provide the language with sufficient features to enable the programmer to write robust programs. An **exception handler** is a piece of program code that is automatically invoked when an exception occurs. The exception handler can take appropriate remedial action, then either resume execution of the program (at the point where the exception occurred or elsewhere) or terminate the program in a controlled manner.

The purpose of exception handling is to allow a programmer to fix exceptions, particularly when the exception is caused by user errors (which are unavoidable). For example, when a file fails to open properly, the program could ask the user if they would prefer to enter the file name again, or quit the program. If this handler is put in an appropriate loop, the program can be made robust to multiple consecutive user errors.

A **fault-tolerant** computer system is capable of providing either full functionality or reduced functionality after a failure has occurred. Software fault tolerance may be provided using exception handling. A computer system that provides a reduced level of service in spite of the occurrence of at least one fault is said to be in a state of **graceful degradation**. Such techniques are of vital importance in the design and implementation of safety-critical computer systems where peoples lives may be put at risk by the malfunction of a computer control system.

On a less emotional note, you should remember that computer users make mistakes when using a computer system. A user may key in the wrong data, or supply data that is inappropriate to your system. To prevent your program from crashing you need to develop a mentality for defensive programming that relies upon exception handling.

An exception can be implicit, in which case it is a signal from the Java Virtual Machine to the program, indicating a violation of a semantic constraint of the Java language. For example, attempting to index outside the bounds of an array would automatically throw an *index out of bounds exception.*

An exception may also be explicitly thrown from within the program, to signal that an error condition exists. For example, if input data was only acceptable within a predefined range, then the program might throw an exception if data was found to lie outside of this range.

In both cases it is essential to grasp the concept that an exception is thrown and must eventually be caught. If you supply an exception handler then the exception may be dealt with in the program, otherwise, the Java interpreter will handle the exception by reporting on its cause and abandoning the program.

When inputting data from the keyboard, we have always adopted the technique of typing a string and converting the string, if necessary, to a value of the appropriate type. For example, integers and real numbers were always input as strings, and then converted to either `int`, `float` or `double` primitive data type. The method that permitted the input of a string was `readLine()` from the class `BufferedReader`. If you examine the signature of this method, you may notice that the method throws an `IOException`. Therefore, whenever `readLine()` was used in a method, such as `main`, it was necessary to state that the method `throws` an `IOException`, since there was no means of handling the exception within the method.

If a method throws an exception, then the exception has to be caught. In all the programs you have written, the Java interpreter has caught any exceptions that might have occurred. Within this chapter you will learn how to write Java code to catch exceptions.

9.2 Exception Classes

An exception is the occurrence of an event that happens when the program is running. An exception is generally an error condition that interrupts the normal execution of a program.

> An exception in Java is treated as an object that is an instance of the superclass `java.lang.Throwable` or an instance of one of its subclasses.

A partial listing of the class `Throwable` follows.

```
public class Throwable extends Object
{
    // Constructors
    public Throwable();
    public Throwable(String  message);

    // Methods
    public Throwable fillInStackTrace();
    public String getMessage();
    public void printStackTrace();
    public void printStackTrace(PrintWriter  s);
    public String toString();


}
```

The functionality of the constructors and methods will be discussed in the context of the program examples found in this chapter.

The superclass `Throwable` has two immediate subclasses, `Error` and `Exception`. Generally, the first of these classes `Error` is a superclass to classes that deal with errors that are generally unrecoverable, for example `VirtualMachineError` which includes such subclasses as `InternalError`, `OutOfMemoryError`, `StackOverflowError` and even `UnknownError`!

However, the second class `Exception` is the superclass to a number of subclasses that support exceptions which may be detected and ultimately recovered from.

Figure 9.1 illustrates a partial class hierarchy between the top level of exception handling classes. However, there are many subclasses of the superclasses `Error`, `Exception` and `RuntimeException`, that are not shown in Figure 9.1. For a complete list of these classes refer to the Java API documentation.

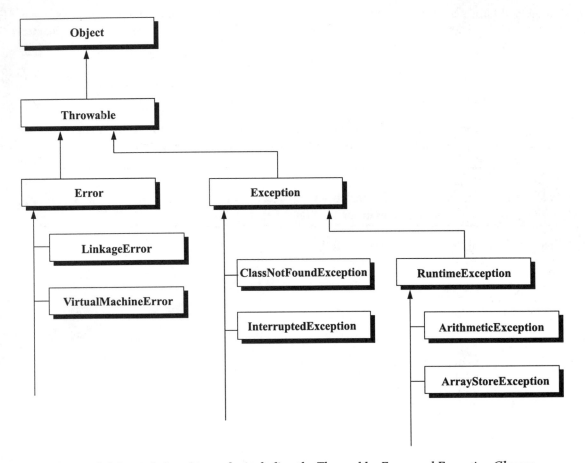

Figure 9.1 Partial class hierarchy including the Throwable, Error and Exception Classes

From Figure 9.1 it is clear that a number of exception classes exist that inherit from the superclass `Throwable`. The Java interpreter is capable of handling all the exceptions that may be generated. Unfortunately, the interpreter abandons the program after having warned of the exceptional condition. We need to be able to catch the exception within the program and handle it ourselves.

9.3 Catching an Exception

Program Example 9.1 illustrates what happens when an arithmetic exception is deliberately created. The test results show that the program has been run twice by the computer. On the first run, valid data was input and the result of the division displayed on the screen. However, on the second run a divisor of value zero was deliberately input to cause a run-time arithmetic exception to be thrown.

When using the `throws` clause, it is sufficient to state only the superclass of all the exceptions that may occur within a method. In Program Example 9.1, both an `ArithmeticException` and an `IOException` may occur. Since both exceptions are subclasses of the class `Exception` only the `Exception` class will be stated in the `throws` clause. Both exceptions are handled by the Java interpreter, to the extent that an error message is displayed and the program abandoned.

Program Example 9.1: The Creation of a Deliberate Arithmetic Exception

```
// chap_9\Ex_1.java
// program to demonstrate creating an exception
// and allowing the Java interpreter to handle it

import java.io.*;

class Ex_1
{
    static BufferedReader keyboard = new
            BufferedReader(new InputStreamReader(System.in));
    static PrintWriter screen = new PrintWriter(System.out,true);

    public static void main(String[] args) throws Exception
    {
        int dividend, divisor, quotient;

        screen.print("dividend? "); screen.flush();
        dividend = new Integer(keyboard.readLine()).intValue();
        screen.print("divisor? "); screen.flush();
        divisor  = new Integer(keyboard.readLine()).intValue();

        // possible arithmetic exception can be thrown
        // if divisor is zero
        quotient = dividend/divisor;
        screen.println("quotient = " + quotient);
    }
}
```

Test results from program being run twice

```
dividend? 25
divisor? 5
quotient = 5

dividend? 25
divisor? 0
java.lang.ArithmeticException: / by zero
        at Ex_1.main(Ex_1.java:24)
```

How can we incorporate into the `main` method, code that will handle the arithmetic exception? The answer is to use a catch block. A **catch** block contains a single parameter whose type is any class from the superclass `Throwable` down through the subclass in the hierarchy.

Catch Block: **catch(***exception-class object***){***statements***}**

The `catch` block is only entered, if an exception object is of the same type as the class stated by the parameter, or the exception object is an instantiation of a subclass of the parameter. For example, `catch(ArithmeticException ae){..}` will only allow an exception `ae` of the type `ArithmeticException` to be caught.

However, `catch(Exception e){..}` will allow an exception `e` of the type `Exception` or any type below `Exception` in the class hierarchy to be caught. Therefore if the exception object was of type `ArithmeticException`, which is a subclass of `Exception`, the exception will be caught.

The statements within the `catch` block may report on what caused the exception and take appropriate action to nullify the error (if appropriate). Since all the exception classes inherit from the class `Throwable`, these subclasses may use the methods defined in `Throwable` in the `catch` block to report on the error.

A **try** clause is used to delimit a block of code where the result of any method calls or other operations might cause an exception. To handle an exception a `try` clause must have at least one `catch` block.

Try Clause: **try** {*statements*}

Figure 9.2 illustrates the flow of control in a method that includes `try` and `catch` blocks, with and without an exception being raised. Where no exception is thrown the statements of the catch block are not executed. The computer by-passes the catch block and program execution resumes at the first statement that follows the end of the catch block (as long as it is not another catch block). However, where an exception is raised by a statement in the try block, the remaining statements in the try block are not executed. Control branches to the appropriate catch block that handles the exception and the statements of the catch block are executed. Control then passes to the next executable statement after the catch block (as long as it is not another catch block).

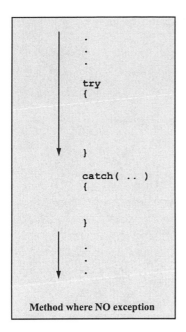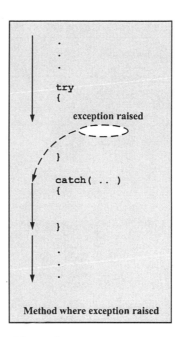

Figure 9.2 Flow of Control

Program Example 9.2, is a modified version of Program Example 9.1. In Program Example 9.2 a catch block has been coded into the `main` method to explicitly catch any arithmetic exception. Both the try block and the catch block have been embedded within a do..while loop controlled by a boolean variable. Only when valid data is input, will it be possible to exit from the loop.

This technique reinforces the point made earlier, that the purpose of exception handling is to allow a programmer to fix exceptions caused by user errors.

The test run indicates the value of the divisor is deliberately chosen to be zero, and an arithmetic exception is thrown when the interpreter attempts to divide the dividend by zero. The Java interpreter executes the code within the catch block associated with the arithmetic exception, then exits the catch block. However, the computer is still within the do..while loop, and the condition to exit from the loop is still false. Only when the divisor is valid is the arithmetic division performed, and the result output. In these circumstances the catch block is never entered as there is no exception and the computer exits from the loop.

In this example the catch block will only handle arithmetic exceptions, therefore, if an `IOException` was thrown it would be handled by the Java interpreter and not the catch block.

Program Example 9.2: The Introduction of try and catch Blocks

```java
// chap_9\Ex_2.java
// program to demonstrate creating an exception and
// catching the exception within the program

import java.io.*;

class Ex_2
{
    static BufferedReader keyboard = new
            BufferedReader(new InputStreamReader(System.in));
    static PrintWriter screen = new PrintWriter(System.out,true);

    public static void main(String[] args) throws Exception
    {
        int dividend, divisor, quotient;
        boolean done = false;

        do
        {
            try
            {
                screen.print("dividend? "); screen.flush();
                dividend = new Integer(keyboard.readLine()).intValue();
                screen.print("divisor? "); screen.flush();
                divisor  = new Integer(keyboard.readLine()).intValue();

                // possible arithmetic exception can be thrown
                // if divisor is zero
                quotient = dividend/divisor;
                screen.println("quotient " + quotient);
                done = true;
            }

            catch(ArithmeticException ae)
            {
                screen.println("\nException " + ae.toString() +" caught\n");
            }

        } while (! done);
    }
}
```

Test results

```
dividend? 25
divisor? 0

Exception java.lang.ArithmeticException: / by zero caught

dividend? 25
divisor? 5
quotient 5
```

Since the class `Arithmetic Exception` inherits from the class `Throwable`, the method `toString()` may be used on objects of type `ArithmeticException`. The purpose of the method `toString()` is to convert an object to a string before it may be printed.

9.4 Catching Multiple Exceptions

It is possible that other exceptions may occur when the previous program is executed. What if the character o was input instead of the digit 0 (zero)? This would generate a `NumberFormatException`, and since there is no catch block to accommodate the exception, the Java interpreter will catch the exception, display a message and terminate the program.

You may include in a method many catch blocks to explicitly catch a number of known exceptions. The single catch block in Program Example 9.2 may be replaced by the following code.

```
catch(ArithmeticException ae)
{
        screen.println("\nException " + ae.toString() + " caught");
}
catch(NumberFormatException nfe)
{
    screen.println("\nException " + nfe.toString() + " caught");
}
```

 When using more than one catch block to explicitly trap exceptions, make sure that the class type for each block is not a superclass. If you need to use a superclass in a block as a "catch all" for any exceptions that you have not explicitly coded, see that the catch block appears as the <u>last</u> block in the sequence.

Alternatively, you may have just the one catch block, with a parameter whose data type is the superclass of all exceptions that are likely to be caught by the block. For example, `catch(Exception e) {..}`. Within this block you will test for the exception object e being a specific instance of an exception class. The comparison between the object and an instance of a specific class is made by using the **instanceof** operator. The syntax of the operator follows.

syntax

instanceof operator: *object* **instanceof** *class*

The `instanceof` operator returns true if the object on its left-hand side is an instance of the class specified on its right-hand side; otherwise `instanceof` returns false.

The `instanceof` operator can also return false if the object is `null`.

The suggestion of the use of two catch blocks in Program Example 9.2 may be replaced by a single catch block having the following code.

```
catch(Exception e)
{
    if (e instanceof ArithmeticException)
    {
        screen.println("\nException " + e.toString() + " caught\n");
    }

    if (e instanceof NumberFormatException)
    {
        screen.println("\nException " + e.toString() + " caught\n");
    }
}
```

Program Example 9.3 is a modified version of Program Example 9.2; the program incorporates the technique of using a single catch block for multiple exceptions. The test results show a divisor of 0 (zero) causing an arithmetic exception; a divisor of o (lower-case letter) causing a number format exception, and finally the correct result of the division.

Program Example 9.3: Multiple Exceptions

```
// chap_9\Ex_3.java
// program to demonstrate creating exceptions and
// catching each exception within the program

import java.io.*;

class Ex_3
{
    static BufferedReader keyboard = new
            BufferedReader(new InputStreamReader(System.in));
    static PrintWriter screen = new PrintWriter(System.out,true);

    public static void main(String[] args) throws Exception
    {
        int dividend, divisor, quotient;
        boolean done = false;

        do
        {
            try
            {
                // possible number format exception can be thrown
                // if numbers are not in integer format
                screen.print("dividend? "); screen.flush();
                dividend = new Integer(keyboard.readLine()).intValue();
                screen.print("divisor? "); screen.flush();
                divisor  = new Integer(keyboard.readLine()).intValue();

                // possible arithmetic exception can be thrown
                // if divisor is zero
                quotient = dividend/divisor;
```

```
                    screen.println("quotient " + quotient);
                    done = true;
                }

            catch(Exception e)
            {
                if (e instanceof ArithmeticException)
                {
                    screen.println("\nException " + e.toString() + " caught\n");
                }

                if (e instanceof NumberFormatException)
                {
                    screen.println("\nException " + e.toString() + " caught\n");
                }
            }

        } while (! done);
    }
}
```

Test results

```
dividend? 25
divisor? 0

Exception java.lang.ArithmeticException: / by zero caught

dividend? 25
divisor? o

Exception java.lang.NumberFormatException: o caught

dividend? 25
divisor? 5
quotient 5
```

9.5 Creating your own Exception Classes

You may recall from the introduction, that a predefined exception may be thrown as a result of a violation of a semantic constraint of the language. Such exceptions are well catered for by the predefined exception classes in the language. However, what if you want to create your own exception classes in response to various exceptions that might be thrown from a suite of your own data validation routines? Using your own exceptions in a program will require you to create your own exception classes. Whatever exception class you define, must be a subclass of the class Throwable. Naturally, you will inherit all the characteristics of the class Throwable, unless you specifically override the methods.

The constructors of the class Throwable are:

```
public Throwable(); // default constructor
public Throwable(String message);
```

If the default constructor is used then any method invoked by the object will always refer to the name of the object. For example, from the instantiation:

`Throwable MyException = new Throwable();` the statement

`screen.println(MyException.toString());` will display the name `MyException`.

If the constructor that takes a string argument is used, for example:

`Throwable MyException = new Throwable("THIS IS MY OWN EXCEPTION");`

the statement `screen.println(MyException.toString());` will display both the name of the exception and the message included as the argument in the constructor. For example,

`MyException: THIS IS MY OWN EXCEPTION`

The instance method `getMessage()` will return the message associated with the argument in the constructor. If the default constructor has been used then the message is returned as `null`. For example, the statement `screen.println(MyException.getMessage());` will display the message `THIS IS MY OWN EXCEPTION`.

If you examine the subclasses of `Throwable`, the majority of these subclasses do not add any further functionality to this class. The classes only redefine the two constructors. Therefore, a typical class definition for your own exception class might be as follows.

```
class MyException extends Throwable
{
    public MyException(){super();}
    public MyException(String s){super(s);}
}
```

Note that it is possible to extend other classes down the hierarchy other than `Throwable`. You may care to be more specific about the type of exception you are extending. For example:

```
class MyException extends RuntimeException{ .. }
```

is a better way to denote the classification of the exception. Since `RuntimeException` is a subclass of `Exception`, and `Exception` is a subclass of `Throwable`, `MyException` must inherit all the functionality of `Throwable`.

9.6 Throwing an Exception

A simple analogy to help you understand the concept of throwing and re-throwing an exception follows.

A person throws a hot potato (the exception) into a small group of people. If the first person to catch the potato is wearing oven mitts (the exception handler), that person does not burn their hands and can safely hold the potato (handle the exception). However, if a person in the group catches the potato, and is not wearing oven mitts (no exception handler present in the method), the potato is too hot to handle and is re-thrown to another person in the group. You can imagine the hot potato being thrown from person to person, until eventually it is caught by a person who can safely hold the potato (handle the exception).

A **throw** statement is executed to indicate that an exception has occurred. The throw statement must specify an exception object to be thrown. An exception object being any object that is instantiated from the class `Throwable` or any subclass or extension of a class in the exception classes hierarchy.

Throw Statement: **throw** *exception-object*

Figure 9.3 illustrates how a thrown exception searches for a handler. The throw statement passes control to a catch block. If there is no catch block in the current method, the computer exits the method and returns to the calling method. Again, if there is no catch block to handle the exception the computer exits the method and returns to the calling method. The process continues to pass up through the calling methods until it finds a catch block capable of handling the exception. Hopefully, you now see the analogy with the hot potato!

If after returning through all the calling methods a catch block cannot be found, the Java interpreter will handle the exception by reporting on what caused the exception, and terminating the program.

A **throws** clause <u>lists</u> the exceptions that can be thrown by a method. Do not get the `throws` clause confused with a `throw` statement, that explicitly invokes an exception.

It is possible to trace the route the computer takes through the methods in attempting to find a catch block to handle the exception. Both instance methods `printStackTrace()` and `printStackTrace(PrintWriter s)` will display the names of the methods that are visited by the computer in the search for an appropriate catch block. The first method takes no argument, therefore, it is assumed the information is displayed on a screen. The second method allows you to specify a stream for writing the information.

Program Example 9.4 implements the logic behind Figure 9.3 and displays the contents of a stack trace showing the route the computer takes to find a suitable catch block.

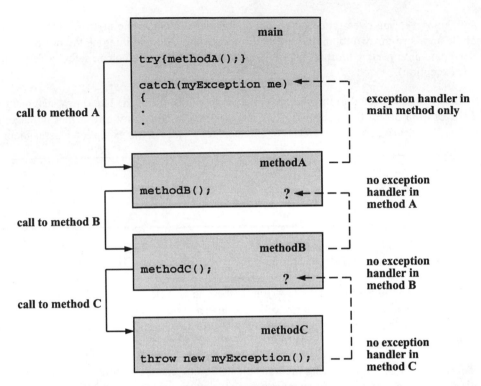

Figure 9.3 An exception searching for a handler

Program Example 9.4: Finding a catch Block

```
// chap_9\Ex_4.java
// program to demonstrate the use of a stack trace

import java.io.*;

class MyException extends Throwable
{
    public MyException(){super();}
}

class Ex_4
{
    static PrintWriter screen = new PrintWriter(System.out,true);

    static public void main(String[] args)
    {
        try
        {
            methodA();
        }
```

```
        catch(MyException me)
        {
            screen.println("The exception has been caught in main.");
            screen.println("The stack trace shows the order in which");
            screen.println("each method has thrown the exception.\n");
            me.printStackTrace(screen);
        }
    }

    static void methodA() throws MyException
    {
        methodB();
    }

    static void methodB() throws MyException
    {
        methodC();
    }

    static void methodC() throws MyException
    {
        // an exception must be instantiated before
        // it can exist; after which it may be thrown
        throw new MyException();
    }
}
```

Test results

```
The exception has been caught in main.
The stack trace shows the order in which
each method has thrown the exception.

MyException
        at Ex_4.methodC(Ex_4.java:45)
        at Ex_4.methodB(Ex_4.java:38)
        at Ex_4.methodA(Ex_4.java:33)
        at Ex_4.main(Ex_4.java:19)
```

It is possible for an exception to be re-thrown from within a catch block. Program Example 9.5 is a modification of Program Example 9.4 to include a second throw clause, but this time within the catch block. Note the instance method `fillInStackTrace()` has also been included in the catch block. The purpose is to supply information to the trace. The method returns an object of the type `this.Throwable`.

Program Example 9.5: Demonstration of Re-throwing an Exception

```java
// chap_9\Ex_5.java
// program to demonstrate the use of a stack trace

import java.io.*;

class MyException extends Throwable
{
    public MyException(){super();}
    public MyException(String s){super(s);}
}

class Ex_5
{
    static PrintWriter screen = new PrintWriter(System.out,true);

    static public void main(String[] args)
    {
        try
        {
            methodA();
        }

        catch(Throwable t)
        {
            screen.println(t.toString()+" caught in method main");
            t.printStackTrace();
            screen.println();
        }
    }

    static void methodA() throws Throwable
    {
        methodB();
    }

    static void methodB() throws Throwable
    {
        try
        {
            methodC();
        }

        catch(MyException me)
        {
            screen.println(me.toString()+" caught in methodB");
            me.printStackTrace();
            screen.println();
            throw me.fillInStackTrace();
        }
    }
```

```
static void methodC() throws MyException
{
    // an exception must be instantiated before
    // it can exist; after which it may be thrown
    throw new MyException("THIS IS MY OWN EXCEPTION");
}
}
```

Test results

```
MyException: THIS IS MY OWN EXCEPTION caught in methodB
MyException: THIS IS MY OWN EXCEPTION
        at Ex_5.methodC(Ex_5.java:56)
        at Ex_5.methodB(Ex_5.java:40)
        at Ex_5.methodA(Ex_5.java:33)
        at Ex_5.main(Ex_5.java:20)

MyException: THIS IS MY OWN EXCEPTION caught in method main
MyException: THIS IS MY OWN EXCEPTION
        at Ex_5.methodB(Ex_5.java:48)
        at Ex_5.methodA(Ex_5.java:33)
        at Ex_5.main(Ex_5.java:20)
```

Note the output from the instance method `printStackTrace` in `methodB` and `main`, showing which methods have been visited.

9.7 Finally

The computer will exit from a `try` block under the following circumstances.

- An exception is thrown.

- The execution of a `break`, `continue` or `return` statement.

- Normally, after the execution of the last statement in the block where there are no exceptions thrown.

Note a **continue** statement causes the computer to branch to the end of the last statement in a loop, but not outside the loop. A **break** statement will cause the computer to branch to outside of the loop. It is <u>not</u> recommended that you make use of either the `break` or `continue` statements since they represent unconditional branching within a program, and generally lead to poor programming style.

Java allows the programmer to define a block of code that is guaranteed to be executed before the computer exits from the method, regardless of whether an exception was thrown or `return` statement executed within a `try` block.

The **finally** block may be used to release any permanent resources the method might have allocated; for example closing any open files. Exit from a `finally` block is normally through a `return` statement.

 Finally Block: **finally** {*statements*}

If there is a local `catch` block to handle an exception being thrown from the `try` block, the code of the `catch` block is executed before the code of the `finally` block. However, if a local `catch` block does not exist to handle the exception, then the code of the `finally` block is executed, and the computer must return to the calling method to find a `catch` clause to handle the exception.

Program Example 9.6 demonstrates how a `finally` block is entered before the program is abandoned by the interpreter. Within the try block the method `failure()` is called. This method throws a valid Java exception, `NullPointerException`, which is usually reserved to signal an attempt to access a field or invoke a method of a null object. However, there is no handler in this program to handle a `NullPointerException`. Normally at this point the interpreter would abandon the program, and display the cause of the error.

However, since a finally block has been included, the computer must execute the statements within this block before abandoning the program.

Program Example 9.6: Example of a finally Block

```
// chap_9\Ex_6
// program to demonstrate the finally clause

import java.io.*;

class MyException extends Exception
{
    public MyException(){}
    public MyException(String s){super(s);}
}

class Ex_6
{
    static PrintWriter screen = new PrintWriter(System.out,true);

    static void failure() throws MyException
    {
        screen.println("Entered failure() method");
        throw new NullPointerException();
    }
```

```
public static void main(String[] args)
{
    try
    {
        screen.println("Entered try block");
        failure();
    }
    catch(MyException me)
    {
        screen.println("Entered catch block with MyException");
    }
    finally
    {
        screen.println("Entered finally block");
        screen.println("Uncaught Exception - NullPointerException");
    }
}
}
```

Test results

```
Entered try block
Entered failure() method
Entered finally block
Uncaught Exception - NullPointerException
java.lang.NullPointerException
        at Ex_6.failure(Ex_6.java:19)
        at Ex_6.main(Ex_6.java:27)
```

9.8 Discussion

When using the throws clause, it is sufficient to state only the superclass of all the exceptions that may occur within a method. Furthermore, Java does not require exceptions that refer to the subclasses of Error and RuntimeException to be declared. Practically any method can generate these exceptions and it would become tedious to have to list all the possible subclasses of exceptions that might be thrown.

Given the restriction just mentioned, how do you know which exceptions to declare in a throws clause? The answer is twofold.

Firstly look at the documentation associated with the class methods you are using. The signatures of these methods state which methods throw exceptions.

Secondly, when developing a program don't declare any exceptions in a throws clause, but wait for the compiler to tell you which exceptions you should have declared.

When developing your own classes state which methods are likely to throw exceptions. Do not handle the exceptions within these classes, but write the appropriate exception handlers in the program that uses the classes. Such exception handlers may be grouped together in one part of the program, thus allowing for a better organization in the layout of your code. In turn this approach must improve program clarity and enhances program modifiability.

Exception handling provides a unified approach for dealing with errors in a program. Adopting exception handling reduces the need to use "home grown" techniques for error detection and recovery.

Never be tempted to use exception handling for purposes other than exception handling, otherwise you can reduce program clarity and program performance. For example, to rely upon the exception EndOfFileException to be thrown in detecting the end of file is a poor substitute for using an appropriate method or variable that specifically detects when the end of a file has been reached.

Remember, with the prudent use of exception handling, a program may continue executing after dealing with an error situation. This helps ensure the software that you write is both robust and reliable.

Case Study: A TextFile Class to Examine the Contents of any Text File

Problem. Create a class TextFile containing the following methods that may be used to list the contents of a text file, and provide information on the number of tokens and the number of lines in the file.

```
class TextFile
{
    // constructor
    public TextFile(String fileName) throws FileNotFoundException,
                                              IOException;

    // instance methods
    public void listFile() throws IOException;
    public int numberOfTokens();
    public int numberOfLines();
}
```

Devise a suitable program to test the constructor and methods of the class TextFile.

Problem Analysis. The problem divides into two distinct parts - the design and implementation of the class TextFile, and the design and implementation of a main method to instantiate an object of type TextFile and invoke the methods of this new class.

In designing a main method you may assume that the name of the file is input as a command line parameter. This in itself can lead to an error prone situation. What if there is no parameter specified, or there are too many parameters? A new exception type CommandLineArgumentsException should be implemented to handle the possibility of either none or too many command line arguments being specified.

This case study illustrates that it is not always possible to continue processing when an exception is caught. When dealing with command line parameters you can hardly ask the user to re-input either a filename or the correct filename, without first abandoning the program.

Analysis of Class TextFile. The constructor is used to instantiate an object of type `TextFile`. Since the object is the file to be processed, the constructor must open the file stated in the command line argument. If the file does not exist the constructor must throw a `FileNotFoundException`.

For the instance methods to be independent of each other, it will be necessary to read the file and count the number of tokens and lines at the instantiation of an object. Once the constructor has established there is a file to be opened, the constructor needs to call a "helper" method `readFile()` to read the contents of the file, and store each line of the file into consecutive cells of a vector (ready for printing at a later stage). The `readFile()` method must also count the number of tokens and count the number of lines in the file.

After instantiation it will not matter in which order the instance methods are invoked, since it will always be possible to get the number of tokens or lines, or list the contents of the file (display the contents of the vector).

To read the contents of the file, it is necessary to read each token from each line in the file, and store each token together with a space separator, in a string buffer. When an end of line token is read, the contents of the string buffer (the complete line) is copied to a cell in the vector.

The `readfile()` method also counts the number of tokens processed and the number of lines of text stored in the vector.

The method `nextToken()` in the `StreamTokenizer` class throws an `IOException`. This exception will not be handled in the class `TextFile` but re-thrown from the "helper" method `readFile()`.

Algorithm for readFile. The only method that requires a detailed algorithm is `readFile()`. The constructor `TextFile` and the methods `listFile()`, `numberOfTokens()` and `numberOfLines()` are so trivial to implement that the inclusion of separate algorithms for these methods is not necessary.

1. read token
2. while token not end of file
3.   while token not end of file and not end of line
4.   if token number
5   append number as string to string buffer
6.   else
7.   append string to string buffer
8.   increase number of tokens by 1
9.   read next token
10.   store contents of string buffer in vector
11.   instantiate new string buffer
12.   read next token
13. trim vector to size
14. calculate number of lines from size of vector

Data Dictionary The class `TextFile` will require instance variables to represent the number of tokens and the number of lines in the input stream, and the vector to store the lines read from the text file.

```
protected int tokens = 0;
protected int lines;
protected Vector dataStore = new Vector();
```

The constructor TextFile requires two local variables to represent the file to be read and the stream tokenizer input stream.

```
FileReader file;
StreamTokenizer inputStream;
```

The method `readFile()`, requires two local variables to represent the string buffer and a token type.

```
StringBuffer buffer;
int tokenType;
```

Desk Check of readFile. Assume the test data is the following two lines of text, with an end of line token before an end of file token.

```
395.95 television
550 music center
```

token	395.95	television	EOL	
token==EOF?	false	false	false	
token==EOL?	false	false	true	
tokens	0	1	2	
buffer		395.95	395.95 television	
dataStore[0]				395.95 television

token	550	music center	EOL	EOF
token==EOF?	false	false	false	true
token==EOL?	false		true	
tokens	2	3	4	
buffer		550	550 music center	
dataStore[1]				550 music center
lines	2			

Coding

```
class TextFile
{
    // instance variables
    protected int tokens = 0;
    protected int lines;
    protected Vector dataStore = new Vector();

    // method to read a text file, token-by-token
    // the tokens are stored as lines of text in a vector
    // the number of tokens and number of lines is calculated
    private void readFile(StreamTokenizer inputStream) throws IOException
    {
        final char SPACE=' ';
        StringBuffer buffer = new StringBuffer();

        inputStream.eolIsSignificant(true);        // set EOL as significant
        int tokenType = inputStream.nextToken();   // read token

        while (tokenType != StreamTokenizer.TT_EOF)
        {
            while (tokenType != StreamTokenizer.TT_EOF &
                    tokenType != StreamTokenizer.TT_EOL)
            {
                if (tokenType == StreamTokenizer.TT_NUMBER)
                    buffer.append(String.valueOf(inputStream.nval)+SPACE);
                else
                    buffer.append(inputStream.sval+SPACE);

                tokens++;
                tokenType = inputStream.nextToken(); // read token
            }

            dataStore.addElement(buffer);            // store buffer in vector
            buffer = new StringBuffer();             // instantiate new buffer

            tokenType = inputStream.nextToken();     // read token
        }

        dataStore.trimToSize();
        lines = dataStore.size();                    // lines = vector size
    }

    // constructor
    public TextFile(String fileName) throws FileNotFoundException,
                                        IOException
    {
        FileReader file = new FileReader(fileName);
        StreamTokenizer inputStream = new StreamTokenizer(file);

        readFile(inputStream);
    }
```

```
    // instance methods
    public void listFile()
    {
        for (int index=0; index != lines; index++)
        {
            IO.screen.println(dataStore.elementAt(index));
        }
    }

    public int numberOfTokens(){return tokens;}
    public int numberOfLines(){return lines;}
}
```

Algorithm of the main method

1. *try*
2.   *if argument missing throw exception*
3.   *instantiate file object*
4.   *listFile*
5.   *print number of tokens*
6.   *print number of lines*
7. *catch*
8.   *print details of exception caught*
9. *finally*
10.   *display prompt to end*

Data Dictionary for main method. The only variable to declare is an object of type `TextFile`.

```
TextFile data;
```

Desk Check of main method. If the test data is the same as used for testing the method `listFile()`, then the output from the program will be a listing of the text file, together with the number of tokens and lines.

In this example, a new exception class is defined `CommandLineArgumentsException`. The class overrides the two constructors of the class `Exception`; and in the implementation both constructors use the constructors of the superclass.

An object of type `CommandLineArgumentsException` is thrown if the number of command line arguments is not correct.

Coding

```
// chap_9\Ex_7

import java.io.*;
import java.util.*;

class IO
{
    static PrintWriter screen = new PrintWriter(System.out,true);
}

class TextFile {..}

class CommandLineArgumentsException extends Exception
{
    public CommandLineArgumentsException(){super();}
    public CommandLineArgumentsException(String s){super(s);}
}

class Ex_7
{
    static final int NUMBER_OF_ARGUMENTS = 1;

    public static void main(String args[]) throws IOException
    {
        try
        {
            // throw an exception if the number of arguments is not correct
            if (args.length != NUMBER_OF_ARGUMENTS)
                throw new CommandLineArgumentsException();

            // constructor TextFile may throw a FileNotFoundException
            TextFile data = new TextFile(args[0]);

            // instance method may throw an IOException
            data.listFile();

            IO.screen.println("\nnumber of tokens read
                             "+data.numberOfTokens());
            IO.screen.println("number of lines processed
                             "+data.numberOfLines());
        }

        catch(Exception e)
        {
            e.printStackTrace();
            return;
        }

        finally
        {
            IO.screen.println("\nPROGRAM TERMINATED\n");
            return;
        }
    }
}
```

The program has been run three times.

On the first run the command line deliberately contained no arguments. The programmer-defined CommandLineArgumentsException was thrown and caught by the handler.

On the second run the command line argument was present, however, the name of the file could not be found in the users directory. A FileNotFoundException was thrown and caught by the handler.

On the third and final run a filename was specified that did exist, and the contents of this file together with the number of tokens and lines processed was listed on the screen.

Test results from program being run three times

```
>java Ex_7
CommandLineArgumentsException
        at Ex_7.main(Ex_7.java:97)

PROGRAM TERMINATED


>java Ex_7 a:\\file.txt
java.io.FileNotFoundException: a:\\file.txt
        at java.io.FileInputStream.<init>(FileInputStream.java:64)
        at java.io.FileReader.<init>(FileReader.java:43)
        at TextFile.<init>(Ex_7.java:57)
        at Ex_7.main(Ex_7.java:100)

PROGRAM TERMINATED


>java Ex_7 a:\\chap_9\\text.txt
395.95 television
550.0 music center
995.95 desk top computer
199.95 microwave oven
299.99 washing machine
149.95 freezer

number of tokens read 17
number of lines processed 6

PROGRAM TERMINATED
```

Summary

- An exception is the occurrence of an event that happens when the program is running.

- In Java, an exception is treated as an object that is an instance of the superclass Throwable, or an instance of one of its subclasses.

- The superclass Throwable has two subclasses Error and Exception.

- There exists a list of subclasses to `RuntimeException`, which itself is a subclass of `Exception`.

- As a general rule, programmers should handle explicit exceptions from the subclass of `Exception` and not the subclass of `Error` or `RuntimeException`.

- All exceptions that are thrown must be eventually caught.

- A method may not always handle an exception, but re-throw it for another method to eventually handle.

- Exceptions are handled using a `catch` block

- Only an exception that is the same class, or a subclass , of the `catch` block parameter may be handled by the `catch` block.

- A `try` clause is used to delimit a block of code where the result of any method calls or other operations might causes an exception.

- If an exception is raised within a `try` block, then the computer branches to the corresponding `catch` block. After the execution of the appropriate `catch` block, the computer does NOT return to the next executable statement in the `try` block, but continues to execute statements that follow the `catch` block.

- When there is no exception raised within a `try` block the corresponding `catch` block is ignored and the computer continues to execute statements after the `catch` block.

- Whenever there are multiple `catch` blocks, the `catch` block with the lowest subclass parameter must be placed first in the order of the `catch` blocks. The `catch` block with a superclass parameter must be placed last in the order of the `catch` blocks. Failure to observe this rule will result in a superclass `catch` block overshadowing a subclass `catch` block and the compiler reporting this occurrence as an error.

- Multiple exceptions may be caught by either the use of multiple `catch` blocks or by a single superclass `catch` block, with sufficient logic to determine which exception was thrown.

- You may create your own exception classes, however, these classes should extend one of the superclasses, such as `Throwable` or `Exception`.

- An exception is explicitly thrown using a `throw` statement. A `throw` statement must specify an exception object to be thrown.

- A `throws` clause lists the exceptions that can be thrown by a method.

- The instance method `toString()` in the class `Throwable` returns as a string the name of the exception.

- The instance method getMessage() in the class Throwable returns the message used in the instantiation of the exception object.

- The instance methods printStackTrace in the class Throwable will display the names of the methods that are visited by the computer in search of the appropriate catch block.

- The instance method fillInStackTrace() in the class Throwable returns the information about the trace.

- Whenever, a block of statements need to be executed before the computer exits from a method, declare these statements in a finally block.

- Good practice dictates that you should state which methods in a class throw exceptions. Write the exception handlers for these exceptions in the program that uses the methods.

Review Questions

1. What is an exception?

2. How is an exception invoked?

3. If a method cannot handle an exception what happens to the exception?

4. Inspect the class java.lang.Math. State which of the class methods throw exceptions, and why you think the methods need to do this.

5. Repeat question (4), but this time look at the methods in the class java.lang.String.

6. Define try, catch and finally blocks.

7. True or false - A RuntimeException is a superclass of an ArithmeticException.

8. True or false - The order of try and catch blocks is of no significance.

9. True or false - A single try block may have corresponding multiple catch blocks.

10. True or false - The throws clause invokes an exception.

11. True or false - A catch clause may have more than one parameter.

12. True or false - Catch blocks must immediately follow a try block.

13. True or false - A catch block is never executed if the corresponding exception is not raised.

14. What is the function of the instance method toString() and when is it used?

15. What does the instanceof operator return?

16. What is the function of the instance method `printStackTrace()`?

17. How should multiple `catch` blocks be arranged?

18. What restrictions are imposed upon creating your own exception class?

19. What is the difference between a `throw` clause and a `throws` clause?

20. If a `catch` block does not exist in a method how is the corresponding `throw` clause handled?

Exercises

21. Detect the error in the following code.

```
try
{
    methodA();
}

methodB();

catch(Throwable t){}
```

22. Once again detect the error in the following code.

```
try
{
    FileReader file = new FileReader("data.bin");
    BufferedReader input = new BufferedReader(file);
}
catch(FileNotFoundException f){System.exit(1);}
Record data = new Record();
data.readRecord(input);
```

23. Is the following structure of `try` and `catch` blocks legal?

```
try
{

    .
    .
    .
    try
    {

        .
        .
        .
    }
    catch(..){}
    .
    .
    .
}
catch (..){}
```

24. Detect the error in the following `catch` block.

```
catch (Error e)
{
    if (e instanceof ArithmeticException) ..
    if (e instanceof ArrayStoreException) ..
}
```

25. Comment upon the legality of the following catch blocks.

```
try
{
    .
    .
    .
}
catch (Throwable t){..}
catch (Exception e){..}
catch (ClassNotFoundException c){..}
catch (InterruptedException i){..}
```

26. Detect the errors in the following code.

```
static public void main(String[] args)
{
    methodA();
}

static void methodA() throw newTypeOfException
{
    .
    .
    .
    throws newTypeOfException;
}
```

27. Desk check the following code. What type of exception will cause the `catch` block to be executed?

```
int[] array = {1,2,3,4,5};
int   index = 0;

for (;;)
{
    try
    {
        screen.println(array[index]);
        index++;
    }
    catch(Exception e)
    {
        e.printStackTrace();
        return;
    }
}
```

Programming Problems

28. Write a program to prove that the order in which `catch` blocks are written is of importance.

29. Write and test separate segments of program code to input a string and throw the appropriate exception if the string cannot be:

(a) converted to a number;
(b) converted to an integer;
(c) converted to a real number.

Allow the number to be re-input until it is accepted as a number in a valid format.

30. Write an exception class for a time of day not represented in the correct 24-hour format. Write a program to input various times in the 24-hour format and throw an exception for those times that are in error.

31. Rewrite the case study from this chapter, however, do not use command line arguments for the input of the filename. Instead, allow a user to type the name of the text file to be processed when the program is running. If the file does not exist allow the user to either enter a new file name or state whether they want to quit the program.

32. A text file contains records with the following fields:

> stock number - 4 digits followed by a modulus-11 check digit;
> quantity of stock - 3 digit positive integer;
> distribution code - 2 digit positive integer.

Create a test data file having records with the stated format. However, you should include in your file a number of records that do not conform to the format. For example, a stock number may have the wrong modulus-11 check digit, implying that the number was incorrectly transcribed; a quantity of stock may not lie within the prescribed limits; and a distribution code that is not a two-digit number.

Write a program to read the records from the stock file, and filter only those records that contain no errors into another file. Before writing each record to the new file, translate the 2 digit distribution code into a textual description of the area for distribution. The names of the distribution points are stored in a one-dimensional array. Beware - this is another source of error, since the distribution code may generate an index out of bounds exception.

Records that are in error should be displayed on the screen stating the nature of the error.
Note. A modulus-11 check digit provides a means for the computer to check that a number has not had any digits transposed when it has been input to the computer. The check digit method will ensure a detection of all transcription and transposition errors and 91% of random errors.

The modulus-11 check digit for a stock number is calculated as follows. Using the code number 9118 as an example - multiply each digit by its associated weight, and calculate the sum of the partial products. The weights are 5,4,3 and 2, with the most significant digit in the number having the weight of 5, and the least significant digit in the number having the weight of 2.

$(5 \times 9) + (4 \times 1) + (3 \times 1) + (2 \times 8) = 68$

The sum 68 is then divided by 11 and the remainder 2 is then subtracted from 11, the result 9 is the check digit. The stock number, including the check digit as the last digit, is 91189. If the value of the check digit is computed to be 10, this is replaced by the letter X.

To check whether a stock number has been entered into the computer correctly, a similar calculation is carried out. Each digit is multiplied by a weight, the check digit has a weight of 1, and the sum of the partial products is calculated.

$(5 \times 9) + (4 \times 1) + (3 \times 1) + (2 \times 8) + (1 \times 9) = 77$

The sum 77 is divided by 11 and the remainder is zero. If the remainder was non-zero then a transcription error would have been made when entering the number into the computer.

Chapter 10
Graphical User Interfaces

This chapter marks a departure away from the traditional input of data via a keyboard and displaying information in textual form on a screen. You will be introduced to many of the components found in Java, that contribute towards the construction of a graphical user interface (GUI).

A **GUI** is an interface between a user and a computer, that makes use of input devices other than the keyboard, and presentation techniques other than alphanumeric characters. Typical GUIs involve the use of windows, icons, menus and pointing devices. The windows can contain control objects such as a slider bar, radio buttons, check boxes and pick lists, as well as textual or graphical information. The objects forming the interface display have attributes such as the ability to be resized, moved around the display, shrunk down to an icon, or given different colors.

By the end of this chapter you should have an understanding of the following topics.

- The hierarchy of components found in the `java.awt` package known as the `Abstract Windowing Toolkit`.

- GUI components such as buttons, menus, lists, and text fields.

- Handling events described in the `java.awt.event` package.

- The layout of components within containers.

- Drawing two-dimensional graphical shapes.

- The interaction of components within a graphical display.

10.1 GUI Example

Before commencing with a detailed discussion of how to build a graphical user interface in Java, it is worthwhile considering what such an interface is likely to contain. Figure 10.1 illustrates a typical GUI for drawing shapes. By the end of this chapter you will have enough knowledge to be able to program the construction of a similar interface.

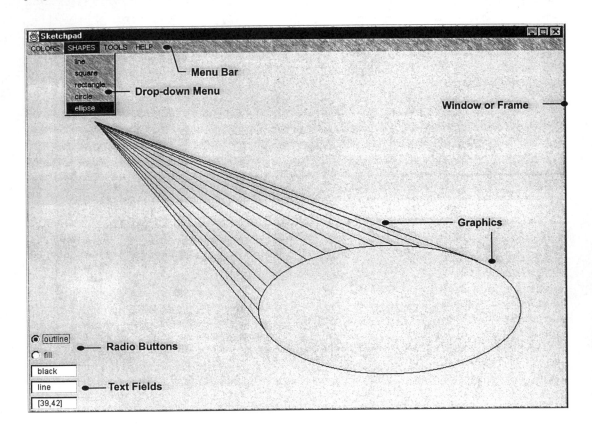

Figure 10.1 Typical components that make up a GUI

A GUI typically consists of a container, such as a window or frame; into which components, such as buttons, menus and text fields are added. The container is also suitable for drawing graphical shapes. Typically, a mouse pointer is used to select items from a menu, or push selected buttons. The information gathered from these components and the positions of the mouse pointer may then be used to perform a function, such as drawing a shape.

In programming a GUI you should always consider how you will implement:

- A container on which to place the components.

- The types of components to use, for example, buttons and drop-down menus.

- A method to capture an interaction between a user and a component.

Within the context of this chapter we will explore each of these three points in detail.

10.2 The AWT Hierarchy of Classes

Figure 10.2 illustrates some of the classes from the Abstract Windowing Toolkit (AWT) found in the package java.awt used to build GUIs.

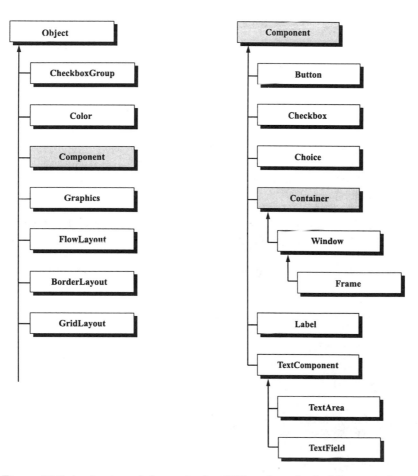

Figure 10.2 A selection of classes in the AWT package for building interfaces

Figure 10.2 indicates that the `Container` class is defined as an abstract class. Remember an abstract class implies that objects of type `Container` cannot be instantiated, since the implementation of many of its methods are found in subclasses further down the hierarchy. One such class that will be used is `Frame`.

Despite `Container` being an abstract class, the class `Frame` inherits all the characteristics of `Container`. Two useful public instance methods to initially consider from the `Container` class are:

```
public Component add(Component comp);
public void setLayout(LayoutManager mgr);
```

The method `add` allows us to place a component into a container such as a `Frame`, and the method `setLayout` allows us to specify a class for laying out components in a particular position within the container.

But `Container` is a subclass of `Component`. Therefore, all the characteristics of the `Component` class are also available to the `Frame` class. Three useful public instance methods to consider from the `Component` class are:

```
public void setSize(int width, int height);
public void setBackground(Color c);
public void setVisible(boolean b);
```

The method `setSize` allows you to change the width and height of a component - in this case `Frame`. Both the width and height are measurements in pixels. A **pixel** is a very small region of a screen representing a picture element. Typically 500 pixels will measure approximately 6 inches (15.25 cm) on a 17 inch monitor.

The method `setBackground` sets the background color of the frame. The argument is of type `Color`. The available colors are described in the class `Color`.

The method `setVisible` allows you to display the frame on the screen, provided the `boolean` argument is set to `true`.

We implement our own class `Gui` that inherits all the characteristics of `Frame`.

```
class Gui extends Frame
{
    // constructor
    public Gui(String s)
    {
        super(s);
        setBackground(Color.yellow);
        setLayout(new FlowLayout());
    }

        .
        .
}
```

The constructor for `Gui` calls a constructor of `Frame` that takes a string argument; sets the background color to yellow and determines the layout pattern for the components in the frame. The class `FlowLayout` arranges components from left to right in rows. It fits as many components as it can in a row before moving on to the next row. A more detailed explanation of the `FlowLayout` manager appears later in the chapter.

We can create an object of type `Gui`, as follows:

```
Gui screen = new Gui("Example 1");
```

The size of the frame is then set to a rectangular shape of 500 pixels by 100 pixels, and made visible on the screen of the monitor.

```
screen.setSize(500,100);
screen.setVisible(true);
```

10.3 Creating a Component

Figure 10.2 illustrates several subclasses of `Component`. For example, `Button`, `Checkbox`, `Label`, and `TextComponent`. Rather than overwhelming you with a full description of these components we will examine just one for now - the `Button`.

The methods of the class `Component` are inherited by many different types of components. For example, the button component will inherit, and may use, methods such as `setBackground`, `setForeground`, `setLocation`, `setName`, `setSize`, and so on.

The `Button` class represents a graphical representation of a push-button that displays a specified textual label. A partial listing of the class `Button` follows showing only the constructors.

```
public class Button extends Component
{
    // Constructors
    public Button();
    public Button(String  label);
    .
    .
}
```

The default constructor `Button()` creates a button with no label; whereas the constructor `Button(String label)` creates a button with the string argument as the label.

An object button is instantiated as follows:

```
Button pushButton = new Button("press me");
```

and placed into the `Gui` container using the `add` method inherited from the `Container` class as follows.

```
add(pushButton);
```

Program Example 10.1 creates an object of type `Gui`, that displays a frame 500x100 pixels in size and contains one button marked *press me*.

Program Example 10.1: Creating a GUI Containing a Single Push-button.

```java
// chap_10\Ex_1.java
// program to demonstrate the construction of a container and a button

import java.awt.*;

class Gui extends Frame
{
    // constructor
    public Gui(String s)
    {
        super(s);
        setBackground(Color.yellow);
        setLayout(new FlowLayout());
        Button pushButton = new Button("press me");
        add(pushButton);
    }
}

class Ex_1
{
    public static void main(String[] args)
    {
        Gui screen = new Gui("Example 1");

        screen.setSize(500,100);
        screen.setVisible(true);
    }
}
```

Test results

Well there you have it. Your first graphical user interface. It is not much to write home about; in fact its pretty useless as it stands. You keep pressing the button as instructed, but nothing happens. Even worse you cannot make the program stop. Help!

10.4 Handling an Event

Let us tackle the problems of the *press me* button being pressed with no response, and not being able to stop Program Example 10.1 from continuous execution. All the time you were pushing the button, by moving the mouse pointer over the *press me* button and clicking on the mouse, you were sending signals to the computer. The signals you were sending to the computer were a result of actions taking place. What was missing from the program was the ability to detect the signals and act upon them.

An **event** is normally associated with an action such as a mouse button click, mouse movement, or a key being pressed on the keyboard. For example, a button when pressed, generates an `ActionEvent` object. `ActionListener` is an interface that contains a single method `actionPerformed(ActionEvent e)` which is automatically invoked when a button is pressed. Because `ActionListener` is an interface, the method `actionPerformed(Action event e)` must be implemented by the user.

An **event listener** acts as a communicator between the button object and the `ActionListener` object. The `addActionListener(ActionListener l)` method notifies the button that the `ActionListener` has implemented an `actionPerformed` method and wants to be notified by the button whenever an action event occurs on the button. In other words, the `ActionListener` is telling the button that it wants its `actionPerformed` method to be called whenever an action event occurs on the button.

The source of the event may be established by invoking the method `getActionCommand()` from the `ActionEvent` class. This way it is possible to determine which of several buttons have been pressed. Note, both classes `ActionEvent` and `ActionListener` can be found in the package `java.awt.event`.

To detect a button being pressed we must do the following.

- Add an action listener for the button. The class Button contains such a method `addActionListener(ActionListener l)`.

- Since `ActionListener` is an interface, its method(s) must be implemented by the appropriate class.

- The implementation of `actionPerformed`, the only method of the `ActionListener` interface determines how the event will be processed.

Program Example 10.2 is a modification of Program Example 10.1, to detect the event of pushing the press me push-button. In this example, when the event resulting from pushing the button has been detected the internal speaker to the computer is activated by printing the Unicode \u0007. This code represents the BELL character.

Program Example 10.2. Detecting an Event.

```java
// chap_10\Ex_2.java
// program to demonstrate handling an event

import java.awt.event.*;
import java.awt.*;
import java.io.*;

class Gui extends Frame implements ActionListener
{
    // constructor
    public Gui(String s)
    {
        super(s);
        setBackground(Color.yellow);
        setLayout(new FlowLayout());
        Button pushButton = new Button("press me");
        add(pushButton);
        pushButton.addActionListener(this);
    }

    public void actionPerformed(ActionEvent event)
    {
        final char BELL = '\u0007';

        if (event.getActionCommand().equals("press me"))
            System.out.print(BELL);
    }
}

class Ex_2
{
    public static void main(String[] args)
    {
        Gui screen = new Gui("Example 2");

        screen.setSize(500,100);
        screen.setVisible(true);
    }
}
```

The output is identical to that depicted for Program Example 10.1. However, when the push-button is pressed, the computer responds with a single note played through the in-built speaker. The problem of stopping the program from running has not yet been solved! Program Example 10.2 was abandoned by keying Control-C in the MSDOS window.

To stop Program Example 10.2 from further execution, it is necessary to detect the action of closing the window. Figure 10.3 illustrates that the window may be closed by either pointing at the drop-down menu item Close and clicking on the mouse button; or by pointing at the close icon **X** in the top right-hand corner of the window and clicking on the mouse button. In either case an event is generated, which needs to be detected.

Figure 10.3 Drop-down menu from a window

The `java.awt.event` package contains the abstract interface `WindowListener`.

```
public abstract interface WindowListener extends EventListener
{
    // public instance methods
    public abstract void windowActivated(WindowEvent e);
    public abstract void windowClosed(WindowEvent e);
    public abstract void windowClosing(WindowEvent e);
    public abstract void windowDeactivated(WindowEvent e);
    public abstract void windowDeiconified(WindowEvent e);
    public abstract void windowIconified(WindowEvent e);
    public abstract void windowOpened(WindowEvent e);
}
```

The class `Window` contains the method `addWindowListener`, to detect an action performed on a window. The event generated by clicking the mouse button over the <u>C</u>lose on the drop-down menu or **X** icon can be detected and will activate the method `windowClosing`. Because `WindowListener` is an interface, it is necessary to implement all the methods contained therein. At present the only method we need to tailor to our needs is `windowClosing` as follows.

```
public void windowClosing(WindowEvent event)
{
    System.exit(0);
}
```

where the **exit** method will permit the program to be terminated.

Program Example 10.3 incorporates the method of detecting the window closing and the *press me* push-button being pushed. Despite the appearance of the results from Program Example 10.3 being identical to those from the previous two programs, you are advised to run the program to appreciate how it differs from Program Example 10.1 and Program Example 10.2.

Program Example 10.3: Creating a GUI Component and Handling Events and Actions

```java
// chap_10\Ex_3.java
// program to demonstrate action listeners and event handlers

import java.awt.*;
import java.awt.event.*;

class Gui extends Frame implements ActionListener, WindowListener
{
    // constructor
    public Gui(String s)
    {
        super(s);
        setBackground(Color.yellow);
        setLayout(new FlowLayout());
        addWindowListener(this);

        Button pushButton = new Button("press me");
        add(pushButton);
        pushButton.addActionListener(this);
    }

    public void windowClosed(WindowEvent event){}
    public void windowDeiconified(WindowEvent event){}
    public void windowIconified(WindowEvent event){}
    public void windowActivated(WindowEvent event){}
    public void windowDeactivated(WindowEvent event){}
    public void windowOpened(WindowEvent event){}

    public void windowClosing(WindowEvent event)
    {
        System.exit(0);
    }

    public void actionPerformed(ActionEvent event)
    {
        final char bell = '\u0007';

        if (event.getActionCommand().equals("press me"))
        {
            System.out.print(bell);
        }
    }
}

class Ex_3
{
    public static void main(String[] args)
    {
        Gui screen = new Gui("Example 3");

        screen.setSize(500,100);
        screen.setVisible(true);
    }
}
```

Before we look at other components that may be used in a GUI, it is worth revising how we deal with events generated by components.

- For every object component, add the corresponding action listener(s).

- Implement the corresponding listener interface(s) to enable the events to be handled by the appropriate listener methods within your GUI class.

NOW DO THIS

To gain confidence in the construction of a GUI, turn to the Exercises at the end of this chapter and attempt question 26.

Component	Events Generated	Listener Interface	Listener Methods
Button	ActionEvent	ActionListener	actionPerformed
Checkbox	ItemEvent	ItemListener	itemStateChanged
CheckboxMenuItem	ItemEvent	ItemListener	itemStateChanged
Choice	ItemEvent	ItemListener	itemStateChanged
Component	ComponentEvent	ComponentListener	componentHidden
.	.	.	componentMoved
.	.	.	componentResized
.	.	.	componentShown
.	FocusEvent	FocusListener	focusGained
.	.	.	focusLost
Container	ContainerEvent	ContainerListener	componentAdded
			componentRemoved
[key]	KeyEvent	KeyListener	keyPressed
.	.	.	keyReleased
.	.	.	keyTyped
List	ActionEvent	ActionListener	actionPerformed
.	ItemEvent	ItemListener	itemStateChanged
MenuItem	ActionEvent	ActionListener	actionPerformed
[mouse]	MouseEvent	MouseListener	mouseClicked
.	.	.	mouseEntered
.	.	.	mouseExited
.	.	.	mousePressed
.	.	.	mouseReleased
.	.	MouseMotionListener	mouseDragged
.	.		mouseMoved
Scrollbar	AdjustmentEvent	AdjustmentListener	adjustmentValueChanged
TextComponent	TextEvent	TextListener	textValueChanged
TextField	ActionEvent	ActionListener	actionPerformed
Window	WindowEvent	WindowListener	windowActivated
			windowClosed
			windowClosing
			windowDeactivated
			windowDeiconified
			windowIconified
			windowOpened

Figure 10.4 Components, events and listener methods

Figure 10.4 lists a number of components from the Abstract Windowing Toolkit. Note that although both a key (from the keyboard) and a mouse are external to the GUI, and not components within the AWT, they are still capable of generating events that must be handled within your program.

10.5 More Components

The AWT package contains a number of specific component classes for building GUIs. These include labels, check boxes, radio buttons, menus, text fields, text areas, lists, and so on. This section explains what some of the components look like, how they are created and how they are used within a GUI. For a full description of each class consult your Java API documentation. Note - in the following examples the layout manager used was FlowLayout, with all the components LEFT justified.

Labels

Labels are text strings that may be used to label other components.

Figure 10.5 An example of Label components

An object from the Label class is instantiated using one of the following constructors.

```
public Label();
public Label(String label);
public Label(String label, int alignment);
```

where alignment is one of the class constants CENTER, LEFT and RIGHT. The labels illustrated in Figure 10.5 were created with the following code. The add instance method is inherited from the class Container. Within the class Container, add is overridden by two other instance methods; however, only one variant will be considered here.

```
public Component add(Component comp);

Label l1 = new Label("NAME:            ", Label.LEFT);
Label l2 = new Label("AGE:     ", Label.CENTER);
Label l3 = new Label("ADDRESS:",Label.RIGHT);

add(l1); add(l2); add(l3);
```

The font used to display any text on the screen, including labels, may be modified by instantiating an object from the class Font, and setting the screen font to the value of the font object, as follows.

```
Font mono = new Font("Monospaced",Font.BOLD,12);

screen.setFont(mono);
```

The constructor for the Font class is:

```
public Font(String name, int style, int size);
```

where name is "Serif", "SansSerif","Monospaced", "Dialog" and "DialogInput"; style is one of the class constants BOLD, ITALIC or PLAIN and size is the point size of the font. A point size of 72 is an inch high character.

Write a program to produce the labels shown in Figure 10.5.

Check Boxes

Checkboxes are components that have two states; on or off (true or false). The Checkboxes illustrated in Figure 10.6 may be selected non-exclusively, implying that any check box may be selected.

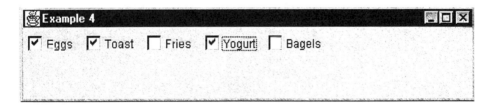

Figure 10.6 An Example of a Check Box component

An object from the Checkbox class is instantiated using one of the following constructors.

```
public Checkbox();
public Checkbox(String label);
public Checkbox(String label, CheckboxGroup group, boolean state);
```

The checkboxes illustrated in Figure 10.6 were created using the following code.

```
Checkbox c1 = new Checkbox("Eggs");
Checkbox c2 = new Checkbox("Toast");
Checkbox c3 = new Checkbox("Fries");
Checkbox c4 = new Checkbox("Yogurt");
Checkbox c5 = new Checkbox("Bagels");
```

```
add(c1); c1.addItemListener(this);
add(c2); c2.addItemListener(this);
add(c3); c3.addItemListener(this);
add(c4); c4.addItemListener(this);
add(c5); c5.addItemListener(this);
```

The mouse is used to point at and click-select the appropriate boxes. Figure 10.6 illustrates that **Eggs**, **Toast** and **Yogurt** have been chosen from the selection. The events of a checkbox are detected by the method `itemStateChanged` from the class `ItemListener`. The class `ItemEvent` contains class constants that specify whether an item is DESELECTED or SELECTED. There are methods to `getStateChange` and `getItem` to determine which item has been pointed at. The `itemStateChanged` method would be implemented as follows.

```
public void itemStateChanged(ItemEvent event)
{
    if (event.getStateChange() == ItemEvent.SELECTED)
    {
        // test to see which item (event.getItem())has been pointed at and
        // react by implementing the functionality for that component
    }
}
```

NOW DO THIS   Write a program to produce the checkboxes shown in Figure 10.6, select any of the boxes and display in the MSDOS/terminal window the value of the items selected.

Radio Buttons

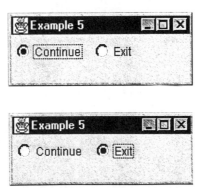

Figure 10.7 An example of radio buttons

Radio buttons unlike check boxes, will only allow one button to be chosen from a series of buttons. Switching any one button on will switch any other button off. To create a set of radio buttons it is first necessary to instantiate an object from the `CheckboxGroup`. The constructor from the CheckboxGroup class is:

```
public CheckboxGroup();
```

The radio buttons illustrated in Figure 10.7 were created using the following code.

```
CheckboxGroup whatNext = new CheckboxGroup();

Checkbox Continue = new Checkbox("Continue", whatNext, true);
Checkbox Exit     = new Checkbox("Exit", whatNext, false);

add(Continue); Continue.addItemListener(this);
add(Exit);     Exit.addItemListener(this);
```

Notice the constructor being used for the Checkbox, is the third constructor described under the heading of Check Boxes.

To give an initial priority to continuing a task, the Checkbox marked Continue, in Figure 10.7, was set at true. When the program starts executing the radio button marked Continue is set to on. Only when the radio button marked Exit is chosen will the Continue button be switched off.

Since we are dealing with Checkbox components, the method of detecting and dealing with events is identical to the previous example.

NOW DO THIS Write a program to produce the radio buttons shown in Figure 10.7, select any button and display in the MSDOS/terminal window the value of the item selected.

Text Fields

A `TextField` allows you to either input or output textual information. Although Figure 10.8 illustrates that labels are used to indicate the nature of the text being input and displayed, it is possible to include such labels within the instantiation of the `TextField` object as a string in the argument list.

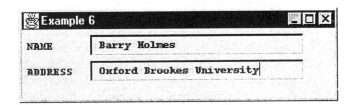

Figure 10.8 An example of editable text fields

An object from the `TextField` class is instantiated using one of the following constructors.

```
public TextField();
public TextField(int columns);
public TextField(String text);
public TextField(String text, int columns);
```

The Java code used to create the window illustrated in Figure 10.8 was as follows.

```
TextField name = new TextField(30);
TextField address = new TextField(30);

add(new Label("NAME    "));
add(name); name.addActionListener(this);
add(new Label("ADDRESS"));
add(address); address.addActionListener(this);
```

After text has been input into the appropriate text field, pressing the return key is an action that generates an event. Provided an action listener is associated with the text field, the event can be handled by implementing the `actionPerformed` method of the `ActionListener` interface.

The instance method `getActionCommand()` may be used to retrieve the string data from any text field. For example, the following code could be used to retrieve the information typed in either text field.

```
public void actionPerformed(ActionEvent event)
{
    String data = event.getActionCommand();
}
```

Alternatively, since the class `TextField` inherits from the class `TextComponent`, the instance method `getText()` from the class `TextComponent` may be used to retrieve text from the fields. For example,

```
public void actionPerformed(ActionEvent event)
{
    nameField = name.getText();
    addressField = address.getText();
}
```

where the `nameField` and `addressField` are described as variables of type `String`.

The obvious drawback of this approach is that you cannot determine from which field the text was input.

Fortunately, help is at hand, if you should want to find the particular source of an event. The class `EventObject` in the package `java.util` contains an instance method `getSource()` that returns a type `Object`. The class `ActionEvent` is a subclass of `AWTEvent`; and `AWTEvent` is a subclass of `EventObject`. Therefore, the instance method `getSource()` is applicable to `ActionEvent` objects. All the events described in the package `java.awt.event` are either subclasses of the class `AWTEvent` or exist further down this hierarchy. In which case the instance method `getSource()` is also applicable to the event classes in the `java.awt.event` package.

With this information it is now possible to discriminate between the text fields being used. For example the `actionPerformed` method may be modified as follows.

```
public void actionPerformed(ActionEvent event)
{
   if (event.getSource() == name)         //referring to the name field
      nameField = name.getText();
   else if (event.getSource() == address) // referring to the address field
      addressField = address.getText();
}
```

> **i** If you have prepared a GUI where data is to be input to a number of fields, you must press the return key after data entry for each field. The cursor, however, will remain at the end of the line of text in the field. To move this cursor to the next field use the TAB key rather than the mouse pointer. This technique is quicker for data entry.

NOW DO THIS Write a program to produce the editable text fields shown in Figure 10.8, input data into the fields and display in the MSDOS/terminal window, the values of the items input.

So far we have looked at the input of data to a text field. However, text fields may be used to display information. If we want to display items in a field, other than labels, then it is possible to use the instance method `setText` from the class `TextComponent`, the format of which follows.

```
public void setText(String text);
```

When data is input to a field, we assume quite correctly, that should we make a mistake in data entry, then we can return to the field and make changes to our data. Being able to edit a field is set as the default. However, if you have displayed information in a field and you do not want the information to be changed by a user, it is possible to prevent any changes being made to the information by using the instance method `setEditable` from the class TextComponent. The signature of the method follows.

```
public void setEditable(boolean value);
```

If a text field is described as follows:

```
TextField information = new TextField();
information.setEditable(false);
information.setText("This field is not for change");
```

then the contents of the field cannot be changed.

Text Areas

If you are inputting, or wanting to display a large amount of text, then a single text field becomes impractical owing to the restricted size of the field. A text area, however, will allow you to input and display a large amount of information. Figure 10.9 illustrates how a poem, The Blackbird, by Thomas Hardy, can be displayed in a text area. An object from the `TextArea` class can be instantiated using the following constructors.

```
public TextArea();
public TextArea(String text);
public TextArea(int rows, int columns);
public TextArea(String text, int rows, int columns);
public TextArea(String text, int rows, int columns, int scrollbars);
```

where the scrollbars parameter in the last constructor is described in the class `TextArea` as the following self-explanatory integer constants.

```
SCROLLBARS_BOTH;
SCROLLBARS_HORIZONTAL_ONLY;
SCROLLBARS_NONE;
SCROLLBARS_VERTICAL_ONLY;
```

The Java code used to display the poem in Figure 10.9 was as follows:

```
String poem =
    "I watched a blackbird on a budding sycamore\n"+
    "One Easter Day, when sap was stirring twigs to the core;\n"+
    "I saw his tongue, and crocus-coloured bill\n"+
    "Parting and closing as he turned his trill;\n"+
    "Then he flew down, seized on a stem of hay,\n"+
    "And upped to where his building scheme was under way,\n"+
    "As if so sure a nest were never shaped on spray.\n\n"+
    "\t\t\t\tThomas Hardy 1840-1928\n";

    TextArea verse = new TextArea(poem,5,45,TextArea.SCROLLBARS_BOTH);

    add(verse);
```

where poem was a string, and the values 5 and 45 indicate that the text area will contain 5 lines, with each line containing up to 45 characters. Notice from figure 10.9 that the vertical and horizontal scroll bars are automatically added to the text area if the size of the text area is too small to accommodate the complete text.

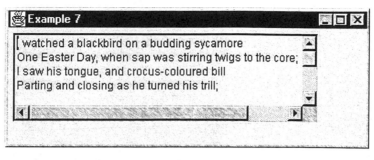

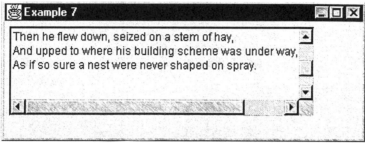

Figure 10.9 A Example of a Scrollable Text Area

Write a program to produce the scrollable text area shown in Figure 10.9.

Scrolling Lists

A scrolling list is illustrated in Figure 10.10. Within a scrolling list, if the number of items in the list is larger than the size of the list box, a scrollbar is automatically inserted to allow inspection of the other items in the list. A scrolling list can be defined to accept either one item at a time or multiple items.

Figure 10.10 An example of a scrolling list

A scrolling list has the following constructors.

```
public List();
public List(int rows, boolean multipleSelections);
```

The Java code used to produce the scrolling lists illustrated in Figure 10.10 follows.

```
List menu = new List(4,true);

menu.add("Eggs");
menu.add("Toast");
menu.add("Fries");
menu.add("Yogurt");
menu.add("Bagels");
menu.add("Pancakes");
menu.add("Coffee");

add(menu);
menu.addActionListener(this);
menu.addItemListener(this);
```

Note. A scrollbar is automatically added to the list if the number of rows is specified to be less than the numbers of items in the list.

You may notice from Figure 10.4 that a list may generate two different types of events. Hence the need to implement an `ActionListener` and an `ItemListener`.

Using a mouse pointer, when you single-click select an item from the menu, a change of state for that item has taken place. This event is handled by the item listener and by the implemented `itemStateChanged` method. To identify which item has been selected use the instance method `getItem()` from the class `java.awt.event.ItemEvent`. The method `getItem()` will return the position of the item in the menu. The first item is located at position 0 (zero), the second item is located at position 1, and so on.

```
public void itemStateChanged(ItemEvent event)
{
    position = ((Integer)event.getItem()).intValue();
}
```

where `position` is declared as a class variable of type `int`.

However, if you double-click select an item, the first click is handled by the item listener, and the second click by the action listener. The following code can be used to determine the name of the item selected from the menu .

```
public void actionPerformed(ActionEvent event)
{
    nameOfItem = event.getActionCommand();
}
```

where `nameOfItem` is declared as a class variable of type `String`.

NOW DO THIS Write a program to produce the scrolling list shown in Figure 10.10. Select items from the list and display in the MSDOS/terminal window, the values of the items selected.

Drop-Down Menus

Figure 10.11 illustrates a drop-down menu. The menu has two parts - a menu bar containing the name of the menu, and a list of menu items.

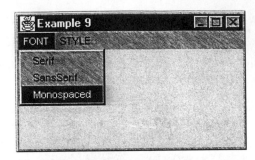

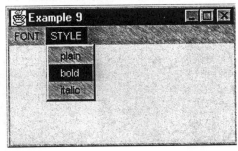

Figure 10.11 Examples of drop-down menus

The constructor for the menu bar is:

```
public MenuBar();
```

and the constructor for the menu is:

```
public Menu();
public Menu(String label);
```

The code used to create the drop-down menus illustrated in Figure 10.11 follows.

```
MenuBar bar = new MenuBar();

Menu font = new Menu("FONT");

font.add("Serif");
font.add("SansSerif");
font.add("Monospaced");

Menu style = new Menu("STYLE");

style.add("plain");
style.add("bold");
style.add("italic");
bar.add(font);
bar.add(style);
this.setMenuBar(bar);
font.addActionListener(this);
style.addActionListener(this);
```

To determine the item selected from the drop-down menu, use the action listener and implement the `actionPerformed` method. The `getActionCommand` will return, as a string, the value of the selected item.

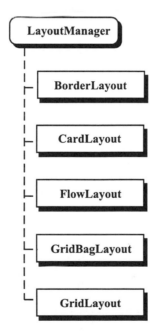

NOW DO THIS   Write a program to produce the drop-down menu illustrated in Figure 10.11. Select any item from the menu and display in the MSDOS/terminal window the value of the item selected.

10.6 Layout Managers

A **layout manager** is an interface (`java.awt.LayoutManager`) that defines the methods necessary for a class to be able to arrange `Component` objects within a `Container` object. There are five layout classes that implement the interface `LayoutManager`.

Figure 10.12 Five implementations of the layout manager

From the five layout classes illustrated in Figure 10.12, we will examine just `FlowLayout` and `GridLayout`. In addition, we will consider how to place components into a container when no layout manager is specified.

We have already briefly introduced the `FlowLayout` class, and used it in implementing the GUI components described in the previous section.

FlowLayout

Figure 10.13 illustrates that when using the `FlowLayout` class, components are added to the container one after another in rows, and when a row is full the next component is added to the next row.

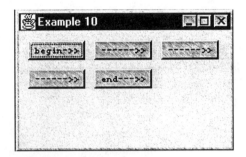

Figure 10.13 An example of buttons using FlowLayout

The `FlowLayout` class has three constructors.

```
public FlowLayout();
public FlowLayout(int align);
public FlowLayout(int align, int hGap, int vGap);
```

The argument `align` may be any one of the three class constants LEFT, RIGHT or CENTER (default), and specifies whether the alignment of the components will be left justified, right justified or centralized with respect to the edge of the frame.

The arguments `hGap` and `vGap` specify the number of horizontal and vertical pixels between components.

The code used to add the buttons to the frame in figure 10.13 is:

```
setLayout(new FlowLayout(FlowLayout.LEFT,10,10));

add(new Button("begin->>"));
add(new Button("------>>"));
add(new Button("------>>"));
add(new Button("------>>"));
add(new Button("end--->>"));
```

which indicates that the layout of the buttons are left justified in the frame, and that each button has a horizontal and vertical separation from the next by 10 pixels.

GridLayout

Figure 10.14 illustrates that when using a GridLayout manager the components are placed into the respective cells of the grid. When the cells of the first row are filled, the components continue to be placed in the next row, and so on, until eventually there are no further components to place on the grid.

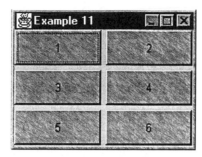

Figure 10.14 An example of buttons using GridLayout

The constructor for the GridLayout class is:

```
public GridLayout(int rows, int columns);
public GridLayout(int rows, int columns, int hGap, int vGap)
                throws IllegalArgumentException;
```

where the parameters rows and columns specifies the size of the grid; and hGap and vGap specify the distance in pixels between the components.

The code used to generate the grid in figure 10.14 is:

```
setLayout(new GridLayout(3,2,5,5));

        for (int counter=1; counter <=6; counter++)
           add(new Button(String.valueOf(counter)));
```

No layout manager

If you need to plan a GUI to your exact requirements, then you may prefer not to use a layout manager. In which case, each component must be placed in the container by the programmer. The following code was used in the constructor to produce the GUI illustrated in Figure 10.15.

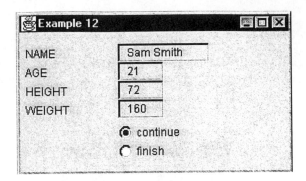

Figure 10.15 An example of no layout manager being used

```
class Form extends Frame implements ActionListener, ItemListener,
                                    WindowListener
{
    static TextField name   = new TextField(20);
    static TextField age    = new TextField(4);
    static TextField height = new TextField(4);
    static TextField weight = new TextField(4);

    public Form(String s)
    {
        super(s);
        setBackground(Color.yellow);
        setForeground(Color.black);
        setLayout(null);

        Label l1 = new Label("NAME  ");
        Label l2 = new Label("AGE    ");
        Label l3 = new Label("HEIGHT");
        Label l4 = new Label("WEIGHT");

        l1.setLocation(10,40);  l1.setSize(100,10);
        l2.setLocation(10,60);  l2.setSize(100,10);
        l3.setLocation(10,80);  l3.setSize(100,10);
        l4.setLocation(10,100); l4.setSize(100,10);

        add(l1); add(l2); add(l3); add(l4);

        name.setLocation(110,35);   name.setSize(100,20);
        age.setLocation(110,55);    age.setSize(50,20);
        height.setLocation(110,75); height.setSize(50,20);
        weight.setLocation(110,95); weight.setSize(50,20);

        add(name); add(age); add(height); add(weight);

        CheckboxGroup whatNext = new CheckboxGroup();

        Checkbox cb1 = new Checkbox("continue",whatNext,true);
        Checkbox cb2 = new Checkbox("finish",whatNext,false);
```

```
      cb1.setLocation(110,120); cb1.setSize(100,20);
      cb2.setLocation(110,140); cb2.setSize(100,20);

      add(cb1); add(cb2);

      name.addActionListener(this);
      age.addActionListener(this);
      height.addActionListener(this);
      weight.addActionListener(this);
      cb1.addItemListener(this);
      cb2.addItemListener(this);
      addWindowListener(this);
   }
   .
   .
   .
}
```

When no layout manager is required you should include a `null` argument in the call to the `setLayout` method.

The `Component` class methods `setLocation` and `setSize` have the following signatures.

```
public void setlocation(int x, int y);
public void setSize(int width, int height);
```

The instance method `setLocation` specifies the location (x, y) of the top left-hand corner of the component in the container. The origin of (0,0) is the top left-hand corner of the container. The instance method `setSize` specifies the width and height of the component. All locations and measurements are specified in pixels.

Case Study: Ben's Breakfast Bar

Problem. If you return to Figure 2.6 you will see a menu for Ben's Breakfast Bar. Write a program to display this menu on the screen, and allow a customer to select/cancel as many items from the menu as the customer wants to order. After the selection has been completed, display a fully itemized check of the items chosen; and display the subtotal, local tax (5% of subtotal) and the total.

Problem Analysis. Before starting a full analysis on how to solve the problem, it is a good idea to have a visual impression of the final output on the screen. The screen layout document is very useful, since it can be used not only to show the types of components being used in the GUI, but also where the components are to be placed in the container.

In the screen layout document that follows, the components `Label`, `List`, `Button` and `TextArea` have been identified. The position on the screen of each component is illustrated by horizontal and vertical coordinates along the edge of the screen layout document.

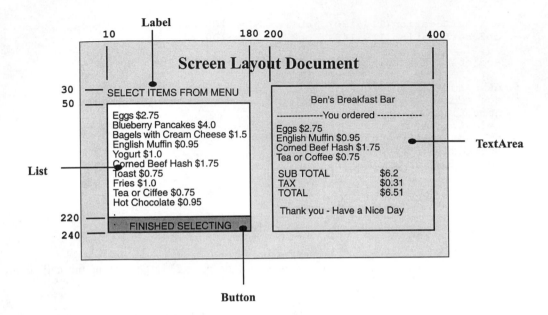

Button

From the screen layout document, it is clear that the menu is to appear in a List, and the check (or bill) to appear in a TextArea alongside the menu. A customer signals their menu selection is complete by pressing the button marked FINISHED SELECTING.

Associated with every List component is a one-dimensional array that stores the indexes of those items in the list that have been selected. The first or top item in the list is index 0 (zero), the next item down the list is index 1, the next item index 2, and so on. Therefore, if Eggs, English Muffin, Corned Beef Hash and Tea or Coffee had been selected from the list, the associated array has stored the indexes 0, 3, 5 and 8. There is an instance method in the class `java.awt.List` called `getSelectedIndexes()` that returns an integer array containing the values of those indexes where selections have been made from the list.

When the button is pressed to indicate that the selection from the menu is complete, the indexes stored in the array returned by `getSelectedIndexes()`, will be used to look-up the names of the items from a separate array of names and look-up the prices of the items from a separate array of prices. The names and the prices can then be used to display the information in the check for the food ordered.

Analysis of Classes. The class we are intending to create is a graphical user interface known as `Gui`. There is only one public method that is of relevance to the user of `Gui`, and that is the constructor. Hence the public face of the `Gui` class is:

```
class Gui extends Frame implements ActionListener, WindowListener
{
    public Gui(String s);
}
```

This description of `Gui` shows that this class is a subclass of `Frame`, and it implements the action and window listeners. The action listener will react in response to the button being pressed, and the window listener will react in response to the frame being closed.

Algorithms.

The starting point for algorithm development is the `Gui` constructor.

1. call super constructor
2. set background color of frame
3. set layout manager (in this case to null since no manager is being used)
4. display label asking customer to select items from the menu
5. set up menu
6. display button to be pressed when customer has finished selecting items
7. add action listener
8. add window listener

Stepwise refinement may be used to expand upon the statement to *set up menu*.

5. set up menu
5.1 for every item in list
5.2   add name and price of item to list
5.3 add menu to Frame container
5.4 add action listener for list

Data Dictionary for the Gui. The `Gui` contains class data that can be accessed by any of the methods within the `Gui` class. These class variables will be the number of items in a menu, arrays used to store the names of the items and the prices of the items; and instantiations of the List and the TextArea components.

```
static final int NUMBER_OF_MENU_ITEMS = 10;

static String[] menuItems = {"Eggs",
                             "Blueberry Pancakes",
                             "Bagels with Cream Cheese",
                             "English Muffin",
                             "Yogurt",
                             "Corned Beef Hash",
                             "Toast",
                             "Fries",
                             "Tea or Coffee",
                             "Hot Chocolate"};

static float[] menuPrices = {2.75f,4.00f,1.50f,0.95f,1.00f,
                             1.75f,0.75f,1.00f,0.75f,0.95f};

List      menu = new List(NUMBER_OF_MENU_ITEMS, true);
TextArea  check = new TextArea();
```

When the button is pressed to signify the end of customer selection, the check is displayed in the text area. The call to the method `displayCheck()` is found in the `actionPerformed` method as part of the `ActionListener` interface. The algorithm to display the check follows.

1. set location and size of text area for check
2. calculate cost of a meal
3. display heading of check
4. display each item selected
5. display the sub total, tax and total
6. display thank you message
7. reset list array of indexes to selected items

2. calculate cost of a meal
2.1 for each cell of selected items array
2.2   increase subtotal by price of selected item
2.3 calculate local tax
2.4 calculate total

4. display each item selected
4.1 for each cell of selected items array
4.2   get item from list and display value

7. reset list array of indexes to selected items
7.1 for each cell of selected items array
7.2   deselect item from list

Data Dictionary. The local data for the method `displayCheck()` contains an array for storing the selected indexes from the List; floating-point variables for the local tax rate, tax calculated, sub total and total.

```
int[] listArray = menu.getSelectedIndexes();
float localTax = 0.05f;
float tax;
float subTotal=0;
float total;
```

Desk Check of cost of meal in displayCheck(). Assume three items are chosen from the list -Eggs, Toast and Hot Chocolate. The array of indexes to selected items `listArray`, will contain just three indexes, `listArray[0]` contains 0 (position of Eggs in the list) and `listArray[1]` contains 6 (position of Toast in the list) and `listArray[2]` contains 9 (position of Hot Chocolate in the list).

index		0	1	2	3
index != listArray.length?		true	true	true	false
listArray[index]		0	6	9	
menuPrices[listArray[index]]		2.75	0.75	0.95	
subtotal	0	2.75	3.50	4.45	
tax				0.22	
total				4.67	

Note - when attempting to output numbers relating to costs it is necessary to convert the floating point numbers to numbers containing only two decimal places, rounded to the nearest cent as appropriate. For this reason it has been necessary to include a method twoDecimalPlaces to convert all prices and costs to the correct format.

Coding

```
// chap_10\Ex_4.java
// lists and text areas - Ben's Breakfast Bar

import java.awt.*;
import java.awt.event.*;

class Gui extends Frame implements ActionListener, WindowListener
{
    static final int NUMBER_OF_MENU_ITEMS = 10;

    List       menu = new List(NUMBER_OF_MENU_ITEMS, true);
    TextArea   check = new TextArea();

    static String[] menuItems = {"Eggs",
                    "Blueberry Pancakes",
                    "Bagels with Cream Cheese",
                    "English Muffin",
                    "Yogurt",
                    "Corned Beef Hash",
                    "Toast",
                    "Fries",
                    "Tea or Coffee",
                    "Hot Chocolate"};

    static float[] menuPrices = {2.75f,4.00f,1.50f,0.95f,1.00f,
                    1.75f,0.75f,1.00f,0.75f,0.95f};

    //-------------------------------------------------------------

    public Gui(String s)
    {
        super(s);
        setBackground(Color.yellow);
        setLayout(null);

        // display label, menu and button
        Label menuLabel = new Label("SELECT ITEMS FROM MENU");
        menuLabel.setLocation(10,30);
```

```
        menuLabel.setSize(180,20);
        add(menuLabel);
        setUpMenu();

        Button button = new Button("FINISHED SELECTING");
        button.setLocation(10,220);
        button.setSize(180,20);
        add(button);
        button.addActionListener(this);
        add(check);
        addWindowListener(this);
    }

    //-----------------------------------------------------------------

    private void setUpMenu()
    // method to display menu on screen
    {
        for (int index=0; index != NUMBER_OF_MENU_ITEMS; index++)
        {
            StringBuffer item = new StringBuffer();

            menu.add(menuItems[index]+" $"+menuPrices[index]);
        }

        menu.setLocation(10,50);
        menu.setSize(180,170);
        add(menu);
        menu.addActionListener(this);
    }

    //-----------------------------------------------------------------

    private void displayCheck()
    // method to display order and costs
    {
        int[] listArray = menu.getSelectedIndexes();
        float localTax = 0.05f;
        float tax;
        float subTotal=0;
        float total;

        check.setLocation(200,30);
        check.setSize(200,240);

        // set the text area to non-edit mode
        check.setEditable(false);

        // calculate cost of meal
        for (int index=0; index != listArray.length; index++)
            subTotal = subTotal + menuPrices[listArray[index]];

        tax = twoDecimalPlaces(localTax*subTotal);
        total = twoDecimalPlaces(subTotal+tax);

        // display costs
        check.append("                BEN'S BREAKFAST BAR\n\n");
```

```java
        check.append("-------------- You ordered ----------\n");
        for (int index=0; index != listArray.length; index++)
        {
            check.append(menu.getItem(listArray[index])+"\n");
        }
        check.append("\n");
        check.append("SUB TOTAL\t$"+String.valueOf(subTotal)+"\n");
        check.append("TAX       \t\t$"+String.valueOf(tax)+"\n");
        check.append("TOTAL     \t\t$"+String.valueOf(total)+"\n\n");
        check.append("Thank you - Have a Nice Day\n\n");

        // reset list array
        for (int index=0; index != listArray.length; index++)
            menu.deselect(listArray[index]);
    }

    //-------------------------------------------------------------

    private float twoDecimalPlaces(float number)
    // function to adjust a floating-point value to only
    // two decimal places with rounding
    {
        final float roundingFraction = 0.005f;
              float newNumber;

        number = number+roundingFraction;
        newNumber = (int)(100.0f * number);
        return newNumber/100.0f;
    }

    //-------------------------------------------------------------

    public void windowClosed(WindowEvent event){}
    public void windowDeiconified(WindowEvent event){}
    public void windowIconified(WindowEvent event){}
    public void windowActivated(WindowEvent event){}
    public void windowDeactivated(WindowEvent event){}
    public void windowOpened(WindowEvent event){}

    public void windowClosing(WindowEvent event)
    {
        System.exit(0);
    }

    //-------------------------------------------------------------

    public void actionPerformed(ActionEvent event)
    {
        Object source = event.getActionCommand();

        if (source.equals("FINISHED SELECTING"))
        {
            displayCheck();
        }
    }
}
```

```
class Ex_4
{
    public static void main(String[] args)
    {
        Gui screen = new Gui("Example 13");
        Font f = new Font("SansSerf",Font.BOLD,11);

        screen.setFont(f);
        screen.setSize(410,300);
        screen.setVisible(true);
    }
}
```

Test results

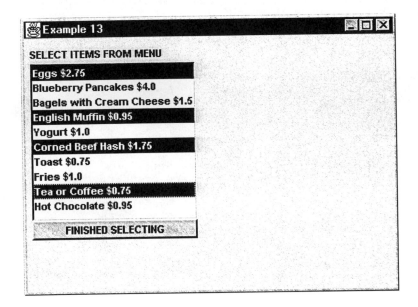

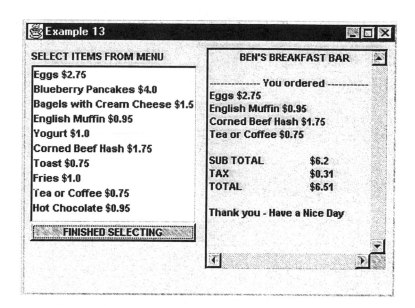

Comment. If Ben changes his menu on a regular basis, you will need to change the hard-coded names of foods/beverages and prices in the two arrays. Under such circumstances the program should be re-written to read the names of foods/beverages and prices from a text file. That way, only the contents of the text file needs to be changed and not the program!

Turn to the Exercises at the end of this chapter and attempt question 27.

Case Study: Simple Calculator

Problem. Design and write a program to mimic a simple calculator. The calculator can perform the operations of addition, subtraction, multiplication and division on positive integer values only. The input of the data for a calculation always follows the predefined sequence of pressing digit keys to input the first number, followed by pressing a single arithmetic operator key; then pressing digit keys to input the second number, followed by pressing the equals key. The answer is then displayed in the text field of the calculator.

Problem Analysis. Once again it is useful to be able to visualize what the calculator will look like on the screen before any programming can begin.

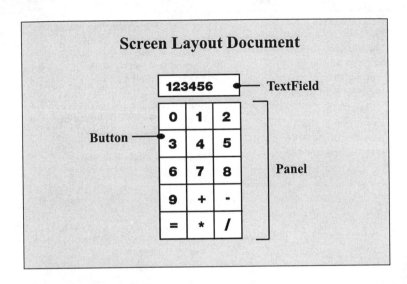

This problem introduces a `Panel`; a new container not mentioned in the earlier part of the chapter. A `Panel` is a class of container that is itself contained within a container. Unlike `Frame`, `Panel` is a container that does not create a separate window of its own. `Panel` is suitable for holding other components, such as buttons in this example. In the creation of the calculator interface, buttons are added to the panel and the panel is added to the frame.

The `Panel` uses a `GridLayout` manager, with 5 rows and 3 columns to add the fifteen buttons to the `Panel` container. On each button is written a digit in the range 0..9; or an operator +,-,* , /, =.

The calculator interface also contains a `TextField` for displaying the numbers that are keyed into the calculator and the result of a computation. Despite the `Panel` using the `GridLayout` manager to arrange the buttons within the `Panel`, both the `Panel` and the `TextField` are added to the `Frame` using the `FlowLayout` manager.

The series of actions that take place in using the calculator follows.

Digits in the range 0..9 are input via the keypad until an arithmetic operator is input. The arithmetic operator is used to mark the completion of the input of the first number. Digits in the range 0..9 are again input until an equal sign is input. The equal sign is used to mark the completion of the input of the second number. The calculator then performs the appropriate arithmetic operation on the two numbers and displays the answer in the text field.

Both numbers are stored in two different `StringBuffers`. Every time a digit is entered at the keypad it is appended to the appropriate buffer, thus building each number a digit at a time. To calculate the result of the arithmetic operation, the numbers in each `StringBuffer` are evaluated as integers and operated upon according to the arithmetic operation specified.

Analysis of Classes. The class we are intending to create is a graphical user interface known as `Calculator`. There is only one public method that is of relevance to the user of `Calculator`, and that is the constructor. Hence the public face of the `Calculator` class is:

```
class Calculator extends Frame implements ActionListener, WindowListener
{
    public Calculator(String s);
}
```

Similar to the previous example, the class `Calculator` is a subclass of `Frame`, and it implements the action and window listeners. The action listener will react in response to any button being pressed, and the window listener will react in response to the frame being closed.

Algorithms. Once again, starting with the constructor for the class.

1. call super constructor
2. set background color of frame
3. add window listener
4. set layout manager for the components in the frame container
5. add text field to the frame container
6. instantiate keypad that represents a panel of buttons
7. set layout manager as GridLayout for the keypad
8. add individual buttons to the keypad panel
9. add keypad panel to the frame container

8. add individual buttons to the keypad panel
8.1 for every button in the keypad
8.2   instantiate button with appropriate value from look-up table
8.3   add action listener for that button
8.4   add the button to the keypad

Data Dictionary for Class Calculator. The GUI contains data that can be accessed by any of the methods within the `Calculator` class. These variables will be the text field to display the answer to a calculation; an array to store the fifteen button components; an array of strings to store the functionality of each key; two string buffers for storing the first number and second number; a character variable to store the operator, and finally a boolean variable to mark when the first number has been input.

```
TextField display = new TextField(10);
Button[] button = new Button[15];

static String[] keys = {" 0 "," 1 "," 2 ",
                        " 3 "," 4 "," 5 ",
                        " 6 "," 7 "," 8 ",
                        " 9 "," + "," - ",
                        " = "," * "," / "};

StringBuffer registerA = new StringBuffer();
StringBuffer registerB = new StringBuffer();

char operator;
boolean firstNumberAlreadyInput = false;
```

When a button is pressed it could signify one of three possible actions; the input of a digit, the input of an operator or the input of an equals sign. The `actionPerformed` method must therefore check for the occurrence of any of the three actions. The algorithm for the `actionPerformed` method follows. Note - since the action of pressing a digit key is more common than pressing either an operator key or an equals key, it makes sense to test for the digit keys before the operator and equals keys.

1.   *get the source of the event*
2.   *for every digit key (keys 0..9)*
3.   *   if source is digit key*
4.   *   if first number already input*
5.   *   append digit to register B*
6.   *   display register B in text field*
7.   *   return*
8.   *   else*
9.   *   append digit to register A*
10. *   display register A in text field*
11. *   return*
12. *for every operator key*
13. *   if source is an operator and not equals key*
14. *   store operator*
15. *   set first number already input flag to true*
16. *   return*
17. *if source is equals key*
18. *   display in text field result of calculation*
19. *   reset all variables used in calculations*

Data Dictionary for actionPerformed. Owing to the layout of the buttons on the keypad, the arithmetic operator keys can be found at indexed positions 10,11,13 and 14 in the `button` array. The equals key is at indexed position 12. In checking for operator keys it is necessary to know the position of the equals key, hence the inclusion of the constant denoting the position of the equals key.

```
final int positionOfEqualsKey = 12;
```

The line of pseudocode

18. display in text field result of calculation

needs to be refined further. This one statement contains not only a call to a method to perform the calculation on the input data, but also to display the result of the calculation in the text field.

18.1 perform arithmetic calculation on data
18.2 display result of calculation

18.1.1 convert contents of register A from a string to an integer value
18.1.2 convert contents of register B from a string to an integer value
18.1.3 switch on operator
18.1.4 case '+': return sum of numbers as a string
18.1.5 case '-': return difference of numbers as a string
18.1.6 case '': return product of numbers as a string*
18.1.7 default: return quotient of numbers as a string

To cater for any attempt to divide by zero it is prudent to set up an exception handler that will audibly warn of the error as well as returning an error message to be displayed in the text field.

Data Dictionary for doCalculation. In order to perform arithmetic upon the contents of register A and register B, it is necessary to introduce two temporary integer variables A and B.

Desk Check. The test data assumes the following string of characters are input via the keypad 19*56=

source	1	9	*	5	6	=
digit	1	9	10	5	6	10
operator			*			
positionOfOperator			13			15
registerA	1	19				
registerB				5	56	
firstNumberAlreadyInput	false		true			false
output	1	19		5	56	1064

Coding

```
// chap_10\Ex_5.java
// program to mimic a calculator

import java.awt.*;
import java.awt.event.*;
import java.io.*;
```

```
class Calculator extends Frame implements ActionListener, WindowListener
{
    private TextField display = new TextField(10);
    private Button[] button = new Button[15];

    static String[] keys = {" 0 "," 1 "," 2 ",
                            " 3 "," 4 "," 5 ",
                            " 6 "," 7 "," 8 ",
                            " 9 "," + "," - ",
                            " = "," * "," / "};

    private StringBuffer registerA = new StringBuffer();
    private StringBuffer registerB = new StringBuffer();

    private char operator;
    private boolean firstNumberAlreadyInput = false;

    //-------------------------------------------------------------------

    // constructor
    public Calculator(String s)
    {
        super(s);
        setBackground(Color.yellow);
        addWindowListener(this);

        // set up display
        setLayout(new FlowLayout(FlowLayout.CENTER));
        add(display);

        Panel keypad = new Panel();
        keypad.setLayout(new GridLayout(5,3));

        // set up keypad
        for (int index=0; index != 15; index++)
        {
            button[index] = new Button(keys[index]);
            button[index].addActionListener(this);
            keypad.add(button[index]);
        }
        add(keypad);
    }

    //-------------------------------------------------------------------

    public void windowClosed(WindowEvent event){}
    public void windowDeiconified(WindowEvent event){}
    public void windowIconified(WindowEvent event){}
    public void windowActivated(WindowEvent event){}
    public void windowDeactivated(WindowEvent event){}
    public void windowOpened(WindowEvent event){}
    public void windowClosing(WindowEvent event)
    {
        System.exit(0);
    }
```

```
// method to detect which key has been pressed
public void actionPerformed(ActionEvent event)
{
    final int positionOfEqualsKey = 12;

    Object source = event.getActionCommand();

    // test for digit in the range 0-9
    for (int digit = 0; digit != 10; digit++)
    {
        if (source.equals(keys[digit]))
        {
            if (firstNumberAlreadyInput)
            {
                registerB.append(String.valueOf(digit));
                display.setText(registerB.toString());
                return;
            }
            else
            {
                registerA.append(String.valueOf(digit));
                display.setText(registerA.toString());
                return;
            }
        }
    }

    // test for an operator
    for (int positionOfOperator=10; positionOfOperator != 15;
            positionOfOperator++)
    {
        // test for +, -, * or /
        if (source.equals(keys[positionOfOperator]) &&
            (positionOfOperator != positionOfEqualsKey))
        {
            operator = keys[positionOfOperator].charAt(1);
            firstNumberAlreadyInput = true;
            return;
        }
    }

    // test for =
    if (source.equals(" = "))
    {
        display.setText(doCalculation());
        registerA.setLength(0);
        registerB.setLength(0);
        firstNumberAlreadyInput = false;
    }
}
```

```
    private String doCalculation()
    {
        final char beep = '\u0007';

        try
        {
            int A = new Integer(registerA.toString()).intValue();
            int B = new Integer(registerB.toString()).intValue();

            switch (operator)
            {
                case '+' : return String.valueOf(A+B);
                case '-' : return String.valueOf(A-B);
                case '*' : return String.valueOf(A*B);
                default  : return String.valueOf(A/B);
            }
        }

        catch(Exception ae)
        {
            System.out.print(beep);
            return "   E R R O R";
        }
    }
}

//------------------------------------------------------------------

class Ex_5
{
    public static void main(String[] args)
    {
        Calculator C = new Calculator("Example 17");

        C.setSize(150,200);
        C.setVisible(true);
    }
}
```

Test results - The specimen output illustrates two displays.

10.7 Graphics

Within the `java.awt` package is a `Graphics` class that will permit drawing a variety of shapes. This is an abstract class, and hence has no constructor, that defines methods for performing line drawing of various shapes, area filling, and other graphical activities.

> A Graphics object cannot be created directly though a constructor - it may be obtained with the `getGraphics()` method of a `Component`.

A partial listing of the `Graphics` class follows, showing some of the methods we will be using in the remainder of this chapter. For a full description of the Graphics class turn to your downloaded Sun documentation.

```
public abstract class java.awt.Graphics extends java.lang.Object
{
   .

   // Methods
   public abstract void clearRect(int  x, int  y, int width, int  height);

   public abstract void drawLine(int  x1, int  y1, int  x2,  int  y2);
   public abstract void drawOval(int  x, int  y, int width, int  height);
   public void drawRect(int  x, int  y,  int  width, int  height);
   public abstract void drawString(String  str, int  x, int  y);

   public abstract void fillOval(int x,int y,int width,int height);
   public abstract void fillRect(int  x, int  y, int  width,  int  height);

   public abstract void setColor(Color  c);
   public abstract void setFont(Font  font);

   public String toString();
   .
   .

}
```

With interactive drawing on the screen, the position of the mouse can provide the coordinates for drawing a shape.

Actions such as, clicking, releasing and pressing the mouse button all generate events that can be detected by the mouse listener. The appropriate method from the `MouseListener` interface is implemented as a means of reacting to the event taking place.

Program Example 10.4 demonstrates how the position of the mouse can be captured and displayed as a set of coordinates on the screen. The methods `getX()` and `getY()` are from the class `MouseEvent`; and the method `drawString` is from the `Graphics` class.

Program Example 10.4: Plotting Mouse Coordinates on the Screen

```java
// chap_10\Ex_6.java
// program to demonstrate the construction of a container
// and mouse events

import java.awt.*;
import java.awt.event.*;

class Gui extends Frame implements WindowListener, MouseListener
{
    // constructor
    public Gui(String s)
    {
        super(s);
        setBackground(Color.yellow);
        addMouseListener(this);
        addWindowListener(this);
    }

    public void mouseClicked(MouseEvent event){}
    public void mouseEntered(MouseEvent event){}
    public void mouseExited(MouseEvent event){}
    public void mouseReleased(MouseEvent event){}

    public void mousePressed(MouseEvent event)
    {
        // get coordinates of mouse
        int x = event.getX();
        int y = event.getY();

        Graphics g = getGraphics();

        // display message on screen
        g.drawString("+ ["+String.valueOf(x)+","+
                        String.valueOf(y)+"]",x,y);
    }

    public void windowClosed(WindowEvent event){}
    public void windowDeiconified(WindowEvent event){}
    public void windowIconified(WindowEvent event){}
    public void windowActivated(WindowEvent event){}
    public void windowDeactivated(WindowEvent event){}
    public void windowOpened(WindowEvent event){}

    public void windowClosing(WindowEvent event)
    {
        System.exit(0);
    }
}
```

```
class Ex_6
{
   public static void main(String[] args)
   {
      Gui screen = new Gui("Example 18");

      screen.setSize(400,300);
      screen.setVisible(true);
   }
}
```

Test results

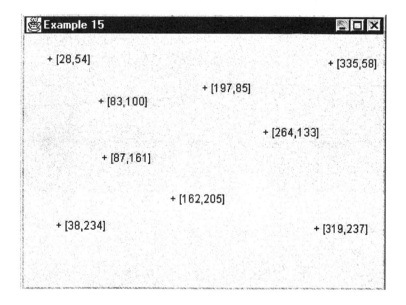

Observation. The origin of coordinates is taken to be the upper left-hand corner of the screen. From Figure 10.16 you will notice that the positive X-axis is to the right of the origin, and the positive Y-axis is directly beneath the origin.

The following technique, known as **rubber banding**, uses a mouse to determine the coordinates of a rectangular shape. To draw a rectangle we must specify the coordinates of the upper left-hand corner of the rectangle, and the width and height of the rectangle as defined by the signature of the drawRect method.

```
public void drawRect(int upperLeftX,  int upperLeftY,
                     int width,       int  height);
```

If a mouse is to be used to specify the coordinates of the upper left-hand corner, and by dragging the mouse (moving the mouse with the button kept pressed) to another location on the screen, to specify the width and height of the rectangle, then it is necessary to listen for two types of events - pressing the mouse button, and dragging the mouse.

Upon detecting the mouse button being pressed it is possible to capture the position of the mouse by using the methods getX() and getY() from the class MouseEvent. When we detect that the mouse is being moved it is also possible to capture the ever changing position of the mouse by using the methods getX() and getY().

The calculations of the coordinates for the upper left-hand corner, and width and height of the rectangle will vary when dragging the mouse either up or down the screen and to the right or left as depicted in Figure 10.16.

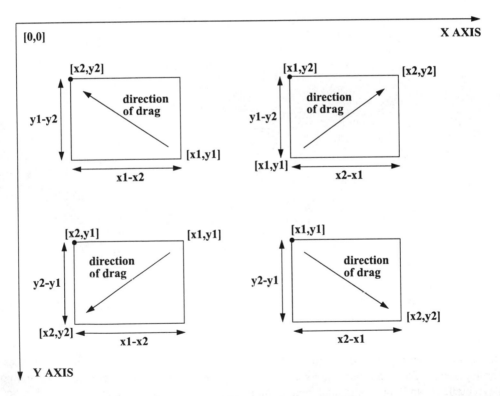

Figure 10.16 Constructing rectangles

To calculate the necessary values for the arguments of the drawRect method use the following technique. The coordinates of the upper left-hand corner, and width and height of the rectangle can be calculated using the following expressions, irrespective of the direction of the movement of the mouse.

```
upperLeftX = Math.min(x1,x2);  upperLeftY = Math.min(y1,y2);
width = Math.abs(x1-x2);       height = Math.abs(y1-y2);
```

Note - the mathematical class method **min** will return the smaller of two numbers, and the method **abs** will return the positive value of the difference between two numbers.

NOW DO THIS

Turn to the Exercises at the end of this chapter and attempt questions 28, 29 and 30.

Case Study: Sketchpad

Problem. Devise a graphical user interface for a drawing package. The package should allow for drawings to be made from a range of two-dimensional shapes using different colors. The shapes may be drawn in outline or filled. There should be a facility to erase parts of a shape or erase the entire screen. Help should be provided in how to use the drawing package and information about the package.

Problem Analysis. The solution to this problem incorporates the techniques of adding such components as a menu bar, drop-down menus, radio buttons, text fields, text areas and the inclusion of an additional window. The techniques of using a mouse to draw shapes on the screen are also incorporated into this drawing package. The screen layout document indicates the position of the components on the screen. The GUI will be similar to that illustrated in Figure 10.1.

Analysis of Classes. The class we are intending to create is a graphical user interface known as Sketchpad. There are two class constants representing the width and height of the interface and one public method, the constructor, that is of relevance to the user of Sketchpad. Hence the public face of the Sketchpad class is:

```
class Sketchpad extends Frame implements ActionListener,
                                         ItemListener,
                                         MouseListener,
                                         MouseMotionListener,
                                         WindowListener
{
   static final int WIDTH = 800;
   static final int HEIGHT = 600;

   public Sketchpad(String s);
}
```

Similar to the previous examples, the class Sketchpad is a subclass of Frame, and it implements the action, item, mouse and window listeners. The action listener will react in response to any button being pressed; the item listener will react to radio buttons being pressed; the mouse listener will react to mouse buttons being operated; the mouse motion listener will react to the movement of the mouse and finally the window listener will react in response to the frame being closed.

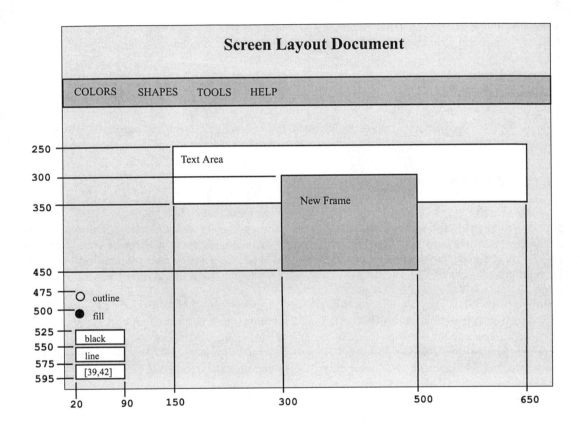

Algorithms. Starting with the class constructor.

1. set background color of frame
2. set null layout manager
3. initialize text fields
4. initialize menu components
5. initialize radio buttons
6. add mouse and window listeners

Items 3, 4 and 5 may be refined into the following pseudocode.

3. initialize text fields
3.1 add textfield to show color of figure
3.2 add textfield to show shape of figure
3.3 add textfield to show position of mouse
3.4 set up text area

4. initialize menu components
4.1 add menu bar
4.2 add colors menu and action listener
4.3 add shapes menu and action listener
4.4 add tools menu and action listener
4.5 add help menu and action listener
4.6 set menu bar

5. initialize radio buttons
5.1 add radio buttons
5.2 add item listener

Data Dictionary for the class constructor. The variables used by `Sketchpad(String s)` are the text fields for the color and shape of the figure and the position of the mouse; the menus for colors, shapes, tools and help; the menu bar; the check box group for the radio buttons; the text area for the information on how to use the sketchpad and the frame for displaying information about the drawing package.

You will notice from the listings of the variables that at this stage it is possible to make decisions about the contents of each menu.

Since many of these variables are used by other methods within the Sketchpad class, it is prudent to declare the variables within the class.

```
// text fields for displaying the chosen color, shape
// and the coordinate position of the mouse
TextField color = new TextField();
TextField shape = new TextField();
TextField position = new TextField();

// check box group for radio buttons
CheckboxGroup fillOutline = new CheckboxGroup();

// contents of the drop-down menus stored in arrays
String[] colorNames =
{"black","blue","cyan","gray","green","magenta","red","white","yellow"};
String[] shapeNames = {"line","square","rectangle","circle","ellipse"};
String[] toolNames  = {"erase","clearpad"};
String[] helpNames  = {"information","about"};

// information about using Sketchpad
String helpText;
```

```
// component for displaying information
TextArea info = new
TextArea(helpText,0,0,TextArea.SCROLLBARS_VERTICAL_ONLY);
// component for displaying information about product
Frame about = new Frame("About Sketchpad");
```

The group of objects that define the menus and radio buttons may be defined locally to the constructor.

```
MenuBar bar = new MenuBar();
Menu colors = new Menu("COLORS");
Menu shapes = new Menu("SHAPES");
Menu tools = new Menu("TOOLS");
Menu help = new Menu("HELP");

Checkbox fill = new Checkbox("fill", fillOutline, false);
Checkbox outline = new Checkbox("outline",fillOutline,true);
```

The various listener methods implement the functionality of the package. The `actionPerformed` method is called by `ActionListener` when an item is chosen from a list. The `itemStateChanged` method is called by `ItemListener` when a radio button is pressed. The `mouseDragged` and `mouseMoved` methods are called by `MouseMotionListener` when the mouse is moved. The `mousePressed` and `mouseReleased` methods are called by `MouseListener` when a mouse button is either pressed or released. Finally, the `windowClosing` method is called by `WindowListener` when the window is being closed.

Algorithm to detect an actionPerformed.

1.   *get source of event*
2.   *for every color*
3.   *if source equals color*
4.   *store name of color*
5.   *write name of color in color text field*
6.   *return*
7.   *for every shape*
8.   *if source equals shape*
9.   *store name of shape*
10.   *write name of shape in shape text field*
11.   *return*
12.   *if source equals "erase"*
13.   *set erasure flag to true*
14.   *return*
15.   *else if source equals "clearpad"*
16.   *remove any open windows*
17.   *clear the current frame*
18.   *return*

19.   *if source equals 'information'*
20.   *display information in text area*
21.   *return*
22.   *else if source equals 'about'*
23.   *display the about window*

Data Dictionary for actionPerformed. There are two local variables to declare, a graphics variable and the source of the event.

```
Graphics g = getGraphics();
Object source = event.getActionCommand();
```

However, the algorithm refers to storing the name of a color and the name of a shape; the algorithm also sets an erasure flag to indicate that erase was chosen from the TOOLS menu. These variables are not declared within the method, but declared within the class.

```
String drawColor; String drawShape;
boolean erasure;
```

The algorithm for `actionPerformed` calls a method to display the *about* window. This is a new window that describes the following facts about the drawing class. The name of the author, title of the class, date the class was written and its use.

Algorithm to displayAboutWindow.

1. set position and size of window
2. set background color and text font
3. set flow layout manager
4. add labels for name, title, date and use
5. make window visible
6. add window listener

Data Dictionary for displayAboutWindow. The method has a formal parameter list containing one parameter, a `Frame` object.

```
protected void displayAboutWindow(Frame about);
```

Algorithm to detect itemStateChanged. This algorithm will be executed if either one of the radio buttons is pressed. The purpose of the button is to show whether the drawing will be an outline or a solid (filled) shape.

1. if event equals 'fill'
2.   set fill flag to true
3. else
4.   set fill flag to false

Data Dictionary for itemStateChanged. This method requires one boolean variable, declared within the class, to indicate whether the drawing is to be solid or an outline.

```
boolean fill;
```

Algorithm to detect mouseDragged. The mouse is dragged when the mouse button is kept pressed and the mouse is moved. This algorithm must always update the current position of the mouse; checking to see if the erasure flag is set and displaying the coordinates of the mouse. A small area of screen is erased by drawing a small solid rectangle in the same color as the background.

1. get coordinates of current mouse position
2. if erasure flag set to true
3.   set current color to the same color as the background color
4.   draw a small solid rectangle at the current mouse position
5. display the coordinates of the mouse

Data Dictionary for mouseDragged. Since a graphic is drawn on the screen to erase a small area of the screen the only local variable is of type Graphics. There are two variables to denote the current position of the mouse on the screen and the erasure flag.

```
Graphics g = getGraphics();       // local variable
int x2, y2;                       // variables declared within the class
boolean erasure;
```

Algorithm to detect mouseMoved.

1. display the coordinates of the mouse

Algorithm to detect mousePressed

1. if erasure flag set true return
2. initialize coordinates of the upper left-hand corner of the rectangular drawing envelope to zero
3. initialize width and height of the rectangular drawing envelope to zero
4. get coordinates of the current mouse position
5. display a reference point on the screen showing where drawing is to begin
6. display the coordinates of the mouse

Data Dictionary for mousePressed. This method initializes four variables that represent the coordinates of the upper left-hand corner of the drawing envelope and the width and height of the drawing envelope. These variables are declared within the class.

```
int upperLeftX, upperLeftY, width, height; // stored within the class
```

Since a graphic is drawn it is necessary to declare a graphic variable local to the method.

```
Graphic g = getGraphics(); // local variable
```

Algorithm to detect mouseReleased. This algorithm triggers the drawing of a shape.

1.   *display coordinates of the mouse*
2.   *if erasure flag set to true*
3.   *reset erasure flag to false*
4.   *return*
5.   *select a color for drawing graphic*
6.   *get coordinates of current mouse position*
7.   *if shape to draw is a line*
8.   *draw line*
9.   *else if shape to draw is a circle*
10.   *call method to draw circle*
11.   *else if shape to draw is an ellipse*
12.   *call method to draw ellipse*
13.   *else if shape to draw is a square*
14.   *call method to draw square*
15.   *else if shape to draw is a rectangle*
16.   *call method to draw rectangle*
17.   *erase reference point of initial position of mouse*

Data Dictionary for mouseReleased. Since a graphic is drawn it is necessary to declare a graphic variable local to the method. Although the method makes reference to the coordinates of the current mouse position [x2,y2], the coordinates of the initial mouse position [x1,y1] and the erasure flag; these variables are declared within the class.

```
Graphic g = getGraphics(); // local variable
```

The algorithm for `mouseReleased` contains a statement to select a color for drawing a graphic. This is a call to a method that translates the color chosen in the COLOR menu to a color for drawing the graphic. The algorithm for this method follows.

Algorithm for selectColor.

1. *for every index in the colors array*
2.   *if the selected color from the menu equals the name in the colors array*
3.   *switch on index value*
4.   *case 0: set color to black*
5.   *case 1: set color to blue*
6.   *case 2: set color to cyan*
7.   *case 3: set color to gray*
8.   *case 4: set color to green*
9.   *case 5: set color to magenta*
10.   *case 6: set color to red*
11.   *case 7: set color to white*
12.   *case 8: set color to yellow*

Data Dictionary for selectColor. The only variable used in this method is the index to the array containing the names of the colors. The declaration of the index is part of the `for` loop.

The algorithm for `mouseReleased` contains statements to call a method to draw a circle, ellipse, square and rectangle. Such a method must calculate the correct parameters of the shape and draw the corresponding shape according to whether outline or fill has been chosen. The method to draw two-dimensional shapes is called `closedShapes`. The algorithm for this method follows.

Algorithm for closedShapes

1.   *calculate the correct parameters for the shape (see figure 10.15)*
2.   *if shape equals a square and fill set*
3.   *draw filled rectangle using horizontal distance only for length of side*
4.   *else if shape equals square and fill not set*
5.   *draw outline of rectangle using horizontal distance only for length of side*
6.   *if shape equals a rectangle and fill set*
7.   *draw filled rectangle*
8.   *else if shape equals rectangle and fill not set*
9.   *draw outline of rectangle*
10.   *if shape equals a circle and fill set*
11.   *draw filled circle using horizontal distance only for width and height of envelope*
12.   *else if shape equals square and fill not set*
13.   *draw outline of circle using horizontal distance for width and height of envelope*
14.   *if shape equals a ellipse and fill set*
15.   *draw filled ellipse*
16.   *else if shape equals ellipse and fill not set*
17.   *draw outline of ellipse*

Data Dictionary for closedShapes. There is a formal parameter list for this method that requires a Graphics object in order to perform the drawing, the name of the chosen shape and whether the shape is to be filled. The signature for the method is:

```
protected void closedShapes(Graphics g, String shape, boolean fill);
```

Algorithm to detect windowClosing.

1. *if event generated by the about window*
2.   *dispose of the about window*
3.   *return*
4. *else*
5.   *exit from the program*

Desk Check. As a means of fully understanding the construction of this software you are advised to desk check each method using your own test data.

Coding

```
// chap_10\Ex_7.java
// drawing program
// program to demonstrate a graphical user interface for drawing shapes

import java.awt.*;
import java.awt.event.*;

class Sketchpad extends Frame implements
      ActionListener,          // menu item
      ItemListener,            // radio buttons
      MouseListener,           // pressing/releasing a mouse button
      MouseMotionListener,     // dragging or moving a mouse
      WindowListener           // closing a window
{
   // size of Sketchpad area
   static final int WIDTH = 800;
   static final int HEIGHT = 600;

   // coordinate of upper-left hand corner of a rectangle
   int upperLeftX, upperLeftY;
   // size of surrounding rectangle
   int width, height;
   // coordinates of two selected points
   int x1,y1,x2,y2;

   // set/reset flags to indicate filling and erasing
   boolean fill = false;
   boolean erasure = false;

   // chosen color and shape - initialized to default values
   String drawColor = new String("black");
   String drawShape = new String("line");

   // text fields for displaying the chosen color, shape
   // and the coordinate position of the mouse
   TextField color = new TextField();
   TextField shape = new TextField();
   TextField position = new TextField();

   CheckboxGroup fillOutline = new CheckboxGroup();

   // contents of the drop-down menus stored in arrays
   String[] colorNames =
   {"black","blue","cyan","gray","green","magenta","red","white","yellow"};
   String[] shapeNames = {"line","square","rectangle","circle","ellipse"};
   String[] toolNames  = {"erase","clearpad"};
   String[] helpNames  = {"information","about"};

   // information about using Sketchpad
   String helpText =
   "Sketchpad allows you to draw different plane shapes over a predefined
   area.\n"+
   "A shape may be either filled or in outline, and in one of eight
   different colors.\n\n"+
   "The position of the mouse on the screen is recorded in the bottom left-
```

```
hand \n"+
"corner of the sketchpad. The choice of color and shape are displayed
also in \n"+
"the left-hand corner of the sketchpad\n\n"+
"The size of a shape is determined by the position of the mouse when the
mouse \n"+
"button is first pressed, followed by the mouse being dragged to the
final position\n"+
"and released. The first press of the mouse button will generate a
reference dot \n"+
"on the screen. This dot will disappear after the mouse button is
released\n\n"+
"Both the square and circle only use the distance measured along the
horizontal \n"+
"axis when determining the size of the shape.\n\n"+
"Upon selecting erase, press the mouse button, and move the mouse over
the area\n"+
"to be erased. Releasing the mouse button will deactivate erasure\n\n"+
"To erase this text area choose clearpad from the TOOLS menu\n\n";

// componet for displaying information
TextArea info = new
TextArea(helpText,0,0,TextArea.SCROLLBARS_VERTICAL_ONLY);
// component for displaying information about product
Frame about = new Frame("About Sketchpad");

//----------------------------------------------------------------------
//helper methods
private void initializeTextFields()
{
    // add textfield to show color of figure
    color.setLocation(5,525);
    color.setSize(70,20);
    color.setBackground(Color.white);
    color.setText(drawColor);
    add(color);

    // add textfield to show shape of figure
    shape.setLocation(5,550);
    shape.setSize(70,20);
    shape.setBackground(Color.white);
    shape.setText(drawShape);
    add(shape);

    // add textfield to show position of mouse
    position.setLocation(5,575);
    position.setSize(70,20);
    position.setBackground(Color.white);
    add(position);

    // set up textfield for information
    info.setLocation(150,250);
    info.setSize(500,100);
    info.setBackground(Color.white);
    info.setEditable(false);
}
```

```java
private void initializeMenuComponents()
{
    // add pull-down menu to menu bar
    MenuBar bar = new MenuBar();

    // add colours menu
    Menu colors = new Menu("COLORS");
    for (int index=0; index != colorNames.length; index++)
        colors.add(colorNames[index]);
    bar.add(colors);
    colors.addActionListener(this);

    // add shapes menu
    Menu shapes = new Menu("SHAPES");
    for (int index=0; index != shapeNames.length; index++)
        shapes.add(shapeNames[index]);
    bar.add(shapes);
    shapes.addActionListener(this);

    // add tools menu
    Menu tools = new Menu("TOOLS");
    for (int index=0; index != toolNames.length; index++)
        tools.add(toolNames[index]);
    bar.add(tools);
    tools.addActionListener(this);

    // add help menu
    Menu help = new Menu("HELP");
    for (int index=0; index != helpNames.length; index++)
        help.add(helpNames[index]);
    bar.add(help);
    help.addActionListener(this);

    setMenuBar(bar);
}

//-------------------------------------------------------------


private void initializeRadioButtons()
{
    // add radio buttons
    Checkbox fill = new Checkbox("fill", fillOutline, false);
    Checkbox outline = new Checkbox("outline",fillOutline,true);

    fill.setLocation(5,500);
    fill.setSize(70,20);
    add(fill);
    fill.addItemListener(this);

    outline.setLocation(5,475);
    outline.setSize(70,20);
    add(outline);
    outline.addItemListener(this);
}
```

```
// constructor
public Sketchpad(String s)
{
    super(s);
    setBackground(Color.yellow);
    setLayout(null);

    initializeTextFields();
    initializeMenuComponents();
    initializeRadioButtons();

    // set up remaining listeners
    addMouseMotionListener(this);
    addMouseListener(this);
    addWindowListener(this);
}

//----------------------------------------------------------------

public void actionPerformed(ActionEvent event)
// method to detect which item is chosen from a menu
{
    Graphics g = getGraphics();
    Object source = event.getActionCommand();

    // check for color chosen
    for (int index=0; index != colorNames.length; index++)
        if (source.equals(colorNames[index]))
        {
            drawColor =colorNames[index];
            color.setText(drawColor);
            return;
        }

    // check for shape chosen
    for (int index=0; index != shapeNames.length; index++)
        if (source.equals(shapeNames[index]))
        {
            drawShape = shapeNames[index];
            shape.setText(drawShape);
            return;
        }

    // check for tools chosen
    if (source.equals("erase"))
    {
        erasure = true;
        return;
    }
    else if (source.equals("clearpad"))
    {
        remove(info);
        g.clearRect(0,0,800,600);
        return;
    }
```

```
      // check for help chosen
      if (source.equals("information"))
      {
         add(info);
         return;
      }
      else if (source.equals("about"))
      {
         displayAboutWindow(about);
      }
   }

   //----------------------------------------------------------------

   public void itemStateChanged(ItemEvent event)
   // method to detect which radio button was pressed
   {
      if (event.getItem() == "fill")
         fill = true;
      else if (event.getItem() == "outline")
         fill = false;
   }

   //----------------------------------------------------------------

   protected void displayAboutWindow(Frame about)
   // method to display information about Sketchpad
   // in new window
   {
      about.setLocation(300,300);
      about.setSize(200,150);
      about.setBackground(Color.cyan);
      about.setFont(new Font("Serif",Font.ITALIC,14));
      about.setLayout(new FlowLayout(FlowLayout.LEFT));

      about.add(new Label("Author: Barry Holmes"));
      about.add(new Label("Title: Sketchpad"));
      about.add(new Label("Date: 1998"));
      about.add(new Label("Use: Demonstration only"));
      about.setVisible(true);
      about.addWindowListener(this);
   }

   //----------------------------------------------------------------

   protected void selectColor(Graphics g)
   // method to change color of graphic to correspond
   // with chosen menu item
   {
      for (int index=0; index != colorNames.length; index++)
      {
         if (drawColor.equals(colorNames[index]))
         {
            switch (index)
            {
               case 0: g.setColor(Color.black);break;
               case 1: g.setColor(Color.blue);break;
```

```
                    case 2: g.setColor(Color.cyan);break;
                    case 3: g.setColor(Color.gray);break;
                    case 4: g.setColor(Color.green);break;
                    case 5: g.setColor(Color.magenta);break;
                    case 6: g.setColor(Color.red);break;
                    case 7: g.setColor(Color.white);break;
                    case 8: g.setColor(Color.yellow);
               }
          }
     }
}

//-------------------------------------------------------------

protected void closedShapes(Graphics g, String shape, boolean fill)
// method to draw a closed shape with the correct orientation
{
     // calculate correct parameters for shape
     upperLeftX = Math.min(x1,x2);
     upperLeftY = Math.min(y1,y2);
     width = Math.abs(x1-x2);
     height = Math.abs(y1-y2);

     // draw appropraite shape
     if (shape.equals("square") && fill)
          g.fillRect(upperLeftX,upperLeftY,width,width);
     else if (shape.equals("square") && !fill)
          g.drawRect(upperLeftX,upperLeftY,width,width);

     else if (shape.equals("rectangle") && fill)
          g.fillRect(upperLeftX,upperLeftY,width,height);
     else if (shape.equals("rectangle") && !fill)
          g.drawRect(upperLeftX,upperLeftY,width,height);

     else if (shape.equals("circle") && fill)
          g.fillOval(upperLeftX,upperLeftY,width,width);
     else if (shape.equals("circle") && !fill)
          g.drawOval(upperLeftX,upperLeftY,width,width);

     else if (shape.equals("ellipse") && fill)
          g.fillOval(upperLeftX,upperLeftY,width,height);
     else if (shape.equals("ellipse") && !fill)
          g.drawOval(upperLeftX,upperLeftY,width,height);
}

//-------------------------------------------------------------

protected void displayMouseCoordinates(int X, int Y)
// method to display the coordinates of the mouse
{
     position.setText("["+String.valueOf(X)+","+String.valueOf(Y)+"]");
}
```

```
public void mouseDragged(MouseEvent event)
// capture coordinates of new mouse position as it is
// dragged across the screen
{
   Graphics g = getGraphics();

   x2=event.getX();
   y2=event.getY();

   // erase a small rectangular area of the window
   // if erase was selected
   if (erasure)
   {
      g.setColor(Color.yellow);
      g.fillRect(x2,y2,5,5);
   }

   displayMouseCoordinates(event.getX(), event.getY());
}

//-------------------------------------------------------------

public void mouseMoved(MouseEvent event)
{
   displayMouseCoordinates(event.getX(), event.getY());
}

//-------------------------------------------------------------
// implemented blank methods
public void mouseClicked(MouseEvent event){}
public void mouseEntered(MouseEvent event){}
public void mouseExited(MouseEvent event){}

//-------------------------------------------------------------
public void mousePressed(MouseEvent event)
// capture initial coordinates of mouse
{
   if (erasure) return;

   upperLeftX=0; upperLeftY=0; width=0; height=0;

   x1=event.getX();
   y1=event.getY();

   Graphics g = getGraphics();

   // display reference point of coordinates (x1,y1)
   g.drawString(".",x1,y1);
   displayMouseCoordinates(event.getX(), event.getY());
}
```

```
public void mouseReleased(MouseEvent event)
// draw the appropriate shape when mouse button released;
// shape will be drawn between the coordinates (x1,y1) and (x2,y2)
{
   Graphics g = getGraphics();
   displayMouseCoordinates(event.getX(), event.getY());
   if (erasure)
   {
      erasure = false;
      return;
   }
   selectColor(g);
   x2=event.getX();
   y2=event.getY();

   if (drawShape.equals("line"))
   {
      g.drawLine(x1,y1,x2,y2);
   }
   else if (drawShape.equals("circle"))
   {
      closedShapes(g,"circle",fill);
   }
   else if (drawShape.equals("ellipse"))
   {
      closedShapes(g,"ellipse",fill);
   }
   else if (drawShape.equals("square"))
   {
      closedShapes(g,"square",fill);
   }
   else if (drawShape.equals("rectangle"))
   {
      closedShapes(g,"rectangle",fill);
   }

   // erase reference point at coordinates (x1,y1)
   g.setColor(Color.yellow);
   g.drawString(".",x1,y1);
   g.setColor(Color.black);
}

//----------------------------------------------------------------
// implemented blank methods
public void windowClosed(WindowEvent event){}
public void windowDeiconified(WindowEvent event){}
public void windowIconified(WindowEvent event){}
public void windowActivated(WindowEvent event){}
public void windowDeactivated(WindowEvent event){}
public void windowOpened(WindowEvent event){}

//----------------------------------------------------------------

public void windowClosing(WindowEvent event)
// method to check which window was closing
{
   if (event.getWindow() == about)
```

```
        {
            about.dispose();
            return;
        }
        else
        {
            System.exit(0);
        }
    }
}


class Ex_7
{
    public static void main(String[] args)
    {
        Sketchpad screen = new Sketchpad("Sketchpad");
        screen.setSize(Sketchpad.WIDTH, Sketchpad.HEIGHT);
        screen.setVisible(true);
    }
}
```

Test results - Sample output from a Sketchpad drawing

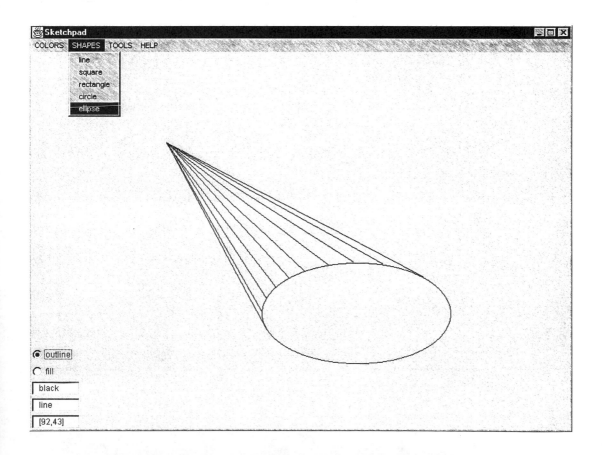

Summary

- A graphical user interface (GUI), replaces the traditional input of data via a keyboard and displaying information in textual form on a screen.

- A GUI typically consists of a container, such as a window or frame; into which components, such as buttons, menus, text fields, and text areas are added.

- The information gathered from the components in a GUI represent data input. Output from a GUI may take the form of drawings, or text written into new windows, or text fields and text areas.

- The Abstract Windowing Toolkit (AWT) contains classes that represent all the GUI components.

- A container class is created by inheriting all the characteristics of the `Frame` class and specifying in the constructor such features as the background color for the container, layout manager used for the components, and so on.

- A GUI component is created by instantiating a variable of the appropriate class to create an object. The object is added to the container using the `add` method from the `Container` class.

- When a user interacts with a GUI component, for example pressing a button; the action of the user creates an event.

- Associated with every event is an event class. The source and characteristics of the event may be obtained through constants and methods found in the appropriate event class. For example, the action of pressing a button generates an `ActionEvent`. The source of the event may be determined from the `getActionCommand()` instance method in the `ActionEvent` class.

- An event is detected through an event listener. Every event has a corresponding event listener whose methods must be implemented in a manner applicable to handling the event for the action on that component. For example, the action of pressing a button generates an `ActionEvent`, that is detected by the `ActionListener`. To react to the button being pressed, it is necessary to implement the `ActionListener` method `actionPerformed` in a way that deals with the button being pressed.

- The event and event listener classes are contained in the package `java.awt.event`.

- The selection of components examined in detail in this chapter have been labels, check boxes, radio buttons, text fields, text areas, scrolling lists, and drop-down menus. If you care to examine the `java.awt package` you may notice these are not the only components available in Java.

- Components are added to the container in a sequence predetermined by the appropriate layout manager in use. If you wish to specify the position and size of each component in the container, then set the layout manager to null.

- A panel is a class of container that is itself contained within a container. A panel does not create a separate window of its own. A panel is used to group like components together, so they may be referred to as a single entity.

- A `Graphics` package is available for drawing shapes. To create an object of type Graphics it is necessary to call the method `getGraphics()`.

Review Questions

1. Using your Sun documentation, how many `Color` constants are specified in the class `java.awt.Color` and what are the colors?

2. True or false - `Component` is an abstract class.

3. True or false - a button component is added to a container using the `add` method from the `Component` class.

4. True or false - `Button`, `Checkbox`, and `Label` classes all inherit from the `Component` class.

5. True or false - a `Frame` inherits from a `Window` class.

6. What instance method would you use to set the size of a `Frame`?

7. How do you make a `Frame` visible?

8. How would you set the background color of a `Frame` to red?

9. How would you set the size and location of a component in a container?

10. True or false - A `Checkbox` generates an `ActionEvent`.

11. True or false - It is not necessary to implement all the listener methods of the `MouseListener` interface.

12. What listener methods must be implemented for the `KeyListener` interface?

13. What is a `Label`?

14. What is non-exclusive check-box selection?

15. How does a radio button differ from a check box?

16. In a program how can you retrieve the chosen items from a List?

17. How do you prevent the displayed text in either a `TextField` or `TextArea` from being overwritten?

18. How can you find the source of an event?

19. What is the difference between `FlowLayout` and `GridLayout`?

20. What is the difference between a mouse being dragged and a mouse being moved?

21. How can you obtain the values of mouse coordinates?

22. How do you detect a window closing?

23. Code a Graphics method to draw a rectangle given the coordinates of the bottom right-hand corner as (x1,y1) and the coordinates of the top left-hand corner as (x2,y2)?

24. What is the fundamental error in the following statement.

```
Graphics g = new Graphics();
```

25. When entering data into text fields what is the quickest method of moving from text field to text field?

Exercises

In questions 26 to 30 inclusive you should write Java code to:

26. Draw a push-button on the screen at coordinates (200,220), having a size of 100x30. The push-button has a red background with the word STOP in white letters. When the push-button is pressed you return back to the operating system prompt. The size of the frame should be 500x500.

27. Set up a scrolling list containing the names of countries. In the same GUI transfer any three countries from the list to a separate text area.

28. Set up two radio buttons marked RED and GREEN, detect which radio button is activated and draw either a corresponding red or green circle on the screen.

29. Set up three text fields labeled Red, Green and Blue. Input numbers in the range 0-255 in each box. Display a square area of the screen that represents the RGB color.

30. Rotate a compass needle on the screen about a fixed point in response to the mouse being moved around the screen.

Programming Problems

31. A computerized minefield, divided into a 10x10 matrix as illustrated in Figure 10.17, may be considered as an object. Devise a class Minefield, containing methods that will allow you to plot a path through the mines and display your route.

The position of the mines is generated at random. The number of mines is also generated at random, and will be a value in the range 1 to 10. A person plotting a path through the minefield is allowed to input pairs of coordinates of a path. The computer generates the starting position at any column in row 9 of the matrix, and the only legal move is to any adjacent cell in the matrix. The idea behind the simulation is to trace a path through a minefield without stepping on a mine, and to finish at the Northern perimeter of the matrix. Only at the end of the simulation should the computer reveal the position of the mines.

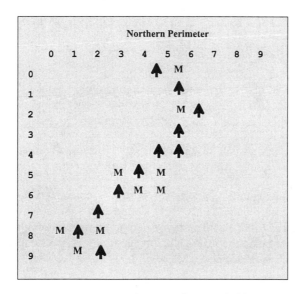

Figure10.17 Matrix of a minefield

Write a program to test the instance methods of the class by simulating tracing a path though the minefield.

32. Create a text file that contains the details of aircraft departures, similar to those in Figure 10.18, from an airport in the USA. The format of a record in the text file is:

```
class Flight
{
    int    departureTime;
    String flightNumber;
    String destination;
}
```

```
              D E P A R T U R E S

    Fri Feb 10 18:59:32 1995

       TIME      FLIGHT        DESTINATION
       1900      BA147         LONDON HEATHROW
       1910      AA202         BOSTON
       1925      AA204         BOSTON
       1930      LU110         MUNICH
       1945      LU120         FRANKFURT
       2000      BA654         LONDON GATWICK
       2015      BA655         IRELAND SHANNON
       2020      AA200         SAN FRANCISCO
       2025      SA156         SINGAPORE
       2035      SA276         HONG KONG
```

Figure 10.18 An example of a departure board

Devise a system that includes classes and a test program, that will read the file containing the records of the flights and output a real-time display of the next ten flights that are scheduled to depart from the airport. Update and display the departures board every minute.

33. Return to your answer to question 38 in Chapter 8. Replace the textual output, with a graphical output that plots the movement of the airplanes on their various courses.

34. Return to the Case Study: Simple Calculator, found in Chapter 10. Rewrite the program to cater for the arithmetic of rational numbers only. You should reuse the class Rational developed from Chapter 7. You should display the fractions being computed as rational numbers, together with the arithmetic operation selected, and the result of the computation. For example the display part of the GUI may resemble the following output.

$$-8/3 + 9/4 = -5/12$$

35. Design an on-line form for the capture of textual data and store the data in a text file. The nature of the data you capture might include name, marital status, date of birth, address, telephone number, driving license number, passport number, social security number, and so on.

36. Write a program to plot the path of a small circle moving around the circumference of a larger circle.

37. Using the polar equation $r = a(1 + e.\cos\theta)$ where $0 \le \theta \le 2\pi$ and the relations $x = r.\sin\theta$, and $y = r.\cos\theta$. Write a program to graphs for e = 0.5, 1 and 2. Select a value for a so that the graphs are large enough to fill the screen. Hint try values of a between 20 and 100.

38. An analysis of examination results at a school gave the following distribution of grades for all subjects taken in one year.

grade	%
A	10
B	25
C	45
D	20

Write a program to represent the distribution of each grade in a pie chart, where each slice of pie is drawn in a different color.

39. The monthly sales figures (units sold) for a computer manufacturing company are as follows.

Jan	Feb	Mar	Apr	May	Jun	Jul	Aug	Sep	Oct	Nov	Dec
20	25	37	27	19	25	34	40	50	60	55	42

Write a program to plot a histogram of the sales.

40. Design a GUI specifically for writing letters. The GUI should have a number of drop-down menus that allow you to select the following items.

The name of a person from a scrolling list. The name is a key to small data base of names and addresses, and the program will retrieve the corresponding address for use in the letter.

Drop-down menus of font names, font sizes, font styles and ink colors.

A drop-down file menu with options to open a file of an existing letter; save the current letter as a new file; clear the GUI to make a new start on a letter; exit the system.

A scrollable and editable text area for writing the letter. Note the computer automatically inserts your name and address and the person's name and address to whom you are writing.

Write a program to implement the GUI.

Chapter 11
Applets

All the program you have written up to this point have been application programs, where each program was compiled into Java byte codes and run using a Java interpreter.

This chapter introduces you to writing applet programs, that are designed to be run either by a Web browser or by an applet viewer. Your knowledge of creating and implementing classes, exception handling and devising graphical user interfaces may also be used in conjunction with writing applets. In addition to these features, an applet will also allow you to access Web sites, play sounds and display images.

By the end of this chapter you should have an understanding of the following topics.

- An introduction to the terminology of the World Wide Web.

- The construction of Applets.

- Multimedia applets for sound and images.

- An introduction to the meaning and use of threads.

- Animation of images.

- The limitations of applets.

11.1 Introduction

The **Internet** is an international network of computers, or more accurately a network of networks. For example, the network at Oxford Brookes University is joined, via the Internet, to other networks all over the world, giving users global access to people and information. The Internet is the hardware of network cables, hubs, repeaters, and so on, that enable computers from all around the world to communicate with one another.

There are various resources available on the Internet, including Email, FTP, Gopher, and Telnet.

Email is an electronic mailing system that allows you to send a message to anyone that is connected to the Internet.

A **File Transfer Protocol** (FTP) server is a computer on the Internet that stores a collection of files. Using FTP software, you can connect to any FTP server, browse through the directories and download files to your local machine. Provided you have the access rights, you can also transfer files from your local machine to the FTP server.

Gopher allows you to search for files and documents about a particular topic.

Telnet provides you with a method to log on to a computer on a remote site. When you telnet to another computer, the resulting link is just like using a terminal at the remote site.

The four Internet resources described (and there are others), all require dedicated software tools, with each resource having its own user interface. As a result, having to use the different Internet resources, with their different interfaces, can at times present a less user-friendly system. The World Wide Web combines many of the Internet resources into a consistent, user-friendly, front end that is much easier to use.

The **World Wide Web** (WWW, Web or W3) is a distributed information service on the Internet, that allows access to documents containing links. Information on the Web is displayed in the form of hypertext and hypermedia documents.

The Web can access information located anywhere in the world. The level of user interaction on the Web ranges from the simple selection and retrieval of Web documents, to the submission of completed forms, the inquiry of databases and the ability to learn from multimedia computer based learning packages.

A **hypertext** document may be entered at many points, and may be browsed in any order by interactively choosing words or key phrases as search parameters for the next text image to be viewed. The word or phrase in a hypertext document is a *hot link*, when selected by using a mouse, causes information relevant to the word or phrase to be displayed.

Hypermedia is a more accurate term than hypertext, since the links in the WWW are not constrained to being text only. Links can also be made with still images, sound and video clips.

```
<html>
<body>

<font face="Arial" size=4>
<marquee width=100% height=5% align="middle" behavior="scroll"
     direction="right" bgcolor="yellow" scrolldelay=0>
... You have reached the home page of Barry Holmes ...
</marquee>

<center><BR><BR>

<a href="http://www.users.globalnet.co.uk/~bjholmes/public_html/">
<img src="bjh.jpg">
</a>

<BR><BR><BR></center>

</font>
<font face="Lucida" size=3 color="red">

<big>Author of Programming Texts on:</big><BR><BR>
<li>Programming with Java (due March 1998)<BR>
<li>Through C to C++ (1997)<BR><BR>

Contact <A href="http://www.jbpub.com">
<tt><big>Jones & Bartlett Publishers</big></tt></A><BR><BR>

<font color="blue">
Also <BR><BR>
<li>Programming with ANSI C (1995)<BR>
<li>Modula-2 Programming (1994)<BR>
<li>Introductory Pascal (1993)<BR>
<li>Structured Programming in COBOL (1991)<BR>
<li>Pascal Programming (1990)<BR><BR>

Contact <A href="http://www.lettsed.co.uk">
<tt><big>Letts Educational</big></tt></A><BR><BR>

<hr color = "black"><br>
<font color="green">
<big>Barry Holmes is a Principal Lecturer in the School of Computing and
Mathematical Sciences at
</big><A href="http://www.brookes.ac.uk">
<tt><big>Oxford Brookes University</big></tt></A><br><br>
He joined the School in 1979, and lectures on computer programming and safety
critical systems courses to undergraduate and postgraduate audiences. <br>
He is a member of the British Computer Society, a Chartered Engineer, and has an
MSc in Computer Science from The City University; <br>
and a BSc in Mathematics and Physics, and a Certificate in Education from the
University of London<br><br>
<hr color = "black"><br>

<img src="/cgi-
bin/Count.cgi?ft=9|frgb=69;139;50|tr=0|trgb=0;0;0|wxh=15;20|md=6|dd=A|st=5|sh=1|df=
bjholmes"
align=absmiddle><br><br>

<font size=1 color="black">
last updated: 16/10/1997<br>

</body>
</html>
```

The **Hyper-Text Mark-up Language** (HTML) is the language that is used to write WWW documents. The listing on the previous page is an example of a Web document written in HTML. The document is the author's home page on the WWW.

In the context of this book you are not expected to understand the syntax of HTML. However, if you would like to know more about HTML then there is an abundance of documentation and tutorials to be found on the Web. You can also download editors from the Web that write the HTML syntax for you, allowing you to concentrate on the contents of the document.

The user-friendly, front end of the Web, is a **browser**. This is the software package that reads and formats the HTML pages to be viewed. There are several popular browsers, such as Sun's HotJava, Netscape's Navigator; and the browser illustrated in Figure 11.1 is Microsoft's Internet Explorer 4.

Figure 11.1 illustrates how the Web browser has interpreted part of the HTML file shown earlier, to create the author's home page.

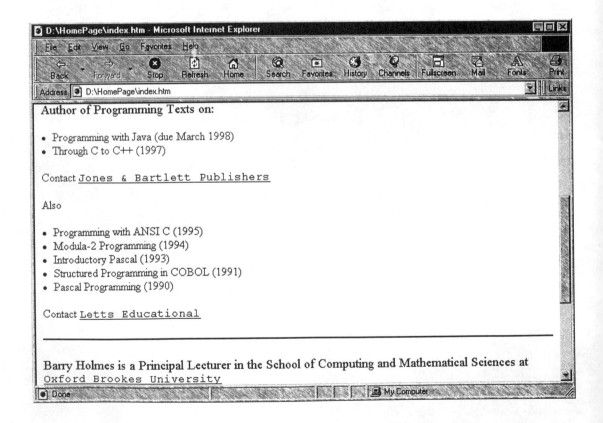

Figure 11.1 An example of running an HTML file on a browser

A Web browser provides the means to perform at least the following tasks.

- Search the Web for information - known as *surfing the net*.

- Use links in a hypertext document to move to different networked sites within the Web.

- Access any site on the Web.

- Send and receive electronic mail (this is a secondary feature and is not available on all browsers).

- Download files from other sites on the Web.

- Interpret a text file written in HTML.

A fifth resource of the Internet, not previously mentioned, is the **Hyper-Text Transfer Protocol** (HTTP). This is the set of rules that define and control the flow of information via the WWW. Both the Web server and Web browser understand the HTTP language, and use it to communicate with one another. Part of the server's job is to store Web documents; the other part is to deliver the documents, over the network, to the Web browser making a request for the documents.

To gain access to other sites on the Web, it is necessary to provide a **Uniform Resource Locator** (URL). Think of a URL as a networked extension of the hierarchical filename concept; not only can you specify a file in a directory, but that file and that directory can exists on any machine on the network. A URL comprises the following four parts that specify the unique address of a document on the WWW.

Resource descriptor	`http:`
Separator	`//`
Resource address	`www.users.globalnet.co.uk`
Pathname	`/~bjholmes`

The full URL is given as: `http://www.users.globalnet.co.uk/~bjholmes`

If you enter this URL on a browser, it is possible to visit my home page on my Web site. If you visit my home page you can mouse-click on hot links to the Jones and Bartlett Web site (the publishers of this book); Oxford Brookes University (where I work) and Letts Educational (another publisher that I write text books for).

11.2 Applets

An **applet** is a Java program designed to be run by a Java-enabled Web browser or an applet viewer. A call to an applet is embedded in an HTML script file. When a Web page is loaded that contains a reference to an applet, the browser downloads the applet from the Web server and executes the applet on the client's machine. Having a piece of software invade your computer from anywhere on the Web is a frightening prospect! To avoid the possibility of the applet causing havoc on your computer, there are certain restrictions imposed on what an applet is allowed to do. Towards the end of this chapter we will briefly discuss what these restrictions are.

Before we embark upon writing applets, it is necessary to consider how an applet is called from an HTML script file. The only small amount of HTML you are expected to remember is enough to call an applet. For example, the following HTML script file calls the file Ex_1.class containing the Java byte codes of the compiled applet. The applet source code would be stored in a file named Ex_1.java, and compiled in the same manner as a Java application program.

```
<HTML>
<BODY>

<APPLET code=Ex_1.class width=900 height=300>
</APPLET>

</BODY>
</HTML>
```

A Java applet is included in a Web page using the <APPLET> tag, which has the following minimal syntax.

syntax

Applet tag: <APPLET code = applet-filename
                       width = pixel-width
                       height = pixel-height>
               </APPLET>

Where the width and height refer to the initial width and height that the applet requires in the browser's window.

The java.applet package contains several classes, one of which is the Applet class. A listing of the Applet class follows.

```
public class Applet extends Panel
{
    // Constructors
    public Applet();

    // Methods
    public void destroy();
    public AppletContext getAppletContext();
    public String getAppletInfo();
    public AudioClip getAudioClip(URL  url);
    public AudioClip getAudioClip(URL  url, String  name);
    public URL getCodeBase();
```

```
        public URL getDocumentBase();
        public Image getImage(URL  url);
        public Image getImage(URL  url, String  name);
        public Locale getLocale();
        public String getParameter(String  name);
        public String[][] getParameterInfo();
        public void init();
        public boolean isActive();
        public void play(URL  url);
        public void play(URL  url, String  name);
        public void resize(Dimension  d);
        public void resize(int  width, int  height);
        public final void setStub(AppletStub  stub);
        public void showStatus(String  msg);
        public void start();
        public void stop();
}
```

To create an applet you must create a subclass of `Applet` and override some or all of the following methods.

`init()` - is called after the constructor is invoked, when the applet first starts.

`start()` - is called when the browser opens the applet's window.

`stop()` - is called when the browser changes to a new HTML page making the applet temporarily hidden.

`destroy()` - is called when the applet exits, and reverses any actions taken by `init()` freeing any resources the applet is holding.

You do not need to explicitly call these methods, they are automatically called for you.

The applet also overrides the `paint()` method from the `java.awt.Component` class to draw an applet on the screen.

There is no `main` method in a Java applet, as there is in a Java application. Hence, it becomes common practice to override methods from the appropriate classes, and allow the system to automatically call the methods.

The Applet class inherits from the Panel class, which in turn inherits from the Container, Component and Object classes respectively. Therefore, within an applet you are at liberty to override any of the methods found in these classes.

Program Example 11.1 illustrates how to write a simple applet for displaying the hackneyed phrase Hello World in an applet viewer window.

Program Example 11.1. The Hello World Applet.

```java
// chap_11\Ex_1.java
// applet to display Hello World in a window

import java.awt.*;
import java.applet.*;

public class Ex_1 extends Applet
{
    // override init() method to set background color of screen
    public void init()
    {
        setBackground(Color.yellow);
    }

    // override paint() method to automatically display information
    // in the applet's window
    public void paint(Graphics g)
    {
        Font font = new Font("Serif", Font.BOLD, 72);

        // set font, and color and display message on
        // the screen at position 250,150
        g.setFont(font);
        g.setColor(Color.blue);
        g.drawString("Hello World",250,150);
    }
}
```

The applet was stored in a source file called Ex_1.java and compiled using the same javac command as for a Java application - for example **javac Ex_1.java**. The compiler produced a Java byte-code file called Ex_1.class. It is the file Ex_1.class that is called from within the HTML script file, saved as **Ex_1.html**, and shown earlier.

After a successful compilation the applet may be run on an applet viewer by using the command **appletviewer Ex_1.html**. Alternatively the applet may be run on a Java-enabled Web browser, by opening the file Ex_1.html in the browser.

Test results

What lessons can we learn from this simple applet?

As you can see, we have used methods from the `Graphics` class, yet no attempt was made to set up a window on which to draw the graphics!

After the program has run, we can close down the window by pointing at the **X** button in the top right-hand corner of the window or invoke the drop-down menu from the applet viewer to close the window; yet no window or event listeners have been declared in the program!

Since Java applets run inside a Web browser or applet viewer, the applets take full advantage of the following facilities offered by the host software.

- Applets may run in the browser's window.

- Event-handling (such as closing down a window) already exists for the browser and may be shared by the applet.

- The Graphics class may be used in the context of the browser's window.

- The interface of the Web browser or applet viewer may also be used to control the applet. For example, stopping the applet from running.

Picking up on this last point, Figure 11.2 illustrates a drop-down menu that may be used to control an applet running on the Sun Applet Viewer.

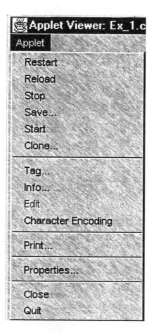

Figure 11.2 Drop-down menu from the applet viewer

The applet is a subclass of the class `java.applet.Applet`, and as such inherits all the methods from the superclass.

The method `init()`, inherited from the superclass has been overridden to set the background color of the applet viewer's window to yellow.

The Web browser or applet viewer invokes the `paint()` method automatically to allow the applet to draw itself in the browser's window. By overriding the `paint()` method we can get the browser to draw what we want.

An HTML script file may pass values to an applet, in the same context as arguments may appear in the command line to run a Java application program. The syntax to define arguments in an HTML script file, to be passed to an applet follows.

---

syntax

Passing parameters to applets:

```
<APPLET code = .. >
<PARAM NAME=parameter-name VALUE=parameter-value>
   .
   .
</APPLET>
```

For example, should we want to modify Program Example 11.1, to accept parameters for defining the size of a character, the font, the color of the letters, the color of the background and the message; then it would be necessary to modify the HTML script file as follows.

```
<HTML>
<BODY>

<APPLET code=Ex_2.class width=900 height=300>

<PARAM NAME=size VALUE="72">
<PARAM NAME=font VALUE="Serif">
<PARAM NAME=color VALUE="yellow">
<PARAM NAME=background VALUE="blue">
<PARAM NAME=message VALUE="The truth is out there!">

</APPLET>

</BODY>
</HTML>
```

Notice that each parameter is given a name, and the value of the parameter is always treated as a string in the HTML script file.

Within the applet, the value of the parameter is obtained by using the `getParameter` applet class method. For example, to obtain the point size of a character you would use:

```
int sizeParameter = Integer.parseInt(getParameter("size"));
```

The `getParameter` method only returns the value of the parameter as a string. Therefore, when dealing with numbers, the string will need to be converted into a number of the appropriate type. In this example the `Integer` class method `parseInt` has been used to convert the string into an integer.

Clearly in the case of the remaining four parameters in the HTML script file, when a parameter is a string type there is no need for any further type conversion. For example,

```
String fontParameter = getParameter("font");
```

The names given to the parameters in the HTML script file, need not be the same as the names given to the variables within the applet.

Notice from Program Example 11.2 that it is perfectly legal to include your own methods in an applet. You are not confined to the predefined methods already mentioned in this chapter. The method `convertColorString`, does just what the name infers, it takes a string parameter that represents the name of a color and returns the appropriate `Color` constant.

Program Example 11.2: Use of Applet Parameters from an HTML Script File.

```
// chap_11\Ex_2.java
// applet to display a message in a window;
// the font style, font size, background and
// foreground colors and the message are input
// as parameters to the applet

import java.awt.*;
import java.applet.*;

public class Ex_2 extends Applet
{
    int    sizeParameter;
    String fontParameter;
    String colorParameter;
    String backgroundParameter;
    String messageParameter;

    private Color convertColorString(String color)
    // method to convert the string name of a color to a Color object
    // if the string name does not exist return the Color black
    {
        if      (color.equals("red"))        return Color.red;
        else if (color.equals("orange"))     return Color.orange;
        else if (color.equals("yellow"))     return Color.yellow;
        else if (color.equals("green"))      return Color.green;
        else if (color.equals("blue"))       return Color.blue;
        else if (color.equals("cyan"))       return Color.cyan;
        else if (color.equals("magenta"))    return Color.magenta;
        else                                 return Color.black;
    }
```

```
// override init method to assign the values of the parameters
// from the HTML file, to variables within the applet
public void init()
{
    sizeParameter = new Integer(getParameter("size")).intValue();
    fontParameter = getParameter("font");
    colorParameter = getParameter("color");
    backgroundParameter = getParameter("background");
    messageParameter = getParameter("message");
}

public void paint(Graphics g)
{
    Font font = new Font(fontParameter, Font.BOLD, sizeParameter);

    // set font, color, background color and display
    // a message on the screen at position 75,150
    g.setFont(font);
    g.setColor(convertColorString(colorParameter));
    setBackground(convertColorString(backgroundParameter));

    g.drawString(messageParameter,75,150);
}
}
```

Test results. The best way to view the output from this program is to run the program. You will then observe that the background is colored blue, and the message is written using the color yellow.

Try editing the parameters in the HTML script file, choose a different point size, colors and a new message. Save the file, and open the HTML script file in either a Web browser or applet viewer. Notice that without changing the Java applet the appearance of the screen has changed.

Program Example 11.3 shows you how to use URLs within an applet to reach the home page of the chosen Web site. The applet displays five buttons on the screen; each button is marked with the name of a Web site. The names of the Web sites are stored in one array, and their corresponding URLs in a second array. Therefore, upon pressing a button, it is a simple matter of finding the index to the array where the name of the Web site is stored and using the value of this index to obtain the URL from the second array.

Notice in this example, that it is necessary to include an `ActionListener` to capture the event of pressing a button, and invoking the `actionPerformed` method.

The java.net.package provides a powerful set of features that allow applets and applications to connect to, and communicate with, other sites on the Internet. The class URL allows the data referred to by the URL to be downloaded. One of the constructors from the URL class has the signature:

```
public URL(String spec) throws MalformedURLException;
```

where the `spec` is the URL for the site. To access the home page for the appropriate Web site we need to use the `showDocument()` method from the abstract interface `AppletContext`. This interface defines the methods that allow an applet to interact with the context of say, a Web browser, in which it runs. Note - the `getAppletContext()` method, from the class `Applet`, returns an `AppletContext` object that is used to invoke the `showDocument()` method.

The code required to retrieve the home page of a Web site follows.

```
try
{
   URL site = new URL(webURLs[index]);
   getAppletContext().showDocument(site);
}
catch (MalformedURLException m){System.exit(1);}
```

Notice from this code, and the constructor's signature that a URL may throw a `MalformedURLException`, that must be handled.

Program Example 11.3: Using an Applet to Connect to Web Sites.

```java
// chap_11\Ex_3.java
// program to display a set of buttons on the screen
// to allow for the selection of different sites on the Web

import java.awt.*;
import java.awt.event.*;
import java.applet.*;
import java.net.*;

public class Ex_3 extends Applet implements ActionListener
{
   // initialize an array with the names of the Web sites
   String[] webSiteNames = {"Oxford Brookes University",
                            "Oxford Computing Laboratory",
                            "Jones & Bartlett",
                            "Java Development",
                            "Windows 95 utilities"};
   // initialize an array with the URLs of the Web sites
   String[] webURLs      = {"http://www.brookes.ac.uk",
                            "http://www.comlab.ox.ac.uk",
                            "http://www.jbpub.com",
                            "http://java.sun.com",
                            "http://www.windows95.com"};
```

```
// array of buttons that will denote the different Web sites
Button[] button = new Button[webSiteNames.length];

// override method init to display the group of buttons
public void init()
{
    setLayout(null);
    setBackground(Color.yellow);

    for (int index=0; index != webSiteNames.length; index++)
    {
        button[index] = new Button(webSiteNames[index]);
        button[index].setLocation(10,25*index);
        button[index].setSize(200,20);
        button[index].setBackground(Color.cyan);
        button[index].addActionListener(this);
        add(button[index]);
    }
}


// use an implementation of the actionPerformed method taken
// from the ActionListener abstract class
public void actionPerformed(ActionEvent event)
{
    // find the name of the button that was pressed
    Object source = event.getActionCommand();

    for (int index=0; index != webSiteNames.length; index++)
    {
        // inspect each web site name in the array of Web site names
        if (source.equals(webSiteNames[index]))
        {
            // display the relevant page from the Web site
            try
            {
                URL site = new URL(webURLs[index]);
                getAppletContext().showDocument(site);
            }
            catch (MalformedURLException m){System.exit(1);}

            return;
        }
    }
}
```

Test results An applet viewer shows you what the layout of the buttons will look like, however, it is no use for running this program. You need to run the program in a Web browser, connected to the Internet. The two illustrations that follow show the applet running in Internet Explorer, and the results of pressing the button marked Jones & Bartlett.

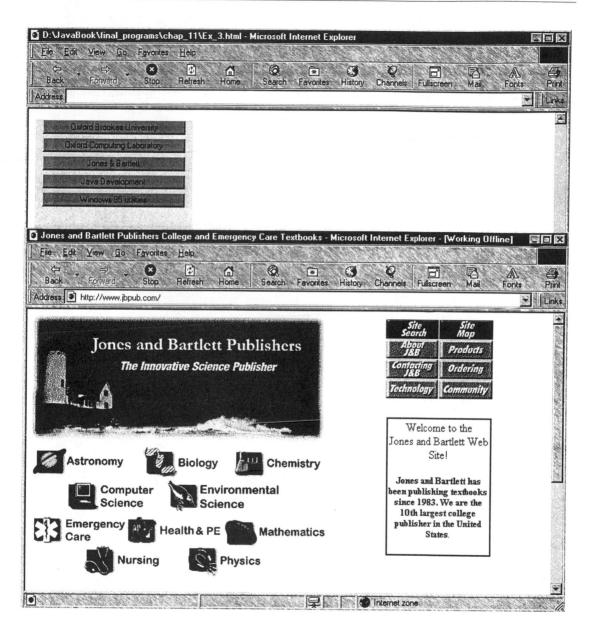

11.3 Playing sounds

If you examine the methods of the Applet class you cannot fail to notice such methods as
getAudioClip, getImage and play. Java applets have the ability to play sounds and display
images on your computer.

Currently the sounds are limited to AU sound files, but WAV files will be included in later versions of the language. **AU sound files** use an audio format developed for Sun workstations and are often used to distribute sound clips via the Web.

Program Example 11.4 uses the same technique to display buttons as Program Example 11.3. However, in this example each button represents the name of a particular sound.

Ten sounds, ranging from a dog barking to a train whistling have been down loaded from the Oxford University Sound Archive. This archive allows you public access to many useful sounds. If you want to visit this site, the URL is:

```
http://www.comlab.ox.ac.uk/archive/sound.html
```

The sounds used in Program Example 11.4 may be found under the hot key <u>Sun demonstration</u> <u>sounds</u> on this site. If you would like to find out more about audio on the Web then you might also like to visit the Oxford University Sound Archive using the URL

```
http://www.comlab.ox.ac.uk/archive/audio.html
```

There are three statements necessary to play an audio clip.

```
AudioClip sound;
sound = getAudioClip(getCodeBase(),"audio\\"+source.toString()+".au");
sound.play();
```

The first statement declares a variable sound of type AudioClip. The class AudioClip is part of the applet package, and contains the following methods.

```
public interface AudioClip
{
    // Methods
    public abstract void loop();
    public abstract void play();
    public abstract void stop();
}
```

The second statement initializes the variable sound with an AudioClip file. The format of the method is:

```
public AudioClip getAudioClip(URL url, String name);
```

where the method getCodebase() returns the URL from which the applet's code was loaded; and the name refers to the directory and filename of a particular AU sound file. The name is composed from a concatenation of the directory (audio) beneath the current directory; the name on the button (source of the event) and the type of file (.au). For example:

```
"audio\\"+source.toString()+".au"
```

The third statement executes the sound variable by playing the contents of the AudioClip file.

Program Example 11.4: Demonstration of Playing Various Sounds

```java
// chap_11\Ex_4.java
// program to demonstrate the use of sound in an applet

import java.awt.*;
import java.awt.event.*;
import java.applet.*;

public class Ex_4 extends Applet implements ActionListener
{
    // initialize an array with the names of the sounds
    String[] soundNames = {"bark","computer","crash","cuckoo","doorbell",
                           "drip","gong", "ring","spacemusic","train"};

    // instantiate an array of buttons
    Button[] button = new Button[soundNames.length];

    AudioClip sound;

    // override init method to display an array of buttons
    // with the names of the sounds written on the buttons
    public void init()
    {
        setLayout(null);
        for (int index=0; index != soundNames.length; index++)
        {
            button[index] = new Button(soundNames[index]);
            button[index].setLocation(10,25*index);
            button[index].setSize(100,20);
            button[index].setBackground(Color.cyan);
            button[index].addActionListener(this);
            add(button[index]);
        }
    }

    // use an implementation of the actionPerformed method taken
    // from the ActionListener abstract class
    public void actionPerformed(ActionEvent event)
    {
        // find the name of the button that was pressed
        Object source = event.getActionCommand();

        for (int index=0; index != soundNames.length; index++)
        {
            // inspect each sound name with the sound names in the array
            if (source.equals(soundNames[index]))
            {
                // play the appropriate audio clip
                sound =
                getAudioClip(getCodeBase(),"audio\\"+source.toString()+".au");
                sound.play();
                return;
            }
        }
    }
}
```

Test results

Obviously the results from this applet can only be heard by running the program on a multi-media computer (one that includes a sound card and speakers), or a Sun Workstation. The layout of the buttons on the applet follows.

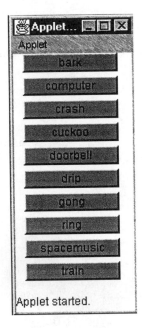

The class `AudioClip` also contains methods to `loop()` - repeatedly play the sound; and `stop()` - terminate the sound. This information has been coded into Program Example 11.5, to allow any sound to be chosen, and played continuously until you press the stop button. A further modification to this program is to change the color of a button to show when it has been pressed and is active.

Program Example 11.5: Playing Sound Continuously.

```
//chap_11\Ex_5.java
// program to demonstrate repeated use of sounds
// in an applet

import java.awt.*;
import java.awt.event.*;
import java.applet.*;

public class Ex_5 extends Applet implements ActionListener
{
    static final int START = 0;
    static final int STOP = 1;

    // initialize array with names of sounds
```

```
      String[] soundNames = {"bark","computer","crash","cuckoo","doorbell",
                             "drip","gong","ring","spacemusic","train"};

      // initialize array with names of functions
      String[] functions = {"START","STOP"};

      // instantiate an array of buttons for sounds
      Button[] button = new Button[soundNames.length];
      // instantiate an array of buttons for functions
      Button[] functionButton = new Button[functions.length];

      AudioClip sound;
      String soundSelected = new String();
      boolean selectionMade = false;
      int selectedButton = 0;
      int selectedFunction = 0;

      // overriden init method to set up and display an array of buttons
      // containing the names of the sounds, and an array of functions

      public void init()
      {
          setLayout(null);

          for (int index=0; index != soundNames.length; index++)
          {
             button[index] = new Button(soundNames[index]);
             button[index].setLocation(10,25*index);
             button[index].setSize(100,20);
             button[index].setBackground(Color.cyan);
             button[index].addActionListener(this);
             add(button[index]);
          }

          for (int index=0; index != functions.length; index++)
          {
             functionButton[index] = new Button(functions[index]);
             functionButton[index].setLocation(150,75*(index+1));
             functionButton[index].setSize(100,40);
             functionButton[index].setBackground(Color.white);
             functionButton[index].addActionListener(this);
             add(functionButton[index]);
          }

      }

      // use an implementation of the actionPerformed method
      // taken from the ActionListener abstract class
      public void actionPerformed(ActionEvent event)
      {
          // find the name of button that was pressed
          Object source = event.getActionCommand();

          // if a sound has been selected then getAudioClip
          if (selectionMade)
             sound = getAudioClip(getCodeBase(), soundSelected);
```

```
// check which function button was pressed
for (int index=0; index != functions.length; index++)
{
    // reset color of function button
    functionButton[selectedFunction].setBackground(Color.white);

    // test to see if either a start or stop button was pressed
    // and whether a sound has been selected
    if (source.equals(functions[index]) && selectionMade)
    {
        // change color of button to show function selected
        functionButton[index].setBackground(Color.yellow);
        selectedFunction = index;

        // implement function to start or stop the sound
        switch (index)
        {
            case START: sound.loop(); return;
            case STOP:  sound.stop(); return;
        }
    }
}


// check which sound button was pressed
for (int index=0; index != soundNames.length; index++)
{
    // reset color of sound buttons
    button[selectedButton].setBackground(Color.cyan);

    // test to see which sound has been chosen
    if (source.equals(soundNames[index]))
    {
        // obtain sound file from directory
        soundSelected = "audio\\"+source.toString()+".au";
        // change color of button to show chosen item
        button[index].setBackground(Color.yellow);

        // update flags to showwhich button was pressed
        // and selection made
        selectedButton = index;
        selectionMade = true;

        return;
    }
}
}
}
```

Test results The illustration indicates that the sound of a doorbell has been chosen and is being played. You can only appreciate this program by running it on a multimedia computer or Sun Workstation.

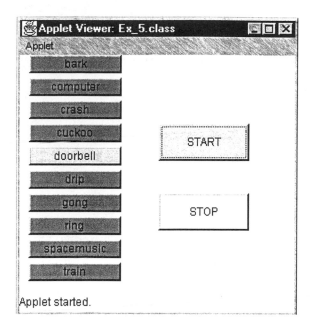

11.4 Displaying images

Let us turn our attention to using applets to display photographs on the screen. Image files are limited to GIF files (Graphic Interchange Format) - a commonly used file compression format developed by CompuServe for transferring graphics files to and from online services; and JPEG files (Joint Photographic Experts Group) an image compression format used to transfer color photographs and images over computer networks. Along with GIF, the JPEG format is one of the most common ways photographs are moved over the Web.

Within the java.awt package is an Image class. An Image object may not be instantiated directly through a constructor; it must be obtained through a call, such as Applet.getImage(). The Graphics class defines several methods for drawing an image; the method used in the following examples has the format:

```
public abstract boolean drawImage(Image img,
                    int x, int y,
                    int width, int height,
                    ImageObserver observer);
```

Program Example 11.6 uses these ideas in a program to display three JPEG images on the screen.

Program Example 11.6: Displaying JPEG Images Using an Applet

```java
// chap_11\Ex_6.java
// applet to display photographic images on the screen

import java.awt.*;
import java.awt.event.*;
import java.applet.*;

public class Ex_6 extends Applet
{
    // declare names of three Image variables
    Image dancers, mask, figure;

    // override init method to assign the image files to the three variables
    public void init()
    {
        dancers = getImage(getDocumentBase(), "images\\fig1.jpg");
        mask    = getImage(getDocumentBase(), "images\\fig2.jpg");
        figure = getImage(getDocumentBase(), "images\\fig3.jpg");
    }

    // display the three images on the screen
    public void paint(Graphics g)
    {
        g.drawImage(dancers,100,100,150,120,this);
        g.drawImage(mask, 300,100,150,120,this);
        g.drawImage(figure, 500,100,150,120, this);
    }
}
```

Test results

Note - the images are taken from the author's own photographic archive.

Program Example 11.7 is an extension of Program Example 11.6 to demonstrate the use of an image map. The image is displayed on the screen at a predefined position using the coordinates of the upper left-hand corner of the image and the width and height of an area in which the image will be scaled and inserted. When a mouse passes over the image, the coordinates of the mouse in relation to parts of the image are known, and the event can be used to display information on the screen relating to that part of the image.

Program Example 11.7 displays a single image of three Balinese musicians. When the mouse passes over each man's image the name of the man is displayed. Only one name is displayed at any one time. Notice that it has been necessary to implement a MouseMotionListener and the mouseDragged method.

Program Example 11.7: Creation of an Image Map.

```java
// chap_11\Ex_7.java
// program to demonstrate image maps

import java.awt.*;
import java.awt.event.*;
import java.applet.*;

public class Ex_7 extends Applet implements MouseMotionListener
{
    // declare single image variable
    Image musicians;

    public void init()
    {
        // get an image from the file and assign to the variable musicians
        musicians = getImage(getDocumentBase(), "images\\fig4.jpg");

        // add motion listener to detect movement of the mouse
        addMouseMotionListener(this);
    }

    // paint single image of musicians
    public void paint(Graphics g)
    {
        g.drawImage(musicians,100,100,200,150,this);
    }

    public void mouseDragged(MouseEvent event){}

    // move the mouse over the picture to display
    // the names of the musicians
    public void mouseMoved(MouseEvent event)
    {
        int x=event.getX();

        Graphics g = getGraphics();

        // erase previous name from window
        g.setColor(Color.white);
        g.fillRect(100,255,200,45);
        g.setColor(Color.black);

        // display the name of the musician if the
        // mouse is positioned near to the person
        if (x<=160)
        {
            g.drawString("Tom",120,275);
        }
        else if (x>160 && x<=240)
```

```
    {
        g.drawString("Dick",200,275);
    }
    else if (x>240 && x<=300)
    {
        g.drawString("Harry",260,275);
    }
  }
}
```

Test results

Harry

![i] Many of the multimedia programs require a large number of media files to be downloaded with an applet. Normally each file is transferred in a uncompressed form. To improve the efficiency of data transfer and data storage all dependent files may be combined into one single compressed Java Archive (JAR) file. The single compressed file can be transferred from the Web server to the Web browser more efficiently. See your JDK documentation for further information.

11.5 Threads

Program Example 11.8 is written to simulate a digital clock, containing a display for hours, minutes and seconds. The class `Calendar` found in the `java.util` package contains many methods and constants to represent the date and time.

The constructors are protected in the `Calendar` class, and it is necessary to use the `getInstance()` method that returns an instance of a `Calendar` subclass. For example,

```
Calendar time=Calendar.getInstance();
```

If you inspect the contents of the Calendar class, you may notice a list of field constants, amongst which you will find the integer class constants HOUR, MINUTE and SECOND. You need to use the instance method get to obtain a value for the three field constants. For example,

```
int hours = time.get(Calendar.HOUR);
int mins = time.get(Calendar.MINUTE);
int secs = time.get(Calendar.SECOND);
```

With this new found knowledge, you may think it is very straightforward to write an applet to regularly sample the time of day, and display the values for hours, minutes and seconds. Indeed the program is straightforward and the chances are you may create a program similar to Program Example 11.8. You may recall that the paint method is called by Java whenever an applet needs to be painted. However, to tell the applet to continuously paint the new time, requires a call to the method repaint() found in the Container class. The repaint() method, in turn automatically calls the update() method that clears the screen and then calls paint.

In the program the paint method is overridden and contains the code to display the time on the screen. After the time (hours, minutes and seconds) has been updated, there always follows a call to repaint.

Program Example 11.8: An Applet to Simulate a Digital Clock

```
// chap_11\Ex_8.java
// applet to demonstrate the need for threads when
// continuously repainting a window

import java.applet.*;
import java.awt.*;
import java.util.*;

public class Ex_8 extends Applet
{
    Font font = new Font("Monospaced",Font.BOLD,16);

    int hours, mins, secs;

    // override the start method, to calculate the time of day
    // and call the repaint() method to display the time
    public void start()
    {
        while (true)
        {
            Calendar time=Calendar.getInstance();

            hours = time.get(Calendar.HOUR);
            mins = time.get(Calendar.MINUTE);
            secs = time.get(Calendar.SECOND);

            repaint();
        }
    }

    // display the time of day on the screen
```

```
    public void paint(Graphics g)
    {
        g.setFont(font);
        g.drawString(String.valueOf(hours)+":"+
                     String.valueOf(mins)+":"+
                     String.valueOf(secs),50,50);
    }
}
```

Test results

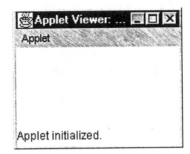

Oh! The results did not work out quite as expected. The applet has displayed a window, however, there is no sight of the time! Also when you attempt to stop the applet running, you continue to press the mouse button over the window close symbol, and if you are lucky, after a short while the window closes and the program stops running. This is not a very satisfactory outcome, to what appeared to be a simple solution to the problem.

What has gone wrong?

An applet does not have a `main` method. Instead we override the methods `init()`, `start()`, `stop()`, and so on; and let the Web browser or applet viewer invoke these overridden methods. In other words, the running of the applet is dependent upon when the browser or viewer decides to execute `init()`, `start()`, `stop()`, etc. An applet, unlike an application, is not in control of itself; it simply responds when told to do so, by the Web browser or applet viewer.

Because the Web browser or applet viewer is in control, it is necessary that the methods you overwrite should take very little time to execute. These methods should not enter into time consuming work.

The method `repaint()` is a request for Java to repaint your applet as soon as it can. The important words are "*as soon as it can*". In Program Example 11.8 the Web browser or applet viewer cannot regain control and find time to execute `repaint()` since it is stuck in an infinite loop. To prove the point, insert the statement `System.out.println("start method");` anywhere inside the `while` loop; recompile the applet, then execute the corresponding HTML source file. We know that the applet window remains blank, but just look at the terminal or MSDOS window - the statement `start method` is displayed over and over again - indicating that the applet is still running, but the Web browser or applet viewer has no spare time to execute the `repaint()` method. Convinced?

All the application programs that we have studied and you have written, have executed in a sequential fashion, from the first instruction to the last instruction in the `main` method, unless an exception occurred, in which case program execution might have been abandoned. A **thread** is a single sequential flow of control. All the programs we have written have had a single thread of execution.

To solve the problem of the digital clock not appearing, we need to allow the applet to run in parallel with the Web browser. In other words we need to give the applet its own thread of execution to run along side the Web browser.

You may wonder how the computer can cope with more than one thread of execution at any one time. Thread objects allow **multithreaded** Java programming, where a single Java Virtual Machine can execute many threads in an interleaved or concurrent manner. Threads independently execute Java code that operates on Java values and objects residing in shared memory.

The computer must share its time between executing the code running in different threads. Unfortunately, different operating systems have different regimes for coping with multithreading. As an example, both Windows 95 and Windows NT give each thread a portion (or slice) of time to use the processor; at the end of the time slice the code running in that thread is suspended (swapped from the processor) and the code for the next thread that is ready to run, is given a slice of time on the processor. The business of running program code on the processor, for different threads of execution, continues in a round-robin manner until program execution is completed, or the program is abandoned.

A thread has a life cycle.

- A thread must be created (born) using an appropriate constructor.

- A thread must be started, however, depending on the availability of the processor, the thread may go into a ready (to be run) state.

- A thread may be running (the program code associated with the thread is being executed on the processor).

- After a thread has been running, it may go into one of several states.

    Ready (to be run when it is the thread's turn and a processor becomes free).
    Sleeping (not requiring the processor until it wakes up after a stated time period).
    Suspended (not requiring the processor until it is resumed at some later time).
    Waiting (not requiring the processor until notified that it may be transferred to a ready state).
    Blocked (not requiring the processor until the completion of an I/O operation).

- A thread may die when it is no longer required. The garbage collector will return the unwanted memory space back to the heap.

There is a class `Thread` in the package `java.lang`. A selection of the methods found in the class `Thread` may be used as follows.

A thread is declared as a variable of type `Thread`. For example `Thread appletThread;` Until the variable has been instantiated it will have a `null` reference.

A thread may be started, for example `appletThread.start();` Don't become confused over the `start()` methods, this one is from the class `Thread`, and not from the class `Applet`. **After a thread has been started it automatically invokes the `run()` method.**

The code of a thread may be executed by ensuring that it is included within the `run()` method. The abstract method `run()` is the only method in the class `java.lang.Runnable`, and must be overridden in the applet containing the thread. **For this reason you must ensure that your applet implements the `Runnable` interface.**

A thread may sleep for a stated number of milliseconds. For example, the thread currently executing the code contained in the `run` method would sleep for 1 second by including the statement `Thread.sleep(1000)`. The danger in sending a thread to sleep stems from the fact that a program may be interrupted (for example, by using the Ctrl C keys to abandon program execution), and the thread needs to be cleared from the system. Whenever, you use the class method `sleep`, always provide an exception handler, should an interrupt exception occur.

A thread may be stopped, for example `appletThread.stop();` Don't become confused over the `stop()` methods, this one is from the class `Thread`, and not from the class `Applet`.

Program Example 11.9 is a modification of Program Example 11.8 and includes a thread for the running of the applet, to allow the Web browser or applet viewer to run in parallel, and hence process the request to repaint the screen.

Notice that the standard applet method `init()` has been used to create a thread and start it running, and `destroy()` has been used to stop a thread. The method `run()` from the `Runnable` interface has also been overridden.

Program Example 11.9: An Applet Running in its Own Thread

```
// chap_11\Ex_9.java
// program to display a digital clock allowing the calculation of
// the time and displaying the value to run in its own thread of
// execution

import java.applet.*;
import java.awt.*;
import java.util.*;

public class Ex_9 extends Applet implements Runnable
{
    Thread appletThread;

    Font font = new Font("Monospaced",Font.BOLD,16);
```

```
    int hours, mins, secs;

    // override the init() method to initialize and start
    // a thread of execution
    public void init()
    {
        if (appletThread == null)
        {
            appletThread = new Thread(this);
            appletThread.start(); // start from class Thread
        }
    }

    // calculate the time of day, and call the repaint method to
    // display the time
    public void run() // implemented from the abstract class Runnable
    {
        while (true)
        {
            Calendar time=Calendar.getInstance();

            hours = time.get(Calendar.HOUR);
            mins = time.get(Calendar.MINUTE);
            secs = time.get(Calendar.SECOND);

            repaint();

            // generate a short pause by letting the thread sleep
            try{Thread.sleep(1000);}
            catch(InterruptedException i){System.exit(1);}
        }
    }

    // override the destroy() method to stop the execution of the thread
    // and nullify the thread
    public void destroy()
    {
        if (appletThread != null)
        {
            appletThread.stop();
            appletThread = null;
        }
    }

    // display the time in the applet's window
    public void paint(Graphics g)
    {
        g.setFont(font);
        g.drawString(String.valueOf(hours)+":"+
                     String.valueOf(mins)+":"+
                     String.valueOf(secs),50,50);
    }
}
```

Test results You are advised to run the program, to verify that it does accurately display the time of day. Because the applet is running in its own thread, the Web browser or applet viewer can react to the mouse button being pressed over the **X** to close the applet window. Closing the applet window will result in the destroy method being called and the thread of execution being terminated.

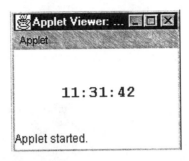

⚠️ Always get into the habit of running an applet in its own thread. You may want to run more than one applet on a Web page so concurrent processing becomes almost mandatory!

There is a great deal more to multithreading and concurrent processing than is mentioned in this chapter. Threads may also be used with applications. You have only been given a brief introduction to the topic in the context of applets.

⚠️ The methods `stop()` and `stop(Throwable)` from the class `java.lang.Thread` have been **deprecated in Java 1.2**. Deprecation means that Sun Microsystems, Inc may not support these methods in future releases of Java. When the programs containing the `stop` method were compiled, using the Java 1.2 Beta release, the deprecation was flagged as a warning after compilation. All the programs containing the `stop` method still ran correctly using the Java 1.2 interpreter.

Case Study: An Example of Multithreading.

Problem. Write a program to display three frames in an applet's window. In each frame is a solid black rectangle that increases in length with time. Associated with each frame is a separate thread of execution. The threads are given different attributes of sleepiness. Some threads may sleep for a long time before doing any active work in increasing the length of the rectangle; other threads require less sleep and are always adding to the length of the rectangle.

Problem Analysis. The time each thread is given to sleep can be calculated as a random number. If the maximum sleeping period of a thread is 5000 ms, then a random number generated between 0.0 and 1.0 will scale the time to sleep between 0 and 5000 ms. You will rarely get three random numbers generated with the same value, therefore, you will nearly always create threads that sleep for longer periods than other threads.

Analysis of classes. The solution to this problem uses three classes. A class to create a Gui object from a frame with a method to increment and draw a solid rectangle.

A class to create a GraphicThread that takes on the attributes of time asleep and a Gui frame, with a method run that implements the Runnable interface. All object of this class will execute the run method automatically. Hence all objects will go through a period of sleeping, followed by drawing their extended rectangle in the frame.

The third class extends the Applet class, its function is to instantiate and start the three threads, and when the applet window is closed destroy the three threads. Since the third class is trivial it will not be discussed further, but implemented directly in the coding section.

The public interfaces of the classes Gui and GraphicThread follow.

```
class Gui extends Frame
{
    // constructor
    public Gui(String s);
    // method to draw a solid rectangle within a frame
    public void draw();
}

class GraphicThread extends Thread implements Runnable
{
    // constructor
    public GraphicThread();
}
```

Notice that the method run is not available for public use from the class GraphicThread. The run method cannot be described as private since it must implement a predefined signature from the Runnable interface.

Algorithm for the constructor Gui

1. set the size of the frame
2. set the location of the frame
3. update the position of the next frame so there is no frame overlap
4. set the background color of the frame

Algorithm for the method draw.

1. get an instance of a graphic
2. set the graphic to the color black
3. increase the length of the rectangle by the incremental length
4. draw the rectangle at a set position within the frame

Data Dictionary for the class Gui. This contains the dimensions of the frame and a rectangle. Since the width and height of the frame never change, these dimensions may be stored as integer constants. Similarly, the width of a rectangle and the amount the rectangle is increased may also be stored as integer constants.

The length of the rectangle is an instance variable, since it applies to each separate frame instantiated, and is initialized to zero. However, the position of the frame with respect to the applet's window must be declared as a static integer variable, to prevent different frames from being drawn one-on-top of another.

```
static final int WIDTH_OF_FRAME     = 800;
static final int HEIGHT_OF_FRAME    = 100;
static final int INCREMENTAL_LENGTH = 5; // size rectangle increases
static final int WIDTH_OF_RECTANGLE = 10;

// unique ordinate position of top-left hand corner for each frame
static int position = 0;
int lengthOfRectangle = 0; // initial length of rectangle
```

Data Dictionary for the method draw. Since this method is responsible for drawing the solid rectangle, there is a need to create a variable of type Graphic. Hence the local declaration of

```
Graphics g = getGraphics();
```

Algorithm for the constructor GraphicThread

1. calculate the time a thread spends asleep by using a random number generator
2. instantiate a new frame for the thread

Algorithm for the method run

1. while true
2.   thread sleeps predefined time
3.   set threads frame visible
4.   draw solid rectangle for threads frame

Data Dictionary for the class GraphicThread. This contains an integer constant representing the maximum time a thread will spend asleep (5000 ms), and a variable representing the time asleep. Since every thread has its own frame, a variable must be declared of type `Gui`.

```
static final int DELAY = 5000; // maximum delay of 5 seconds
int timeAsleep;                // time a thread spend asleep
Gui threadFrame;
```

Desk Check. Up to now all our desk checking activities have been confined to programs that run in a single thread. In this example we have three threads to consider. In constructing a table of results it is helpful to show elapsed time over a short period.

During this time period different events of drawing and sleeping will take place for each thread. We may assume that the time spent asleep for each thread is 1s, 2s and 3s respectively; and the amount of drawing a thread can perform in 1s is just one rectangle.

The test data represents the time spent asleep for each thread. Let thread1=1s; thread2=2s and thread3=3s.

time interval	0	1	2	3	4	5	6	7	8	9
thread1 (position)	0									
asleep	1									
lengthOfRectangle	0	5	10	15	20	25	30	35	40	45
thread2 (position)	100									
asleep	2									
lengthOfRectangle	0	0	5	5	10	10	15	15	20	20
thread3 (position)	200									
asleep	3									
lengthOfRectangle	0	0	0	5	5	5	10	10	10	15

Coding

```
// chap_11\Ex_10.java
// applet to demonstrate three threads of execution;
// each thread makes different rates of progress in drawing a
// solid rectangle in its own window;
// the thread given less time to sleep will draw the longest
// rectangle compared with the thread that sleeps for longer periods
// of time

import java.applet.*;
import java.awt.*;

class Gui extends Frame
{
    static final int WIDTH_OF_FRAME     = 800;
    static final int HEIGHT_OF_FRAME    = 100;
    static final int INCREMENTAL_LENGTH = 5; // size rectangle increases
    static final int WIDTH_OF_RECTANGLE = 10;

    // unique ordinate position of top-left hand corner for each frame
    static int position = 0;

    int lengthOfRectangle = 0; // initial length of rectangle

    //-----------------------------------------------------------------

    public Gui(String s)
    {
        super(s);
        // set up attributes of a single frame
        setSize(WIDTH_OF_FRAME,HEIGHT_OF_FRAME);
        setLocation(100,position);
        position = position+100;
        setBackground(Color.yellow);
    }

    //-----------------------------------------------------------------

    public void draw()
    // method to draw a black rectangle in the frame
    {
        Graphics g = getGraphics();

        g.setColor(Color.black);
        lengthOfRectangle=lengthOfRectangle+INCREMENTAL_LENGTH;
        g.fillRect(10,50,lengthOfRectangle,WIDTH_OF_RECTANGLE);
    }
}

    //-----------------------------------------------------------------

class GraphicThread extends Thread implements Runnable
{
    static final int DELAY = 5000; // maximum delay of 5 seconds
    int timeAsleep;                 // time a thread spend asleep
    Gui threadFrame;                // the frame used by a thread
```

```
    public GraphicThread()
    {
        super();
        // calculate sleep time for thread
        timeAsleep = (int)(DELAY*Math.random());

        // instantiate and set the attributes of a frame
        threadFrame = new
        Gui("Thread sleeps for "+String.valueOf(timeAsleep)+" milliseconds");

    }

    //------------------------------------------------------------------
    // each thread will be scheduled an amount of time to run by the
    // operating system however some threads will remain asleep during
    // their allocated amount of time
    public void run()
    {
        while (true)
        {
            try{sleep(timeAsleep);}
            catch(InterruptedException i){System.exit(1);}
            // set frame visible and extend length of rectangle
            threadFrame.setVisible(true);
            threadFrame.draw();
        }
    }
}

//--------------------------------------------------------------------------

public class Ex 10 extends Applet
{
    GraphicThread firstThread, secondThread, thirdThread;

    // override init() method to instantiate and start three threads
    public void init()
    {
        firstThread = new GraphicThread();
        secondThread = new GraphicThread();
        thirdThread = new GraphicThread();

        firstThread.start();
        secondThread.start();
        thirdThread.start();
    }

    //------------------------------------------------------------------
    // override destroy() method to stop the three threads running
    public void destroy()
    {
        firstThread.stop();
        secondThread.stop();
        thirdThread.stop();
    }
}
```

Test results Once again you are advised to run this program to gain a better insight into the functionality of threads. If you edit the program so that none of the threads sleep, you will get an idea of how your operating system schedules the running of many threads.

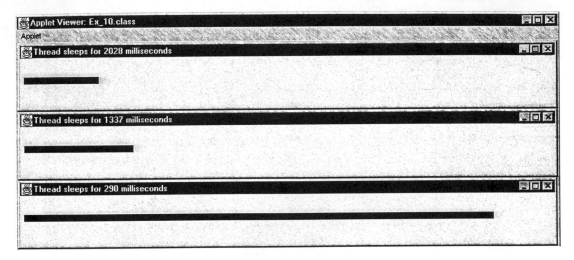

Case Study: Ships at Sea Revisited

Problem. Before commencing this extension to the Case Study: Ships at Sea - An example of Inheritance, you are advised to return to Chapter 8, and familiarize yourself with its contents. The example just cries out for a graphical user interface to display the positions of the ships over a period of time. Now that you have a knowledge of GUIs and applets, it is possible to extend the case study to include a graphical display in an applet window rather than a textual display in an MSDOS/terminal window.

Problem Analysis. This solution to this problem emphasizes the power of object-oriented programming. Most of the work has already been successfully completed in Chapter 8. The classes `Ship`, `Ferry`, `Liner` and `Time` require no further modification, and may be reused in this new case study. The class containing the `shipData` and `main` methods is the only class requiring modification.

The new problem requires that we address the following areas.

Use a graphical user interface with a Y-axis that is in the opposite direction to the Y-axis in the original problem. This means that all Y-axis values must be subtracted from the height of the screen. The height of the screen may be passed as a parameter from the HTML script file to the applet.

Use a thread to control the running of the applet.

Incorporate an element of real-time delay into the simulation to plot the movement of the ships across the screen. The solution is to allow the thread to sleep for a predetermined time (1000ms).

Analysis of classes. The only class that must be modified is the one containing the `main` method. In using applets the `main` method will conveniently be replaced by the `run` method implemented from the `Runnable` interface. The innards of the `main` method are literally transplanted into the `run` method. The algorithm for the `shipData` method is unchanged, only it must cater for displaying details of any ship in the window of the applet.

Coding

```
//chap_11\Ex_11.java
// simulation of ships at sea

import java.awt.*;
import java.applet.*;
import java.util.*;

abstract class Ship {..}

class Ferry extends Ship {..}

class Liner extends Ship {..}

class Time {..}

public class Ex_11 extends Applet implements Runnable
{
    int     yAxisLength;
    Thread appletThread;
    Font small = new Font("Serif",Font.PLAIN,9);

    // simulation over 1416 minutes
    final int MAX_SIMULATION_TIME = 1416;
    // simulate movement every 60 minutes
    final int TIME_INTERVAL = 60;

    public void init()
    {
        setBackground(Color.yellow);
        yAxisLength = Integer.parseInt(getParameter("lengthOfYAxis"));

        if (appletThread == null)
        {
            appletThread = new Thread(this);
            appletThread.start();
        }
    }


    public void destroy()
    {
        if (appletThread != null)
        {
            appletThread.stop();
            appletThread = null;
        }
    }
```

```
protected void shipData(Ship object, Time time)
// method to display the data on any type of ship
{
    int x, y; // coordinates of position of ship

    Graphics g = getGraphics();

    g.setFont(small);
    g.setColor(Color.black);

    // get position of ship
    // correct y axis value for plotting on screen
    x=object.getX();
    y=yAxisLength - object.getY();

    // display the details of a ship
    g.drawString("+ "+object.getName()+" "+
            String.valueOf(time.getHours())+":"+
            String.valueOf(time.getMinutes())+" "+
            String.valueOf(object.getDirection())+" "+
            String.valueOf(object.getSpeed()),x,y);

    // real-time delay
    try{Thread.sleep(1000);}
    catch(InterruptedException i){System.exit(1);}
}

//-----------------------------------------------------------------

public void run()
{

    // instantiate ships
    // VIKING; x,y [0,100];  bearing 75; speed 25
    // QEII;   x,y [900,100]; bearing 310; speed 45
    Ferry rollOnRollOff = new Ferry("VIKING",0,100,60,25);
    Liner queenElizabeth2  = new Liner("QEII",900,100,310,45);

    // instantiate time
    Time simulationTime = new Time(TIME_INTERVAL);

    // display data on ships
    do
    {
        shipData(rollOnRollOff,simulationTime);
        rollOnRollOff.calculateNewPosition(TIME_INTERVAL);
        shipData(queenElizabeth2,simulationTime);
        queenElizabeth2.calculateNewPosition(TIME_INTERVAL);
        simulationTime.update();
    } while (simulationTime.elapsedTime() <= MAX_SIMULATION_TIME/2);

    // change course and speed of ships
    rollOnRollOff.changeCourse(20);
    rollOnRollOff.changeSpeed(15);
    queenElizabeth2.changeCourse(35);
    queenElizabeth2.changeSpeed(30);
```

```
// display data on ships
do
{
    shipData(rollOnRollOff,simulationTime);
    rollOnRollOff.calculateNewPosition(TIME_INTERVAL);
    shipData(queenElizabeth2,simulationTime);
    queenElizabeth2.calculateNewPosition(TIME_INTERVAL);
    simulationTime.update();
} while (simulationTime.elapsedTime() <= MAX_SIMULATION_TIME);
}
}
```

Test results

11.6 Animation

You may recall seeing childrens' books in which a series of single pictures are drawn on say the odd numbered pages of the book, where each picture differs very slightly from the previous picture. By rapidly thumbing through the pages, from the first page to the last, it is possible to get the illusion of movement or animation of the drawn figures.

Because applets and applications are capable of displaying images, it is possible in Java to display a sequence of images, one after another, to form an animation.

The technique involves the sequence of displaying an image, followed by erasing the image, and displaying a similar image to the first apart from some minor alteration to the image. The technique is repeated until all images have been shown.

This technique is fine in theory, but very disappointing to implement in practice since it suffers from the following problems.

- When the images are being loaded they are frequently displayed as partial images.

- There is a considerable amount of flicker caused by an image being cleared from the screen and a new image being drawn on the screen.

Let us tackle these problems by looking at a worked example to store a series of GIF images, 36 images to be precise, in an array, and display each image from the array. The first four images are shown in Figure 11.3. The image is the 3-D word *JAVA*, produced using a drawing package, with each image being saved as a GIF file. Notice that each image differs slightly from the previous image, in so much as the image is being rotated clockwise.

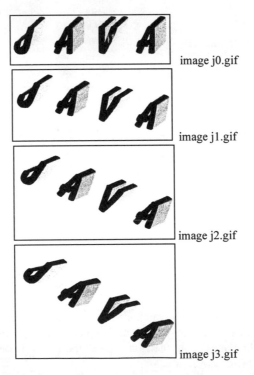

image j0.gif

image j1.gif

image j2.gif

image j3.gif

Figure 11.3 A selection of GIF images used in the animation of Program Example 11.12

The images are stored in the following array:

```
Image[] gifImages = new Image[36];
```

where each image needs to be retrieved from a file and stored at in the appropriate cell of the array. The storage is such that j0.gif is stored in gifImages[0]; j1.gif is stored in gifImages[1]; and so on. The code you may intuitively write to perform this operation follows.

```
for (int index=0; index != gifImages.length; index++)
{
    gifImages[index] =
    getImage(getDocumentBase(), "images\\j"+index+".gif");
}
```

where images is a sub-directory that contains the 36 GIF files. Using this approach results in partial images being displayed by the Web browser or applet viewer when each image is being loaded into the array. The solution is to use methods from the MediaTracker class to keep track of the status of any number of Image objects. To eliminate partial images being displayed use MediaTracker to load one or more images and wait until those images have been completely loaded and are ready to use. A partial listing of the MediaTracker class follows. For the full documentation refer to the Sun JDK API documentation.

```
public class MediaTracker extends Object
{
    // Fields
    public final static int ABORTED;
    public final static int COMPLETE;
    public final static int ERRORED;
    public final static int LOADING;

    // Constructor
    public MediaTracker(Component  comp);

    // Methods
    public void addImage(Image  image, int  id);
    public boolean checkAll();
    public boolean checkID(int  id);
    public boolean isErrorAny();
    public synchronized void removeImage(Image image, int id);
    public int statusAll(boolean  load);
    public int statusID(int  id, boolean  load);
    public void waitForAll() throws InterruptedException;
    public void waitForID(int  id) throws InterruptedException;
       .
       .
       .
}
```

The meaning of a selection of these methods follows.

addImage() method registers an image to be loaded and tracked and assigns it a specified identifier value.

isErrorAny() method checks whether any errors have occurred when loading images.

`waitForAll()` method loads all images and returns when all images have been loaded or received an error. Since you are putting the applet into a waiting state this method is capable of throwing an interrupted exception that may occur during the running of the applet.

`statusAll()` method returns the status of all images, and returns one of the field constants.

The first attempt at writing code to retrieve and store the GIF images in an array can now be rewritten making full use of the methods in the `MediaTracker` class.

```
MediaTracker tracker = new MediaTracker(this);

for (int index=0; index != gifImages.length; index++)
{
    gifImages[index] =
    getImage(getDocumentBase(), "images\\j"+index+".gif");
    tracker.addImage(gifImages[index],index);
}

try
{
    tracker.waitForAll();
}
catch (InterruptedException e){}
```

This code has cured the problem of partial images appearing when the images are being loaded into the array.

Now to tackle the problem of image flicker. Once again the code you may intuitively write to display the images on the screen might follow the same technique as for displaying the digital clock. You override the `paint` method with the code required to display each image; and you call the `repaint()` method from within an overridden `run()` method. Your code might look something like this.

```
public void paint(Graphics g)
{
    // draw image on the applet's screen
    g.drawImage(gifImages[index],0,0,width,height,this);
}
```

Note `index` is a class variable that is incremented from within the `run()` method. The `run()` method may be overridden with the following code.

```
public void run()
{
    Graphics g = getGraphics();

    while (true)
    {
        repaint();
        index++;
        index = index % 36;
```

```
        try{appletThread.sleep(50);} catch (InterruptedException e){}
    }
}
```

The code will produce an animation, however, there is a discernible flicker between the drawing and clearing of the images. The call to `repaint()` automatically calls the method `update()`. The `update()` method clears the area of the screen in use, and then automatically calls the `paint()` method. The `update()` method is the method responsible for the flicker - since you perceive an image, followed by a blank screen, followed by another image.

A trick to reduce flicker is not to use `repaint()`, but to override the `paint()` method with a technique called graphical double-buffering. The `paint()` method is then called directly.

Graphical double-buffering uses two drawing areas - one off screen and the other on the applet's screen. All erasure of images and drawing of images is performed off screen; the created off screen image is then drawn on applet's screen. Using this technique there is no erasure of images on the applet's screen, hence flicker is reduced. The technique requires two instance variables being declared, one to hold the image off screen, and one to hold the graphics off screen. For example:

```
Image offScreenImage;
Graphics offScreenGraphics;
```

During the applet's initialization phase, both these objects can be initialized with values. For example:

```
offScreenImage = createImage(width,height);
offScreenGraphics = offScreenImage.getGraphics();
```

where `createImage(width, height)` from the `Component` class will create an image that may be used off screen. The `getGraphics()` method returns a `Graphics` object that can be used for drawing into off screen images.

The `paint()` method is overridden as follows.

```
public void paint(Graphics g)
{
    int topLeftX=100;   // abscissa of top left-hand corner of image
    int topLeftY=100;   // ordinate top left-hand corner of image

    // get width and height of image and scale by 50%
    int imageWidth = (gifImages[index].getWidth(this))/2;
    int imageHeight = (gifImages[index].getHeight(this))/2;

    // erase previous image from off screen graphics area
    offScreenGraphics.setColor(Color.white);
    offScreenGraphics.fillRect(0,0,width,height);

    // draw next image in off screen graphics area
    offScreenGraphics.drawImage(gifImages[index], topLeftX, topLeftY,
                        imageWidth, imageHeight, this);
```

```
    // draw image on the applet's screen
    g.drawImage(offScreenImage,0,0,width,height,this);
}
```

Notice that the size of the image has been scaled to 50% of its normal height and width. This makes the image easier to display within the boundaries of a Web browser or applet viewer.

Program Example 11.12 brings together the points discussed, and demonstrates the animation of the 36 GIF files.

Program Example 11.10: Applet Illustrating Animation of GIF Files

```java
// chap_11\Ex_12.java
// program to demonstrate animation techniques

import java.awt.*;
import java.applet.*;


public class Ex_12 extends Applet implements Runnable
{
    static final int NUMBER_OF_FRAMES = 36;
    static final int TIME_ASLEEP = 50; // 50 milliseconds sleep time

    Image[] gifImages = new Image[NUMBER_OF_FRAMES];

    int index = 0;     // index to gifImages array
    int width = 500;   // width of offscreen graphics area
    int height = 500;  // height of offscreen graphics area

    Image        offScreenImage;
    Graphics     offScreenGraphics;
    MediaTracker tracker;
    Thread appletThread;

    public void init()
    {
        // load images into array
        tracker = new MediaTracker(this);
        for (int index=0; index != gifImages.length; index++)
        {
            gifImages[index] =
            getImage(getDocumentBase(), "images\\j"+index+".gif");
            tracker.addImage(gifImages[index],index);
        }

        try
        {
            tracker.waitForAll();
        }
        catch (InterruptedException e){}

        offScreenImage = createImage(width,height);
        offScreenGraphics = offScreenImage.getGraphics();
    }
```

```
public void paint(Graphics g)
{
    int topLeftX=100;   // abscissa of top left-hand corner of image
    int topLeftY=100;   // ordinate top left-hand corner of image

    // get width and height of image and scale by 50%
    int imageWidth = (gifImages[index].getWidth(this))/2;
    int imageHeight = (gifImages[index].getHeight(this))/2;

    // erase previous image from off screen graphics area
    offScreenGraphics.setColor(Color.white);
    offScreenGraphics.fillRect(0,0,width,height);

    // draw next image in off screen graphics area
    offScreenGraphics.drawImage(gifImages[index],
                                topLeftX, topLeftY,
                                imageWidth, imageHeight,
                                this);

    // draw image on the applet's screen
    g.drawImage(offScreenImage,0,0,width,height,this);
}

// create new thread
public void start()
{
    if (appletThread == null)
    {
        appletThread=new Thread(this);
        appletThread.start();
    }
}

// override run() method to display the images on the screen
public void run()
{
    Graphics g = getGraphics();
    while (true)
    {
        paint(g);
        index++;
        index = index % NUMBER_OF_FRAMES;

        try{appletThread.sleep(TIME_ASLEEP);}
        catch (InterruptedException e){}
    }
}

public void destroy()
{
    if (appletThread != null)
    {
        appletThread.stop();
        appletThread=null;
    }
}
}
```

Test results The results of this applet are best viewed with the applet running. The 3-D word *JAVA* rotates. The way in which each rectangle containing a GIF file is drawn results in the strange rotational effect.

11.7 Restrictions

You have probably noticed by now, that when you surf the Web and download documents your browser literally comes into life with superb text and graphics, displayed in brilliant colors, possibly with sound, photographs, videos and animated pictures. You now know that the text is based on an HTML script file; the photographs and some animation are likely to come from GIF files, however, there may be a number of applets that have been downloaded and are running on your computer.

As mentioned earlier in this chapter, to avoid the possibility of a downloaded applet causing havoc on your computer, there are certain restrictions imposed on what an applet is allowed to do.

Different Web browsers and applet viewers may impose different security restrictions on applets. Applets downloaded over the network must be considered as **untrusted code**, and you should assume that any applet will be restricted by the following security measures. Applets that are considered to be untrusted code <u>cannot</u> perform the following operations.

- Access the local file system on your computer.
- Perform networking operations.
- Use system facilities.
- Use certain AWT facilities.
- Access certain system properties.
- Create threads or access threads or thread groups outside of the thread group in which the applet is running.
- Access certain classes and packages.

When an applet is loaded from the file system on your computer, it is assumed that the code is likely to be more trustworthy than an anonymous downloaded applet over the network. For this reason Web browsers and applet viewers may relax some of the restrictions listed above.

> It is possible to attach a digital signature to a Java Archive (JAR) file, as a means of specifying the applet(s) contained within the JAR file have trusted code. The Web browser may then grant special privileges to such applet(s). See your JDK documentation for further information.

Summary

- The Internet is an international network of computers, where the structure permits networks within networks. The Internet refers to the hardware needed to support the linking together of many computers to form networks; and the linking of the networks together.

- There are various resources available on the Internet - Email, File Transfer Protocol (FTP), Gopher, Telnet and Hyper-Text Transfer Protocol (HTTP).

- The World Wide Web (WWW) is a distributed information service on the Internet, that uses browsers to interpret documents written in Hyper-Text Mark-up Language (HTML).

- An HTML script file may contain references to text, images, video clips and applets.

- A Uniform Resource Locator (URL) is a means of addressing any site on the Web.

- An applet is a program designed to be run by a Java-enabled Web browser or applet viewer.

- There are two parts to creating an applet. The applet code itself, that is compiled using a Java compiler. An HTML file that contains a call to the applet, together with any parameters that the applet requires. The HTML file is executed by the Web browser of applet viewer.

- The Applet class contains a set of methods that may be overridden by a subclass of the Applet class. The most important standard methods to override are - `init()`, `start()`, `stop()`, and `destroy()`.

- There is no concept of a `main` method in an applet as there is with an application. Control of the computer must be made through automatic calls to the standard methods of the applet.

- Applets run in either a Web browser or an applet viewer, and make use such facilities as the browser's window to implement GUI's and draw graphics; the browser's event handling of its window; and the browser's interface for controlling the applet.

- Both HTML files and applets may be used to incorporate multimedia into Web-based documents.

- An applet may set up listeners to control input and output in a graphical user interface.

- The position of a mouse may be used in conjunction with an image map to trigger other media being shown or played.

- A thread is a single sequential flow of control. Since the Web browser or applet viewer controls the applet, it is important for an applet to have at least one thread to run in, to allow the browser time to perform useful work, such as implementing `repaint`.

- A thread has a life cycle - it is created, starts, runs, enters any of the states of being ready to be run, asleep, suspended, waiting or blocked, and eventually must die.

- An applet that uses threads must ensure that the functionality of the applet is controlled from within the `run` method.

- Images may be animated within applets. To ensure flicker-free animation do not clear the image on the browser's drawing surface, instead clear the image behind the scenes, by using double buffering.

- To prevent images from being partially shown during the loading process, use the MediaTracker class to monitor the loading of the images.

- An applet may gain access to any site on the Web by using the URL of the site.

- Applets that are downloaded to a local machine have severe restrictions of access imposed upon them, as a means of protecting the host machine from untrusted code.

- Applets that have been loaded from a local machine are regarded as being trustworthy and are subject to less stringent restrictions.

Review Questions

1. What is the Internet, and how does it differ from the Word Wide Web?

2. Describe any three resources on the Internet.

3. What is hypertext, and how does it differ from hypermedia?

4. What is a HTML script file, and why is it used?

5. True or false - a Web browser interprets an HTML script file.

6. True of false - an applet does not require an HTML script file in order that it might run.

7. True or false - a Web browser and an applet viewer have the same functionality.

8. Describe three tasks that a Web browser will enable you to perform.

9. What is a Hyper-Text Transfer Protocol (HTTP)?

10. Discuss the format and purpose of a Uniform Resource Locator (URL).

11. What is the purpose of the parameters width and height in a HTML applet tag?

12. True or false - you must override the standard methods `init()`, `start()`, `stop()` and `destroy()` in an applet before it can be executed.

13. True or false - there is no `main` method in an applet.

14. State two advantages of running an applet in a Web browser or applet viewer compared with an application.

15. What is the purpose of NAME and VALUE in an HTML parameter tag?

16. How do you play an audio clip in an applet?

17. What is an image map?

18. Why is it important for an applet to run in its own thread?

19. Discuss briefly the life cycle of a thread.

20. What is the major causes of flicker in image animation when using applets?

21. Discuss graphical double buffering.

22. What is the purpose of a MediaTracker object?

23. State any three limitations imposed upon an applet that is downloaded from the Web to a local computer.

Exercises

24. Comment upon the error in the following URL - `java.sun.com`

25. The following HTML script contains errors. What are the errors?

```
<BODY>
<APPLET> code=Ex_25.java>
</HTML>
```

26. Desk check the following HTML script file and applet.

```
<HTML>
<BODY>
<APPLET code=Ex_26.class width=500 height=300>
<PARAM NAME=url VALUE="http://www.windows95.com">
</APPLET>
</BODY>
</HTML>
```

```
public class Ex_26 extends Applet
{
    public void init()
    {
        try
        {
            URL site = new URL(getParameter("url"));
            getAppletContext().showDocument(site);
        }
        catch (MalformedURLException m){System.exit(1);}
    }
}
```

What do the HTML script file and applet do? How could you change the value of the URL without having to edit and re-compile the applet?

27. Desk check the following code. Explain any errors that you find.

```
public class Ex_27 extends Applet
{
    String name;

    public void paint()
    {
        Font font = new Font("Monospaced, Font.ITALIC, 36);

        setFont(font);
        setBackground(yellow);
        setColor(red);
        drawString(name);
    }
}
```

28. Rewrite the applet in question 27, so that it is error free; supply a value for the variable name from the parameter list in the corresponding HTML script file.

29. Modify your program in question 28 to cater for a value for the variable name being input at the time of running the applet.

30. Return to the Case Study: Simple Calculator from Chapter 10, and modify the source code to run as an applet. You will also need to create an HTML script file to call the applet.

31. If the value of the String variable source is "dialtone", and the AU sound file dialtone.au is stored in the same directory as the applet containing the following statements:

```
AudioClip sound = getAudioClip(getCodebase(), souce+"au");
sound.play();
```

Why doesn't the applet make a sound when it is executed? (This is a very simple error, but one that is very easy to make!).

32. Comment upon the errors in the following applet. Rewrite the code using a thread to control the repainting of the screen.

```
public class Ex_32 extends Applet
{
    Thread appletThread;
    int length = 1;

    public start()
    {
        while (true)
        {
            repaint();
            length++;

            Thread.sleep(5000);
        }
    }

    public void paint(Graphics g)
    {
        g.fillRect(10,50,length,5);
    }
}
```

33. In this chapter HTML has been talked about and used, however, there has been no formal tutorial about the syntax of the language. Using your Web browser, do a Web search on the words **HTML tutorial**. You will discover a lot of very useful tutorials out there. Either teach yourself HTML on-line, or download the tutorial information for further study off-line.

34. Write an HTML script file for your own home page on a Web server. This file should contain textual information about yourself, photographs, and possibly sound and video clips. Use your Web browser to verify that your HTML script file functions correctly.

Programming Problems

35. Improve the digital clock applet. The clock should be given a set of buttons, to control an alarm.

36. Design and write a program to display an analog clock on the screen. Give the clock a sweeping seconds hand and program the clock to chime every quarter hour as well as hourly.

37. Design and write a program to display the buttons from a digital telephone. As you dial a number play the correct tone. After say inputting a six digit number the program plays either a ringing or busy tone. Download the tone dialing sounds from a sound archive of your choice.

38. Design and write your own space invaders game. Control a gun sight by moving the mouse over the enemy space-craft to zap the invaders. Invader space craft should be generated at random intervals and at random positions on the screen. Display on the screen the number of seconds

remaining before the game finishes and the number of invaders space craft zapped. You might also allow different levels of difficulty.

This problem gives you plenty of opportunity to experiment with sounds and graphics. Remember to use threads in this problem.

39. Design and write an applet to play tic-tac-toe.

40. Design and write an HTML script file that includes applets to produce a multimedia-based computer-assisted learning package on a subject of your choice.

Chapter 12
Algorithms and
Data Structures

The final chapter introduces you to a number of algorithms and data structures you may find useful when you continue to develop programs using Java.

Many of the techniques, methods and data structures discussed in this chapter form part of a computer science course. Their inclusion here is for completeness, and to explain how Java supports these concepts.

By the end of the chapter you should have an understanding of the following topics.

- The technique of calling a method recursively.

- Using recursion in sorting and searching algorithms.

- Creating dynamic structures such as linked lists.

- Using queues and stacks in processing data.

12.1 Recursion

You are already familiar with the process of calling one method from within another method. For example, from within the method main other methods can be called. The calling of one method from within another method is quite acceptable. But what if the method being called from within a method, is the same method? When the method is in effect calling itself, the technique is known as **recursion**.

Program Example 12.1 introduces the subject of recursion with a method that uses a variable level as a counter. Rather than constructing a loop, the value of level is updated and output in the method, and the method is then called recursively to repeat updating level and to output the value of level again. The method is called recursively until level becomes equal to 5.

Because of the nature of recursion, it is then possible to return through each recursive level and display the value of level associated with the recursive call.

Program Example 12.1 Recursive Calls to a Method

```java
// chap_12\Ex_1.java
// program to demonstrate recursive calls and returns

import java.io.*;

class Ex_1
{
    static PrintWriter screen = new PrintWriter(System.out, true);

    // recusive method
    static void output(int level)
    {
        level++;
        screen.println("recursive call to level " + level);

        if (level < 5)
            // recursive call to higher level
            output(level);
        else
            // return to lower level
            return;

        screen.println("returning through level " + level);
    }

    static public void main(String[] args) throws IOException
    {
        output(0);
    }
}
```

Test results

```
recursive call to level 1
recursive call to level 2
recursive call to level 3
recursive call to level 4
recursive call to level 5
returning through level 4
returning through level 3
returning through level 2
returning through level 1
```

Figure 12.1 illustrates that a recursive call to a method produces another instance or level of the method, depicted by the code being superimposed upon the calling code.

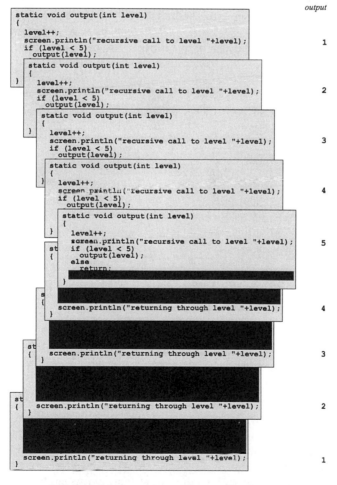

Figure 12.1 Recursive calls to method output

The remaining code after `output(level)` is not shown in the recursive calls to levels 1,2,3 and 4, since this is not yet executed. Level 5 serves as the terminating case in which the parameter `level` is equal to 5. No further recursion is possible and the code

```
if (level < 5)
    output(level);
else
    return;
```

will cause the `return` statement to be executed. The computer must return through each level or instance of the code before the program can finish. Since the computer is returning to the method that invoked the call, the next statement after the call, `output(level)`, will be executed. However, `output(level)` was in one branch of a selection; therefore, the next statement to be executed `screen.println("returning through level "+level);` will be after the selection statement. Consequently, all the code that had been executed is now blacked-out in Figure 12.1, because it will not be used as the computer returns through the levels, or instances, of the method. Notice also, that within each level the value of `level` remains what it was when the method was originally invoked. Hence, in returning through the levels, the parameter `level` is output as 4,3,2 and 1 respectively.

You may wonder how the computer remembers the values of the parameters at each level of recursion, and where to return to from a level of recursion?

The computer stores information in a stack. A **stack** operates on a LIFO principle in which the computer stores and removes information from one end of the stack only. The computer associates a stack frame with each level of recursion. A **stack frame** contains the values of the parameters and local variables for any one level of recursion, and the memory address of where the computer should return to after the level of recursion is complete. Figure 12.2 illustrates a single stack frame for Program Example 12.1. This stack frame contains a value for the `level` parameter and the next statement after the method call. In this example it is not practical to include the memory address of the statement that follows the method call.

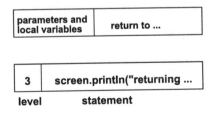

Figure 12.2 An example of a stack frame

Figure 12.3 illustrates how each frame is stored at the top of a stack for each recursive call to the method `output`, and how each frame is removed from the stack as the computer returns through the levels of recursion. Figure 12.3 should be read first from the top left to bottom left, which represents how frames are stored on the stack at each recursive call. After the terminating case level=5 has been reached, the figure should be read from bottom right to top right where the computer removes each frame from the top of the stack. The removed frame contains the level number of the values of the parameter for that particular instance of recursion, and the statement of where to return after that instance of recursion is complete.

The computer continues to remove frames from the stack as it returns through each level of recursion until the stack is empty and the computer has returned to the end of the main method.

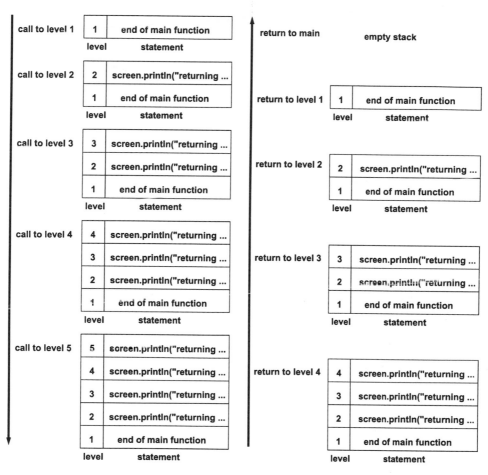

Figure 12.3 Use of a stack to store data for each level

It is tempting to offer a simple definition of recursion as a method that calls itself. However this definition is incomplete, since there is no mention of how the called method stops repeatedly calling itself, and how every recursive level contributes towards the overall solution to the problem.

Recursion may be regarded as a technique for performing a method R, by performing a similar method Ri, where the method Ri is exactly the same in nature as the original method R. Thus method R recursively calls method R_1; method R_1 recursively calls method R_2; and so on until method Rn-1 recursively calls method Rn, where each recursive call contributes towards the overall solution to the problem.

Eventually the recursive calls must lead to a solution R_n, which cannot allow for further recursive calls because a terminating criterion has been reached.

You should always address the following three questions before constructing a recursive solution.

• How can you define a solution where each recursive call contributes towards the overall solution to the problem?

• What instance or level of the solution can serve as the terminating case?

• Does the manner in which the recursive solution execute, ensure that this terminating case will always be reached?

In the context of Program Example 12.1, consider the three questions about constructing a recursive algorithm.

The algorithm represents counting forwards from 1 to 5, and counting in reverse from 4 to 1. The recursive solution is a repetitive solution, in so much as it will display the value of the counter after each call to a level of recursion, and display the value of the counter when returning back through each level of recursion.

The terminating case is when level is equal to 5. No further recursion is possible, and all values in the range 1 to 5 have been output.

Since the variable `level` is being increased by 1 after each recursive call, `level` will eventually become equal to 5.

Two further examples on the use of recursion follow. Program Example 12.2 illustrates how a method can be called recursively to output the contents of a string backwards.

Program Example 12.2: Recursively Writing a String Backwards

```java
// chap_12\Ex_2.java
// program to print a string backwards

import java.io.*;

class Ex_2
{
    static PrintWriter screen = new PrintWriter(System.out, true);

    static void writeBackwards(StringBuffer alphaString, int index)
    {
        if (index >= 0)
        {
            screen.print(alphaString.charAt(index));
            screen.flush();

            // recursive call
            writeBackwards(alphaString, index-1);
        }

        // return to lower level from this point in the program
    }

    static public void main(String[] args) throws IOException
    {
        StringBuffer alphabet = new
        StringBuffer("abcdefghijklmnopqrstuvwxyz");

        writeBackwards(alphabet, 25);
    }
}
```

Test results

```
zyxwvutsrqponmlkjihgfedcba
```

We can make two observations about Program Example 12.2. The identifier `index` is set at the last cell of the string buffer, and the contents z, output. The index is then reduced by 1 and a recursive call to `writeBackwards` outputs y; index is then reduced by 1 and `writeBackwards` is recursively called again. The output of characters continues until the index is less than zero, in which case the condition to terminate recursion `index >= 0` becomes false.

The recursive call `writeBackwards(alpha, index-1)` is the last executable statement of the method `writeBackwards`, and although the computer must return through each level of the method `writeBackwards`, no further output is possible.

The final program in this section illustrates how a method may be called recursively to calculate the factorial value of a number.

Factorial n, written as n!, is defined as : n*(n-1)*(n-2) .. 3*2*1. hence 5!=5*4*3*2*1 = 120.

Program Example 12.3: Calculating the Factorial Value of a Number

```
// chap_12\Ex_3.java
// program to calculate the factorial of a number

import java.io.*;

class Ex_3
{
    static BufferedReader keyboard =
    new BufferedReader(new InputStreamReader(System.in));
    static PrintWriter screen = new PrintWriter(System.out, true);

    // recursive method to calculate the factorial value
    // of a number
    static long factorial(int n)
    {
        if (n == 0)
            // return to lower level with a value for the method
            // being returned as 1
            return 1;
        else
            // the recursive call needs to be made before the
            // computer can return to a lower level
            return n*factorial(n-1);
    }

    static public void main(String[] args) throws IOException
    {
        int number;

        screen.print("Input a number in the range 1..12 "); screen.flush();
        number = new Integer(keyboard.readLine()).intValue();

        while (number >=1 && number <= 12)
        {
            // call to method
            screen.println(number+"!\t"+factorial(number));
            screen.print("Input a number in the range 1..12 ");
            screen.flush();
            number = new Integer(keyboard.readLine()).intValue();
        }
    }
}
```

Test results

```
Input a number in the range 1..12 3
3!      6
Input a number in the range 1..12 4
4!      24
Input a number in the range 1..12 5
5!      120
Input a number in the range 1..12 6
6!      720
Input a number in the range 1..12 0
```

In Program Example 12.3 the value of the factorial of a number cannot be calculated until the method has recursively reached `factorial(0)`. Upon returning to the lower level of `factorial(1)`, the value `1*factorial(0)` can then be calculated. Returning to the lower level of `factorial(2)`, the value `2*factorial(1)` can then be calculated. Finally, returning to the lower level of `factorial(3)`, the value `3*factorial(2)` can be calculated.

You are advised to desk check Program Example 12.3 to fully appreciate the comments made.

You may wonder when you should use recursion in preference to iteration?

Recursion can be used as an alternative to iteration; however, recursion is not a wise choice if it merely replaces straightforward iteration. The true power of recursion is its use in solving problems for which there is no simple non-recursive solution.

Recursion is a powerful problem-solving tool, that compared with iteration, can lead to succinct solutions to the most complex problems. Recursion's strength will be demonstrated later in this chapter in searching and sorting algorithms. Recursion may also be used in the context of dynamic data structures, such as linked lists.

There are however, drawbacks related to efficiency when recursion is compared with iteration. These drawbacks may be summarized as follows.

- There is an overhead of the extra memory space associated with a call to a method. Memory space must be set aside for storing parameters, local variables, and the return address of the next statement to be executed in the calling method. Recall for a moment the use of the stack frame for storing this information. Every time a recursive call is made the computer must allocate memory space to store the information. This overhead is magnified by a recursive method, since a single initial call to the method can generate a large number of recursive calls. For example the method factorial(n) generates n recursive calls.

- There is the overhead of the computer time it takes to make recursive method calls. Although fast computers make this overhead negligible.

- Finally, some recursive algorithms can be inherently inefficient in the way they process data. This inefficiency has nothing to do with how recursion is implemented on a computer, but is tied to the method of solution in the algorithm.

12.2 Sorting

You have already been introduced to the Bubble Sort algorithm in Chapter 8. The main reason for its introduction was to show you how an interface might be used in sorting numbers as well as strings. The Bubble Sort was not an efficient algorithm for sorting data, and we now turn our attention to efficient methods for sorting data. In this section one non-recursive method and one recursive method for sorting numbers held in an array will be explained. Both methods will be compared in terms of efficiency to sort differing amounts of data.

Selection Sort

Figure 12.4 illustrates the movement of integers in a one-dimensional array, when a selection sort is used to place the integers into ascending order (lowest to highest values). The contents of the cells from 0 to 4 are inspected for the largest number (18), which is swapped with the number in cell 4. the contents of the cells from 0 to 3 are inspected for the largest number (15), which is swapped with the number in cell 3. The contents of the cells from 0 to 2 are inspected for the largest number (13), which is swapped with the number in cell 2. The contents of the cells from 0 to 1 are inspected for the largest number (8), which is swapped with the number in cell 1. When only the contents of cell 0 remains to be inspected the numbers are assumed to have been sorted into ascending order.

To generalize, if N represents the number of integers to be sorted, in the cells of an array from subscripts 0 to N-1, the largest number in the cells subscripted 0 to N-1 is found and swapped with the number in cell N-1. The process is repeated with N being decreased by 1 each time until N=0.

0	18		0	13		0	13		0	8		0	7
1	7		1	7		1	7		1	7		1	8
2	15		2	15		2	8		2	13		2	13
3	8		3	8		3	15		3	15		3	15
4	13		4	18		4	18		4	18		4	18
N=5			N=4			N=3			N=2			N=1	

Figure 12.4 A Selection Sort

Although the selection sort can be implemented as a single method, it is clearer if the implementation is based upon two methods. The first method `positionOfLargest` will return the subscript of the largest number in an array `numbers` of size `limit`.

The second method `selectionSort` calls the first method to find the largest number in the N-element array, where N is equal to size. This number is then swapped with the number at the end of the array. The process is repeated for N-1 elements, then N-2 elements, and so on, until N is reduced to zero.

You are advised to desk check Program Example 12.4 using the test data illustrated in Figure 12.4.

Program Example 12.4 Sorting Numbers into Ascending Order using the Selection Sort

```java
// chap_12\Ex_4.java
// program to demonstrate a selection sort

import java.io.*;

class SortingAlgorithms
{
    static int positionOfLargest(int[] array, int limit)
    // method to return the position of the largest item
    // in the array with bounds 0..limit
    {
        int largest = array[0];
        int indexOfLargest = 0;

        for (int index=1; index <= limit; index++)
        {
            if (array[index]> largest)
            {
                largest = array[index];
                indexOfLargest = index;
            }
        }

        return indexOfLargest;
    }

    public static void selectionSort(int[] array)
    // method to sort the contents of an array into ascending order
    {
        int temporary;
        int position;
        int size=array.length;

        for (int index=size-1; index > 0; index--)
        {
            position=positionOfLargest(array, index);

            // swap numbers
            if (index != position)
            {
                temporary = array[index];
                array[index] = array[position];
                array[position] = temporary;
            }
        }
    }
}
```

```
class Ex_4
{
    static PrintWriter screen = new PrintWriter(System.out, true);

    // method to display the contents of an array
    static void displayArray(int[] array)
    {
        for (int index=0; index != array.length; index++)
        {
            screen.print(array[index] +"\t");
            screen.flush();
        }
    }

    static public void main(String[] args) throws IOException
    {

        int[] array = {18,7,15,8,13};

        screen.println("Contents of array BEFORE being sorted\n");
        displayArray(array);

        // sort data stored in array
        SortingAlgorithms.selectionSort(array);

        screen.println("\n\n                    AFTER being sorted\n");
        displayArray(array);
    }
}
```

Test results

```
Contents of array BEFORE being sorted

18       7       15      8       13

                   AFTER being sorted

7        8       13      15      18
```

In attempting to compare the efficiency of two algorithms for solving the same problem, in this case sorting, we want to see which algorithm is the more time efficient. Intuitively, you might want to code both algorithms and perform a comparison on the time it takes to run both programs. However, there are problems with this approach.

How should the algorithms be coded? In comparing the running times, we are comparing the implementations of the algorithms and not the algorithms.

What computer should you use? The operations used by one algorithm might run faster on one machine than on another.

What data should be used to compare the two algorithms? The values of the data will influence the timings of the algorithms. Ideally our analysis should be independent of specific data.

To analyze algorithms independently of specific implementations, computers or data, the time requirement of an algorithm is taken to be a function of the size of the problem. Size is measured as the number of items in an array, the number of records in a file, and so on. We need to establish how quickly an algorithm's time requirement grows as a function of the size of the problem. For example, making the statement that *algorithm A requires time proportional to N^2* is exactly the kind of statement that characterizes the inherent efficiency of an algorithm, and is independent of such factors as implementations, computers and specific data.

In analyzing the efficiency of the selection sort we will look at the number of comparisons on the data being sorted.

If there are N items of data, then

the number of comparisons on the first pass through the array is N-1;
the number of comparisons on the second pass through the array is N-2;
the number of comparisons on the third pass through the array is N-3;
.

.

the number of comparisons on the N-1th pass through the array is 1.

The selection sort algorithm is blind to the original order of the numbers. The number of comparisons, regardless of the order of the numbers, will be the sum of the sequence of numbers (N-1)+(N-2)+(N-3)+...+1 which as the sum of a series is N(N-1)/2. Don't worry, you are not expected to know the mathematics of summing a series! Expanding this expression, the number of comparisons is $N^2/2$ - $N/2$. If we omit the fractional part of this expression, we may conclude that the selection sort has an order of magnitude of N^2 comparisons and is referred to as a quadratic algorithm. The time it takes to sort an array will be proportional to the amount of work the computer must do to compare and swap data.

The algorithm is suitable for sorting only a small amount of data; otherwise, the time taken to complete the sorting algorithm, proportional to N^2, will become lengthy.

Quicksort

By way of a contrast to the selection sort, the next sorting algorithm is normally considerably quicker in sorting data stored in an array. The algorithm is recursive, and is known as the Quicksort created by C.A.R.Hoare and described in his paper "Quicksort" (Computer Journal, Vol.5, No.1,1962).

Figure 12.5 illustrates integers stored in a one-dimensional array, with subscript bounds `first` `..` `last`. Quicksort relies upon a routine to find a value, known as a pivot, in the array. When the pivot is placed into its correct position in the array, all the numbers between the subscripts `first` `..` `pivotIndex-1` are less than or equal to its value and all the numbers between the subscripts `pivotIndex+1` `..` `last` are greater than its value.

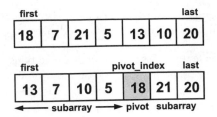

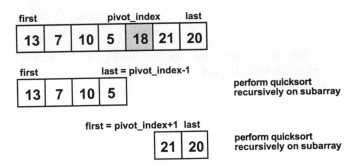

Figure 12.5 Properties of a pivot value

The array has been divided into two subarrays by the pivot value. Since the pivot is in its correct position with respect to the remainder of the data, there is no need to include this value in any further data to be sorted. The problem has been reduced to sorting two subarrays as depicted in Figure 12.6.

Figure 12.6 Quicksort performed on subarrays

Quicksort is then applied recursively to the left subarray contained between subscripts first .. pivotIndex-1 and then recursively to the right subarray contained between subscripts pivotIndex+1 .. last. The algorithm can be expressed by the following method.

```
public static void quicksort(int[] array, int first, int last)
{
    int pivotIndex;

    if (first < last)
    {
        pivotIndex = partition(array, first, last);
        quicksort(array, first, pivotIndex-1);
        quicksort(array, pivotIndex+1, last);
    }
}
```

The recursive algorithm is applicable only when the (first < last). If (first == last), then there is only one element in the subarray and is therefore sorted. The case when (first > last) indicates that the array bounds do not classify a subarray.

Figure 12.7 illustrates the operations on the array that are necessary to move the pivot to its correct position in the array.

A value for the pivot is chosen from the array. When we are selecting the pivot, if the arrays are initially randomly ordered, then it really does not matter which element is used as the pivot value. In this example the pivot is chosen to be the first number in the array.

```
pivot = array[first];
```

In order to access the array from different ends, the subscripts lo and hi are used. In figure 12.7 lo is initialized to first and will be incremented to move up the array (to the right); hi is initialized to last and will be decremented to move down the array (to the left).

```
lo = first;
hi = last;
```

The value contained in the array at lo is compared with the pivot. If this value is less than or equal to the pivot, the value of lo is increased by 1. The comparison continues while the value in the array at subscript lo is less than or equal to the pivot and the value of lo has not exceeded the subscript last.

```
while ((lo <= last) && (array[lo] <= pivot)) lo++;
```

Because of short-circuit evaluation of conditional statements it is important that the condition (lo <= last) appears before (array[lo] <= pivot) otherwise as lo increases beyond the limits of the array, an exception will be thrown.

When the comparisons stop because the value in the array at subscript lo is greater than the pivot, or lo exceeds last, attention must switch to the data at the subscript hi. The value contained in the array at hi is compared with the pivot. If this value is greater than the pivot, the value of hi is decreased by 1. The comparison continues while the value in the array at subscript hi is greater than the pivot.

```
while (array[hi] > pivot) hi--;
```

When the comparisons stop because the value in the array at subscript hi is less than or equal to the pivot, the two values in the array at subscripts hi and lo are swapped as long as lo is less than hi. The subscripts lo and hi are then increased and decreased respectively.

```
if (lo < hi)
{
    swap(array,lo,hi);
    lo++; hi--;
}
```

As long as the subscripts `lo` and `hi` do not cross over each other, the algorithm is repeated with `lo` moving up the array to the right and `hi` moving down the array to the left. When this condition becomes false, the iteration ceases and the pivot value is moved to its correct place in the array by using the method `swap(array,first,hi)`.

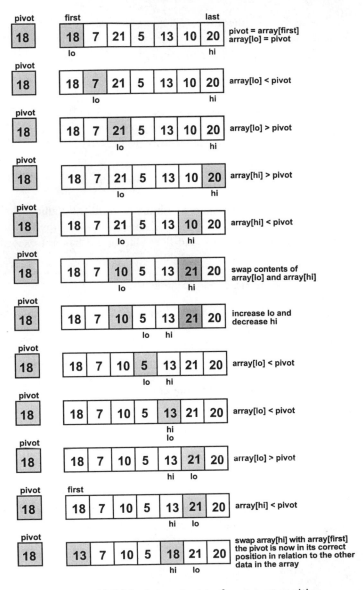

Figure 12.7 Moving a pivot to the correct position

The following program demonstrates the Quicksort on an array of integers.

Program Example 12.5: Demonstration of the Quicksort

```java
// chap_12\Ex_5.java
// program to demonstrate a Quicksort

import java.io.*;

class SortingAlgorithms
{
    // method to exchange the value of array[i] and array[j]
    static void swap(int[] array, int i, int j)
    {
        int temporary = array[i];

        array[i] - array[j];
        array[j] = temporary;
    }


    // method to return the subscript of array, such that all
    // values less than or equal to array[subscript] are stored
    // in the range first..subscript-1 and all the values greater
    // than array[subscript] are stored in the range subscript+1..last
    static int partition(int[] array, int first, int last)

    {
        int pivot = array[first];
        int lo = first;
        int hi = last;

        while (lo <= hi)
        {
            while ((lo <= last) && (array[lo] <= pivot)) lo++;

            while (array[hi] > pivot) hi--;

            if (lo < hi)
            {
                swap(array,lo,hi);
                lo++;
                hi--;
            }
        }

        swap(array,first,hi);
        return hi;
    }
```

```
    // method to sort an array with subscripts first..last, by
    // recursively sorting the smaller array first..pivotIndex-1
    // followed by recursively sorting the smaller array pivotIndex+1..last
    public static void quicksort(int[] array, int first, int last)
    {
        int pivotIndex;

        if (first < last)
        {
            pivotIndex = partition(array, first, last);

            quicksort(array, first, pivotIndex-1);
            quicksort(array, pivotIndex+1, last);
        }
    }
}


class Ex_5
{

    static PrintWriter screen = new PrintWriter(System.out, true);

    // display contents of array
    static void displayArray(int[] array)
    {
        for (int index=0; index != array.length; index++)
        {
            screen.print(array[index] +"\t");
            screen.flush();
        }
    }

    static public void main(String[] args) throws IOException
    {
        int[] array = {18,7,21,5,13,10,20};

        int size = array.length;

        screen.println("Contents of array BEFORE being sorted\n");
        displayArray(array);

        SortingAlgorithms.quicksort(array,0,size-1);

        screen.println("\n\n                    AFTER being sorted\n");
        displayArray(array);
    }
}
```

Test results

```
Contents of array BEFORE being sorted

18       7       21       5       13       10       20

                   AFTER being sorted

5        7       10       13       18       20       21
```

The Quicksort algorithm works more efficiently for some arrays than it does for others. The best results are found when the partitioning process splits each subarray into two subarrays of approximately the same size. In such cases the time to perform a Quicksort is proportional to the order of $N\log_2 N$ where N is the number of elements to be sorted. Using the best-case scenario it is quite easy to justify the $N\log_2 N$ figure.

If the number of elements in the array is N, and each time we partition a subarray it is divided into exactly equal parts, then while the first partition of the original array of length N (=2^m) will require 2^m comparisons, the partition of two half arrays of length 2^{m-1} will each require 2^{m-1} comparisons and so on.

Thus the total number of comparisons is: $2^m + 2(2^{m-1}) + 2^2(2^{m-2}) + .. + 2^{m-1}.2 = N\log_2 N$

The worst results occur when the array is already sorted, and the partition will result in a one-element left subarray and an N-1 element right subarray. The element in the left subarray is in its correct position in the array. The partition must then be applied to the right subarray. As expected this produces a one element subarray and an N-2 element right subarray. Continuing through the array, the number of comparisons becomes $(N-1) + (N-2) + .. 3 + 2 + 1 = \frac{1}{2} N(N-1)$. This approximates to the order of N^2.

In such cases the time to perform the Quicksort is no faster than the time to perform a selection sort; since the efficiency has deteriorated to the order N^2. Figure 12.8 illustrates the comparative average-case efficiency of the selection sort and the Quicksort for increasing values of N. Notice that the time to sort identical arrays is proportional to N^2 and $N\log_2 N$ respectively, and increases dramatically for the selection sort as the number of elements N increases.

N	N^2 Selection sort	$N\log_2 N$ Quicksort
32	1024	160
64	4096	384
128	16384	896
256	65536	2048
512	262144	4608

Figure 12.8 Average-case efficiency of sorting algorithms

12.3 Searching

The concept of searching was first introduced in Chapter 7. In this section, we will cover in detail two major methods, the sequential search and the binary search.

Sequential Search

When the information held in an array is sorted into search key order, it is not always necessary to search through the entire array before discovering that the information is not present. Consider for a moment the following information held in the array depicted in Figure 12.9. Alphabetically Adams is before Davies; Davies is before Evans; Evans is before Farthing, and so on.

0	Adams	18 Milestone Road
1	Davies	72 Sherwood Avenue
2	Evans	433 Lake Street
3	Farthing	10 Almond Avenue
4	Fielding	21 Turnpike Boulevard
5	Hewitt	30 Chester Street
6	Jones	336 Cornwallis Road
7	Mowbray	45 Brookside Avenue
8	Peters	113 Flemming Road
9	Quayle	212 Wiltshire Boulevard
10	Rankin	732 High Road

Figure 12.9 An array of records

If we search the contents of the sequential array for the key Ellis, then we must perform the following comparisons, illustrated in Figure 12.10, before we discover that Ellis is not in the array. Ellis is alphabetically greater than both Adams and Davies, so may be found further on in the array. Ellis is alphabetically less than Evans; therefore, an entry for Ellis cannot exist in the array because the names are ordered into alphabetical sequence. By sorting the contents of the array into alphabetical order on the name of each person, only three key comparisons are necessary to discover that Ellis does not exist in the array. If the array was not sorted by name, then we would have to compare every name in the array before we discovered that Ellis does not exist in the array.

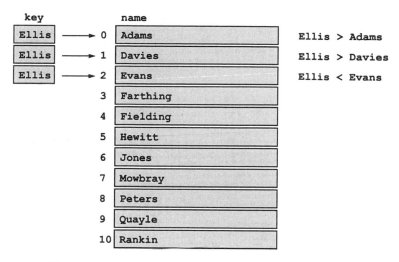

Figure 12.10 A sequential search on an array of records

Assuming that the records are stored into consecutive array locations from 0 to 10, the following algorithm is used in searching for a surname in the array.

```
// method to search for a key in an array containing ordered data
static public int sequential(Record[] array, int size, String nameKey)
{
        int index = 0;
        int resultOfComparison;

        while (index < size)
        {
                // compare search key with key in array
                resultOfComparison=nameKey.compareTo(array[index].name);

                // keys match
                if (resultOfComparison == 0)
                        return index;
                // search key less than key in array, therefore,
                // cannot exist in array
                else if (resultOfComparison < 0)
                        return size;
                // search key greater than key in array, therefore,
                // key may exists further down the array
                else
                        index++;
        }

        // return the size of the array to show that no key
        // match was possible
        return size;
}
```

The index used to access each cell of the array is initialized to 0, the first cell position of the array.

While the value of the index is within the limits of the array [0..10], the search for the key continues. In the cell being examined, if the key is equal to the surname, the position in the array of the located record, that is the value of the index, is returned.

In the cell being examined, if the key is less than the name field, then the surname cannot exist in the array; the search must stop, and the size of the array is returned. The size of the array is not a legal subscript to the array, and is used to signify that no match for the key was found.

In the cell being examined, if the key is greater than the name of the field, then the surname may exist further down the array and the value of the index is increased to retrieve the contents of the next cell.

The algorithm is implemented as the method `sequential` in the class `SearchingAlgorithms`. The following program stores in alphabetical order of surname, eleven records containing surnames and addresses in a one-dimensional array. A user is invited to input a name, and the array is searched for a key match. If the key is found, the corresponding address is output.

Program Example 12.6 Sequential Search on an Array of Records

```java
// chap_12\Ex_6.java
// program to demonstrate a sequential search of an array of records

import java.io.*;

class Record
{
    String name;
    String address;
}

//-------------------------------------------------------------------

class SearchingAlgorithms
{
    // method to search the records of an ordered array
    // for a key; if not found return the size of the array
    // otherwise return the position in the array of the match
    static public int sequential(Record[] array,int size,String nameKey)
    {
        int index = 0;
        int resultOfComparison;

        while (index < size)
        {
            // compare key with key in array
            resultOfComparison=nameKey.compareTo(array[index].name);

            // keys match
            if (resultOfComparison == 0)
                return index;
```

```
            // search key less than key in array, therefore,
            // key cannot exist in array
            else if (resultOfComparison < 0)
                return size;

            // search key greater than key in array, therefore,
            // key may exist further down the array
            else
                index++;
        }

        // return the size of the array to show that no key
        // match was possible
        return size;
    }
}

//-------------------------------------------------------------------------

class Ex_6
{

    static BufferedReader keyboard = new
            BufferedReader(new InputStreamReader(System.in));
    static PrintWriter screen = new PrintWriter(System.out, true);

    static final int MAX_RECORDS = 50;

    static public void main(String[] args) throws IOException
    {
        // text input file and stream
        FileReader file = new
        FileReader("a:\\chap_12\\names.txt");
        StreamTokenizer inputStream = new StreamTokenizer(file);

        Record[] array = new Record[MAX_RECORDS];

        int tokenType = inputStream.nextToken();
        int index = 0;
        int size;

        // build array of records from text file
        while (tokenType != StreamTokenizer.TT_EOF)
        {
            array[index] = new Record();

            array[index].name = inputStream.sval;
            inputStream.nextToken();
            array[index].address = inputStream.sval;

            index++;
            tokenType = inputStream.nextToken();
        }

        size = index; // number of records stored in the array
        file.close();
```

```
// search for a name

String   nameKey;
boolean  found;
int      position;

do
{
    screen.print("name? "); screen.flush();
    nameKey = keyboard.readLine();

    position = SearchingAlgorithms.sequential(array,
                                              size,
                                              nameKey);

    if (position != size)
        screen.println("address "
                        +array[position].address);
    else
        screen.println("name not found");
} while (position != size);
    }
}
```

Test results

```
name? Quayle
address 212 Wiltshire Boulevard
name? Fielding
address 21 Turnpike Boulevard
name? Ellis
name not found
```

Binary Search

This algorithm also requires the keys to be sorted prior to the search, and the information is stored in an array. From Figure 12.11, the array is divided into two parts by the midpoint. The midpoint is calculated as (first+last)/2, and in this example it is assigned to the variable location. The key Quayle is compared with the key at location. Since Quayle > Hewitt, Quayle may be found in the lower subarray within the bounds (location+1..last). The process is repeated with a new midpoint being calculated as (location+1+last)/2 and assigned to the variable location. The key Quayle is compared with the key at the location. Since Quayle > Peters, Quayle may be found in the lower subarray within the bounds (location+1..last). The process is repeated again with a new midpoint being calculated. Note when a sublist contains an even number of keys, the midpoint may be taken to be the next lowest key from the center. A match for the key Quayle exists at location = 9. If the value for first had exceeded the value for last, then no match can be found for the key. Notice that only three comparisons are necessary, compared with ten comparisons, if a serial or sequential search had been performed.

A binary search can be implemented succinctly using recursion. (The algorithm may also be implemented using repetition). The search involves calculating a midpoint from the lowest and highest indexes of an array, and if the key is in the lower half of the subarray repeating the process within the array bounds (first..location-1). However, if the key is in the upper half of the subarray, we repeat the process within the bounds (location+1..last). Recursion continues until the bounds of the subarray cross (first > last), or a match for the key is found.

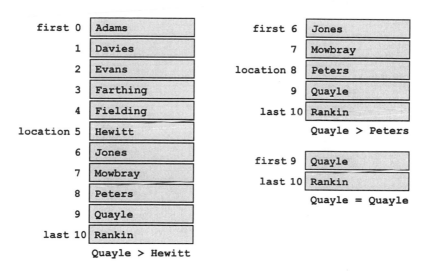

Figure 12.11 A binary search for a surname in an array

The method binary has the following signature.

```
static public int binary(Record[] array,
                         String nameKey,
                         int first,
                         int last);
```

where array is the one-dimensional array to be searched, nameKey is a string to be matched with the keys in the array; first and last are as described. The method returns an integer indicating the location of the key match. If there is no match the method returns the size of the array.

The following program uses the binary search to locate the address of a person when given the surname. The results are similar to those given in Program Example 12.6.

Program Example 12.7: Binary Search of an Array of Records

```java
// chap_12\Ex_7.java
// program to demonstrate a binary search

import java.io.*;

class Record
{
   String name;
   String address;
}

//-----------------------------------------------------------------------
// method to binary search the records of an ordered array for a key
class SearchingAlgorithms
{
    static public int binary(Record[] array,
                             String    nameKey,
                             int       first,
                             int       last)

    {
      // key not found in array
      if (first > last)
         return array.length;
      else
      {
         // calculate midpoint
         int index = (first+last)/2;
         // keys match
         if (nameKey.compareTo(array[index].name) == 0)
            return index;
         // key in lower half of array
         else if (nameKey.compareTo(array[index].name) < 0)
             return binary(array, nameKey, first, index-1);
         // key in upper half of array
         else
             return binary(array, nameKey, index+1, last);
      }
    }
}

//-----------------------------------------------------------------------

class Ex_7
{
    static BufferedReader keyboard =
    new BufferedReader(new InputStreamReader(System.in));
    static PrintWriter screen = new PrintWriter(System.out, true);
    static final int MAX_RECORDS = 50;

    static public void main(String[] args) throws IOException
    {
       // text input file and stream
       FileReader file =
       new FileReader("a:\\chap_12\\names.txt");
```

```
        StreamTokenizer inputStream = new StreamTokenizer(file);

        Record[] array = new Record[MAX_RECORDS];

        int tokenType = inputStream.nextToken();
        int index = 0;
        int size;

        // build array of records from text file
        while (tokenType != StreamTokenizer.TT_EOF)
        {
            array[index] = new Record();

            array[index].name = inputStream.sval;
            inputStream.nextToken();
            array[index].address = inputStream.sval;

            index++;
            tokenType = inputStream.nextToken();
        }

        size = index; // number of records stored in the array
        file.close();

        // search for a name

        String  nameKey;
        int indexOfMatch;
        int first=0;
        int last = size-1;

        do
        {
            screen.print("name? "); screen.flush();
            nameKey = keyboard.readLine();

            indexOfMatch = SearchingAlgorithms.binary(array,
                                                      nameKey,
                                                      first,
                                                      last);

            if (indexOfMatch < size)
                screen.println("address " +array[indexOfMatch].address);
            else
                screen.println("name not found");
        } while (indexOfMatch < size);
    }
}
```

Finally, Figure 12.12 illustrates the performance of a sequential search and a binary search for different amounts of data.

If there are N records in an array, then applying a sequential search will result in the worst search time proportional to N comparisons of keys, since we will need to search through the entire array.

However, using the binary search, if there are N records in an array then the average number of key comparisons will be $\log_2 N$.

To justify this last statistic, consider an array containing 8 records. Provided the key can be matched with a record in the array, the worst possible scenario is obtained as follows. We find the mid-point and make a key comparison; divide the array by 2 giving 4 records, find the mid-point and make a key comparison; divide the array by 2 giving 2 records, find the mid-point and make a key comparison. You are left with just one record - the one you are searching for! The number of key comparisons we made was 3 - $\log_2(8) = 3$. If the array contained N records then it would be necessary to make $\log_2 N$ comparisons.

N	N sequential search	$\log_2 N$ binary search
32	32	5
64	64	6
128	128	7
256	256	8
512	512	9

Figure 12.12 Worst-case efficiency of searching algorithms

12.4 Linked Lists

Figure 12.13 illustrates a record containing two variables; the first `datum` may store an item of any type, and the second `link` is a reference to another record of the same type. The figure illustrates that the record structure known as a `Node`, is made reference to by a variable named `head`. Doesn't this storage model look familiar to you? Yes - the reference to the data is the same model as an object is stored in memory. The record may be designated as an object of the class `Node`. The declaration `Node head = new Node();` would create the structure shown in Figure 12.13.

Since the record contains the field `link`, that is a reference to another record of the same data type `Node`, the record is known as a **self-referential structure**.

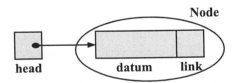

Figure 12.13 A single node

The class `Node` may be defined as follows.

```
class Node
{
    private Object datum;
    private Node    link;

    public Node(Object item, Node pointer)
    {
        datum = item;
        link = pointer;
    }
}
```

A linked list is a sequence of nodes in which each node is linked or connected to the node following it, as illustrated in Figure 12.14. This list has a head referencing the first node in the list. The first node contains the word *apple* and a reference to the second node in the list. The second node contains the word *banana* and a reference to the third node in the list. The third node contains the word *date* and a null reference. The null reference indicates that the link does not reference another node, and the list is terminated. To summarize, the linked list illustrated in figure 12.14 has the following constructional features.

- A named reference variable head that points to the first node in the linked list.

- A list in which the order of the nodes is determined by an explicit reference field within each record, rather than by the physical order of the components in memory (as in the case of an array).

- A null reference indicating the end of the linked list.

Figure 12.14 An example of a linked list

A linked list may be used in preference to an array for storing data in the main memory when the following circumstances apply.

- The number of data records to be stored is not known in advance of the program being executed. The linked list is truly a dynamic data structure, since main memory is allocated for storing the records at runtime without having to specify the number of nodes in the list. Although it was stated in Chapter 5 that an array could be dynamic, it was still necessary to specify at runtime the maximum number of elements the array would hold.

- Nodes need to be inserted into a list or deleted from a list. During the insertion or deletion of nodes in a linked list, there is no movement of the data records in memory, only changes in reference (link) values. By contrast, the insertion or deletion of records in an array would involve the movement of the records in main memory.

Since a linked list in Java, may be thought of as a collection of objects, the implementation of the data structure is very straightforward. To build the linked list shown in Figure 12.15 is simply a matter of specifying three objects as follows.

```
Node head = null;

head = new Node("date", head);
head = new Node("banana", head);
head = new Node("apple", head);
```

Figure 12.15 illustrates how this code is used to build the linked list. What you need to understand is that the constructor `Node(Object item, Node pointer);` uses the link pointer to "join together" the nodes. Initially, `head` is set to a `null` reference. This value is passed to the first constructor, and the resultant node object is then assigned to `head`. This new value of head is then passed as an argument to the second constructor to preserve the link with the previous object, and the second new object is then assigned to head. Notice that the first object has been pushed down the list. Finally, the new value of head is passed as an argument to the third constructor to preserve the link with the previous object, and the third new object is assigned to head.

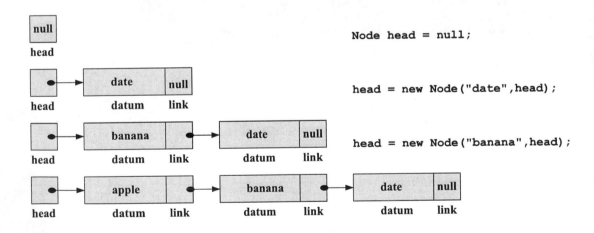

Figure 12.15 Building a linked list

Now that the linked list has been built, it is possible to traverse the list, starting at the head, and finishing when the `null` reference in the last object is detected. Each time we visit a node the contents of the datum field may be displayed. The following code traverses a linked list and displays the data stored at each node.

```
Node temporary = head;

while (temporary != null)
{
    screen.println(temporary.datum);
    temporary = temporary.link;
}
```

You are advised to desk check this code, using the data from Figure 12.15, before progressing with the remainder of this section.

If you inspect the code we used to build the linked list, it is clearly very repetitive. The only part of the code to change are the arguments used in the constructors. If these arguments are represented in a program as variables, then it is possible to build a linked list of any number of nodes (subject to the size of the memory allocated to building objects!). Program Example 12.8 builds and displays a linked list.

Program Example 12.8: Creation and Traversal of a Linked List.

```
// chap_12\Ex_8.java
// program to demonstrate the creation of a linked list

import java.io.*;

class Node
{
    static PrintWriter screen = new PrintWriter(System.out, true);

    private Object datum;
    private Node    link;

    public Node(){}

    public Node(Object item, Node pointer)
    {
        datum = item;
        link = pointer;
    }

    public void displayList()
    {
        Node temporary = this;

        while (temporary != null)
        {
            screen.println(temporary.datum);
            temporary = temporary.link;
        }
    }
}
```

```
class Ex_8
{

    static BufferedReader keyboard =
    new BufferedReader(new InputStreamReader(System.in));
    static PrintWriter screen = new PrintWriter(System.out, true);

    static public void main(String[] args) throws IOException
    {

        Node list=null;
        String datum;

        // input data at keyboard to build linked list
        screen.print("datum? "); screen.flush();
        datum = keyboard.readLine();
        while (! datum.equals("quit"))
        {
            list = new Node(datum,list);
            screen.print("datum? "); screen.flush();
            datum = keyboard.readLine();
        }

        // display contents of list
        list.displayList();
    }
}
```

Test results

```
datum? apple
datum? banana
datum? grape
datum? date
datum? fig
datum? melon
datum? peach
datum? quince
datum? quit
quince
peach
melon
fig
date
grape
banana
apple
```

A linked list is a data structure that may be represented as an abstract data type. Having defined the class of Node in the previous program, a LinkedList class should nest the class Node, thereby inherit all the properties of a Node, and in addition be able to offer methods to insert a node into the list, delete a node from the list, return the number of nodes and whether the list is empty. In the definition of the LinkedList class that follows, the method to display the linked list has been removed from the class Node and implemented in the class LinkedList.

```
class LinkedList
{
    public LinkedList()
    public void insert(Object datum)
    public boolean delete(Object scrap)
    public void displayList()
    public boolean isEmpty()
    public int nodes()
}
```

Figure 12.16 illustrates the variables used to build and maintain a linked list LL. Within the implementation of the class LinkedList these variables are defined as follows.

```
private Node head;
private Node tail;
private Node temporary;
```

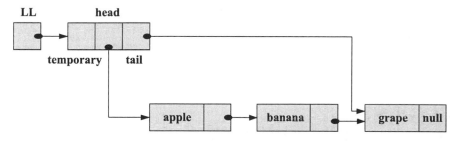

Figure 12.16 Class variables associated with the linked list

The code used to insert a node into the linked list follows. This should be read in conjunction with Figure 12.17. Each drawing in this figure depicts the effects of the following code.

```
public void insert(Object datum)
{
    if (head==null) // list empty
    {
        head=new Node(datum,head);
        tail=head;
    }
    else
    {
        temporary = new Node(datum,temporary);
        tail.link = temporary;
        tail = temporary;
        temporary = null;
    }
    nodeCount++;
}
```

Notice that the nodes are inserted into the linked list in a First In First Out (FIFO) order, unlike the previous algorithm where the nodes were inserted into the linked list in a Last In First Out (LIFO) order; assuming that nodes may be removed only from the head of the linked list.

After the insertion of a node a class variable `nodeCount` is increased.

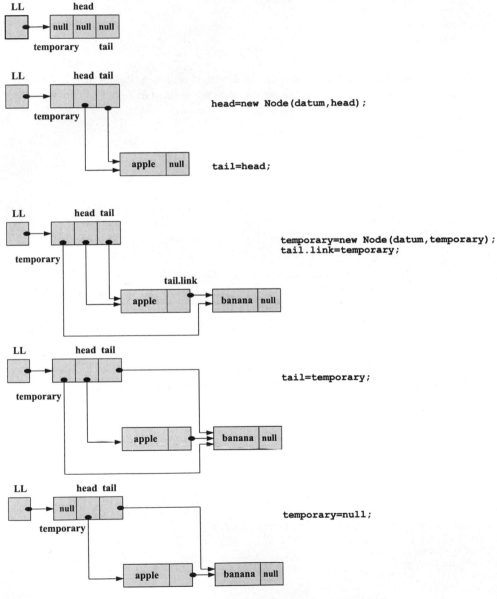

Figure 12.17 Insertion of nodes into a linked list

The removal of any node from any position in the linked list, is slightly more tricky than the removal of a node from the head of the list.

There are three cases to consider.

- The removal of a node at the head of the list, in which case the head must point to the next node in the list if one exists. The value of the head of the list must always be preserved, otherwise, there is no means of accessing the linked list.

- The removal of a node from the list, but excluding the head or tail nodes. In this situation, the previous node to the one being removed must point to the successor node (the node after the one to be removed).

- The removal of the last node in the list, in which case the penultimate node becomes the last node in the list.

The code used to delete any node from the linked list follows. Notice that it is necessary to include two local references in this code, one to point at the current node (the node being inspected), and one to point at the previous node (the node previously inspected if not at the head of the list).

```
public boolean delete(Object scrap)
{
    Node previous = head;

        for (Node current=head; current != null; current=current.link)
        {
            // node to be deleted is at the head of the list
            if (current.datum.equals(scrap) && previous==current)
            {
                head = current.link;
                if (head == null) tail = null;
                nodeCount--;
                return true;
            }

            // node to be deleted is after the first node and before the last
            else if (current.datum.equals(scrap) && (current.link != null))
            {
                previous.link = current.link;
                nodeCount--;
                return true;
            }

            // node to be deleted is at the end of the list
            else if (current.datum.equals(scrap) && (current.link == null))
            {
                tail = previous;
                previous.link = null;
                nodeCount--;
                return true;
            }
```

```
        previous = current;
    }

    return false;
}
```

You are recommended to desk check the code using the data supplied in Figures 12.18, 12.19 and 12.20.

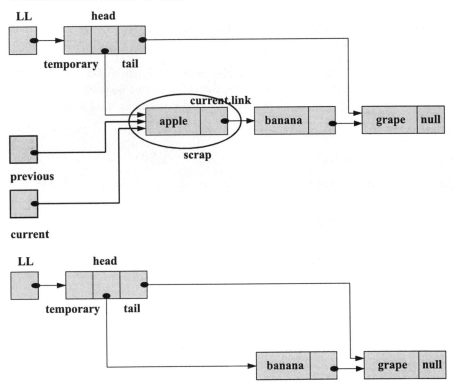

Figure 12.18 Deleting a node from the front of a linked list

To delete the any node between the fiest and last nodes in the linked list

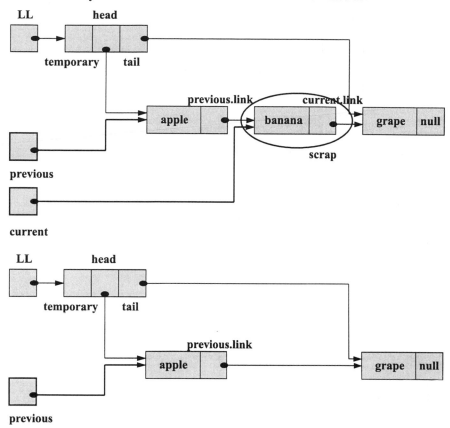

Figure 12.19 Deleting a node other than at the head or tail

To delete the node from the tail of a linked list

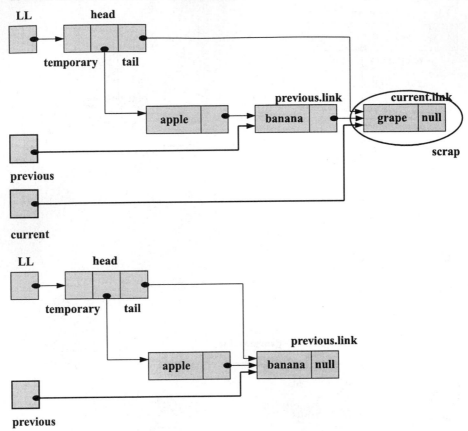

Figure 12.20 Deleting a tail node

Program example 12.9 illustrates the methods of the class `LinkedList`.

Program Example 12.9: Maintenance of a Linked List

```java
// chap_12\Ex_9.java
// program to demonstrate the creation and maintenance of a linked list

import java.io.*;

class IO
{
   static BufferedReader keyboard = new
           BufferedReader(new InputStreamReader(System.in));
   static PrintWriter screen = new PrintWriter(System.out, true);
}

//-----------------------------------------------------------------------

class LinkedList
{
   class Node
   {
      protected Object datum;
      protected Node    link;

      public Node(){}

      public Node(Object item, Node pointer)
      {
         datum = item;
         link = pointer;
      }
   }

   //----------------------------- ------------------------------------------

   private Node head;
   private Node tail;
   private Node temporary;
   private int nodeCount = 0;

   //-----------------------------------------------------------------------
   // constructor
   public LinkedList()
   {
      head = null;
      tail = null;
      temporary = null;
   }

   //-----------------------------------------------------------------------
   // method to insert an object into the linked list;
   // the algorithm will allow for multiple entries
   // of the same object
   public void insert(Object datum)
   {
      if (head==null) // list empty
      {
         head=new Node(datum,head);
```

```
            tail=head;
    }
    else
    {
        temporary = new Node(datum,temporary);
        tail.link = temporary;
        tail = temporary;
        temporary = null;
    }
    nodeCount++;
}

//----------------------------------------------------------------
// method to delete an object from the linked list
public boolean delete(Object scrap)
{
    Node previous = head;

    // for every node in the linked list
    for (Node current=head; current != null; current=current.link)
    {
        // node to be deleted is at the head of the list
        if (current.datum.equals(scrap) && previous==current)
        {
            head = current.link;
            if (head == null) tail = null;
            nodeCount--;
            return true;
        }
        // node to be deleted is after the first node and before the last
        else if (current.datum.equals(scrap) && (current.link != null))
        {
            previous.link = current.link;
            nodeCount--;
            return true;
        }
        // node to be deleted is at the end of the list
        else if (current.datum.equals(scrap) && (current.link == null))
        {
            tail = previous;
            previous.link = null;
            nodeCount--;
            return true;
        }

        previous = current;
    }

    return false;
}
```

```java
   // method to display the contents of a linked list
   // from the first node through to the last node
   public void displayList()
   {
      Node temporary = head;

      if (head == null)
      {
         IO.screen.println("linked list is empty");
         return;
      }

      while (temporary != null)
      {
         IO.screen.println(temporary.datum);
         temporary = temporary.link;
      }
   }

   //------------------------------------------------------------
   // method to return true if the linked list is empty
   // otherwise return false
   public boolean isEmpty()
   {
      return (nodeCount == 0);
   }

   //------------------------------------------------------------
   // method to return the number of nodes in the linked list
   public int nodes()
   {
      return nodeCount;
   }
}


class Ex_9
{
   // method to display a menu to insert data into the linked list,
   // delete data from the list, display the conetnts of the linked list
   // or exit from the program
   static private char menu()
   {
      char response = '\u0000';

      IO.screen.println("Do you want to ");
      IO.screen.print("[I]nsert, [D]elete, [L]ist, [E]xit? ");
      IO.screen.flush();

      boolean done=false;

      do
      {
         try
         {
            String data = IO.keyboard.readLine();
            response = Character.toUpperCase(data.charAt(0));
```

```
            done=true;
        }

    catch (Exception e)
    {
        IO.screen.println("Please input a single character
                        I, D, L or E");
    }
} while (! done);

return response;
}

//-------------------------------------------------------------------

static public void main(String[] args) throws IOException
{

    LinkedList list = new LinkedList();
    String datum;
    char choice;

    // get information from menu
    choice = menu();

    for (;;)
    {
        // select to [I]nsert an item into the list
        //           [D]elete an item from the list
        //           [L]ist the contents of the linked list
        //           [E]xit from the program
        switch (choice)
        {
            case 'I' :  {
                        IO.screen.println("type quit to finish input");
                        IO.screen.print("datum? ");
                        IO.screen.flush();
                        datum = IO.keyboard.readLine();
                        while (! datum.equals("quit"))
                        {
                            list.insert(datum);
                            IO.screen.print("datum? ");
                            IO.screen.flush();
                            datum = IO.keyboard.readLine();
                        }
                        break;
                        }
            case 'D' :  {
                        // if list is empty deletion is not possible
                        if (list.isEmpty())
                        {
                            IO.screen.println("linked list is empty");
                            break;
                        }
                        IO.screen.println("type quit to finish input");
                        IO.screen.print("delete? ");
                        IO.screen.flush();
```

```
                              datum = IO.keyboard.readLine();
                              while (! datum.equals("quit"))
                              {
                                     if (list.delete(datum))
                                     {
                                            IO.screen.println(datum+" was
                                                          scrapped!");
                                     }

                                     // if list is empty deletion is not possible
                                     if (list.isEmpty())
                                     {
                                            IO.screen.println("linked list is
                                                          empty");
                                            break;
                                     }

                                     IO.screen.print("delete? ");
                                     IO.screen.flush();
                                     datum = IO.keyboard.readLine();
                              }
                              break;
                       }
                case 'L' :  {
                              list.displayList();
                              IO.screen.println("number of nodes "+list.nodes());
                              break;
                       }
                case 'E'  : System.exit(0);
          }

          // get information from menu
          choice = menu();
       }
    }
}
```

Test results

```
Do you want to
[I]nsert, [D]elete, [L]ist, [E]xit? l
linked list is empty
number of nodes 0
Do you want to
[I]nsert, [D]elete, [L]ist, [E]xit? i
type quit to finish input
datum? apple
datum? banana
datum? date
datum? fig
datum? grape
datum? melon
datum? quit
Do you want to
[I]nsert, [D]elete, [L]ist, [E]xit? l
apple
banana
```

```
date
fig
grape
melon
number of nodes 6
Do you want to
[I]nsert, [D]elete, [L]ist, [E]xit? d
type quit to finish input
delete? apple
apple was scrapped!
delete? melon
melon was scrapped!
delete? fig
fig was scrapped!
delete? quit
Do you want to
[I]nsert, [D]elete, [L]ist, [E]xit? l
banana
date
grape
number of nodes 3
Do you want to
[I]nsert, [D]elete, [L]ist, [E]xit? e
```

12.5 Queues

Queues are a familiar aspect of everyday life. People often queue (wait in line) for a bus or to queue to be served in a bank. There are many examples in computing of the use of queues. In a real-time system, queues of processes wait to use a processor, or queues of jobs wait to use a separate resource such as a printer. The general concept of a queue is a line of objects that has a front and a rear. The first object in the queue is said to be at the front of the queue, whereas the last object in the queue is said to be at the rear of the queue. In a first-in-first-out queue (FIFO queue), an object can join the queue only at the rear and leave only at the front.

Queues can be built out of linked lists. To allow a node to join a FIFO queue requires a new node to be inserted into the tail of the linked list; to allow a node to exit from a FIFO queue requires a node to be deleted from the front of the linked list. You have already seen the existence of this code in the LinkedList class, where it catered for inserting nodes into the rear of the list and removing nodes from the front of the list. Figure 12.21 indicates the insertion and deletion of the nodes into a FIFO queue.

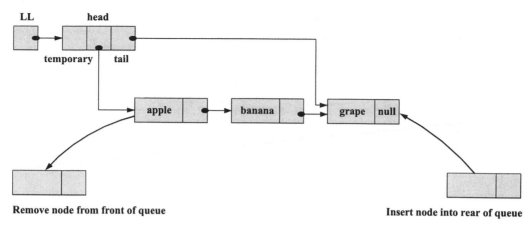

Figure 12.21 *Using a linked list to implement a FIFO queue*

Turn to the Exercises at the end of this chapter and answer question 22.

12.6 Stacks

You first met the term stack in Chapter 9, where reference was made to such methods as `fillInStackTrace` and `printStackTrace`. If you remember the stack trace gave you a list of methods the computer entered in attempting to look for an exception handler. The output from the stack trace was always displayed in the order of visiting the methods, with the last method visited being displayed first. This is a typical characteristic of a stack in which the last item stored in the stack will be the first item to be retrieved from the stack.

Your second encounter with a stack was in this chapter, where you were introduced to a stack frame for storing parameters, local variables and return memory addresses, when calling a method recursively.

Figure 12.22 illustrates a stack in which members can join and leave at one end only. The stack operates on a last-in-first-out (LIFO) principle. The entry/exit point of the stack is known as the stack top. An item that joins the stack is said to be **pushed** on to the stack. An item that leaves the stack is said to be **popped** from the stack. It is also possible to **peek** (look at) at an item on the stack without removing the item.

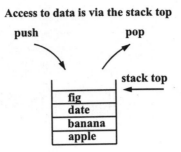

Figure 12.22 Access to a stack is from one end only

Figure 12.23 illustrates the movement of the stack top, and data as it is pushed and popped to and from the stack

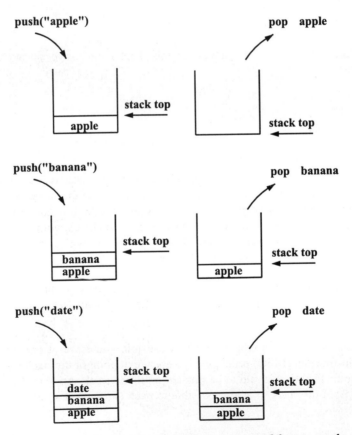

Figure 12.23 Pushing and popping items to and from a stack

You may create a stack from a linked list, in fact we have already gone part way in doing so. If you examine the code in the class `LinkedList` you may observe that we can already insert and delete a node from the front of a linked list. If we treat the front of the linked list as the stack top, then we already have the code we need for manipulating data on a stack.

Alternatively, the Java `util` package contains the following `Stack` class.

```
public class Stack extends Vector
{
    // Constructors
    public Stack();

    // Methods
    public boolean empty();
    public Object peek();
    public Object pop();
    public Object push(Object  item);
    public int search(Object  o);
}
```

Program Example 12.10 demonstrates how data may be inserted into a stack, inspected and removed from the stack.

Program Example 12.10 Use of the Stack Class.

```
// chap_12\Ex_10.java
// program to demonstrate storing and retrieving data from a stack

import java.io.*;
import java.util.*;

class Ex_10
{
    static BufferedReader keyboard =
    new BufferedReader(new InputStreamReader(System.in));
    static PrintWriter screen = new PrintWriter(System.out, true);

    static public void main(String[] args) throws IOException
    {
        Stack pile = new Stack();

        String datum;

        // input data and store on stack
        screen.print("datum? "); screen.flush();
        datum = keyboard.readLine();
        while (! datum.equals("quit"))
        {
            pile.push(datum);
            screen.print("datum? "); screen.flush();
            datum = keyboard.readLine();
        }
```

```
        // inspect the value at the top of the stack
        screen.println("top of stack contains "+pile.peek().toString());

        // search for a single item in the stack
        screen.print("search for? "); screen.flush();
        datum = keyboard.readLine();
        screen.println("position of "+datum+" in stack is "+
                        pile.search(datum));

        // display the contents of the stack
        while (! pile.empty())
        {
            screen.println(pile.pop().toString());
        }
    }
}
```

Test results

```
datum? apple
datum? banana
datum? grape
datum? fig
datum? melon
datum? quit
top of stack contains melon
search for? fig
position of fig in stack is 2
melon
fig
grape
banana
apple
```

Case Study: Converting Infix Notation to Reverse Polish Notation

Problem. Normal algebraic notation is often termed infix notation, since the binary arithmetic operator appears between the two operands to which it is being applied. Infix notation may require parenthesis to specify the desired order of operations. For example, in the expression a/b+c, the division will occur first followed by the addition. If we want the addition to occur first, we must parenthesize the expression as a/(b+c).

Using postfix notation (also called reverse Polish notation after the nationality of its originator Jan Lukasiewicz), the need for parenthesis is eliminated because the operator is placed directly after the two operands to which it applies.

The infix expression a/b+c would be written as the postfix expression ab/c+, which is interpreted as divide a by b and add c to the result.

The infix expression a/(b+c) would be written as abc+/ in postfix notation, which is interpreted as add b to c then divide that result into a.

Write a program to convert arithmetic expressions written in infix notation to reverse Polish notation.

Problem Analysis. In compiler writing it is more convenient to evaluate arithmetic expressions written in reverse Polish notation, than it is to evaluate arithmetic expressions written in infix notation. The following algorithm, known as the Railway Shunting Yard algorithm since data are shunted to and from a stack, can be used to convert infix notations to reverse Polish notations.

The operators [and] are used to delimit the infix expression. For example, the expression a*(b+c/d) will be coded as [a*(b+c/d)]. The algorithm uses operator priorities as defined in Figure 12.24.

operator	priority
[	0
(	1
–	2
+	2
/	3
*	3
^	4

Figure 12.24 Operator priorities

Use Figure 12.25 to trace the following explanation of the algorithm.

Diagram (i) If brackets [or (are encountered, each is pushed on to the stack.

Diagram (ii) All operands that are encountered , for example a, b and c are stored in a string buffer.

Diagrams (iii), (iv) and (v) When an operator is encountered, its priority is compared with that of the operator's priority at the top of the stack.

Diagram (vi) If when comparing priorities the operator encountered is not greater than the operator on the stack, the stack operator is popped and displayed. This process is repeated until the encountered operator has a higher priority than the stack top operator. The encountered operator is then pushed on to the stack.

Diagrams (v) and (vi) When a) is encountered, all the operators up to, but not including (, are popped from the stack one at a time and stored in a string buffer. The operator (is then deleted from the stack.

Diagrams (vi) and (vii) When the operator] is encountered, all the remaining operators, up to but not including [, are popped from the stack one at a time and stored in a string buffer. The string of characters that is displayed will be the reverse Polish string.

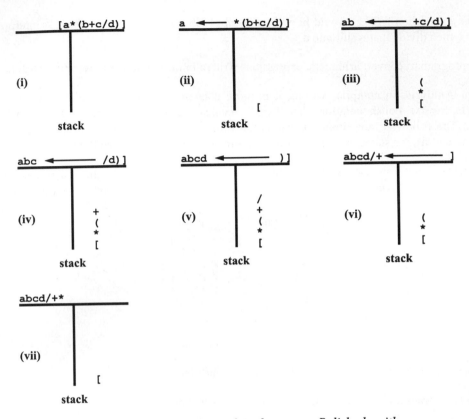

Figure 12.25 The use of a stack in the reverse Polish algorithm

Analysis of classes. Naturally the Java class Stack will be used in the solution to this problem. However, the algorithm to convert an infix string to reverse Polish will be an instance method in a class ReversePolish whose public interface follow.

```
class ReversePolish
{
    // constructor
    public ReversePolish(String infixExpression);

    // method to return a reverse Polish string
    public String toReversePolish();
}
```

Algorithm for the constructor ReversePolish

1. copy formal parameter string to local variable of type string buffer.

Data Dictionary for the class ReversePolish. The class contains two variables of type string buffer, one to store the infix string and a second to store the reverse Polish string.

```
private StringBuffer infixString   = new StringBuffer();
private StringBuffer postfixString = new StringBuffer();
```

Algorithm for the method toReversePolish

1.	*for every character in the infix expression*
2.	*if next character is closing parenthesis ')'*
3.	*pop operator from stack*
4.	*while operator not opening parenthesis '('*
5.	*store operator in string buffer*
6.	*pop operator from stack*
7.	*else if next character is closing bracket ']'*
8.	*pop operator from stack*
9.	*while operator not opening bracket '['*
10.	*store operator in string buffer*
11.	*pop operator from stack*
12.	*else if next character is opening parenthesis '(' or opening bracket '['*
13.	*push next character on to stack*
14.	*else if next character arithmetic operator*
15.	*while priority of next character is < = to priority of stack top operator*
16.	*pop operator from stack*
17.	*store operator in string buffer*
18.	*push next character on to stack*
19.	*else*
20.	*store next character in string buffer*

Data Dictionary for the method toReversePolish. This contains variables to represent the next character in the infix string, the length of the infix expression, a stack and an operator popped from the stack.

```
char nextCharacter;
char operator='\u0000';
int lengthOfExpression;
Stack siding = new Stack();
```

In line 15 of the algorithm to convert an infix string to a reverse Polish string, there is a reference made to the priority of a character and the priority of the stack-top operator. From this statement you may deduce the need to include a private method to take an operator as a parameter and return the priority of that operator.

Algorithm for the private method priority.

1. switch operator
2.   [: return 0
3.   (: return 1
4.   -, +   : return 2
*5.   /, *   : return 3*
6.   ^   : return 4
7.   default : return -1

Desk Check of the method analysis. The test data is [a*(b+c/d)].

Diagram (Figure 12.25)	(i)	(ii)			(iii)		(iv)	
nextCharacter	[	a	*	(	b	+	c	/
nextCharacter == ')'?	false	false	false	false	false	false	false	false
nextCharacter == ']'?	false	false	false	false	false	false	false	false
nextCharacter == '(' | '['?	true	false	false	true	false	false	false	false
arithmetic operator?		false	true		false	true	false	true
popped operator								
operator != '('								
operator != '['								
priority <= priority stack top			false			false		false
contents of stack	[		[*	[*(		[*(+		[*(+/
contents of string buffer	a			ab		abc		

Diagram (Figure 12.25)	(v)	(vi)			(vii)	
nextCharacter	d	)			]	
nextCharacter == ')'?	false	true			false	
nextCharacter == ']'?	false				true	
nextCharacter == '(' | '['?	false					
arithmetic operator?	false					
popped operator		/	+	(	*	[
operator != '('		false	false	false	true	
operator != '['						false
priority <= priority stack top						
contents of stack		[*(+	[*(	[*	[	
character stored in buffer	abcd	abcd/	abcd/+		abcd/+*	

Coding

```
// chap_12\Ex_11.java

import java.io.*;
import java.util.*;

class ReversePolish
{
    private StringBuffer infixString   = new StringBuffer();
    private StringBuffer postfixString = new StringBuffer();

    //------------------------------------------------------------------
    // constructor
    public ReversePolish(String infixExpression)
    {
        infixString.append(infixExpression);
    }

    //------------------------------------------------------------------
    // method to return a reverse Polish string
    public String toReversePolish()
    {
        char     nextCharacter;
        char     operator='\u0000';

        int lengthOfExpression = infixString.length();

        // instantiate stack object siding
        Stack siding = new Stack();

        for (int index=0; index != lengthOfExpression; index++)
        {
            // get next nextCharacter from
            nextCharacter = infixString.charAt(index);

            if (nextCharacter == ')')
            {
                // pop character from stack
                operator = ((Character)siding.pop()).charValue();
                while (operator != '(')
                {
                    // store operator in string buffer
                    postfixString.append(operator);
                    // pop character from stack
                    operator = ((Character)siding.pop()).charValue();
                }
            }
            else if (nextCharacter == ']')
            {
                // pop character from stack
                operator = ((Character)siding.pop()).charValue();
                while (operator != '[')
                {
                    // store operator in string buffer
                    postfixString.append(operator);
                    // pop character from stack
```

```java
                 operator = ((Character)siding.pop()).charValue();
           }
     }
     else if (nextCharacter == '(' || nextCharacter == '[')
     {
         // push character on to stack
         siding.push(new Character(nextCharacter));
     }
     else if (nextCharacter == '^' || nextCharacter == '*' ||
                nextCharacter == '/' || nextCharacter == '+' ||
              nextCharacter == '-')
     {
         while (priority(nextCharacter) <=
                  priority(((Character)siding.peek()).charValue()))
         {
            // pop character from stack
            operator = ((Character)siding.pop()).charValue();
            // store operator in string buffer
            postfixString.append(operator);
         }

         // push character on to stack
         siding.push(new Character(nextCharacter));
     }
     else
         // store operand in string buffer
         postfixString.append(nextCharacter);
 }

 return postfixString.toString();
}

//------------------------------------------------------------------
// method to return the priority of an operator
private int priority(char operator)
{
   switch (operator)
   {
   case '[': return 0;
   case '(': return 1;
   case '-': case '+': return 2;
   case '/': case '*': return 3;
   case '^': return 4;
   default : return -1;
   }
 }
}
```

```
class Ex_11
{
    static PrintWriter screen = new PrintWriter(System.out, true);

    public static void main(String[] args)
    {
        // instantiate reverse polish objects
        ReversePolish e1 = new ReversePolish("[a*b+c]");
        ReversePolish e2 = new ReversePolish("[a*(b+c/d)]");
        ReversePolish e3 = new ReversePolish("[a*b+c/d]");
        ReversePolish e4 = new ReversePolish("[u+f*t]");
        ReversePolish e5 = new ReversePolish("[b^2-4*a*c]");
        ReversePolish e6 = new ReversePolish("[h*(a+4*b+c)/3]");
        ReversePolish e7 = new ReversePolish("[w*1-1/(w*c)]");

        // display reverse Polish strings
        screen.println(e1.toReversePolish());
        screen.println(e2.toReversePolish());
        screen.println(e3.toReversePolish());
        screen.println(e4.toReversePolish());
        screen.println(e5.toReversePolish());
        screen.println(e6.toReversePolish());
        screen.println(e7.toReversePolish());
    }
}
```

Test Results

```
ab*c+
abcd/+*
ab*cd/+
uft*+
b2^4a*c*-
ha4b*+c+*3/
w1*1wo*/-
```

Summary

- A recursive method will repeatedly call itself until a criterion for termination is satisfied.

- The computer must return through each level of the recursive method that has been invoked.

- In the selection sort the largest item of data found in the cells 0..N-1 of an array is transferred to cell N-1. The algorithm is repeated for the items of data in cells 0 .. N-2, and the largest item of data is transferred to cell N-2. The algorithm is repeated until there is only one number to consider in cell 0.

- In the Quicksort algorithm an array is divided into two partitions by a pivot key. Keys in each partition are compared with the pivot key for an ordered sequence. When an ordered sequence in each partition is no longer possible, the offending keys are swapped. Further comparisons and swapping of keys continues until each key in each partition has been compared. All the keys in one partition will be less than or equal to the pivot key, and all the keys in the other partition will be greater than the pivot key. The partitions themselves are not yet ordered. The algorithm is then applied to each partition recursively until the subpartitions contain only one item of data.

- Searching for data held in an array is made more efficient when the data is ordered on key value. If the value of the key is greater than the item being inspected, then the key may be found further on in the array. However, if the value of the key is less than the item being inspected, then the key cannot exist in the array and the search must be abandoned.

- The binary search algorithm relies upon the fact that the contents of the array must be ordered. The technique repeatedly divides an array into smaller arrays that are likely to contain the key until either a key match is possible or the array cannot be subdivided further.

- For large amounts of data a Quicksort ($Nlog_2N$) is an efficient algorithm for sorting data, and a binary search (log_2N) is an efficient algorithm for searching for a datum.

- A node may be regarded as a self-referential record, since it contains a field with a reference to the same record.

- A linked list is a sequence of nodes in which each node is linked or connected to the node following it. A named reference variable points to the first node in the linked list. A null reference is used to indicate the end of the linked list.

- A linked list offers the following advantages over an array:

  A list is created at run-time through dynamic memory allocation.

  The insertion and deletion of nodes in a list requires changing reference variables and not moving data about main memory.

- A linked list may be used to represent queues and stacks.

- A FIFO queue will have records inserted into the tail of a linked list and records accessed and deleted from the head of the linked list.

- A stack is a data structure in which access to objects is from one end only. A stack works on the LIFO principle that the last object inserted into the stack is the first object removed from the stack. Objects are said to be pushed onto the stack (for storage) and popped from the stack (for access and removal). See `java.util.Stack`.

Review Questions

1. What is a recursive call to a method?

2. True of false - the computer must pass back through each level of recursion before returning to the initial method.

3. True or false - a stack is a queue of objects with access to the queue from both ends.

4. In recursion, what is normally contained in a stack frame?

5. How does the computer use stack frames when executing recursive calls to a method?

6. When would you use iteration in place of recursion.

7. If an array contained 1024 integers, proportionally how long would it take to sort the numbers using a selection sort compared with a Quicksort?

8. What changes would you make to the selection sort to reverse the order of the sorted numbers, that is highest to lowest?

9. What is a sequential search?

10. What is the proportional saving in time when using a sequential search versus a binary search to search for an item that does not exists?

11. True or false - the contents of an array do not need to be ordered when using a binary search?

12. How many key comparisons are necessary in a binary search when there are 1024 items in an array and the key does not exist in the array?

13. Explain the term self-referential structure.

14. How do you make reference to a linked list?

15. Why is it easier to insert or delete nodes in a linked list rather than to insert or delete records in an array?

16. Give three methods for implementing a stack using the Java language.

Exercises

17. Desk check the following segment of code and comment upon your observations.

```
void counter(int N)
{
   N++;
   screen.println(N);
   counter(N);
}

public static void main(String[] args)
{
   int N = 0;

   counter(N);
}
```

18. Write a recursive method to raise a number to a power, for example $X^n = X*X^{n-1}$ where n > 0.

19. Write a recursive method to find the greatest common divisor of two positive integers.

20. Write a recursive method to generate the first fifteen numbers in a Fibonacci series where the nth element is the sum of the (n-2) and (n-1) elements for n > 2, for example, 1 1 2 3 5 8 13 21 ...

21. Estimate the time it would take to Bubble sort an array of N items.

22. Implement a class Queue, based upon a linked list, that allows objects to join at the rear of the list and leave from the front of the list. In addition to the constructor, you should devise methods to test whether the queue is empty, insert and delete objects from the queue, and display the values of the objects in the list.

Programming Problems

23. Write a program to simulate a queue of customers at a single check-out in a supermarket. Your simulation would cater for the arrival of at least twenty customers. Use a random number generator to produce a number in the range 1-100, to represent a cumulative percentage. This value can be used to obtain the inter-arrival and service times of customers in the queue from the following tables.

Inter-arrival time distribution (time between customers arriving at the rear of the queue).

time interval	cumulative %
0.1 - 1.0	8
1.1 - 2.0	25
2.1 - 3.0	50
3.1 - 4.0	70
4.1 - 5.0	85
5.1 - 6.0	89
6.1 - 7.0	93
7.1 - 8.0	95
8.1 - 9.0	97
9.1 - 10.0	100

Thus given a random number of, say 33, would yield an inter-arrival time of between 2.1 and 3.0 minutes. The mean value of this range can be taken giving an inter-arrival time of 2.55 minutes.

Service time distribution (time spent at the check-out and not in the queue)

time interval	cumulative %
1.0 - 1.5	15
1.5 - 2.0	40
2.0 - 2.5	60
2.5 - 3.0	75
3.0 - 3.5	85
3.5 - 4.0	90
4.0 - 4.5	95
4.5 - 5.0	100

The same method of generating a service time is used as for generating an inter-arrival time, a random number of, say 84, would yield a service time of between 3.0 - 3.5 minutes. The mean value of 3.25 minutes is used.

Use the class Queue, implemented in question 22, to simulate the customers waiting to be served. In each node, store a customer number, time of arrival and the time to be spend at the check-out. Each time a customer has completed a transaction at the check-out, display the time elapsed since the customer had joined the queue and the present size of the queue.

24. Write a program to create a linked list of nonzero integer random numbers stored in key disorder. Build a second linked list that contains the integers from the first linked list sorted into key order. Find the largest number in the first linked list and copy this to the second linked list. As each integer is used from the first linked list, delete it from the first linked list. Repeat the process until the first linked list is empty. Display the contents of the second linked list.

25. Figure 12.26 illustrates a circular doubly-linked list structure containing a dummy node at the head of the list.

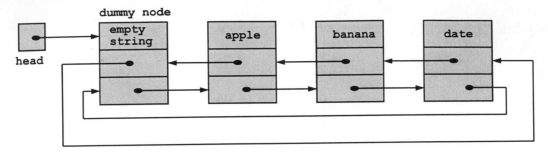

Figure 12.26 A circular double linked list

Rewrite Program Example 12.9 to maintain data in this structure. Examine the contents of the list both in forwards and backwards order.

26. The following strings are examples of infix and postfix expressions.

infix	postfix
a*b+c	ab*c+
a*(b+c/d)	abcd/+*
a*b+c/d	ab*cd/+
u+f*t	uft*+

The values of operands from these expressions are stored in a linked list similar to that illustrated in Figure 12.27. The following algorithm evaluates a postfix expression. Traverse the expression from left to right and continue to push operands on a stack until an operator is encountered. For a binary operator, pop two operands from the stack, evaluate the result, and push the answer back to the stack. Continue traversing the postfix expression until the end of the string; then pop the contents of the stack and display this value.

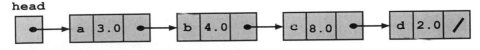

Figure 12.27 A linked list for storing operands

Write a program to input a postfix expression together with values for the operands of the expression and store the operands together with their respective values in a linked list. Using the postfix expression given in this question, check each answer by evaluating by hand, the equivalent infix expression using the values of the same operands.

Design and write applets, containing suitable graphical users interfaces, as answers to questions 27, 28, 29 and 30.

27. Demonstrate recursion graphically, by using the ideas taken from Figures 12.1 and 12.3. Show how each recursive level relates to the contents of a stack frame.

28. Demonstrate graphically, the efficiency of sorting a large number of integers using the bubble sort, selection sort and Quicksort.

29. Demonstrate graphically, the efficiency of searching for a key to a record in an array, using a serial search (the records not sorted on any key), a sequential search and a binary search.

30. Demonstrate graphically, the Railway Shunting Yard algorithm, explained in the Case Study: Converting Infix Notation to Reverse Polish Notation.

Bibliography

Bishop, J. Java Gently, Addison-Wesley 1997

Booch, G. Object Oriented Design, Benjamin Cummings 1991

Davis, S. Learn Java Now, Microsoft Press 1996

Deitel, H. & Deitel, P. Java How to Program, Prentice Hall 1997

Dictionary of Computing, Oxford University Press 1996

Flanagan, D. Java In a Nutshell, O'Reilly & Associates Inc 1997

Gosling, J. The Java Language Specification, Addison-Wesley 1996

Holmes, B. Through C to C++, Jones and Bartlett 1997

Lemay, L. & Perkins, C. Teach Yourself Java in 21 Days, Sams.net 1996

Meyer, B. Object-oriented Software Construction, Prentice Hall 1988

542

Appendix A - Answers to selected questions

Chapter 1

41. Figure 1.24 - Zone is an integer; One-Way, Half-Fare, Monthly-Pass and Family-Fare are all real numbers.

```
int     zone;
float oneWay, halfFare, monthlyPass, familyFare;
```

Figure 1.25 - city is a string; high and low temperatures are both integers; abbreviations are strings.

```
String    city;
int       high, low;
String    weatherCondition;
```

42.
(b) `net-pay` embedded hyphen is illegal
(d) `cost of paper` embedded spaces are illegal
(f) `?X?Y` characters other than alphabetic, numeric digits, underscore or $ are illegal
(g) `1856AD` identifier must begin with a non-digit legal character
(h) `float` is a keyword, therefore, an illegal identifier

43. (a) `String` (b) `char` (c) `int` (d) `long` (e) `double` (f) `float` (g) `int` (f) `double`

44. (a) 0041 (b) 004D (c) 002A (d) 0061 (e) 006D (f) 0039

45. (a) -8.74458E+02 (b) +1.23456E-03 (c) 1.23456789E+08

46.
(a) 0.3016E+40 would result in the number being too large to be stored as float
(b) -0.456E-42 would result in the number being too small to be distinguished from zero

47.
(a) `final int intNumber = -45678;`
(b) `final int hexNumber = 0xFABC;`
(c) `String city = new String("The Big Apple");`
(d) `final char uniChar = '\u0041';`

48.
(a) 255   (b) 6700   (c) 0x73   (d) 0x730F

49.

(a)
A	B	C	D
36	36	36	36

(b)
A	B	C	D
10	14	29	89

(c)
A	B
48	50

(d)
X	Y
19	-13

(e)
X	Y	Z
18	3	54

(f)
A	B
12.5	2.0

(g)
A	B	X
16	3	5

assuming A, B and X are integers

(h)
C	D	Y
19	5	4

(i)
D
35

50.
(a)   (A+B)/C
(b)   (W-X)/(Y+Z)
(c)   (D-B)/(2*A)
(d)   (A*A+B*B)/2
(e)   (A-B)*(C-D)
(f)   B*B-(4*A*C)
(g)   (A*X*X)+(B*X)+C

51.
(a)   X+(2/Y)+4
(b)   (A*B)/(C+2)
(c)   ((U/V)*W/X)
(d)   (B*B)-(4*A*C)
(e)   (A/B)+(C/D)+(E/F)

52. Note in the answers the underscore _ represents the position of the cursor

(a)   `Hello World`

(b)   `‾        name:`

(c)   `‾        name: Mickey Mouse`

(d)   `‾`
        `a=3  b=4  c=5`

(e)   `‾`
        `area covered 635.8658_`
(f)   `ABC`

        `‾`

53.

(a) The object screen is missing; the comma should be replaced by a +
        `screen.println("value of beta is " + beta);`
(b) The delimiters should be double quotes - `"X"`.
(c) The wrapper class should be `Integer`.

54.

(a) The argument for the sin method must be `double`. The literal constant should be specified as 2.0.
(b) The name of the class should be included when calling a class method - `Math.log(1.4793)`.
(c) If you inspect the Java documentation there is no class method `valueOf` that takes a `String` argument.
(d) The method `toLowerCase()` must be invoked by an object of type `String` and not the class `String`.

55.

(a) Hierarchy diagram for the wrapper class `java.lang.Float`

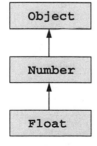

(b) Hierarchy diagram for the class `java.io.BufferedOutputStream`

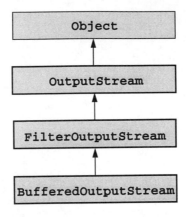

Chapter 2.

21.

```
// program to display an input message
// chap_2\Ans_21.java

import java.io.*;

class Ans_21
{
    static BufferedReader keyboard = new
            BufferedReader(new InputStreamReader(System.in));
    static PrintWriter screen = new PrintWriter(System.out, true);

    public static void main(String[] args) throws IOException
    {
        String message;

        // input message
        screen.print("Message? "); screen.flush();
        message = keyboard.readLine();

        // display message
        screen.println("\n\n" + message + "\n\n");
    }
}
```

22.

```java
// program to calculate the time to reach a town
// chap_2\Ans_22.java

import java.io.*;

class Ans_22
{
    static BufferedReader keyboard = new
            BufferedReader(new InputStreamReader(System.in));
    static PrintWriter screen = new PrintWriter(System.out, true);

    public static void main(String[] args) throws IOException
    {
        int distance;
        int speed;
        float time;

        // input data
        screen.print("Distance to town? "); screen.flush();
        distance = new Integer(keyboard.readLine()).intValue();

        screen.print("Speed of travel? "); screen.flush();
        speed = new Integer(keyboard.readLine()).intValue();

        // calculate time
        time = (float)distance / (float)speed;

        // display time to arrive
        screen.println("Traveling time " + time + " hours");
    }
}
```

23.

```java
// modification to question 22
// chap_2\Ans_23.java

import java.io.*;

class Ans_23
{
    static BufferedReader keyboard = new
            BufferedReader(new InputStreamReader(System.in));
    static PrintWriter screen = new PrintWriter(System.out, true);

    public static void main(String[] args) throws IOException
    {
        int distance;
        int speed;
        float time;
        String town;

        // input data
        screen.print("Name of town? "); screen.flush();
```

```
        town = keyboard.readLine();

        screen.print("Distance to " + town + "? "); screen.flush();
        distance = new Integer(keyboard.readLine()).intValue();

        screen.print("Speed of travel? "); screen.flush();
        speed = new Integer(keyboard.readLine()).intValue();

        // calculate time
        time = (float)distance / (float)speed;

        // display time to arrive
        screen.println("Time to reach " + town + " " + time + " hours");
    }
}
```

24.

```
// program to convert Fahrenheit to Centigrade
// chap_2\Ans_24.java

import java.io.*;

class Ans_24
{
    static BufferedReader keyboard = new
            BufferedReader(new InputStreamReader(System.in));
    static PrintWriter screen = new PrintWriter(System.out, true);

    public static void main(String[] args) throws IOException
    {
        int Fahrenheit;
        int Celsius;

        // input temperature
        screen.print("Input temperature in degrees Fahrenheit ");
        screen.flush();
        Fahrenheit = new Integer(keyboard.readLine()).intValue();

        // convert to Centigrade
        Celsius = (Fahrenheit - 32) * 5 / 9;

        // display result
        screen.println("Equivalent temperature " + Celsius + " C");
    }
}
```

25.

```java
// program to convert elapsed seconds to hours, minutes and seconds
// chap_2\Ans_25.java

import java.io.*;

class Ans_25
{
    static BufferedReader keyboard = new
            BufferedReader(new InputStreamReader(System.in));
    static PrintWriter screen = new PrintWriter(System.out, true);

    public static void main(String[] args) throws IOException
    {
        int elapsedTime;
        int hours;
        int minutes;
        int seconds;

        // input elspased time in seconds
        screen.print("Input number of seconds since Midnight ");
        screen.flush();
        elapsedTime = new Integer(keyboard.readLine()).intValue();

        // calculate current time in hours, minutes and seconds
        hours = elapsedTime / 3600;
        seconds = elapsedTime % 3600;

        minutes = seconds / 60;
        seconds = seconds % 60;

        // display time of day
        screen.println(hours + ":" + minutes + ":" + seconds);
    }
}
```

26.

```java
// program to calculate surface area and volume of a sphere
// chap_2\Ans_26.java

import java.io.*;

class Ans_26
{
    static BufferedReader keyboard = new
            BufferedReader(new InputStreamReader(System.in));
    static PrintWriter screen = new PrintWriter(System.out, true);

    public static void main(String[] args) throws IOException
    {
        float radius;
        float surfaceArea;
        float volume;
```

```
        // input radius of sphere
        screen.print("Radius of sphere? "); screen.flush();
        radius = new Float(keyboard.readLine()).floatValue();

        // calculate surface area and volume of sphere
        surfaceArea = 4.0f * (float) Math.PI * radius * radius;
        volume = radius * surfaceArea / 3.0f;

        // display surface area and volume of sphere
        screen.println("Surface Area " + surfaceArea +"\nVolume " + volume);
    }
}
```

Chapter 3.

15. (a) false (b) true (c) true (d) false (e) true (f) true (g) true

16. (a) X==Y (b) X!=Y (c) A<=B (d) Q<=T (e) X>=Y (f) (X<=Y && A!=B)
(g) (A>18 && H>68 && W>75) (h) (G<100 && G>50) (i) (H<50 || H>100)

17.

	A	B	C	output
(a)	16	16	32	y
(b)	16	-18	32	x
(c)	-2	-4	16	z

18. (a) capital letters (b) error in data (c) small letters

19.

```
if (y > 25)
{
    x = 16;
    screen.println("x = " + x);
}
else
    y = 20;
```

20.

1. *input length of side 1*
2. *input length of side 2*
3. *input length of side 3*
4. *input length of side 4*
5. *input internal angle*
6. *if internal angle is a right angle*

7.　　*if side 1 equals side 2 and side 2 equal side 3 and side 3 equals side 4*
8.　　　　*output square*
9.　　*else if side 1 equals side 3 and side 2 equals side 4*
10.　　　*output rectangle*
11.　*else*
12.　　　*output irregular*
13. *else*
14.　　*if side 1 equals side 2 and side 2 equal side 3 and side 3 equals side 4*
15.　　　*output rhombus*
16.　　*else if side 1 equals side 3 and side 2 equals side 4*
17.　　　*output parallelogram*
18.　*else*
19.　　　*output irregular*

Test data.

side 1	side 2	side 3	side 4	internal angle
1	1	1	1	90
1	2	1	2	90
1	1	1	1	120
1	2	1	2	120
1	1.5	2	1.75	90
1	1.5	2	1.75	120

Desk check

side 1	1	1	1	1
side 2	1	2	1	2
side 3	1	1	1	1
side 4	1	2	1	2
internal angle	90	90	120	120
right angle?	true	true	false	false
all sides equal?	true	false	true	false
opposite sides equal?		true		true
shape	square	rectangle	rhombus	parallelogram

side 1	1	1
side 2	1	1
side 3	2	2
side 4	2	2
internal angle	90	120
right angle?	true	false
all sides equal?	false	false
opposite sides equal?	false	false
shape	irregular	irregular

26.

```java
// chap_3\Ans_26.java
// program to determine shape

import java.io.*;

class Ans_26
{
    static BufferedReader keyboard = new
            BufferedReader(new InputStreamReader(System.in));
    static PrintWriter screen = new PrintWriter(System.out, true);

    public static void main(String[] args) throws IOException
    {
        int side1, side2, side3, side4;
        int angle;

        // input lengths of sides
        screen.println("Input the lengths of the four sides ");
        screen.print("side 1 "); screen.flush();
        side1 = new Integer(keyboard.readLine()).intValue();
        screen.print("side 2 "); screen.flush();
        side2 = new Integer(keyboard.readLine()).intValue();
        screen.print("side 3 "); screen.flush();
        side3 = new Integer(keyboard.readLine()).intValue();
        screen.print("side 4 "); screen.flush();
        side4 = new Integer(keyboard.readLine()).intValue();

        // input internal angle
        screen.print("Input internal angle "); screen.flush();
        angle = new Integer(keyboard.readLine()).intValue();

        // analyze data
        if (angle == 90)
        {
            if (side1 == side2 && side2 == side3 && side3 == side4)
                screen.println("SQUARE");
            else if (side1 == side3 && side2 == side4)
                screen.println("RECTANGLE");
            else
                screen.println("IRREGULAR");
        }
        else
        {
            if (side1 == side2 && side2 == side3 && side3 == side4)
                screen.println("RHOMBUS");
            else if (side1 == side3 && side2 == side4)
                screen.println("PARALLELOGRAM");
            else
                screen.println("IRREGULAR");
        }
    }
}
```

Chapter 4.

12. Output from the `while` loop is

      1   3   5   7   9

13. The loop is a validation loop; termination from the loop is only possible when a digit in the range 0 to 9 is input.

14. Output from the `for` loop is

abcdefghijklmnopqrstuvwxyz

15 (a) This is a classical error of placing a semicolon after the condition in the `while` loop. The result of this error is to create an infinite loop.

(b) This is a similar error to that found in (a); the semicolon at the end of the statement
```
for (i=10; i>0; i--);
```
marks the end of the scope of the `for` statement. The behavior of the segment of code differs from that of (a), the value of i will be counted down to zero, and the line `T minus 0 and counting` will be output.

16.

```
for (x=30; x>=3; x--)
   screen.println(x);
```

17.

1. input decimal number D
2. do
3.   divide D by 16 giving quotient Q and remainder R
4.   if remainder R > 9
5.   R is assigned the character whose decimal code is R+55
6.   else
7.   R is assigned the character whose decimal code is R+48
8.   output R as the next least significant digit of the hexadecimal value
9.   assign Q to D
10. while Q is not zero

Desk Check

D	3947		246		15	
Q	246		15		0	
R	11	66	6	54	15	70
R>9?	true		false		true	
output		B		6		F
Q != 0		true		true		false

Note. By adding 48 to R, you are creating the decimal code for the character that represents the digit R; by adding 55 to R, you are creating the decimal code for the character that represents the hexadecimal digit from A..F.

The value of the remainder is displayed with the least significant digit of the hexadecimal number first and finally the most significant digit last. Therefore, when it comes to writing a program for this algorithm it is necessary to reverse the output, by printing from right to left and not left to right in the conventional sense.

26.

```
// chap_4\Ans_26.java
// program to convert a decimal number to a hexadecimal number

import java.io.*;

class Ans_26
{
    static BufferedReader keyboard = new
            BufferedReader(new InputStreamReader(System.in));
    static PrintWriter screen       = new PrintWriter(System.out, true);

    public static void main(String[] args) throws IOException
    {
        final int NUMBER_BASE = 16;
        final String SPACE = new String(" ");

        int decimalNumber;
        int quotient;
        int remainder;
        int printingPosition = 6;

        // input number
        screen.print("Input decimal number "); screen.flush();
        decimalNumber = new Integer(keyboard.readLine()).intValue();

        do
        {
            quotient = decimalNumber / NUMBER_BASE;
            remainder = decimalNumber % NUMBER_BASE;

            // convert remainder into appropriate character code
```

```
          if (remainder > 9)
             remainder = remainder+55;
          else
             remainder = remainder+48;

          // generate printing position
          for (int index=1; index < printingPosition; index++)
             screen.print(SPACE); screen.flush();

          screen.print((char)remainder + "\r"); screen.flush();
          printingPosition--;
          decimalNumber = quotient;

       }while (quotient != 0);
    }
}
```

Chapter 5.

19.

alpha[0]	-10						
alpha[1]	16						
alpha[2]	19						
alpha[3]	-15						
alpha[4]	20						
index		0	1	2	3	4	5
value	0	-10	6	25	10	30	

The final value of the identifier value is 30.

20. -31

21. The type declaration is wrong. The correct answer is:
```
     String string = "abracadabra";
```

22. The method `toCharArray()` will store a string as a sequence of characters in a one-dimensional array. Therefore, the string "Ten green bottles standing on the wall." will be stored as consecutive characters in the character array `string` as follows.

string[0]	T
string[1]	e
string[2]	n
string[3]	(space)
string[4]	g

.

.

23. Length of the array `string` is 39.

24.

numbers[0]	5				5
numbers[1]	2				2
numbers[2]	8				8
numbers[3]	7			8	8
numbers[4]	0		2		2
numbers[5]	3	5			5
left	0	1	2	3	
right	5	4	3	2	
left <= right?	true	true	true	false	

25.   5   12   9

26.   143

27.

70	18	36	23
35	21	98	36

28.

```
int[][] array = new int[4][];
```
declares a one-dimensional array with 4 rows capable of storing integer numbers.

```
for (int i=0; i < array.length; i++)
{
```
for each element of the array

```
   array[i] = new int[i+1];
```
allocate a new array

```
   for (int j=0; j<i+1; j++)
   {
```
for each element of the new array

```
      array[i][j] = i+j;
```
initialize the contents to a value

```
   }
}
```

array[0][0]	0
array[1][0]	1
array[1][1]	2
array[2][0]	2
array[2][1]	3

array[2][2]   4

array[3][0]   3
array[3][1]   4
array[3][2]   5
array[3][3]   6

Contents of array

```
0
12
234
3456
```

29.

(a) `contains` - tests if the specified object is a component in this vector.
(b) `copyInto` - copies the components of this vector into the specified array.
(c) `isEmpty` - tests if this vector has no components.
(d) `lastIndexOf` - returns the index of the last occurrence of the specified object in this vector.

30.

`Vector dataStore = new Vector(1);`	instantiate the object dataStore containing 1 cell.
`dataStore.addElement("Sybil");`	insert the string "Sybil" into cell 0
`dataStore.addElement("Basil");`	the vector will double in size, to just 2 cells, and the string "Basil" will be inserted into cell 1
`dataStore.addElement("Polly");`	the vector will double in size, to just 4 cells, and the string "Polly" will be inserted into cell 2.

Chapter 6.

26.   25   Note - the method returns the sum of A and B.

27.   Hello World   Note - the argument Hello World is passed to the parameter message.

28.   38   Note - the arguments 25 and 13 are passed to the parameters A and B.

29.   [main]   A=41 B=29
       [valueOnly]   A=40 B=30

30.   [main]   40   30
       Note - the array data is passed by reference, therefore, any changes to the array parameter, also results in changes to the array data.

31.

(a)   Missing parenthesis in call to `alpha` - should be `alpha();`
(b)   No formal parameter list in the method `beta`.
(c)   The order of the arguments is wrong - an integer argument must <u>follow</u> a character argument in the method call to `delta`.
(d)   The data type of the arguments in the call to `gamma` does not match the formal parameters in the method `gamma`.

32. The method alpha does not return a value (void), therefore, return 2*number cannot be possible. The method signature should be changed to `static int alpha(int number);`

33.   56   Note - the class scope version of global is hidden by the declaration within the block.

34.

```
//· chap_6\Ans_34.java
// program to display a message a set number of times

import java.io.*;

class Ans_34
{
    static BufferedReader keyboard = new
            BufferedReader(new InputStreamReader(System.in));
    static PrintWriter screen = new PrintWriter(System.out, true);

    //-------------------------------------------------------------

    // class method to display a message a number of times
    static void displayMessage(String message, int numberOfTimes)
    {
        for (int counter=1; counter <= numberOfTimes; counter++)
            screen.println(message);
    }

    //-------------------------------------------------------------

    static public void main(String[] args) throws IOException
    {
        String message;
        int numberOfTimes;

        screen.print("What is your message? "); screen.flush();
        message = keyboard.readLine();
        screen.print("How many times do you want "+message+" repeated? ");
        screen.flush();

        numberOfTimes = new Integer(keyboard.readLine()).intValue();
        displayMessage(message, numberOfTimes);
    }
}
```

37.

```java
// chap_6\Ans_37.java
// program to calculate number of ways of selecting a team

import java.io.*;

class Ans_37
{
    static BufferedReader keyboard = new
            BufferedReader(new InputStreamReader(System.in));
    static PrintWriter screen = new PrintWriter(System.out, true);

    //------------------------------------------------------------------

    // class method to return N!
    static long factorial(int N)
    {
        long factorialValue = 1;

        while (N != 1)
        {
            factorialValue = factorialValue * (long)N;
            N--;
        }

        return factorialValue;
    }

    //------------------------------------------------------------------

    // class method to calculate the number of ways of selecting a team
    // of R players from N players
    static long selection(int R, int N)
    {
        return (factorial(N) / (factorial(R) * factorial(N-R)));
    }

    //------------------------------------------------------------------

    static public void main(String[] args) throws IOException
    {
        int numberOfPlayers;
        int sizeOfTeam;

        screen.print("Input the number of players "); screen.flush();
        numberOfPlayers = new Integer(keyboard.readLine()).intValue();

        screen.print("Input the size of the team "); screen.flush();
        sizeOfTeam = new Integer(keyboard.readLine()).intValue();

        screen.println("Number of ways of selecting a team of "+ sizeOfTeam +
                    " players from " + numberOfPlayers + " is " +
                        selection(sizeOfTeam, numberOfPlayers));
    }
}
```

Chapter 7.

26.   value of x is 0
        value of x is 1
        value of x is 2

27.   value of x is 0
        value of x is 1
        value of x is 1

28. In this answer it is necessary to create a private helper method to return whether a rational number is positive, in addition to the public method that tests whether one rational number is greater than another rational number.

```
private boolean positive(Rational number)
{
    return (number.numerator > 0 && number.denominator > 0);
}

public boolean greaterThan(Rational x)
{
    if (positive(this) && !positive(x)) return true;
    if (!positive(this) && positive(x)) return false;

    // subtract rational numbers
    numerator = this.numerator * x.denominator -
                x.numerator * this.denominator;
    denominator = this.denominator * x.denominator;

    // create temporary rational number
    Rational difference = new Rational(numerator, denominator);

    if (positive(this) && positive(x) && positive(difference))
        return true;
    if (positive(this) && positive(x) && !positive(difference))
        return false;
    if (!positive(this) && !positive(x) && positive(difference))
        return true;
    if (!positive(this) && !positive(x) && !positive(difference))
        return false;

    return true;
}
```

29. The code will compile without errors. The logical error is the absence of any instantiation for an object of type Date. Without this instantiation array[index] will contain a null pointer in each cell. Although the program segment compiles, it cannot be executed. Not only will it produce a null pointer exception at run time, but there is no main method present.

30. The rewritten code from question 29 contains a static initializer.

```
class Date
{
   int month;
   int day;
   int year;
}

class Question_30
{
   static Date[] array = new Date[10];

   static
   {
      for (int index=0; index != 10; index++)
      {
         Date value = new Date();

         value.month = 1;
         value.day   = 1;
         value.year  = 2000;

         array[index]=value;
      }
   }
}
```

31.

```java
// chap_7\Ans_31.java
// program to create a Circle class

import java.io.*;

class Circle
{
   // instance variable
   int radiusOfCircle;

   // constructor
   public Circle(int radius)
   {
      radiusOfCircle = radius;
   }

   // instance methods
   public float circumference()
   {
      return (float)(2 * Math.PI * radiusOfCircle);
   }

   public float area()
   {
      return (float)(Math.PI * radiusOfCircle * radiusOfCircle);
   }
```

```
    public float sphericalVolume()
    {
        return (float)(4.0/3.0*Math.PI*Math.pow((double)radiusOfCircle,3.0));
    }
}


class Ans_31
{
    static PrintWriter screen = new PrintWriter(System.out,true);

    public static void main(String[] args)
    {
        Circle ring = new Circle(10);

        screen.println("circumference "+ring.circumference());
        screen.println("area          "+ring.area());
        screen.println("volume        "+ring.sphericalVolume());
    }
}
```

Chapter 8.

31. The output from the program is:

```
A
B
C
```

A hierarchical relationship exists between the classes A, B and C. When the constructor for class C is invoked, the system will automatically chain the constructor calls to classes B and A. The constructor in class A is executed first, followed by the constructor for class B and finally the constructor for class C.

32. The output from the program is:

```
X in class C 45
X in class C 45
X in class B 35
X in class B 35
X in class A 25
```

This problem is all about how to access shadowed variables in a hierarchy of classes. variable X in class C, may be accessed directly using the name X, or by using the implicit this object, this.X. Access to the variable X in class B (the superclass of class C) is made possible by using the reserved word super, super.X. Access is also possible by casting class B, ((B)this).X. A similar technique is used to access the variable X in class A, ((A)this).X.

33. The output from the program is:

```
value of X in class A 25
value of X in class B 35
```

This is a problem of accessing shadowed variables, and overriding superclass methods. The variable object of type B is instantiated. The call to `getX` invokes the instance method in class B, which calls the getX method from class A. The getX method in class A, returns the value of X (25) in A. This value is displayed from class B. The computer then returns the value of the variable X (35) in B to the main method. The value of X from class B is then displayed.

34. The output from the program is:

```
value of constant from interface A 65
value of constant from class B 45
```

This is a problem of accessing constants from an interface and a class. Since class C implements the interface A, the constants defined in the interface may be used without qualification in class C. However, since there is no hierarchical relationship between class B and class C, it is necessary to qualify the constant from class B.

35. The output from the program is:

```
value of constant from interface A 65
value of constant from interface B 75
value of constant from interface C 85
```

This is a problem of inheritance of constants from interfaces. Interface C inherits from interface A and from interface B. This implies that the constants from both interfaces are now accessible in interface C. Class D implements interface C, therefore, has access to all the constants defined in interfaces A, B and C.

Chapter 9.

21. A catch block must immediately follow the corresponding try block.

22. The declaration of the object `input` has taken place in a try block, and consequently is not visible outside of this block. Any attempt to access the variable `input` outside of the try block will generate a syntax error.

23. Yes. The outer try block is followed by a catch block, and the inner try block is followed by a catch block, therefore, the structure is legal.

24. The class `Error` is not a superclass of either the classes `ArithmeticException` or `ArrayStoreException`, therefore, the `instanceof` operator is not valid.

25. The statements are legal, however, the class Throwable, in the first catch block, is the superclass of all the classes in the subsequent catch blocks. As a consequence, only the first block will ever be executed when an exception is raised. The superclass should appear as the last class in this program segment. the arrangement of the classes in the blocks should be ClassNotFoundException, InterruptedException, Exception and Throwable.

26. The throw and throws clauses should be interchanged. A throws clause lists the exceptions that can be thrown by a method. The throw statement explicitly invokes an exception. The throw statement must instantiate an exception object to be thrown.

27. By desk checking the code it soon becomes clear that the value of the index goes out of bounds as soon as it becomes 5. The exception to cause the catch block to be executed is ArrayIndexOutOfBoundsException.

Chapter 10.

26.

```
// chap_10\Ans_26.java
// program to demonstrate the construction of a button

import java.awt.*;
import java.awt.event.*;

class Gui extends Frame implements ActionListener
{
    // constructor
    public Gui(String s)
    {
        super(s);
        setLayout(null);

        Button pushButton = new Button("STOP");
        pushButton.setLocation(200,220);
        pushButton.setSize(100,30);
        pushButton.setBackground(Color.red);
        pushButton.setForeground(Color.white);

        add(pushButton);
        pushButton.addActionListener(this);
    }

    public void actionPerformed(ActionEvent event)
    {
        if (event.getActionCommand().equals("STOP"))
        {
            System.exit(0);
        }
    }
}
```

```
class Ans_26
{
    public static void main(String[] args)
    {
        Gui screen = new Gui("Answer 26");

        screen.setSize(500,500);
        screen.setVisible(true);
    }
}
```

27.

```
// chap_10\Ans_27.java
// lists and text areas

import java.awt.*;
import java.awt.event.*;

class Gui extends Frame implements ItemListener, WindowListener
{
    static final int NUMBER_OF_MENU_ITEMS = 10;
    static final int MAX_SELECTION = 3;

    List        countries = new List(NUMBER_OF_MENU_ITEMS, true);
    TextArea    selection = new TextArea();
    int         counter = 0;

    static String[] countryNames = {"Australia",
                                    "Brazil",
                                    "Chile",
                                    "France",
                                    "Greece",
                                    "Japan",
                                    "Norway",
                                    "Spain",
                                    "Switzerland",
                                    "Zimbabwe"};

    public Gui(String s)
    {
        super(s);
        setBackground(Color.yellow);
        setLayout(null);

        // display list
        setUpList();

        // display selection
        add(selection);
        addWindowListener(this);
    }

    // method to display the countries on screen
    private void setUpList()
    {
        for (int index=0; index != NUMBER_OF_MENU_ITEMS; index++)
```

```
        {
            countries.add(countryNames[index]);
        }

        countries.setLocation(10,50);
        countries.setSize(100,50);
        add(countries);
        countries.addItemListener(this);
    }

    // method to display the selected countries
    private void displaySelection()
    {
        int[] listArray = countries.getSelectedIndexes();

        selection.setLocation(200,50);
        selection.setSize(100,75);
        selection.setEditable(false);

        // display selected countries
        for (int index=0; index != listArray.length; index++)
        {
            selection.append(countries.getItem(listArray[index])+"\n");
        }
    }

    public void windowClosed(WindowEvent event){}
    public void windowDeiconified(WindowEvent event){}
    public void windowIconified(WindowEvent event){}
    public void windowActivated(WindowEvent event){}
    public void windowDeactivated(WindowEvent event){}
    public void windowOpened(WindowEvent event){}

    public void windowClosing(WindowEvent event)
    {
        System.exit(0);
    }

    // method to detect when a selection has been made and increase
    // the counter by 1; when three countries have been selected
    // display the selection in a text area
    public void itemStateChanged(ItemEvent event)
    {
        if (event.getStateChange() == ItemEvent.SELECTED) counter++;

        if (counter==MAX_SELECTION)
        {
            displaySelection();
        }
    }
}
```

```
class Ans_27
{
   public static void main(String[] args)
   {
      Gui screen = new Gui("Example 30");

      screen.setSize(400,200);
      screen.setVisible(true);
   }
}
```

28.

```
// chap_10\Ans_28.java
// program to set up two radio buttons
// and display a colored circle showing
// which radio button is pressed

import java.awt.*;
import java.awt.event.*;

class Gui extends Frame implements ItemListener, WindowListener
{
   // constructor
   public Gui(String s)
   {
      super(s);
      setLayout(new FlowLayout());
      CheckboxGroup radioGroup = new CheckboxGroup();

      Checkbox red = new Checkbox("RED", radioGroup, false);
      Checkbox green = new Checkbox("GREEN", radioGroup, false);

      add(red);    red.addItemListener(this);
      add(green);  green.addItemListener(this);

      addWindowListener(this);
   }

   // detect a radio button being pressed
   // and draw the apropriate circle
   public void itemStateChanged(ItemEvent event)
   {
      Graphics g = getGraphics();
      if (event.getItem() == "RED")
      {
         g.setColor(Color.red);
         g.fillOval(200,200,100,100);
      }
      else
      {
         g.setColor(Color.green);
         g.fillOval(200,200,100,100);
      }

   }
```

```
    public void windowClosed(WindowEvent event){}
    public void windowDeiconified(WindowEvent event){}
    public void windowIconified(WindowEvent event){}
    public void windowActivated(WindowEvent event){}
    public void windowDeactivated(WindowEvent event){}
    public void windowOpened(WindowEvent event){}

    public void windowClosing(WindowEvent event)
    {
        System.exit(0);
    }
}

class Ans_28
{
    public static void main(String[] args)
    {
        Gui screen = new Gui("Answer 27");

        screen.setSize(500,500);
        screen.setVisible(true);
    }
}
```

29.

```
// chap_10\Ans_29.java
// program to input RGB color data via three text fields
// and display the color in a rectangle

import java.awt.*;
import java.awt.event.*;
import java.io.*;

class Gui extends Frame implements ActionListener, WindowListener
{
    static PrintWriter screen = new PrintWriter(System.out,true);

    // define name and size of each text field
    TextField rcd = new TextField(5);
    TextField green = new TextField(5);
    TextField blue = new TextField(5);

    // initialize the contents of each text field
    String redField ="0";
    String greenField ="0";
    String blueField ="0";

    Color value;

    // constructor
    public Gui(String s)
    {
        super(s);
        setLayout(new FlowLayout());
```

```
    // display text fields
    add(new Label("Red        "));
    add(red);
    red.addActionListener(this);

    add(new Label("Green       "));
    add(green);
    green.addActionListener(this);

    add(new Label("Blue        "));
    add(blue);
    blue.addActionListener(this);

    addWindowListener(this);
}

// if numeric value for color is not in range return
// zero, otherwise return value of color
static int validateColor(int colorValue)
{
    if (colorValue < 0 || colorValue > 255)
        return 0;
    else
        return colorValue;
}

public void actionPerformed(ActionEvent event)
{
    Graphics g = getGraphics();

    int redValue, greenValue, blueValue;

    // capture data
    if (event.getSource() == red)
        redField = new String(red.getText());
    if (event.getSource() == green)
        greenField = new String(green.getText());
    if (event.getSource() == blue)
        blueField = new String(blue.getText());

    // convert captured data to numbers and validate value
    redValue = validateColor(new Integer(redField).intValue());
    greenValue = validateColor(new Integer(greenField).intValue());
    blueValue = validateColor(new Integer(blueField).intValue());

    // create an RGB color
    value = new Color(redValue, greenValue, blueValue);

    // display color
    g.setColor(value);
    g.fillRect(100,100,300,50);
}

public void windowClosed(WindowEvent event){}
public void windowDeiconified(WindowEvent event){}
public void windowIconified(WindowEvent event){}
```

```
   public void windowActivated(WindowEvent event){}
   public void windowDeactivated(WindowEvent event){}
   public void windowOpened(WindowEvent event){}

   public void windowClosing(WindowEvent event)
   {
      System.exit(0);
   }
}

class Ans_29
{
   public static void main(String[] args)
   {
      Gui screen = new Gui("Answer 28");

      screen.setSize(500,200);
      screen.setVisible(true);
   }
}
```

30.

```
// chap_10\Ans_30.java
// program to simulate a directional compass

import java.awt.*;
import java.awt.event.*;

class Gui extends Frame implements MouseListener, MouseMotionListener
{
   // center of compass
   int x=500;
   int y=400;

   // half-length of compass needle
   int halfLength=50;

   // old coordinates of mouse prior to new position
   int xOld = 0;
   int yOld = 0;

   // constructor
   public Gui(String s)
   {
      super(s);
      addMouseListener(this);
      addMouseMotionListener(this);
   }


   public void mouseDragged(MouseEvent event){}
```

```java
public void mouseMoved(MouseEvent event)
{
   // get current coordinates of mouse
   int xValue=event.getX();
   int yValue=event.getY();

   // erase old position of compass needle
   drawNeedle(xOld,yOld,Color.white);
   // draw new position of compass needle
   drawNeedle(xValue, yValue, Color.red);
   drawCompassPoints();
}


// draw a needle on the screen using the color hue, at the
// position corresponding to the coordinates of the mouse
public void drawNeedle(int xValue, int yValue, Color hue)
{
   Graphics g = getGraphics();

   double angle;
   int vertDist, horizDist;
   int x1,y1,x2,y2;

   // calculate the angle of compass needle to the horizontal
   angle = Math.atan((double)Math.abs(yValue-y)/Math.abs(xValue-x));

   // calculate the horizontal and vertical distances of the tip of the
   // needle from the centre of the needle
   vertDist = (int)(halfLength * Math.sin(angle));
   horizDist = (int)(halfLength * Math.cos(angle));

   // calculate the coordinates of the ends of the compass needle with
   // respect to the position of the mouse
   if ((xValue>x && yValue<y) || (xValue<x && yValue > y))
   {
      x1=x-horizDist; y1=y+vertDist;
      x2=x+horizDist; y2=y-vertDist;

   }
   else
   {
      x1=x-horizDist; y1=y-vertDist;
      x2=x+horizDist; y2=y+vertDist;
   }


   // draw the compass needle
   g.setColor(hue);
   g.drawLine(x1,y1,x2,y2);

   // store the current coordinates of the mouse
   xOld=xValue;
   yOld=yValue;
}
```

```
    // display the points of the compass
    private void drawCompassPoints()
    {
        Graphics g = getGraphics();

        g.setColor(Color.black);
        g.drawLine(x-30,y,x+30,y);
        g.drawLine(x,y-50,x,y+50);
        g.drawString("N",x-4,y-52);
        g.fillOval(x-2,y-2,4,4);
    }

    public void mouseClicked(MouseEvent event){}
    public void mouseEntered(MouseEvent event){}
    public void mouseExited(MouseEvent event){}
    public void mouseReleased(MouseEvent event){}

    public void mousePressed(MouseEvent event)
    {
        System.exit(0);
    }
}

class Ans_30
{
    public static void main(String[] args)
    {
        Gui screen = new Gui("Example 29");

        screen.setSize(1000,800);
        screen.setVisible(true);
    }
}
```

Chapter 11.

24. The resource descriptor and separator are missing. The correct URL is:

http://java.sun.com

25. The HTML, APPLET and BODY tags are not nested correctly; there is no width and height specified for the applet window. The filename for the applet is incorrect; it should refer to the bytecode file and not the java source code file. The correct code is:

```
<HTML>
<BODY>
<APPLET code=Ex_25.class width=900 height=300>
</APPLET>
</BODY>
</HTML>
```

26. The HTML file provides a parameter for the applet. The value of the parameter is a URL. The applet attempts to link to the Web-site specified by the URL and display the home page of the site. If the URL is incorrect, the computer will exit from the applet.

To change the URL, and hence Web site to visit, simply edit the value specified in the HTML file.

27. If the code in the question represents the contents of the source file, then the need to import classes from the packages java.awt and java.applet are missing.

The name given to the applet class must match the name given to the applet file. Since this is an answer it might be better to rename the class Ans_27, and hence filename Ans_27.java.

The variable name is not initialized in the declaration. Without any parameter passing from the corresponding HTML file, the name cannot take a value, and will result in a run-time error.

The paint method must take a formal parameter of type Graphics. This parameter is absent from the methods setFont, setColor and drawString.

A string terminator " is missing after the font name Monospaced.

The drawString method does not contain coordinates of where to draw the string on the screen.

28.

```java
// chap_11\Ans_27.java

import java.awt.*;
import java.applet.*;

public class Ans_27 extends Applet
{
    String name;

    public void init()
    {
        name = getParameter("name");
    }

    public void paint(Graphics g)
    {
        Font font = new Font("Monospaced", Font.ITALIC, 36);

        g.setFont(font);
        setBackground(Color.yellow);
        g.setColor(Color.red);
        g.drawString(name, 75,100);
    }
}
```

```
<HTML>
<BODY>
<APPLET code=Ans_27.class width=700 height=250>
<PARAM NAME=name VALUE="Programming with Java">
</APPLET>
</BODY>
</HTML>
```

29.

```
// chap_11\Ans_29.java

import java.awt.*;
import java.awt.event.*;
import java.applet.*;

public class Ans_29 extends Applet implements ActionListener
{
        TextField nameField = new TextField(30);

        public void init()
        {
                add(new Label("NAME "));
                add(nameField);
                nameField.addActionListener(this);
                setBackground(Color.yellow);
        }

        public void actionPerformed(ActionEvent event)
        {
                Font font   = new Font("Monospaced", Font.ITALIC, 36);
                String name = nameField.getText();

                Graphics g = getGraphics();

                g.setFont(font);
                g.setColor(Color.red);
                g.drawString(name,75,100);
        }
}

<HTML>
<BODY>
<APPLET code=Ans_29.class width=700 height=250>
</APPLET>
</BODY>
</HTML>
```

30. The source code requires very little modification. The class Calculator does not require a WindowListener or any of the methods associated with a window, for example windowClosed, windowClosing, etc can be deleted from the class.

An applet replaces the main program as follows.

```
// chap_11\Ans_30.java
// program to mimic a calculator
       .
       .

import java.applet.*;

class calculator extends Frame implements ActionListener
{
      public calculator(String s){..}

      public void actionPerformed(ActionEvent event){..}

      private String doCalculation(){..}
}


public class Ans_30 extends Applet
{
      public void init()
      {
            calculator C = new calculator("Example 32");

            C.setSize(150,200);
            C.setVisible(true);
      }
}
```

31. The error is forget to include the dot (.) separator between the name of the file and the postfix abbreviation. For example, the file is normally referred to by dialtone.au, the coding source+"au" will result in the filename being constructed as dialtoneau, which of course does not exist. The code requires an amendment of **source+".au"**.

32. The errors are as follows.

The applet needs to implement the Runnable interface, and the run() method must be overridden in the applet. Without this implementation the code of a thread cannot be executed.

There is no code to correctly start a thread or stop a thread.

The reference to a thread sleeping, without any means of trapping an interrupted exception, will generate a syntax error.

The correct solution to this program follows.
```
// chap_11\Ans_32.java

import java.awt.*;
import java.applet.*;
```

```
public class Ans_32 extends Applet implements Runnable
{
    Thread appletThread;

    int length=1;

    public void start()
    {
        if (appletThread == null)
        {
            appletThread = new Thread(this);
            appletThread.start();
        }
    }

    public void run()
    {
        while (true)
        {
            repaint();
            length++;

            try{Thread.sleep(50);}
            catch(InterruptedException i){System.exit(1);}
        }
    }

    public void stop()
    {
        if (appletThread != null)
        {
            appletThread.stop();
            appletThread=null;
        }
    }

    public void paint(Graphics g)
    {
        //g.setColor(Color.black);
        g.fillRect(10,50,length,5);
    }
}
```

Chapter 12.

17. The most serious problem is that the recursive method counter does not contain a terminating condition. Consequently, the recursive call to counter(N) will continue recursion until the stack cannot hold any more data.

19.

```
// chap_12\Ans_19.java

import java.io.*;

class Ans_19
{
    static BufferedReader keyboard = new
            BufferedReader(new InputStreamReader(System.in));
    static PrintWriter screen = new PrintWriter(System.out,true);

    // method to return the greatest common divisor between two numbers
    static int greatestCommonDivisor(int first, int second)
    {
        int remainder;

        remainder = first % second;

        if (remainder == 0)
            return second;
        else
            return greatestCommonDivisor(second, remainder);
    }

    static public void main(String[] args) throws IOException
    {
        int first, second;

        screen.print("first? "); screen.flush();
        first = new Integer(keyboard.readLine()).intValue();
        screen.print("second? "); screen.flush();
        second = new Integer(keyboard.readLine()).intValue();

        screen.println("Greatest common divisor is
                    "+greatestCommonDivisor(first,second));
    }
}
```

21.

The maximum number of passes through an array containing N items is N-1. However, on the first pass there are N-1 comparisons between the items; on the second pass there are N-2 comparisons and on the third pass N-3 comparisons, and so on. Eventually, on the final pass there will be just 1 comparison between two items. Summing the series:

$(N-1) + (N-2) + (N-3) + .. + 3 + 2 + 1 = N(N-1)/2$. The expression may be approximated to a time proportional to N^2, which is the same as the selection sort.

Index